First Dads

First Dads

Parenting and Politics from
George Washington to Barack Obama

JOSHUA KENDALL

GRAND CENTRAL
PUBLISHING

NEW YORK   BOSTON

Grand Central Publishing
Hachette Book Group
1290 Avenue of the Americas
New York, NY 10104

www.HachetteBookGroup.com

Printed in the United States of America

RRD-C

First Edition: May 2016
10 9 8 7 6 5 4 3 2 1

Grand Central Publishing is a division of Hachette Book Group, Inc.
The Grand Central Publishing name and logo is a trademark of Hachette Book Group, Inc.

The Hachette Speakers Bureau provides a wide range of authors for speaking events. To find out more, go to www.hachettespeakersbureau.com or call (866) 376-6591.

The publisher is not responsible for websites (or their content) that are not owned by the publisher.

Library of Congress Cataloging-in-Publication Data

Names: Kendall, Joshua C., 1960- author.
Title: First dads : parenting and politics from George Washington to Barack Obama / Joshua Kendall.
Description: New York : Grand Central Publishing, 2016. | Includes bibliographical references and index.
Identifiers: LCCN 2015050559 | ISBN 9781455551958 (hardcover) | ISBN 9781478909217 (audio download) | ISBN 9781455551965 (ebook)
Subjects: LCSH: Presidents—Family relationships—United States—History. | Presidents—United States—History. | Children of presidents—United States—History. | Presidents—United States—Biography. | Children of presidents—United States—Biography.
Classification: LCC E176.45 .K46 2016 | DDC 973.09/9—dc23 LC record available at http://lccn.loc.gov/2015050559

In Memoriam
George B. Kendall (1925–2014)

Contents

Prologue

The Sense and Sensibility of James Garfield

"It Is a Most Innocent and Intense Passion"

[The President's] emotional state is a matter of continual public commentary, as is the manner in which his personal and official families conduct themselves. The media bring across the President not as some neutral administrator or corporate executive to be assessed by his production, but as a special being with mysterious dimensions.

James David Barber, *The Presidential Character*, 1972

Early on the morning of Saturday, July 2, 1881, a tense President James Garfield rushed into the White House bedroom shared by his two teenage sons, Harry and Jim, who were both still half asleep. As a startled seventeen-year-old Harry later wrote in his diary, "[He] told us of the responsibilities and cares of his office, and then turn[ed] as quickly as he could from work to recreation."

The President began singing a line from Gilbert and Sullivan's recent hit, *HMS Pinafore*, "I mixed these babies up." The muscular six-foot, 185-pound Garfield then grabbed his two sons and carried them around the room, "as if we were in fact two babies," added Harry.

Fifteen-year-old Jim initiated the next round of amusement. The agile and accomplished gymnast, who knew his way around both the trapeze and the springboard, did a flip-flop on the bed, daring his father to follow suit. "You are the President of the United States, but you can't do that." Not only did Garfield acquit himself admirably, he then upped the ante by walking around stiff-kneed on his fingers and his toes. While Jim managed to match his father's feat, Harry came up a bit short.

Just a couple of hours later, the "three bachelors" were scheduled to travel to Elberon, a resort in southern New Jersey where Garfield's wife, Lucretia, was staying with the couple's three younger children, Molly, 14, Irwin, 10, and Abram, 8, as she recuperated from malaria. The trio's ultimate destination was Williams College in western Massachusetts, where the President was to attend his twenty-fifth reunion and the two teenagers, both recently accepted into the Class of 1885, were to register as freshmen.

Despite his wife's serious illness, four months into his presidency, Garfield was earning high satisfaction ratings from his five domestic subjects. He brought in a grandmother—his mother, Eliza—to help look after them. Not trusting the public schools, the scholarly Chief Executive, who was steeped in Latin and Greek, had imported a special tutor from the Montana Territory named Dr. Hawkes. The easygoing President enjoyed playing croquet with his children. He also liked to read to them—Shakespeare's plays were common fare. The President also had a remarkable knack for defusing family crises. In June, he was alarmed to learn that Harry was "dead in love" with Lulu Rockwell, the teenage daughter of his longtime friend and colleague, Col. Almon Rockwell. After encouraging his wife to counsel Harry to "avoid such absorption," Garfield decided no further action was necessary. "He [Harry] feels powerless to draw back... [but] it is a most innocent and intense passion," he wrote in his diary on June 11, "which, of course, at his age, can't last." The President's hunch would prove correct, and the young couple would eventually break up without suffering any ill effects.

That summer morning, Garfield and his boys never managed to board their 9:30 train. Soon after arriving at Washington's Baltimore and Pennsylvania railroad station, the President was shot by anarchist Charles Guiteau. The wounds were ultimately fatal, and he died eleven weeks later.

As with the Kennedy administration, similarly cut short by a bullet, Garfield's presidency is now associated with a string of "might have beens." The nine-time Ohio Congressman ran on a platform that featured strong stands on both civil rights and civil-service reform. In his inaugural address, Garfield called "the elevation of the Negro race from slavery to full rights of citizenship...the most important political change...since the adoption of the Constitution" and promised to fight those who would deny Negroes freedom of the ballot. And to clean up the civil service, he recommended passing a law "to fix the tenure of minor offices...and prescribe the grounds upon which removals shall be made." While we can only speculate about what Garfield might have achieved had he survived, given what we know about how he governed his own children, his loss appears even more tragic. It would take a couple more generations for Americans to elect another President as deeply committed to the full rights of the least powerful among us.

Perhaps no job on earth is more taxing than President of the United States. Faced with a barrage of conflicting and urgent demands, America's Chief Executive must be able to pivot from one crisis to another at a moment's notice. Since these constant challenges primarily test emotional rather than intellectual resources, scholars have often turned to an analysis of character to make sense of the successes and failures of Presidents past and the suitability of potential Presidents future. The landmark study in the field is the 1972 treatise *The Presidential Character: Predicting Performance in the White House*, written by the late Duke University political scientist James David Barber. According to Barber, one cannot understand a President solely by focusing on how he handled a particular predicament—say, an economic collapse or a war—or a set of predicaments. One must also come to grips with his worldview and interpersonal style—the raw material out of which he is made. "The issues will change," asserts Barber, "[but] the character of the President will last."

Unfortunately, in the last few decades, the popular news media have perverted the concept of character, reducing it to a simplistic moral category—little more than a synonym for marital fidelity. Pundits now often speak of the "character question"—as if some presidential candidates may be too depraved even to possess one. The "Karacter Kops"—to use the derisive term coined by the late Richard Ben Cramer, which refers to reporters intent on generating headlines by digging up unsavory incidents in the lives of politicians—have taken over. In his recent book *All the Truth Is Out: The Week Politics Went Tabloid* (2014), Matt Bai, the former chief political correspondent for the *New York Times Magazine*, identifies 1987 as the turning point. By quickly transforming Gary Hart from a Democratic front-runner into a political has-been with its wall-to-wall coverage of his alleged affair with Donna Rice, the *Miami Herald*, argues Bai, forever debased the way in which America vets its presidential hopefuls. "The finest political journalists of a generation," he concludes, "surrendered all at once to the idea that politics had become another form of celebrity-driven entertainment, while simultaneously disdaining the kind of reporting that such a thirst for entertainment made necessary." But our quadrennial electoral contests, in sharp contrast to spectacles launched in Hollywood, do have enormous consequences for people in all corners of the globe. And our cultural arbiters can and must do a better job of informing us about the qualifications of those who wish to lead our nation.

This book starts from the premise that character, as traditionally defined, both counts and is worth resuscitating as a critical variable in political analysis. In an attempt to bring a fresh perspective to presidential leadership, it focuses on an often overlooked window onto character—fathering.

Of the forty-three men who have assumed the role of the father of our country, thirty-eight have produced progeny. (The other five— George Washington, James Madison, Andrew Jackson, James Polk, and James Buchanan, our only bachelor President—all reared adopted children.) The manner in which each President carried out his parental responsibilities reveals much about both his beliefs and aspirations as well as about his psychological makeup. A major reason for the oversight in exploring this most personal of presidential duties is that the nearly two hundred First Children "have been *purposely* excluded" by many biographers, as one historian has noted. But evidence about the precise nature of these parent-child relationships abounds in the letters and diaries available in archives. And scholars are gradually beginning to appreciate just how valuable this line of inquiry can be. In a recent study, *Founders as Fathers: The Private Lives and Politics of the American Revolutionaries* (2014), historian Lorri Glover addresses the family lives of several Virginia revolutionaries, including George Washington, Patrick Henry, Thomas Jefferson, and James Madison. "To a large degree," she emphasizes, "these Virginians became founders *because* they were fathers, responsible...for...the preservation of social order and civic justice...And *how* they headed their families shaped and was shaped by their leadership of the American Republic." Remarkably, the same can be said for all our Presidents.

Fatherhood offers more than just a useful lens through which to examine the men who have held the presidency. It has also influenced the very nature of the institution itself. After all, a key reason why George Washington was unanimously elected as our first President was that he had not fathered any children of his own. (Washington was, however, a stepfather to children and grandchildren resulting from his wife's first marriage.) "You will become," Gouverneur Morris reminded the childless former General in December 1788, "the Father to more than three Millions of Children." America was founded on the idea that its Chief Executive would hold power only temporarily; unlike a monarch, he would not be able to pass the reins of power directly to his heirs. As Washington noted in an early draft of his first inaugural address:

> It will be recollected that the Divine Providence hath not seen fit, that my blood should be transmitted or my name perpetuated by the endearing, though sometimes seducing channel of immediate offspring. I have no child for whom I could wish to make a provision—no family to build in greatness upon my country's ruins...let my personal enemies if I am so unfortunate as to have served such a return from reform from any one of my countrymen, point to the sinister object or to the earthly consideration beyond the hope of rendering some little service to our parent country, that could have persuaded me to accept this appointment.

As for the final layout of the President's home, it was Theodore Roosevelt's desire for more space to play with his children that turned out to be the raison d'etre for the West Wing (the three-story office building located within the White House). The rambunctious TR staged family pillow fights in the White House where he also played bear, using an upturned table for his den. As that astute student of the presidency, Richard M. Nixon, once observed, "From John Adams to Theodore Roosevelt the President and his staff worked in the White House itself. But TR's family of six children and their menagerie of cats, dogs, raccoons, snakes, a pony, and a bear proved too much."

Even more important, the fathering experiences of Presidents have also changed the course of American history. As TR's Secretary of War, William Howard Taft was torn between whether to run for President or to ask for a Supreme Court appointment. He ended up choosing the executive branch over the judicial in part because he thought a stint as President would be more beneficial for his sons, Robert (later a Senator and formidable presidential candidate in his own right) and Charles. And consider the sad turn of events in the presidency of Calvin

Coolidge. In July 1924, just as Coolidge began running for a full term of his own, his beloved second son, Calvin Coolidge Jr., died suddenly at sixteen from blood poisoning. "Silent Cal" blamed himself and went into a deep funk, from which he never recovered. "When he went," Coolidge later wrote, "the power and the glory of the presidency went with him."

In some cases, the behavior of the father closely mirrors that of the President. As a head of household, John Adams was an outlier—an extreme authoritarian—and this demanding perfectionist ruled as willfully over his four children as he did over the rest of the nation. The overbearing President who gave us the Alien and Sedition Acts also alienated his second son, Charles, who would struggle with depression and alcoholism as an adult. Yet, in his first-born son, John Quincy, who later served as Secretary of State as well as President, this "tiger dad" produced a superachiever who remained both forever grateful for his old man's constant prodding and seemingly intimidated by it. "The first and deepest of all my wishes," the sixth President once wrote, "is to give satisfaction to my parents." But sometimes the father and the President seem to be two entirely different people. Ronald Reagan was an emotionally distant father who expressed his frustration with his children not by blowing up but by withdrawing. Late in life, Reagan described himself as "a good father [who]...maybe...should have been sterner than I was." As President, Reagan forged a deep bond with a huge segment of the public as well as with other world leaders such as Mikhail Gorbachev and Margaret Thatcher, but this preoccupied dad had trouble connecting with his four children, all of whom openly rebelled against him. The same was true for that other Great Communicator, Franklin D. Roosevelt. A self-absorbed man who rarely spent much time with his family—partly as a result of his long battle with polio—Roosevelt repeatedly faced public relations disasters caused by his adult children during his presidency; these father-son rifts had a distinct Oedipal flavor. While his second son, Elliott, took a job with William Randolph Hearst, the media mogul who was constantly at war with the Roosevelt administration, his third son, Franklin Jr., married into the Republican DuPont family, which was also doing everything in its power to throw FDR out of office.

According to child-development experts, most parents—and Presidents are no exception—fall into three broad categories: authoritarian, authoritative, and permissive. While authoritarian parents such as John Adams wield authority over children by issuing orders, permissive parents do not set any rules at all. In contrast, authoritative parents provide support, but also set appropriate limits and thus are likely to raise the most emotionally healthy offspring. What authoritarian and permissive parents have in common is that they do not engage much with children; neither group understands the politics of negotiation (at least within the privacy of their own homes). However, authoritative parents are good listeners who take in all the particulars before deciding how to respond to a given situation. Before the midtwentieth century, when child-rearing norms underwent drastic changes, authoritative parents—particularly fathers—were relatively uncommon; and of our first two dozen Presidents, Garfield was a rara avis, one who was emotionally attuned to his children. Ulysses S. Grant was one of many permissive dads to inhabit the White House. As his wife, Julia, observed, this fearless military leader felt uncomfortable denying his four children just about anything. "The General had no idea of the government of the children. He would have allowed them to do pretty much as they pleased (hunt, fish, swim, etc.) provided it did not interfere with any duty."

Each chapter of this book discusses a group of Presidents with similar fathering experiences, containing both in-depth profiles of three illustrative main characters as well as brief sketches of a few minor characters. Parenting style was just one consideration in devising the categories. I also took into account determining circumstances in the President's life—such as whether he was forced to live apart from his children for a long period of time and whether he suffered the loss of any children. Chapter One covers the "preoccupied" style of fathering—which characterizes more First Dads than any other. Focusing on FDR, Lyndon B. Johnson, and Jimmy Carter, it underlines how Presidents have often been so busy building their careers that they were unable to attend to the daily concerns of their children. Chapter Two explores the "playful pals," such as Ulysses Grant, TR, and Woodrow Wilson, who bonded with their children primarily through play. In Chapter Three, we learn about "double-dealing dads," such as John Tyler, Grover Cleveland, and Warren Harding, who fathered illegitimate children. Chapter Four addresses tiger dads, including both John Adams and his eldest son, John Quincy Adams, as well as Dwight Eisenhower. Chapter Five reveals how Franklin Pierce, William McKinley, and Calvin Coolidge were each profoundly affected by the death of a child. In Chapter Six, I present the authoritative or nurturing dads, such as Rutherford B. Hayes, Harry Truman, and Barack Obama. Throughout the book, I stress new over familiar material. In Chapter Three, rather than discussing in detail the mulatto children of Thomas Jefferson, about whom much has been written, I focus on those of another pre–Civil War Virginian, John Tyler, whose family life has rarely been examined. In addition, some Presidents are mentioned in more than one chapter. For example, George Herbert Walker Bush makes a brief appearance in both Chapter One and Chapter Five, since this preoccupied dad was also forever changed by the loss of his three-year-old daughter, Robin, in 1953.

Surprisingly, as a group, the children of Presidents have not fared all that well. Tragedies abound. As numerous commentators have observed, these famous scions somehow seem cursed. Compared to cohorts born in similar socioeconomic circumstances, they have endured more early deaths and have experienced more psychiatric problems, such as depression and substance abuse. Their divorce rates have also been staggeringly high, and a few have committed suicide. Many were haunted by the gnawing feeling that they could never match up to their illustrious fathers. As Theodore Roosevelt Jr. put it, "Don't you think it handicaps a boy to be the son of a man like my father?"

But my emphasis is not on the struggles of the First Children, but on the experiences of their fathers; and what they can teach us about both the inner lives and the political fortunes of the men who have led the country. While Franklin Roosevelt's five children were also emotionally handicapped, our longest-serving President might never have made it to the White House had he not been able to lean on his eldest son, James, time and time again.

1

The Preoccupied

"I Should Like to Have Your Opinion on It"

Heads of state have little time to be heads of families...father was too
busy building his political career to play a regular role in our upbringing.

James Roosevelt, FDR's second child

Jimmy, would you care to come along and lend me your arm?"

The request from Franklin Delano Roosevelt was one that his
sixteen-year-old son, then a sophomore at Groton, could not think of
refusing. "I accepted, of course," James Roosevelt later wrote, "aware
that I would have to lend him not only my arm but also whatever
strength I had."

It was June 1924, and FDR was planning to make his return to public life at the Democratic National Convention at Madison Square
Garden. Since coming down with polio three years earlier, the ambitious former Assistant Secretary of the Navy under Wilson had focused
almost exclusively on regaining his health and stamina. During his con-
valescence, FDR, who had run for Vice President in 1920, was forced
to satisfy himself with part-time leadership posts such as the presidency
of the Boy Scout Foundation and the chairmanship of the American
Legion Campaign. Then in early 1924, the forty-three-year-old father of
five—in addition to James, his other children were Anna, 18, Elliott, 14,
Franklin Jr., 9, and John, 8—dipped back into politics when he began
managing the presidential campaign of New York Governor Al Smith.

And now FDR himself was to nominate Smith from the convention floor. There was only one catch. He could no longer walk. And if he slipped (or spoke from his wheelchair), he would forever identify himself to his fellow Americans as an invalid. The idea to use this speech to carve out a political future had originated with Louis Howe, the former journalist who emerged as FDR's right-hand man after the onset of his illness. Aware of the risk, FDR initially balked before gradually coming around.

Relying on his teenage son James, whom he appointed an alternate delegate to the Convention as "his page and prop," FDR would manage to bring about his own resurrection. His words would generate such a thunderous response that eight years later when he won the nomination, FDR decided to fly to Chicago to accept it in person—breaking a long-held precedent. James was also at his side in that rousing speech when the Democratic standard-bearer first promised Americans "a New Deal."

In the days immediately preceding his appearance at the 1924 Convention in New York, James worked steadfastly with FDR to make all the necessary preparations. With his legs weighed down by fourteen pounds of steel braces, FDR could walk only by relying on friendly arms or crutches and propelling himself forward with his considerable upper-body strength. At the family's Manhattan town house on East Sixty-Fifth Street, father and son marked out a walking path of fifteen feet—the exact distance that FDR would have to tread in Madison Square Garden—and FDR practiced taking steps by leaning on James with his left arm and using a crutch with his stronger right arm. The younger Roosevelt learned to walk slowly so that his strides could match his father's. Every morning, they arrived early at the Convention, so that James could place FDR in his aisle seat before anyone could notice the wheelchair. Once seated, FDR had to depend on his son to run his errands and serve as his bridge to fellow delegates. "I was responsive to his every wish," noted James, who regretted that he was kept too busy to flirt with the attractive niece of the Convention's chairman, Senator Thomas Walsh.

At a few minutes past noon on Wednesday, June 25, James helped carry a laughing FDR up a flight of stairs to a chair on the speaker's platform. Right before "taking off," FDR startled bystanders by whispering to a delegate from Pennsylvania, "Shake the rostrum." The reason? FDR wanted to be sure that it was sturdy enough to lean on during his speech. Then James and Thomas Lynch, the head of Governor Smith's Tax Bureau, helped FDR to his feet. The heavily perspiring nominator pushed down so hard on his son with his right arm that a little blood started trickling out from near James's shoulder. After James stuck crutches under both of his father's armpits, FDR was on his own. Swinging himself forward, he acknowledged the audience of 15,000—about 2,000 over the arena's normal seating capacity—by smiling rather than waving. Suddenly a roar went up "that fairly lifted the Madison Square Garden roof," as one paper reported. "At that moment I was so damned proud of him," James noted, "that it was with difficulty that I kept myself from bursting into tears."

Nearly a decade before he reassured Americans in his inaugural address that "the only thing we have to fear is fear itself," FDR energized his party by arguing that Smith "is the most dangerous adversary that the Republican Party ever had to fear." As FDR joked, Smith "got one million more votes than I did"—a line that referred to Smith's close loss in the Governor's race in 1920, the same year that FDR and the Democratic standard-bearer James Cox were trounced in the statewide presidential contest. Convinced of Smith's "spotless integrity," he praised the nominee as "a Happy Warrior." Though a Smith speechwriter had suggested this allusion to the British poet William Wordsworth, FDR uttered it with authority. And as the audience immediately sensed, the moniker applied more to the speaker than to the candidate.

FDR finished by listing all the reasons for nominating "our own Alfred E. Smith"—a flourish that sent most of the delegates into a frenzy. The hour-long cheering prompted Will Rogers to ruminate about the state of "our civilization." "Why," the celebrated columnist and performer wondered, "if they ever took a sanity test at a political convention, 98 percent would be removed to an asylum." Another five thousand people who had been listening to the speech in neighboring Madison Square Park, where it was broadcast on three radio wagons, also erupted in a bedlam not seen in New York since Armistice Day. Throughout the city, revelers began singing and dancing in the streets.

While the throngs were ostensibly going wild for the native son Smith, it was his nominator who actually won the hearts and minds of New Yorkers that day. As the *New York Times* concluded after the delegates had dispersed, "No one who attended the sessions... would dispute the statement that the most popular man in the convention was Franklin D. Roosevelt," noting that on "his appearance each time, there was a spontaneous burst of applause."

Though he would not run for elective office until 1928 when he replaced Smith as New York's Governor, FDR knew right away that he had succeeded in reigniting his political career. At his hotel the night after his speech, he said, "Well James, we made it." The son was pleased by the father's triumph, but he had a slightly different take. "It was he who made it, of course," James later wrote, "not we."

Like a number of Presidents, FDR was so focused on climbing and staying on top of the political ladder that he sometimes could not distinguish between his own struggles and those of his offspring. For FDR, this tendency was particularly pronounced; after all, in the last two decades of his life, he often experienced James as both a physical as well as an emotional extension of himself. To his eldest son, the thirty-second President revealed a vulnerable side of his complex personality, which he did his best to hide from the public—the anxious and plodding striver who needed reassurance, if not nurturing. The night he defeated Hoover, FDR asked James to pray for him, acknowledging that he feared that "I may not have the strength to do this job." This topsy-turvy parent-child relationship would persist well into his presidency. Early in his second term, FDR asked James, then the head of his own insurance company, to serve as his "legs" (personal assistant) in Washington. In response to his wife, Eleanor, who worried that the press might object, FDR quipped, "Why should I be deprived of my eldest son's help and of the pleasure of having him with me just because I am President?" Known in Washington by such sobriquets as "Assistant President" and "the Grand Vizier of Loose Ends," James faithfully served his father for a year and a half before returning to the private sector.

During World War II, FDR turned to his eldest child, Anna, to be his supporter-in-chief. Giving up her own career as a staff writer on the *Seattle Post-Intelligencer*, she moved into the Lincoln Suite in the White House. Until FDR's death a year and a half later, she was constantly at his side. Though the attractive, leggy Anna—who was described in the press as a blond version of Katharine Hepburn—had no title and received no salary, this adoring daughter was eager to do whatever the President desired. "It was immaterial to me," Anna later wrote, "whether my job was helping him to plan the 1944 campaign, pouring tea for General de Gaulle or filling Father's empty cigarette case."

"My mother worshipped FDR," Ellie Roosevelt Seagraves, Anna's first child, who lived in the White House for several years, told me in a recent interview. "Her father was her ideal man, and she loved being around him." Washington insiders referred to Anna as her father's "expediter," the aide who both got people in to see the President and got the President to do things. Supreme Court Justice William Douglas, a leading contender for the vice presidential nomination in 1944, was convinced that Anna had nixed his chance to run on the Democratic ticket, leading *Life* to speculate that "Truman is partly Anna's creation." "Daddy's girl," the magazine asserted in early 1945, "[is] running Daddy."

As President, FDR was simply too busy to provide much guidance to any of his children. As Eleanor Roosevelt recalled in her autobiography, when her three younger sons—whose ages ranged from sixteen to twenty-two when he was first elected President—wanted to have a private conversation with him, they needed to make an appointment.

On one occasion, when one of his adolescent sons entered the Oval Office, FDR was seated at his desk, reading. As this young man talked, the President appeared to be listening, but then he said, "This is a most important document. I should like to have your opinion on it." After making a comment on the text, his humiliated son quickly departed; not long after, he told his mother, "Never again will I talk to Father about anything personal."

As James Roosevelt noted in his memoir, he had not one, but three fathers: "Pa-pa" (the pre-polio), "Pa" (the post-polio), and FDR (the political leader). But all three were preoccupied. Even the vigorous "Pa-pa," whom the legendary football coach Walter Camp once described as "beautifully built...with the leg muscles of an athlete," was, as James later conceded, "a somewhat self-centered man." He too was not a homebody, and James and his siblings could always tell that his main interests lay elsewhere. And they hardly saw "Pa" during his years of recovery. "During this time...we had no tangible father," James observed, "no father-in-being, whom we could touch and talk to at will—only an abstract symbol, a cheery letter writer, off somewhere on a houseboat or at Warm Springs, fighting by himself to do what had to be done."

In all three incarnations, FDR was not somebody with whom his children could ever have a real relationship, based on mutual give-and-take. While he could be warm and entertaining, he could not develop emotional intimacy with them or with anyone else for that matter. As Henry Wallace, the Vice President during his third term, put it in a formulation that was later echoed by his children, "He doesn't know any man and no man knows him. Even his own family doesn't know anything about him." Fathering was not something that came naturally; it was a role that FDR played in short spurts. When his children and grandchildren were young, he would not hesitate to invite them to snuggle with him under the covers. Anna's third child, John Boettiger Jr., recently told me that he used to love when the President lifted him up onto his bed so that they could spend a few minutes together reading the comics. "He was a consummate performer," said Boettiger, who was born in 1939 and was living in the White House at the time of his grandfather's death. During his Fireside Chats, this Great Communicator left huge numbers of Americans feeling as if he understood their particular problems. But FDR's "simply stupendous" charm—to use the assessment rendered by a Hyde Park neighbor in Thomas Wolfe's roman à clef, *Of Time and the River*—was not enough to make his own children feel that same degree of empathy. As Anna noted, her father "had the ability to relate to groups of people or individuals who had problems...[but] the apparent lack of ability to relate with the same consistent warmth and interest to an individual who was [his] child."

The President who led the country for twelve years consistently inspired trust and confidence—if not love—in his fellow citizens. When FDR died suddenly in April 1945, many Americans were heartbroken, feeling as if they had lost their own father. But in his own children, FDR often sowed confusion and alienation.

———

All Presidents are by definition preoccupied. They have a lot on their minds. But a significant number were also preoccupied long before they ever reached the White House; after all, a single-minded focus, bolstered by fierce ambition, is the most direct path to getting there. As Jack Carter, Jimmy Carter's eldest son, put it in 2003, "Dad's been— you know, Dad has been one track...I mean he had his own thing to do, and I don't think you get to be President unless you're driven." Preoccupied dads come in three different flavors—the absentee dad, the workaholic, and the distant dad—and most preoccupied First Dads combine features of all three subtypes. Cut from the same cloth as his mentor, FDR, Lyndon B. Johnson, who was a game-changing Senate majority leader before becoming President, often quipped, "I never think about politics more than eighteen hours a day." By devoting all those hours to his obsession, Johnson rarely saw his daughters—Lynda and Luci—when they were little. In his pre-presidential years, Jimmy Carter was also a nonstop doer, whether employed as a naval officer or as a state senator cum peanut farmer. FDR, Johnson, and Carter all cared deeply about their children, but attending to their daily concerns was rarely a primary concern. These three Presidents were all much more comfortable forging political rather than personal bonds.

Martin Van Buren also threw himself headfirst into his work long before becoming President in 1837. During the three previous decades, he held several other prominent posts, including U.S. Senator, Secretary of State, and Vice President, and his life consisted of "incessant activity and excitement, professional, political and social," as one family member later put it. In 1807, Van Buren had married his childhood sweetheart, Hannah Hoes, with whom he had four sons. As a young lawyer who doubled as a state legislator, Van Buren was constantly away from the family home in Hudson, New York, attending cases in either Albany or New York City. After Hannah died of tuberculosis in 1819, Van Buren, who would never remarry, farmed out all four boys to various relatives. "This kind of domestic life," wrote his major biographer, "was scarcely suitable to the mental health and development of his children."

James Polk and his wife, Sarah, did not have any children, but Polk helped raise his nephew, Marshall Tate Polk Jr. As the new President promised the teenager's mother—his sister, Laura—in 1846, "You may rest assured that I will give to Marshall all the attention and paternal care which you could do, if you were present with him." During his term in office, "Marsh," as Polk called his ward, attended college and spent vacations at the Executive Mansion. The well-meaning but driven Polk, who banned dancing in the people's house and believed that "no President who performs his duties faithfully and conscientiously can have any leisure," expected the youngster to be as conscientious as he was. Upon discovering that Marshall had little interest in his studies, Polk had a hard time relating to him. In 1848, after his nephew dropped out of Georgetown and a couple of other colleges,

Polk shipped him off to West Point, where he graduated in 1852 as a second lieutenant. Marshall would meet a tragic end. Three decades later, while serving as state treasurer of Tennessee, he was convicted of embezzling hundreds of thousands of dollars. He died of heart troubles before beginning his prison term.

Obsessed with carving out a military career since childhood, Zachary Taylor served as an army officer for nearly forty years before winning the presidency in 1848. Stationed at frontier outposts in various present-day states including Wisconsin, Louisiana, Minnesota, Florida, and Texas, Taylor endured frequent separations from his wife and four surviving children. In the early 1830s when his second daughter, Knox, was being wooed by Lieutenant Jefferson Davis—then a recent West Point graduate under Taylor's command at Fort Crawford—the Colonel initially protested, saying, "I'll be damned if another daughter of mine shall marry into the army. I know enough of the family life of officers. I scarcely know my own children, or they me." (Sadly, Knox died of malaria just two months after her wedding to the future President of the Confederacy.) Taylor would not see his only son, Richard, later a prominent Confederate General, for a period of six years—from 1840, when the fourteen-year-old left for a New England boarding school, until 1846, when he was finishing up his studies at Yale.

William Howard Taft also did not experience much face time with his three children—Robert (the future Senator), Helen, and Charles. In 1892, at the age of only thirty-four, Taft was appointed to the Federal Circuit Court by President Benjamin Harrison. For the next eight years, while his family lived in Cincinnati, the young judge was often away hearing cases in Kentucky, Tennessee, and Michigan. Though the children did move to Manila when Taft served as Governor of the Philippines from 1901 to 1903, they were often separated from their father, who frequently had to travel to other Asian cities on government business. Without much supervision from either of their parents, the children tended to develop solitary pursuits. The young Robert would while away hours playing chess with himself. Devouring books, both he and his sister later became formidable intellectuals. (Robert finished first in his class at both Yale College and at Harvard Law School; after obtaining her Ph.D. in history at Yale, Helen was appointed the Dean of Bryn Mawr College.) In the summer of 1903, Taft shipped the fourteen-year-old Robert halfway around the world by himself so that he could attend boarding school in Connecticut—a fact that startled the San Francisco reporters who covered the trip. When father and son finally had a brief reunion seven months later in New York, Theodore Roosevelt's new Secretary of War had trouble figuring out that the "fine looking modest, well dressed boy" who marched into his hotel room was his own flesh and blood.

Orphaned at eight, Herbert Hoover grew up among Quaker relatives in Iowa and Oregon, who insisted that he do long hours of physically demanding farm work. He never did get a firm handle on parent-child bonding. Five weeks after the birth of each of his two sons, Herbert Jr. and Allan, the energetic engineering executive and efficiency expert took his family on long international trips. Since its newest members could not articulate their concerns, he assumed that they did not have any. "Traveling with babies," Hoover later noted in his memoir, "is easier than with most grown-ups." By the early 1910s, Hoover was independently wealthy and he placed his school-aged boys with nannies and servants as he continued to travel around the world with his wife, Lou, for both business and pleasure. In August 1914, Hoover's public life began when he immersed himself in relief work in Europe. While the boys eventually joined their parents in London, Hoover often took long trips to the Continent. When Hoover served as Harding's Secretary of Commerce, his sons attended high school back in Palo Alto. For updates on their lives, he would rely on the summaries of important milestones provided by his paid caregivers. In 1931, during Hoover's third year in the White House, the twenty-eight-year-old Herbert Jr., a recent Harvard Business School grad with a wife and three children, came down with tuberculosis. During his son's ten-month stay at a sanitarium in Asheville, North Carolina, the President could manage only one visit.

In the early 1950s, when Richard Nixon's two daughters, Tricia and Julie, were toddlers, the conscientious young Senator, who had clocked twenty-hour days during the Alger Hiss hearings in 1948, stayed in his office most evenings; family dinners were a rarity. "Maybe if he gets through early enough he'll come back home," said Earl Chapman, a friend of his wife, Pat, "but many times he'll curl up on the couch and get a few hours' sleep. Then he'll get a little breakfast and shave, and go right down to the Senate chambers." As Vice President, this loner, who had trouble making close friends, also did not interact much with his daughters as he kept a busy travel schedule. After his loss to JFK in the 1960 election, Nixon took a job with a Los Angeles law firm and promised his wife that he would finally become a more involved father. But this never happened. He was soon both back on the speaking circuit and swamped with various writing projects, including a book (*Six Crises*) and a newspaper column for the *Times-Mirror* syndicate. Reflecting back on his first year out of politics since 1946, Nixon later wrote, "One of my reasons for moving to California was to have more time with Pat and the girls, but I think I saw them even less that year than I had when we were in Washington."

Ronald Reagan also was often too preoccupied with his own concerns to be able to understand what his children might be experiencing. On July 12, 1954, while shooting on location one of his final pictures, *Cattle Queen of Montana*, Reagan wrote Patti, his twenty-one-month-old daughter, a nine-paragraph letter. Perhaps it was fortunate that the toddler lacked the cognitive skills to absorb its contents; had she done so, she might well have had a temper tantrum. The emotional needs of the missive's intended recipient failed to register. Missing his new wife, Nancy Davis, whom he had married just two years earlier, Reagan, who was then also raising a daughter, Maureen, and an adoptive son, Michael, with his first wife, Jane Wyman, wrote of his "longing so great that it seemed as if I'd die of pain if I couldn't reach out and touch your Mommie." To Patti, Reagan highlighted not his devotion, but her duty: "I'm counting on you to take care of your Mommie and keep her safe for me." In the decades to come, Patti would rarely feel acknowledged by her father. "[His] presence," she once said, "felt like absence." While Ron, his other child with Nancy, has fond memories of swimming and playing catch with his father, he, too, felt the distance, noting that "there is something that [Dad] holds back. You get just so far."

The hardworking George Herbert Walker Bush was constantly on the go. After settling in Texas in 1948, the budding oil man and his wife, Barbara, kept shuttling back east, entrusting the care of their children to family friends for long stretches of time. In the middle of 1959, as the couple organized the five-hundred-mile move from Midland to Houston while Barbara was pregnant with their last child (Dorothy), they farmed out their four sons for four months. Thirteen-year-old George went to Scotland to visit a family friend, and the six-year-old Jeb, along with four-year-old Neal and three-year-old Marvin, stayed with a babysitter. As Jeb Bush later recalled of that summer, "At least we weren't put in a kennel." When this consummate networker ran for the U.S. Senate in 1964, "there was no coffee gathering or chamber of commerce banquet too small for him to attend," as former President George W. Bush later put it. That spring, Bush also missed George Jr.'s graduation from Andover. "Even when we were growing up in Houston," Jeb has stated, "Dad wasn't at home at night to play catch...It was a matriarchal family...He was hardly around." Accustomed to not seeing his father, Jeb chose to stay in Houston to finish the ninth grade when the rest of the family accompanied the first-term Congressman to Washington in 1967. On those rare occasions when he stayed put, Bush could be playful and entertaining. For this reason, Jeb has also credited his father with inventing "quality time." But there was never much quantity.

On July 14, 1987, the day before the forty-year-old, four-time Governor of Arkansas was expected to announce his candidacy for the

Democratic nomination for President, Bill Clinton had a sudden change of heart. Surprising his supporters, he decided not to throw his hat in the ring, explaining that he was worried about the impact of the constant campaigning on his seven-year-old daughter, Chelsea. "I've seen a lot of kids grow up under these pressures and a long, long time ago I made a promise to myself that if I was ever lucky enough to have a child, she would never grow up wondering who her father was." Clinton's critics have long been skeptical about this claim, since earlier that month, key aides had expressed concern that he made a ripe target for the press, which had just booted Gary Hart out of the race for his philandering. Whatever the true reason for the Arkansas Governor's about-face that summer, his deep affection for his daughter cannot be questioned. But this peripatetic politician, who emerged as a prominent national figure after becoming head of the National Governors Association in 1986, did not get to dote on Chelsea much during her early years. Making the most of every opportunity, Clinton turned drives between the Governor's Mansion and church into story hour. After reading the schoolgirl her favorite book on one ride, he turned to two friends in the car and asked, "Is that okay? The way I was reading to her?" While Clinton, like FDR, never doubted his ability to charm the American people, the once-neglected child was insecure about whether he could win his own daughter's love.

———

As a Harvard undergraduate, Franklin Roosevelt modeled himself both politically and personally on his fifth cousin, Theodore Roosevelt, then the President and the man whom he "admired most on earth." FDR, too, would insist on having six children—a wish that would scare off Alice Sohier, the alluring Boston Brahmin whom he was courting a couple of years before his marriage to TR's niece, Eleanor. Like TR, "Pa-pa," the first incarnation of FDR the dad, would also enjoy roughhousing with all his children, including his daughter Anna. While perched atop his shoulders, the six-year-old Anna once fell as he

skipped from stone to stone on a stream outside Washington—an incident that she later described as "disastrous." The polio-impaired "Pa"
would still engage in Indian wrestling with his boys, as he continued
to maintain his considerable upper-body strength.

But in stark contrast to TR, who was a constant presence in the
lives of his six children, FDR was far from an involved dad. In fact,
the President who attempted to bring America back from the Great
Depression by placing heretofore unheard-of regulations on the
nation's economy was a laissez-faire parent. "Father's attitude on
nurses [nannies]," James later wrote of his youth, "and other household
affairs was strictly hands off." FDR was happy to pass all the responsibility for his children's welfare to Eleanor and his mother, Sara, who
lived in an adjacent Manhattan town house in the early years of their
marriage. His eldest child, Anna, asserted that she was raised "more
by my grandmother than by my parents"—a sentiment that was shared
by her siblings. When FDR's children needed something, they typically asked his mother. FDR's detachment from their daily lives bor-
dered on neglect. Several of the English nannies hired by Sara were
unfit to rear children; one, whom James called "Old Battleax," was
both physically and emotionally abusive. During her brief reign of terror, this nurse tried to teach Anna how to act like "a little lady" by
periodically pushing her to the ground and kneeling on her chest.
Convinced that James was not being truthful when he reported that he
had brushed his teeth, she once forced him to dress in his sister's cloth-
ing and walk up and down East Sixty-Fifth Street wearing a sign reading, I AM A LIAR. "Old Battleax" also punished Franklin Jr. by locking
him in a closet for hours on end. Though the compassionate FDR was
furious when he discovered what she had done to his namesake, who
later developed a severe case of claustrophobia, he declined to take any
action. Eleanor was the one who fired "Old Battleax," but only after
finding a stash of her empty whiskey bottles. In his own family, FDR
was less an executive than a passive bystander. "When Old Battleax
finally went," James observed, "Father was as happy as any of us kids."

While FDR loved his children, he could not or would not offer them much protection.

The Hyde Park Roosevelts were a matriarchy. To emphasize her authority, the whimsical Sara, a formidable presence until her death at eighty-six in 1941, would remind the children, "Your mother only bore you." In contrast to her husband, Eleanor would push back against Sara, but only on rare occasions. Well intentioned but impulsive, FDR's mother spoiled all five children. Her gifts included European trips, horses, fancy watches, and oodles of cash. When Franklin Jr. smashed up the modest roadster that his parents had given him as a high school graduation present, Sara immediately replaced it with a souped-up model. FDR felt that he had no choice but to defer to his mother's wishes because her funds—derived from the wealth she had inherited from his father, who had died when he was eighteen— financed his lavish lifestyle.

A lifelong public servant, FDR never earned much money himself. Until the early 1930s, when he built the Little White House in Warm Springs, this powerful politician still did not have a home of his own. Springwood, the Hyde Park mansion where he had been born, would always remain "Granny's home," as James emphasized. "She laid down the rules, and all of us—even Father and Mother—accepted them."

In nearly all family matters, Sara was the decider. She even dictated how FDR was to resolve his marital conflicts. In 1918, after his wife discovered that he had been carrying on an affair with Lucy Mercer, a former governess, for two years, Sara took Eleanor's side. Concerned that a divorce would endanger his political career, his mother threatened to disinherit him unless he ended the relationship. The bond that would connect the Roosevelts from then on would not be love, but politics—"the obtaining and exercise of power," as his second son, Elliott, later put it. Or, to use James's formulation, their parents were "business partners…not…husband and wife…[who] had an armed truce that endured to the day he died."

As a family disciplinarian, FDR was "the world's worst," as Elliott observed. Eleanor, in contrast, tried to set some limits and advocated the occasional spanking. But nearly every time she called upon her husband to be an enforcer, he took the "let's not and say we did" approach. Once, when a school-aged Elliott insulted his tutor, she asked Franklin to deal firmly with the situation. "Father sat me on his knee," recalled Elliott, "put his arm around me affectionately, and we began talking about everything except what I had said." When asked about the matter by Eleanor, FDR responded, "Everything is settled." Elliott recalled only one spanking from his father; when he would not attend church, FDR grazed him with a hairbrush.

With his children, FDR was even-tempered and rarely raised his voice. It was not that he never got upset; but he knew how to defuse his own anger with humor so as to avoid acting on it. At the end of his first term in the White House, Eleanor noticed that Franklin Jr., then a student at Harvard, had racked up a hefty bill from a Cambridge physician who was treating his stubborn case of hemorrhoids. By way of explanation, she passed on a note to FDR's secretary, Missy LeHand: "He [Franklin Jr.] went eleven times. But apparently it does not depend upon how many times you go, it depends entirely on the cure. I know FDR will have a fit!" After taking a peek at both documents, FDR informed LeHand of his executive decision by jotting down the following words: "Pay it. Have had the fit."

FDR hated to say no. Uncomfortable with conflict, he disliked leaving anyone disappointed. When the young Franklin Jr. got a ticket for speeding, FDR "revoked" his license for an indefinite period. But when his son asked him to limit the suspension to a couple of weeks, he not only capitulated, but also insisted that Eleanor was to blame for the very idea of the punishment. Some of these traits—such as his distaste for direct confrontation—would later surface in the Oval Office. When speaking about an issue with his advisors, he would rarely disagree with anyone. He would then set aside some time to reflect on all the suggestions before doing whatever he felt was right. When a lobbyist came in to pitch some idea for which he had no use, FDR would not get into an argument but would change the subject by telling a few of his favorite anecdotes. "He didn't know how to be disagreeable," explained Anna's daughter, Ellie Seagraves.

FDR was keenly aware of how the sudden demise of "Pa-pa" on August 10, 1921, terrified his children. That afternoon, FDR had gone sailing with Anna, James, and Elliott near the family's summer home on Campobello Island. Upon their return, he felt chills and went to bed early without eating dinner. For the next month, FDR remained squirreled away in his bedroom. Despite his intense pain and discomfort—in the early stages of his polio, he even lost control of his bowels—he smiled whenever he noticed his children in the hallway outside his door. On September 13, 1921, as four island residents carried him out of the house on a stretcher so that he could be whisked off to Manhattan's Presbyterian Hospital, he made a semblance of a wave with his mostly useless left hand, uttering, "I'll be seeing you chicks soon!" Over the next few months, he continued to do whatever he could to ease their distress. Once he returned to the family's Manhattan residence that fall, he had his bed moved so that he and Elliott could exchange glances as his middle child skated to elementary school. When James came home from Groton at Christmas, the immobile FDR gripped his son hard to show that his arms had not lost their strength. "I cried a bit," James later recalled, "but with Pa squeezing me and slapping me on the back and carrying on enthusiastically on how 'grand' I looked, I soon was chattering right along with him."

But both the short-term and the long-term effects of his illness on the family were considerable. To accommodate his new live-in assistant, Louis Howe, Anna had to exchange her capacious third-floor bedroom (and private bathroom) for a tiny room on the fourth floor. And with round-the-clock nursing care now needed, seven-year-old Franklin Jr. and five-year-old John were exiled to a fourth-floor room in Sara's town house next door. The children's anger soon started spilling out. To taunt the gruff Howe, who liked to read his morning newspapers propped up against the lazy Susan at the center of the kitchen table, Franklin Jr. and John kept gently rotating the gizmo, prompting the former journalist to snap, "Why do you need so much butter?" FDR's polio ended up affecting his two youngest children the most. "Unfortunately, neither Franklin Jr. nor John ever had the opportunities the three oldest children had," Elliott later wrote, "to achieve a communion of spirit with our father."

As FDR disengaged himself more and more from all his children, their alienation would continue to grow. If "Pa-pa" related to them like an uncle, then "Pa" resembled a sibling. While he called Anna "Sister," or "Sis," he would refer to Franklin Jr. as "Brother" or "Brud." Though FDR was now over forty, within his own family, he identified himself much more as a son than as a father. It was as if he were the eldest brother who had gone off to war, but in his case the battle was not with a foreign enemy but with his own body. During his years of rehabilitation in the 1920s, he wrote more letters to his mother, who now wielded more financial power over the family than ever, than to his children; Sara often served as the go-between, whom he would ask to "kiss the chicks."

"Looking back on this period," James wrote in his memoir, "I must say…that…neither Anna, my brothers nor I had the guidance and training that…Father would have given us had he not been involved in his own struggle." Due to his long stays in Warm Springs, for most of the 1920s, FDR was away from his children for more than six months a year. And his periodic visits could not make up for his almost complete unavailability the rest of the time. In the summer of 1924, the eighteen-year-old Anna was annoyed when both her grandmother and mother bullied her into making her debut in Newport. "I couldn't go to Father on this," Anna told an interviewer decades later. "He wouldn't give me the time of day." In February 1925, eight-year-old John called his father "a thief." "You may not remember," his furious youngest son wrote, "but you took long ago my black pen. Please write mother and tell her where it is." Feeling completely disconnected from his father, John did not even bother asking him for a reply.

As FDR's chicks hatched, they were all ill equipped to manage the transition to adulthood. In contemporary parlance, the five Roosevelt children received so little attention from their parents that they would all go on to develop lifelong cases of attention-deficit disorder. Impulsivity would reign in nearly all their decisions—particularly in their choices in mates and paramours. (During his presidency, the sexual escapades of his first three sons were well known to Washington insiders.) Like the aimless Jazz Age hedonists depicted in F. Scott Fitzgerald's *The Great Gatsby*, FDR's offspring, too, "were careless people . . . [who] smashed up things and people and then retreated back to their money or their vast carelessness." Feeling ignored and squeezed out by her parents, Anna left the nest at the earliest opportunity. Less than a year after her debut, she married Curtis Dall, a stockbroker with Lehman Brothers who was ten years her senior. "I got married when I did," she later admitted, "because I wanted to get out." While FDR attended the wedding in Hyde Park, James again became his father's legs, as he walked "Sister" down the aisle. The mismatched couple would have two children—Eleanor (Ellie) and Curtis—before their divorce in 1934. In the end, the five Roosevelt children would marry a total of nineteen different spouses and produce twenty-eight grandchildren. Like his elder brother Elliott, Franklin Jr. would divorce four times (his authorship of a mildly successful 1940 pop song, "The Rest of My Life," about marital bliss, notwithstanding). Several of the Roosevelt spouses would be emotionally unstable; two would commit suicide after exiting the family via divorce—Anna's second husband, John Boettiger Sr., and Franklin Jr.'s first wife, Ethel DuPont. And Irene Owens, the third of James's four wives, nearly murdered him. In 1969, as their twelve-year marriage was winding down, she would stab the sixty-one-year-old businessman eight times. By the time of FDR's death, both Anna and James had started second families, and the not-yet-thirty-five-year-old Elliott was already hitched to his third wife.

Due to their inability to focus, higher education and the Roosevelt children never did mix too well. While FDR wanted Anna to complete four years of college, her postsecondary education was limited to a four-month program in agriculture at Cornell. James followed his father to Harvard, but he had trouble getting the "Gentleman's C's" that FDR expected. "Things seem to be going fairly well," James reported to FDR in October 1926, two months into his freshman year, "although I find the work just as hard as it was at Groton and of course much harder to study because of the many distractions and interruptions." He complained that "German...is a continuous struggle and a bore because the instructor is a perfect ham" (in contrast to his English instructor, whom he called a "wow"). He flunked this language course and was put on academic probation the following year. Though his father then urged him "to reconsider carefully the organization of your time and your method of work," James's grades did not improve, and he came up a few credits short at the end of his senior year. Unable to enroll in Harvard Law without a degree, James attended Boston University School of Law for a year before dropping out. Only Franklin Jr. and John would actually obtain a Harvard sheepskin. After eking his way through Groton, Elliott spent a year at the Hun School, where he finally passed his college examinations and was accepted into Princeton. But the following fall, he stunned his parents by taking a job with a Manhattan advertising firm. "In my judgment what Elliott needs," FDR wrote a Groton official after his last term there, "is the definite understanding that an objective simply has to be reached." This was a lesson that his middle child, who would drift from career to career, never quite managed to master.

Like FDR the President, FDR the father—the overscheduled political heavyweight who succeeded "Pa-pa" and "Pa"—would also be a crisis manager. Time and time again, his children would embarrass themselves publicly or get involved in some scrape or other. The first First Family incident occurred on the night of FDR's inauguration. On March 4, 1933, at close to midnight, an inebriated John, then finishing up at Groton, startled the Washington police by driving a jalopy right up to the front door of the White House. Not believing that he was the President's son, a sergeant immediately shooed John away—forcing the adolescent to spend the night in a hotel—an incident which was widely covered by the national press. During his first summer in the Oval Office, Elliott ignored FDR's advice and divorced his first wife, Elizabeth Donner, the daughter of a Pennsylvania steel magnate, after just a year and a half. Moreover, five days after finalizing the settlement in a Nevada courtroom, the twenty-two-year-old got remarried to Ruth Googins, a Texas heiress. This sequence of events would titillate the entire nation, but FDR's only rebuke was a mild one; that Christmas, he failed to invite the newlyweds to the White House. Fences were soon mended, even though in his new job as a columnist for the Hearst papers, Elliott often fulminated against his father's policies.

FDR's high-spirited, hypomanic temperament, which successfully defused so many economic, political, and military challenges, was also well suited to addressing this set of knotty domestic issues. Loyal and forgiving, the pragmatic problem solver never lost his cool—no matter what the provocation. But he was so adept at damage control that his sons had little incentive to mend their ways. Franklin Jr. could not seem to stop his nasty habit of smashing up his car and injuring others in the process. In March 1934, FDR enlisted his presidential staff to help his namesake defend himself against the lawsuit filed by sixty-year-old Margaret O'Leary, who had suffered a lacerated scalp and a concussion along with a broken thumb and ankle when the Harvard student ran her over in front of Boston's Faulkner Hospital.

Franklin Jr. would later face a similar suit in New York and rack up speeding tickets in four other states. As the Associated Press reported in 1935, according to its tabulations, Franklin Jr.'s "accident and speeding record since his advent to Harvard in 1933 resembled the French war debt." In August 1937, John was involved in a small international kerfuffle. As papers across the country reported, the soon-to-be Harvard senior soused the Mayor of Cannes in champagne before proceeding to hit him over the head with flowers during a town festival. Despite pressure from the American embassy to retract his charges, the

Frenchman stuck to his guns. FDR chose to believe John, who, in a missive back home, denied any involvement, claiming that he "wasn't *yet* plastered" (italics mine) at the time of the alleged encounter; on that occasion, John noted, he waited until the wee hours of the morning to begin his serious drinking. The President remained unruffled even when he received a letter from his Harvard classmate, attorney Alfred Sharon, describing John's behavior as "a low record for vulgarity for all time."

In his effort to make sense of his children's irresponsible behavior, FDR laid all the blame on his day job. "One of the worst things in the world is being the child of a President," he told an aide in 1934. "It's a terrible life they lead." But their lives may well have been much worse if he had not possessed the power and the savvy to bail them out time and time again.

FDR's interactions with his wayward sons illustrate his unflappability. This President did not get too caught up in the furor of the moment. In contrast, his eldest son, James, who left the private sector to become his father's secretary in early 1937, literally could not stomach negative publicity. In July 1938, painful ulcers forced him to check himself into the Mayo Clinic. James had been shaken by a recent investigative piece in the *Saturday Evening Post* contending that he had used the family name to earn somewhere between $250,000 and $1 million a year as an insurance agent before coming to Washington. With FDR's canny coaching, James was able to parry these attacks. He released his tax returns showing that he never made more than $50,000 and gave a series of interviews in which he spoke of his frustration with the effort to "smear me...and...the President." But while FDR did not flinch, the stress almost broke his son. In September 1938, James went back to Minnesota to undergo a two-hour surgery in which doctors removed two-thirds of his stomach.

During his second stay in the Mayo Clinic, James, then married to Betsey Cushing, a daughter of the pioneering neurosurgeon Harvey Cushing, fell in love with Romelle Schneider, one of his nurses. That fall, as James was recuperating on a ranch in California, he was startled to receive a visit from Harry Hopkins, FDR's chief aide, who tried to dissuade him from divorcing Betsey. For this President, the personal and the political had long been entwined. FDR had grown attached to Betsey, who often served as a White House hostess during the couple's stay in the capital. Like his mother, FDR did not see anything wrong in meddling in the marital conflicts of his offspring. And since he did not like to address conflict directly, he preferred to hide behind his personal emissary, Hopkins. James had had enough. For the first time in his life, he stood up to his father. Though the son remained polite, he immediately submitted a letter of resignation; he also continued his affair with Romelle, whom he would marry two years later. "[Franklin and Eleanor] were more successful as politicians than as parents," James later observed. "It is as admirable, but imperfect people that I see my parents."

At ten o'clock in the evening of Monday, January 22, 1945, the private train carrying FDR left Washington. With Germany about to surrender, the President was headed to the Crimea to help shape the postwar world with the two other members of the "Big Three"—Joseph Stalin and Winston Churchill.

In the President's entourage were his daughter, Anna, plus a half-dozen aides, including the head of the Office of War Mobilization, Jimmy Byrnes; his press secretary, Steve Early; his Democratic Party crony, Ed Flynn, who hailed from Bronx, New York; and his longtime friend, General "Pa" Watson (who, in James's absence, often helped FDR stand up on important occasions). Various top-ranking administration officials, such as Army Chief of Staff Gen. George Marshall and U.S. Ambassador to the Soviet Union Averell Harriman, would also attend the conference, but they would meet up with the President on the other side of the Atlantic. As Anna later observed, the traveling party consisted mostly of assistants who "just sit on their fannies, and play gin rummy."

Two days earlier, on the bitterly cold twentieth, with James just a few feet to his left, FDR became the first President to take the oath of office on the south portico of the White House. Like his three younger brothers, James was then a full-time soldier, serving as a Marine Colonel in the Philippines. While Elliott was an army pilot, both Franklin Jr. and John were in the navy. James was the only Roosevelt whom the Commander in Chief had ordered to return home for the weekend. FDR was eager for his eldest son to be at his side, just as he had been at his three previous inaugurations. In another nod to sentiment, FDR also made special arrangements so that all thirteen of his grandchildren—the offspring of eight different sets of parents—could attend the ceremony. Simplicity was the order of the day. Highlighting the lessons of the war, FDR's inaugural contained only 551 words. "We have learned," the President declared, "to be citizens of the world."

While the New York Times described FDR as "a happy warrior" who showed "no outward signs of illness," he was already suffering from both heart disease and severe hypertension. The full extent of his frail health was then a secret, known only to a select few such as Anna; Dr. Ross McIntire, his personal physician; and Dr. Howard Bruenn, his cardiologist. FDR was now having trouble carrying out basic tasks. While sitting in the Green Room a few minutes before the inaugural luncheon in the State Dining Room, the President reported to James that he felt chills. Gripping his son's arm, he stated, "Jimmy, I can't take this unless you get me a stiff drink." When James came back with a half tumbler of whiskey, the President downed it in an instant before proceeding to the reception. Though worried about his condition, FDR was not about to miss the chance to negotiate with Stalin face-to-face.

Realizing that she was to see history in the making, Anna was delighted to be crossing the Atlantic. She was also surprised. Like most of his aides, she thought that if any family member were to join FDR, it would be Eleanor or Elliott. His wife had asked, but he had turned her down. "If you go," the President told her, "they will all feel they have to make a great fuss, but if Anna goes it will be simpler," noting that both Churchill and Harriman were also bringing their daughters.

But the real reason had to do with his conviction that Eleanor could not tend to his emotional needs the way his children could. As Elliott once put it, "[On his trips], Pop liked to have a member of the family along, somebody, with whom he could chat, and to whom he could let his hair down." This was a role Eleanor refused to play, as she insisted on being his colleague rather than his caretaker. While FDR initially considered taking Elliott, who had attended the first "Big Three" summit in Tehran, his second son was suddenly a persona non grata with the American people.

Earlier that month, Elliott got embroiled in "L'Affaire Blaze," a scandal that made headlines across the country. In Memphis, three soldiers on leave had been bumped from an army transport plane to make room for Elliott's 130-pound bull mastiff, Blaze, which was flown back to his new bride, wife number three, the Hollywood star Faye Emerson. While Elliott, who then headed the 325th Photographic Reconnaissance Wing in Europe, had not actually requested special treatment for the pooch, he was viciously attacked in the papers, with many writers demanding that he be court-martialed. Ever loyal, the unflappable President went ahead that week with his plan to nominate Elliott, who had also flown on dozens of combat missions, to become a Brigadier General—an appointment that would soon be unanimously approved. But given this public-relations disaster, FDR did not think it wise to have Elliott represent his country on the international stage.

At 6 A.M. on Tuesday, January 23, the train reached Norfolk. A couple of hours later, the President and his daughter boarded the USS *Quincy* in Newport News. Aided by a strong northwest wind, the ship headed out to sea at about 8:30 A.M. Later that morning, as father and daughter were seated next to each other on deck, the President pointed to a spot on the Virginia coastline and said rather matter-of-factly, "Over there is where Lucy grew up."

Lucy, as Anna knew all too well, was his former mistress, Lucy Mercer Rutherford. In 1924, a tearful Eleanor had acknowledged the affair to the seventeen-year-old Anna, who readily identified with her mother's outrage. While FDR had seen little of Lucy in the intervening decades, when her husband, Winthrop Rutherford, became frail—he died in March 1944—he resumed the friendship. The President was now also including Anna in some of his dinners with Lucy. Even though FDR was tugging at his daughter's allegiance to her mother—had Eleanor known about these visits with Lucy, she would have been furious—Anna did not say a word. Anna, who was terrified about her father's weak heart, had "made up her mind," as *Life* put it in early 1945, "that it was her duty to get him to relax." If FDR felt a need to see Lucy, or to allude to the depth of his feeling toward his old flame, Anna would not think of protesting. By way of explanation, she later said, "The private lives of [my parents] were not my business." Realizing that FDR was terminally ill, Anna was reluctant to challenge anything he said or did. "My mother felt his 'magic,' and just wanted to be close and to be of help," John Boettiger Jr., Anna's third child, explained to me.

The trip was so top secret that Anna had to keep most of the details from her husband, John Boettiger Sr. A Lieutenant Colonel in the army, he was on leave in the White House so that he could take care of John Jr. while she was away. "So far," she wrote him on the twenty-third, "I haven't been able to find out if it's safe to mention name and type of ship, convoy and where we started to sea." It was not even clear to her until a few days later in what city the summit would be held.

The following Tuesday, January 30, was FDR's sixty-third birthday. Anna choreographed the party, which delighted everyone on board, especially the President. "Anna made the dinner a gala occasion," observed his aide, Jimmy Byrnes. She topped it off with five birthday cakes—with each one representing an electoral victory; the small fifth cake was decorated with icing in the shape of "1948?" Given her father's tenuous hold on life, Anna knew that he would never run again, but she was eager to make him feel—at least for this evening—as if he could always count on the affection of the American people. The perpetually tired FDR—even though he was getting ten hours of rest a night, he reported never feeling "slept out"—enjoyed the conversation and the jokes and also won all the money at poker. Two days later, the ship reached Malta, its final destination.

On February 3, the President and his aides flew to the Saki airfield, where they met Churchill. Though Yalta was just eighty miles away, the ride along a highway guarded by Soviet troops would take six hours. "Look! How many of them [soldiers] are girls!" an excited Anna told her father. Obsessed with making every leg of the journey as comfortable as possible for FDR, she insisted on sitting next to him so that he would feel free to doze off whenever he wanted.

That evening, they settled into their new quarters in Livadia Palace, which had undergone a few recent metamorphoses. Originally built to be the Czar's summer home, it had resurfaced after the October Revolution as a rest home for tubercular patients before being converted into Nazi Headquarters during the German occupation. As the unofficial chair of the conference, FDR slept in the Czar's former bedroom in the fifty-room mansion. Anna was stationed in a small cubicle at the end of the opposite wing and had to walk a block to take a bath. Before the conference started, a boorish Soviet intelligence agent made a pass at her, causing her father to compare him to some "big businessmen" he knew. Anna was not too distraught, as she knew how to stand up for herself. Though FDR's daughter was sensitive and personable, she was "not a soft nor meek person," Mary Roosevelt, James's fifth wife, who got to know Anna in the 1970s, told me.

The next day, Anna was put in charge of arranging the meals. She quickly realized that this assignment meant tending to the emotional quirks not just of her father, but of the other powerful men in his circle. When Adm. William Leahy, the Chief of Staff to the Commander in Chief, discovered that he was not invited to the informal lunch that she had set up, Anna was forced to issue an apology. "This has given me my first cue," she wrote in her diary, "that I'm going to have to watch certain people's feelings very carefully in this business of eating with the Pres!" By lunchtime, Anna was also "sitting on tacks" as she began making the preparations for the formal dinner that her father was to host that night. Even though she did not yet have a guest list, she asked the maître d'hotel to set the table for the maximum of fourteen. Her plan would have worked smoothly had not Jimmy Byrnes erupted in a temper tantrum just before dinner was to be served. Enraged that FDR had not invited him to attend the first negotiating session that afternoon, Byrnes decided to express his pique by snubbing the President that evening. The irritated aide also instructed her to give FDR this news. Anna did not care whether Byrnes ate with the President, but she knew that the presence of thirteen men at the table "would give the superstitious FDR ten fits." Rather than bothering "FDR and Uncle Joe with this little problem," Anna spent twenty minutes sweet-talking Byrnes, who gave up his protest. The dinner, which lasted past midnight, went swimmingly. By the end, Stalin had warmed up to the idea of the proposed new international organization—soon to be called the United Nations—as long as the great powers had more say than the small powers.

Anna's daily tasks also included entertaining her father. Every morning at nine, after checking in with his various aides, she would bounce into FDR's room to "fill him in with any gossip…which might be amusing or interesting to him." On February 5, FDR enjoyed learning from his daughter that his son Franklin Jr., then still married to Ethel DuPont, was having an affair with Harriman's daughter, Kathleen. As James later noted in his memoir, FDR himself loved the affection of "admiring and attractive ladies," and tales of his namesake's infidelity, rather than alarming him, might well have given the President a vicarious thrill.

But first and foremost, the First Daughter had to be vigilant that the ailing FDR did not overtax himself. She was terrified about the possibility of a sudden health crisis. "Just between you and me," Anna wrote her husband on February 5, "we are having to watch OM [old man] very carefully from the physical standpoint. He gets all wound up, seems to thoroughly enjoy it all, but wants too many people around, and then won't go to bed early enough...[I am]...trying my best to keep abreast as much as possible of what is actually taking place at the Conf so that I will know who should and who should not see OM... And the biggest difficulty in handling the situation here is that we [his two doctors and I] can, of course, tell no one of the ticker trouble. It's truly worrisome and there's not a helluva lot anyone can do about it. (Better tear off and destroy this paragraph)." Had not Anna performed this role so conscientiously, FDR might not have lived another two and a half months.

In fact, she might well have been personally responsible for having kept him alive up until that point. The previous March, when FDR came down with a 104-degree fever in the White House, an alarmed Anna learned that Ross McIntire had not been taking his blood pressure regularly and demanded that the doctor set up a medical exam at Bethesda Naval Hospital. Diagnosed with congestive heart failure, FDR immediately began taking digitalis. Upon doctors' orders, he also cut his drinking down by about half—to one and a half cocktails per evening—and his smoking by about 80 percent—to just five or six cigarettes a day.

For most of the conference, Anna was a bystander rather than a participant. She often did not even eat during the meals that she had organized. But on February 8, along with her two counterparts, Kathleen Harriman and Sarah Churchill, Anna attended the festive dinner hosted by Stalin at Yusupov Palace. During the long proceedings—the guests stayed until 2 A.M.—a staggering total of forty-five toasts were exchanged. The Soviet strongman was in an uncharacteristically ebullient mood. After praising Churchill as "the bravest governmental figure in the world," Stalin proposed a toast to FDR's health, noting that the American President has been "the chief forger of the implements that have led to the mobilization of the world against Hitler." In response, a sanguine FDR described the dinner as a "family gathering," noting that "though each of the national leaders present is pursuing the interests of

his people in a different way, we are all dedicated to providing all the
people of the world a glimpse of opportunity and hope."

At Yalta, the most powerful man in the world did fall back on some
of the same negotiating strategies that he had long used at the family dinner table in Hyde Park. Avoiding conflict wherever possible, he
tried to promote the welfare of the group by relying on his own idi-
osyncratic mix of charm and cajolery. His achievements were considerable. During the eight days of plenary sessions, FDR did get Stalin to
support the conference in San Francisco that would launch the United
Nations. Stalin also accepted the President's idea to give veto power
to members of the Security Council. With the President's help, Churchill persuaded Stalin to allow the French to have a sector in occupied
Germany. In private meetings with Stalin, FDR also managed to enlist
Russia in the war against Japan.

But on the fate of Poland and the rest of Eastern Europe, FDR did
prove much too conciliatory. The resulting communiqué, the Declaration on Liberated Europe, which proposed free elections "broadly
representative of all democratic elements" in the countries once occupied by Germany, was too fuzzy, and Stalin would quickly renege on
his promises. FDR was not unaware of the problem. As he summed up
the conference for Adolph Berle, an original New Deal Brain Truster,
"I didn't say the result was good. I said it was the best I could do." Stalin would have proved an enormous challenge for any President, but
FDR was limited by his own personality style, which precluded aggressive face-to-face confrontation. He could be tough with his enemies,
but not with his allies, which Stalin was at that moment. His "ticker
trouble," to which many historians have assigned the entire blame,
probably played just a small role. As Dr. Bruenn recorded in his medical notes, after a tough round of negotiations on Poland on the day of
Stalin's dinner, FDR's heart suffered a brief bout of pulsus alternans
(alternating strong and weak beats)—his only health scare during the
trip. But without Anna's conscientious care—her legwork—the President might have been barely able to function at all.

On March 1, just thirty-six hours after returning to American shores, FDR, accompanied by Eleanor, Anna, and his son-in-law John Boettiger Sr., settled into a limousine at the White House. His destination was the Capitol, where he was to give "a personal report" on Yalta to a joint session of Congress. He began the hour-long speech with an explanation of why he spoke from a chair, noting his need "to carry about ten pounds of steel at the bottom of my legs." This was the first time that FDR had publicly alluded to his bout with polio. After twenty-one years—ever since his reemergence at Madison Square Garden in 1924—his "splendid deception" was over. For the wan President, this was no time to worry about his personal appearance. He was keenly aware that his former boss, Woodrow Wilson, had failed to convince the Senate to ratify the Treaty of Versailles, thus dooming the League of Nations. "This time," the President insisted, "we are not making the mistake of waiting until the end of the war to set up the machinery of peace." FDR concluded by expressing his hope that his recent diplomatic efforts would help build "that better world in which our children and grandchildren, yours and mine, the children and grandchildren of the whole world must live and can live." But FDR himself would no longer be living by April 25, when delegates from fifty countries convened in San Francisco to establish the United Nations.

While FDR's children would not endure another world war, their lives, particularly in the decade immediately following his death, would often be tumultuous. After the war, Anna and her husband started the *Arizona Times*, a publishing venture that quickly went belly-up. So did their marriage when Anna discovered that a distraught Boettiger, who suffered from chronic depression, had been seeing other women. In 1950, a year after remarrying, Boettiger committed suicide by jumping out the window of a Manhattan hotel. Broke and plagued by various health ills, including desert fever, which she acquired during her sojourn in the southwest, Anna needed several years to get back on her feet.

James's first postwar foray into politics was a disaster; in 1950, Earl Warren beat him by more than a million votes in the California

Governor's race. A few years later, FDR's eldest son was humiliated when his second wife, Romelle Schneider, aired his dirty laundry in public. As their divorce was being finalized, she provided evidence that he had carried on affairs with a dozen women during the marriage. And during custody hearings, Romelle disclosed her husband's confession that he led "a very unhappy life arising from his lack of parental attention as a child . . . [and] was not aware of the meaning of a normal home and family life." Despite all the bad publicity, James managed to win a Congressional seat in 1954, which he held on to for a dozen years. "He found his niche as a Congressman," said his first son with Romelle, James Roosevelt Jr., who also told me of his pride that his father served as the floor manager for the 1964 Civil Rights Bill.

Elliott would continue to be trapped in the soap-opera-like existence of his own creation. On Christmas Day, 1948, his third wife, actress Faye Emerson, slit her wrists at Hyde Park, an event which left his mother shaken. "None of you children experienced security," a guilt-ridden Eleanor told him. "Father was the one who could comfort all of you, and he fell ill before your eleventh birthday."

Franklin Jr. was the first member of the next generation to be a success at the ballot box, becoming a Congressman from New York in 1949. However, his political career essentially ended in 1954 when he lost the race for state Attorney General. A little over a decade later, Franklin Jr. could not even win the Democratic nomination for Governor; running on the Liberal Party ticket, he came in a distant third to Republican Nelson Rockefeller. Franklin Jr. would turn his love of fast cars into a vocation, as he maintained a Fiat distributorship for many years.

John would continue his rebellious ways. After the war, the press revealed that he would have registered as a conscientious objector had not his mother talked him out of it at the last minute. "But you have a responsibility," Eleanor insisted, "to your father and the country such as no other boy would have." In 1952, John came out as a staunch Republican. Acknowledging that he had voted for Dewey in 1948, he began giving speeches for Eisenhower. John would also differentiate himself from the rest of the family by marrying only twice and leading a quiet existence as a Manhattan stockbroker.

By the mid-1950s, relationships among all the children were frosty. "There was no trace of kinship," reported Elliott on the last meeting of all the siblings after Eleanor's death in 1962. A decade later, James and Elliott feuded bitterly over their parents' legacy by publishing a series of competing memoirs.

In contrast to her brothers, Anna would eventually enjoy a remarkably stable and productive life, becoming, as one relative put it, "almost happy." After settling into a satisfying marriage with the physician James Halsted in 1952, she carved out a successful career in medical public relations. She also devoted herself to numerous philanthropies, such as the Wiltwyck School for Boys, the country's first interracial school for emotionally disturbed children, which had been founded by her mother. Her fund-raising efforts resulted in a new campus for this residential reform school, whose distinguished alumni included boxer Floyd Patterson and activist Claude Brown, author of the bestselling novel *Manchild in the Promised Land*. Though she and her brothers had grown up among plenty rather than poverty, they could readily identify with the struggles of inner-city youth. "Yet on a personal level," James observed, "there was something missing from our lives, which even the most disadvantaged youngster may have…We never had the day-to-day discipline, supervision and attention most children get from their parents."

Anna, who died of throat cancer in 1975 at the age of sixty-nine, was perhaps the least scarred of the five children. "This was not a family that typically had much psychological insight or self-awareness. My mother was an exception; she had a relatively rich interior life," explained her son, John Boettiger Jr., who went on to earn a Ph.D. in clinical psychology. As FDR's eldest child, she got to spend fifteen years with the physically vibrant "Pa-pa." "He would ride horseback with me and point out different varieties of birds as they darted by,"

Anna later recalled of her early memories of Hyde Park. "I loved those rides and the companionship...It's hard to equate those days with the post-polio days when family life was busy and complicated." Likewise, during his years in the Wilson administration, her father would often escort her to school, inquiring about her favorite books along the way. These fond memories appear to have given her a solid emotional foundation, which her siblings lacked.

On Saturday morning, July 2, 1955, forty-six-year-old Texas Senator Lyndon Johnson called a press conference. With Congress about to adjourn for the year, the second-youngest majority leader in Senate history wanted to highlight his stunning list of legislative achievements over the past six months. Thanks to his remarkable powers of persuasion, combined with his inimitable ability to reach across the aisle, the Eighty-Fourth Congress managed to bump up the minimum wage to $1 an hour, finance the interstate highway system, and increase foreign aid.

Having secured his place as the second most powerful man in Washington, Johnson was now officially presidential timber. That Saturday's *Orlando Sentinel* featured an editorial urging him to run against Eisenhower in 1956. Observing that "the Democratic party is in a pretty sorry-looking pickle," the paper declared, "The people want a new name, a new face, a man with a general rather than a specific appeal...This man is Lyndon Johnson." The *Washington Post* was about to publish its own story about Johnson's presidential prospects.

After abruptly ending the session when the AP reporter brought up the charged topic of immigration reform—which he did not wish to talk about—Johnson scarfed down a lunch of franks and beans along with some cantaloupe. That afternoon, he headed off to Huntland Farms, the swanky Middleburg, Virginia, estate of his buddy, Texas real estate tycoon George Brown, where he planned to spend the holiday weekend. At about six o'clock, while Brown was passing out the cocktails, Johnson began experiencing extreme physical discomfort, which he first attributed to indigestion. "My arms are heavy and I feel like someone's sitting on my chest," he told fellow Senator Clinton Anderson of New Mexico. An alarmed Anderson, who was on the mend from a recent heart attack, blurted out, "Lyndon, you're having a coronary," and he suggested calling a doctor immediately. Concerned that any public disclosure of illness could thwart his presidential aspirations, Johnson initially nixed that idea. But the pain refused to subside. A couple of hours later, an ambulance took Johnson to the cardiac unit at Bethesda Naval Hospital. His wife, Lady Bird, was already waiting for him at the entrance to the emergency room, as she had dashed out of their two-story colonial house on Washington's Thirtieth Place as soon as Brown called her with the disturbing news.

"My mother faced an excruciating decision," Johnson's younger daughter, Luci, recently told me. "July second happened to be my eighth birthday, and I was sick in bed with a fever of 104. She could either stay with me or rush to her sick husband. I now realize that she must have been scared silly."

While waiting for the elevator to take him up to the cardiac unit on the seventh floor, Johnson suddenly went into shock. He became, as Lady Bird later put it, "as gray as the cement sidewalk...I was horrified. He was no longer Lyndon." She then called Luci and her eleven-year-old sister, Lynda, to say that she was not coming home. That night, the family's cook, Zephyr Wright, whom the Johnsons had first hired in 1942 when she was a student at Wiley College, watched over the girls. Lady Bird stayed with LBJ day and night until his discharge from the hospital in early August.

Both Lynda Bird and Luci Baines Johnson were used to long separations from their parents. Like the Roosevelts, the Johnsons were dedicated to public service long before their White House years. First elected to a House seat in 1937—three years after his marriage— Johnson expected Lady Bird to be his full-time political helpmate. During the war, she ran his Congressional office. Even when her children were toddlers, she was constantly on the road giving speeches on behalf of LBJ. "You either have to cut the pattern to suit your husband or to suit your children," Lady Bird stated. "Lyndon is the leader. Lyndon sets the pattern. I execute what he wants. Lyndon's wishes dominate our household." For most wives of her era, caring for one's husband or one's children was not necessarily an either/or proposition, but the chronically needy LBJ issued incessant demands. "He expected her to devote every waking hour to him, which she did," said a family friend. The girls were raised by a committee, which, in addition to the cook, Zephyr Wright, included the African-American couple Helen and Gene Williams, personal assistants who lived with the family from 1950 to 1961. Their official surrogate mother was Willie Day Taylor, a former staffer, who, as Johnson admitted, also pitched in and "nursed" him. Though Lynda and Luci often felt neglected and abandoned, they were in good hands. "Luci and I fell in love with each other on first sight," remarked Taylor.

In late August 1955, the Johnsons relocated to the family's ranch in Fredericksburg, Texas, where LBJ spent the next few months recuperating. Forced to reflect, he realized his life "was so lopsided as to be ridiculous. After all, there was something in the world besides my job." That fall, he began to acquaint himself with his girls, whom he hardly knew. As he recounted in a magazine article, "My Heart Attack Taught Me How to Live," published the following summer, "We played games together—they could give me stiff competition at dominoes—and took turns reading aloud from their books. We watched our favorite television programs together. I was pleased beyond words by their ready acceptance of me. Why, they liked me!" Unlike most fathers, the woefully insecure LBJ was shocked to discover that his daughters were eager to attach to him.

Though Lyndon Johnson was an expert in forging political alliances, he never fully understood basic human connection. His half-baked ideas about parent-child bonding reveal an almost crippling level of anxiety in all interpersonal relationships in which he did not exercise complete control. A few days before Lynda's birth, he admitted "how nervous I am about this." When the infant developed colic, Johnson was thrown into such a tizzy that he suggested to Lady Bird that they call on their Rock Creek Park neighbor, J. Edgar Hoover, for help. (Fortunately, he was quickly brought back to reality by his wife, who reminded him that this was not a matter that the unmarried FBI Director could handle; the couple eventually got some tips from the wife of a local doctor.)

One Sunday morning, when Lynda was three and Luci was still an infant, LBJ was lying in bed discussing strategy for his first Senate campaign with his aide, Joe Phipps, who was seated next to him. Lady Bird suddenly brought in the girls for some quick kisses, and Johnson enjoyed playing with them for a few minutes. According to Phipps, after Lynda and Luci then proceeded to crawl all over him, Johnson lost control. When the girls would not respond to his efforts to calm them down, he yelled, "Bird! Bird! Come get these little sons of bitches off my bed!" In everyday social interactions, this master Congressional negotiator did not have a clue about how to conduct himself. But Johnson's emotional obtuseness may well have been responsible for his impressive legislative achievements as majority leader and later as President. In his theory of human motivation, affection was totally missing. As Johnson saw it, fellow politicians went along with you not because they liked you but because they either feared you or wanted something from you.

As soon as LBJ returned to the Senate floor in January 1956, he worked as hard as ever. In fact, his brush with mortality only added to his sense of urgency. "We Johnson boys die young" was a favorite refrain. A victim of two heart attacks, LBJ's father, Sam Johnson, had died two weeks after his fiftieth birthday. Once again, LBJ lost touch with Lynda and Luci. Whenever he was around them, he was sweet, but those occasions were few and far between. Recalling the late 1950s, Luci recently asserted, "I didn't see him period"—a statement that is only a slight exaggeration. Desperate for more bonding, his daughters were willing to do practically anything to reel him back in. As they eventually figured out, if they wanted to connect, they would have to do it through politics. As a teenager, Lynda devoured his favorite publication, the *Congressional Record*, in order to have something to talk to him about. In 1964, when LBJ was running against Barry Goldwater to stay in the White House, Luci did not hesitate to go out on the hustings to campaign for her father. That year, the seventeen-year-old performed "daddy duty," as she referred to her speaking gigs, in twenty-six states all by her lonesome. But whenever she returned from a trip, LBJ gave her his undivided attention. "My father would ask me to tell him about three new people whom I had met; and then to name three things that were important to them. He also wanted to know what I had learned along the way and he expected me to respond with a laundry list," emphasized Luci. After conducting this examination, the former English instructor at Houston's Sam Houston High would give his daughter a letter grade. "His girls loved their dad and always wanted to get an A-plus," recalled former Johnson staffer Tom Johnson (no relation), the journalist and publisher who ran CNN in the 1990s.

Luci's seventeenth birthday—July 2, 1964—was also a momentous day—and not just for herself and her family, but for the entire nation.

A few months earlier, without any parental prodding or assistance, the enterprising high school junior landed a three-day-a-week summer job at the office of her optometrist, Dr. Robert A. Kraskin, doing visual training. Dr. Kraskin's specialty was behavioral optometry, and in the past year, he had managed to clear up her own longstanding vision problems. With her daily commute, Luci made history, as she became the first presidential child to "set out in a White House car to 'punch a clock' and earn a salary," as the *Washington Star* society columnist Betty Beale put it. (While FDR Jr. had toiled at a yeast factory the summer after his junior year at Harvard, his worksite was located in Belleville, New Jersey.)

Luci decided to take her birthday off to sleep late and "wash my hair," as she informed the curious White House press corps. That morning, she got a special invitation from her parents to join them at breakfast, where her mother presented her with her gifts—a nightgown and robe along with a wig imported from Europe.

At 12:10 P.M., LBJ sat down and wrote her a card, which he sent along with a yellow rose. "It was the only handwritten note I ever got from my father," recalled Luci. With his political identity trumping his paternal identity, Johnson chose to conclude it not with "Dad," but with his standard presidential signature, which he would affix that evening to the Civil Rights Act of 1964. "That was the best birthday present. He was everyone's daddy that day," she added.

Luci and Lynda had lunch with their mother in her bedroom. Zephyr made a lemon birthday cake, which Luci cut before remembering that photographers would want to capture it for posterity. In the official pictures taken a few hours later, a big hole in the cake is readily apparent.

At about two that afternoon, the House of Representatives approved the Senate's version of the bill by a vote of 289 to 126. Though the Democrats held a large majority in both houses of Congress, Johnson had garnered bipartisan support. Of the 171 Republicans in the House, 136 voted for the bill. After hearing the news, Johnson decided to hold a signing ceremony just before 7 P.M. in the East Room of the White House (the same room in which Luci's half-eaten cake had been shown to the world). Surrounded by two hundred dignitaries, including numerous Congressional leaders from both parties and several prominent civil rights leaders such as Dr. Martin Luther King Jr., A. Phillip Randolph, and Roy Wilkins, LBJ gave a ten-minute televised address. "Let us close the springs of racial poison," Johnson concluded. "Let us hasten that day when [we]...will be free to do the great works ordained for this nation by the just and wise God who is the father of us all."

After giving away seventy-five pens as mementos, LBJ turned to his wife, saying, "Do you remember that nine years ago I had a heart attack?"

"Congratulations on your anniversary," she responded.

LBJ then quipped, "Lucy is seventeen and I am nine."

When Luci was alone with her father a few minutes later, she asked why he gave the first pen to Republican Senator Everett Dirksen rather than to one of the civil rights leaders. "You don't get it, do you?" said LBJ, eager to give his daughter a lesson in how to forge political bonds. "I didn't have to do anything to convince them. It was Everett Dirksen... bringing the people he brought with him that made the difference, and made the civil rights leaders' dream and my dream, come true."

That evening, Bill Moyers noticed that LBJ was not upbeat, but depressed. "I think," the President lamented to his special assistant, "that we've just delivered the South to the Republican Party for the rest of my life, and yours." Seeking some relief, LBJ called Lady Bird. "What do you think?" he asked. "We might just get off to Texas tonight." After a quick dinner, the couple boarded a helicopter on the south lawn to go to Andrews Air Force Base, from where they flew directly to the ranch in the JetStar, the small Lockheed aircraft LBJ used for trips home. Before packing her bags, Lady Bird arranged for Willie Day Taylor to watch over Luci. Once again, LBJ's younger daughter would spend the evening of her birthday apart from her parents.

At two o'clock on the afternoon of July 2, 1965—her eighteenth birthday—Luci Baines Johnson stood next to Fr. James Montgomery at the front of Washington's Saint Matthew's Cathedral, where nearly two years earlier an entire nation had paid tribute to a fallen President. In the house of worship that afternoon were twenty of Luci's friends, including her beau, Patrick Nugent, a recent graduate of Marquette University, along with a few elderly ladies in black dresses, a couple of nuns, and about a dozen supplicants. So, too, was the President of the United States, accompanied by his wife and twenty-one-year-old daughter, Lynda Bird, who had just flown in from the West Coast. For about ten minutes, Luci professed her faith by reading aloud the

Nicene Creed and a couple of other sacred texts. Then Father Montgomery tipped her head back into the baptismal fountain. "If you have not already been baptized," he declared, "then I baptize thee in the name of the Father, the Son, and the Holy Spirit." Now an adult, Luci was "determined not to divorce herself from her family," but she still wanted to chart her own course.

Though Luci would remain a dutiful daughter, she had often felt boxed in by her busy and high-profile parents. In the summer of 1964, as she was campaigning against Republican presidential nominee Barry Goldwater, the seventeen-year-old told *Seventeen* magazine, "You know I'll never really be Luci Johnson. I'll always be Lyndon Johnson's daughter. Let's face it. If I ever do anything great, it'll be because I'm the President's daughter." On her application to Georgetown University, where she planned to study nursing, she described her father's occupation as "government employee."

But her frustration with the self-absorbed and egotistical LBJ, who insisted that the three female Johnsons all share his initials, had actually begun long before her White House years. At just ten, his younger daughter changed the last letter of her first name from *y* to the "swinging *i*," as one reporter would later put it. "It was my little way," Luci recently admitted to me, "to keep my identity. I wanted to be me, too."

This independent streak also manifested itself in her choice of religion. At thirteen, she began practicing Catholicism, even though her mother was Episcopalian and her father belonged to the Disciples of Christ. In the fall of 1964, she embarked on a course of instruction in the Catholic faith from Father Montgomery, which culminated in her conversion nine months later. Both her parents publicly asserted that they supported Luci's decision, but in private, they expressed reservations. However, by now, Luci had learned how to negotiate with her father. Having watched a master at work, she would borrow a couple of elements from his playbook—including charm. Luci knew that snuggling up to her father and throwing her arms around him while blurting out, "There you are, handsome!" could often help her cause.

At the conclusion of the brief service, Luci stayed for her first confession, but LBJ, Lady Bird, and Lynda went back to the White House. "I could not help but think," Lady Bird later wrote in her diary, "we went in four and came out three." That afternoon, Luci celebrated her birthday at a "come as you are" party in the White House Solarium attended by thirty friends. Once again, Willie Day Taylor was called upon to play "Mama," as Luci's parents were nowhere in sight. After taking a helicopter for New York, where LBJ addressed the National Education Association, the Johnsons flew to the ranch that evening. On the plane to Texas, LBJ lectured his wife for three hours about politics and legislative procedure, as was his wont. Alluding to the recently passed Elementary and Secondary School Act, which provided federal funds for the education of underprivileged children, he noted that "putting the Catholics and the Protestants and the Jews together in the Education Bill" was perhaps his finest achievement. Of the new Catholic in the family, he spoke not a word.

A little more than a year later, on August 6, 1966, LBJ and Lady Bird were back at a Catholic church to watch Luci go through another significant rite of passage. The occasion was her wedding to the twenty-two-year-old National Guardsman, Patrick Nugent, at Washington's Shrine of the Immaculate Conception, the seventh largest church in the world. This step, too, was one that LBJ and his wife had initially opposed, as they both considered Luci too young. After turning her down the previous October, LBJ gave his consent at Christmas when Nugent presented his daughter with a diamond engagement ring. With some seven hundred guests in attendance, the "ceremony [was] unmatched in size, splendor and ritual," reported the *New York Times* in its front-page story, "by the wedding of any other Presidential daughter in American history." Everything about the event was Texas sized, including the seven-tiered cake served up later that afternoon in the Blue Room reception, which weighed in at three hundred pounds. The three national TV networks all devoted three hours to live coverage. Immediately after taking their vows, the couple greeted the President and Mrs. Johnson, who were seated in a front pew before walking over to see the groom's mother, Tillie. As Luci and her husband made their way down the aisle, she attended to a little bit of family business, stopping to plant a kiss on the cheek of her father's key Congressional ally, the Republican Senate leader, Everett Dirksen. The Nugents would have four children, but divorced in 1979. Like Anna Roosevelt, Luci also had been too eager to seek a refuge from her dysfunctional family. "I was desperately trying to be normal," she explained in 1994. "One way out of the fishbowl was to marry."

A year and a half later, the twenty-three-year-old Lynda married twenty-eight-year-old Marine Captain Charles Robb in an Episcopal ceremony in the East Room. While the outgoing Luci was, as presidential aide Tom Johnson later put it, "the good press daughter," the shy Lynda rarely said much. In a casual aside, which was often repeated in the papers, LBJ had once described Lynda as the smart one and Luci as the pretty one. While Luci laughed off her epithet ("By gosh, do y'all think I'm dumb?" she would say), Lynda became very self-conscious and began to "doubt whether she was pretty," as Lady Bird later acknowledged. However, the image of LBJ's elder daughter underwent a major metamorphosis when soon after Luci's wedding, she started a highly publicized romance with Hollywood A-lister George Hamilton, which lasted about a year. In accounting for Lynda's selection in a mate, Tom Johnson has suggested that somewhere in the back of her mind may have lurked a desire to help her father, then mired in an unpopular war. "The President said what he really needed," observed this trusted aide decades later, "was one of his daughters marrying a soldier going off to Vietnam." In fact, Robb, who was set to be shipped off to the war in a few months, would do two tours of duty as a Marine Commander. At the beginning of the service, the Reverend Gerald MacAllister asked who was giving away the bride, to which the President replied, "Her mother and I." All five hundred onlookers were stunned that this Civil Rights President also harbored a closet feminist within. "I had never realized," Lynda later stated, "that he was that progressive." The Robbs would have three children. After his return from Vietnam, Robb went into politics. In 1981, he was elected Governor of Virginia and he later served two terms as a Virginia Senator.

On June 21, 1967, Luci gave birth to LBJ's first grandchild, Patrick Lyndon, known as "Lyn." Upon seeing the infant for the first time a few days later at a Catholic hospital in Austin, the President was quick to notice that the boy did not share his preoccupations. "Patrick Lyndon," LBJ told an interviewer, "doesn't seem to be nearly as concerned with the world's problems as I am." Unable to contain his excitement, the President repeatedly injected the newest family member into his extensive negotiations that week with Soviet Premier Alexei Kosygin. After their first five-and-a-half-hour meeting, LBJ stated, "[Kosygin] has been a grandfather longer than I have. And he and I agreed that we wanted a world of peace for our grandchildren."

As the President became increasingly rattled by the failure of his military efforts in Southeast Asia, he often turned to Lyn for comfort. In moments of stress, he would bark out to an aide, "Go find Lyn." "As soon as I brought my son into the Oval Office," Luci told me, "my father would get down on his hands and knees and start playing patty cake." On Lyn's first birthday, LBJ arranged for his grandson to conduct his own Rose Garden press conference. Seated behind a tiny table, the toddler appeared in a red, white, and blue jumper. Around his neck hung a White House pass containing his picture and identification. (Unbeknownst to the press, the pass also contained a signed letter from LBJ's former DC neighbor, FBI Director J. Edgar Hoover, stating that "nothing derogatory was found in the files of the FBI against Patrick Lyndon Nugent.") Before cutting a piece of cake with a pocket knife, the President stated, "You've got the platform. Anything you want to tell them?" After issuing a quick "no comment," Lyn turned his attention to trying to eat the candle.

Once LBJ retired to the ranch in 1969, Luci was worried that her father would become unhinged without the daily political battles to which he had been accustomed during his three and a half decades as a public servant. "But he discovered play," she noted. "That was a word that was not in his vocabulary." While he no longer applied the famous "Johnson treatment" to any wavering Congressmen, he still used it on his daughters. As a young mother, Luci continued to do volunteer work for Head Start, which she had begun in 1965, the year this celebrated Great Society program was launched. Given her interest in behavioral optometry, she was conducting visual screenings for preschool children. But her father felt she was not doing enough. He also wanted her to do screenings at a site near the ranch, which was thirty miles from her Austin home. When Luci alluded to the inconvenience, Johnson went into overdrive. "'What, you don't love your father?' he said," as she recently told me. "'You don't love those kids?' It was easier to do what he wanted you to do."

As much as Luci still loves her father and remains proud of his legislative successes, she is also aware that his intensity has left scars. After becoming engaged to her second husband, the Scottish-born financial advisor Ian Turpin, in the early 1980s, she traveled to England to meet his family. At an afternoon tea, she gave a brief speech in which she thanked his relatives for their warm welcome. Afterward, she expected Ian to give her an evaluation, but none was forthcoming. "I was anxious that I had upset Ian by doing something wrong. Then it dawned on me that I was waiting for him to give me a grade just as my father used to do. I had to learn that not every family does that," Luci recalled with a laugh.

————————

"I had a discussion with my daughter, Amy, the other day," President Jimmy Carter said halfway into his one and only debate with Republican challenger Ronald Reagan, "before I came here to ask her what the important issue was. She said she thought nuclear weaponry and the control of nuclear arms."

The date was Tuesday, October 28, 1980. The site was the Cleveland Convention Center Music Hall, where the two candidates squared off before 120 million television viewers. In the Gallup poll released the day before, Carter had led Reagan by three points, but the following Tuesday, he would be booted out of the White House by ten. "Until the night before the election, we thought we were going to win," Carter's second son, Chip, told me. While Carter's quick aside about his daughter was not the only reason for this dramatic reversal, it was a major contributing factor. For Reagan, this was the gaffe that kept on giving. Two days later, in a speech in Milwaukee, in response to chants of "Amy, Amy," Reagan delighted a cheering crowd by milking it. "Oy, I know he [Carter] touched our hearts—all of us—the other night. I remember when Patti and Ron were tiny kids. We used to talk about nuclear power." The next night, *Tonight Show* host Johnny Carson promised viewers, "This will be a significant monologue because I asked Amy Carter what she thought were the most important issues to make jokes about." Seizing on the momentum, Republican operatives passed out bumper stickers: ASK AMY, SHE KNOWS.

Carter had intended to showcase his thirteen-year-old daughter as a thoughtful and informed citizen of the world. After a phone call a couple of days earlier, in which Amy asked him to clarify what a megaton bomb was, the President noted proudly in his diary, "She discusses international issues…almost like an adult." During a strategy session on the afternoon of the debate, his advisors warned him not to allude to this father-daughter exchange, because it would sound contrived. But Carter remained convinced that this "splendid idea" would humanize him. Little did the President realize that he would come across as a laughingstock, a wimp either unwilling or unable to wield his paternal say-so. That Carter was, in fact, anything but a softie as a parent did not matter. This clunker reinforced what Democratic pollster Patrick Caddell identified in a June campaign memo as a widespread critique of the President: "not in control of government, doesn't seem to want to use his power and authority." At the time, America's power seemed to be rapidly declining, as Iran's Ayatollah Ruhollah Khomeini had been holding fifty-two Americans hostage for nearly a year and the Soviets had just helped themselves to Afghanistan. These words pushed many voters over the edge. If Carter could let Amy tell him what to do, even this once, how could they possibly trust him to stand up to petty dictators in foreign lands, much less Soviet leader Leonid Brezhnev? When the White House Communications Director Gerald Rafshoon saw the debate on TV, he chose to laugh rather than cry about the President's cluelessness. "It's so bad," he said to himself, "that it's funny."

This disconnect between what Carter thought he was doing and the message that he actually communicated to millions of Americans highlights just how preoccupied this First Dad was. For Carter, as for FDR and LBJ, politics had long been a 24/7 obsession and his primary way of connecting with everyone, including his children. Like Anna Roosevelt and Luci Johnson, Amy Carter also needed to immerse herself in policy minutiae simply to get her father's attention. He had little idea how to relate to her quotidian concerns. When she returned from the Thaddeus Stevens Elementary School in the late afternoon, he could not just chitchat about her ups and downs. The President felt compelled to turn her report about her day into actionable intelligence. "I even derived useful information from Amy," he boasted in his 1982 presidential memoir, *Keeping Faith*, "as she described her experiences in public schools. What would improve the school lunch program? How could we help the children who could not speak English? Were the students being immunized against contagious diseases? What was being done to challenge the bright students in the class or to give extra help to the slow ones?" Even more remarkable, Carter described these complex queries as "the normal questions of interest to any family." This President's missionary zeal to improve the world simply blinded him to the way most "normal" families behaved. No doubt the parents of most of Amy's classmates probably stopped at much more basic questions such as whether their child could stand the school lunch and if not, how they might help—say, by providing a homemade sandwich or a piece of fruit.

In contrast to both FDR and LBJ, Carter would survive long after he left the White House. To his credit, decades later, he would realize just how self-absorbed he had been while serving as an elected official. "Perhaps like most other people," Carter acknowledged in *Sharing Good Times* (2004), "I have had to overcome a self-centered inclination to live on my own terms, sometimes obsessed with intense ambition, bringing others into the private recesses of my life only reluctantly." He later felt regret for his frequent inability to treat Amy and her three elder brothers—as well as his wife, Rosalynn—as separate individuals with their own unique hopes and fears. As Carter acknowledged, he had long assumed that every member of his family would automatically be thrilled with whatever he did to chase his career goals.

In this 2004 memoir, he was embarrassed to provide a "most vivid example of this strange relationship" with his wife and children. On October 1, 1962, his thirty-eighth birthday, the gentleman farmer was about to dash out of the house when Rosalynn, noticing that he had exchanged his overalls for a "Sunday suit," asked him where he was going. He then admitted that he was off to the county courthouse to sign up to run for the Georgia State Senate. Lost in his own internal musings, Carter had not considered it necessary to mention to anyone in the family his plans for the immediate future.

And his decision to enter politics would soon have a major impact on both Rosalynn and their three sons—Jack, Chip, and Jeff, then aged between fifteen and ten. (Amy was not born until 1967.) After winning the seat, Carter would spend several months a year in Atlanta, forcing Rosalynn and the boys to run the farm in Plains by themselves. It took a long time, but Carter eventually figured out how to forge two-way connections with members of his own family—something which, he has admitted, "did not come easy for me." As a senior citizen, Carter also finally learned how to enter into the inner world of a younger person and to nurture. "Rosalynn and I have become better parents and grandparents," ran his 2004 mea culpa, "as we've learned more about the interests, peculiarities, and sometimes the partially concealed problems and needs of the other two generations in our family." But by

sticking his wife into the same category as himself, this heartfelt confession seems to be a tad misleading. By all indications, Rosalynn was
never quite as out of touch with the rest of the family as he once was.

———————

Just as FDR the father can be divided into three phases, Carter fits
neatly into four: the absentee navy dad; the farming dad; the political dad; and the post-presidential, generative dad, granddad, and
great-granddad.

Carter's three sons were all born while he served in the navy, and
he rarely spent time with any of them until his discharge in 1953.
While the family was living in Norfolk, where Jack was born in 1947,
Carter spent all week and one-third of his weekends aboard the USS
Wyoming. Looking back over his seven years in the navy—which also
included stints in New London, Pearl Harbor (where Chip, whose
name means "baby" in Hawaiian, was born in 1950), San Diego, New
London again (where Jeff was born in 1952), and Schenectady—Carter
estimates that he was typically aboard ship about twenty-five days a
month. Due to what Carter later called his "almost total obsession
with my [military] career," his wife handled "all family responsibilities"
by herself. But even when he was physically present, Carter was not
emotionally available either to his wife or his children, as he has also
acknowledged. The exhausted and often lonely Rosalynn, who was just
nineteen at the time of their marriage, was forced to hide her crying
spells. "Tears... instead of being persuasive or eliciting sympathy," she
observed in 1984, "had quite the opposite effect on Jimmy. He had
and still has no patience with tears, thinking instead that one makes
the best of whatever situation—and with a smile." Habituated to a
military work environment, Carter could not change when he was off
duty. He became an autocratic head of household who, as he noted in
1996, held the "expectation that those junior to me would honor my
commands."

Carter's second phase of fathering began after his sudden move back to his native Georgia. In the summer of 1953, he took a one-week leave from his work in Adm. Hyman Rickover's nuclear submarine program to visit his father, James Earl Carter Sr., known as Earl, who was dying of pancreatic cancer. An autodidact who had dropped out of school after the tenth grade, the athletic Earl was a successful businessman who ran the family's 360-acre farm in Plains. A former director of the Rural Electrification Agency and a member of the county board of education, the fifty-eight-year-old had recently won a seat in the Georgia House of Representatives. While Carter was engaging in long conversations with his father, he was moved by the stream of visitors, black and white, who stopped by to bring some food or fresh flowers. "A surprising number," Carter later observed, "wanted to recount how my father's personal influence, community service, and many secret acts of generosity had affected their lives." Carter experienced the same "aha" moment as the Jimmy Stewart character at the end of Frank Capra's immortal 1946 Christmas movie, It's a Wonderful Life—except that Carter realized that it was his father, not himself, who enjoyed an idyllic existence in his small hometown. Inspired by Earl's example, Carter soon resigned from the navy and took over the farm, vowing to become a pillar of the Plains community.

Moving into a public housing project, where the family would live for the next eight years, Carter put his boys to work as soon as they were able. That first year in Plains, six-year-old Jack put in ten-hour days on Saturdays, answering the phones in his father's office, for which he was paid—albeit just ten cents an hour (sixty-five cents less than the federal minimum wage at the time). In the summers, Jack cleaned out the warehouse, and in peanut season—September and October—he dropped everything to do the harvesting. "You just sort of worked until you couldn't work," his eldest son recalled in 2003, "and then went home and slept until you woke up and then went back." As a preteen, Jack took on even more grueling tasks, such as unloading 115-pound bags of land plaster (a fertilizer). He also learned how to drive the four-wheelers that hauled the peanuts. His younger brothers—Chip and Jeff—followed him up the same employment ladder. "I labored very hard around Labor Day," recalled Chip. "When I was fourteen, I often ran a peanut driver for twelve hours straight at night. I once worked fifty hours in a row—with just a few naps."

While long hours of toil were not uncommon among farm boys of their generation, Carter was a particularly demanding taskmaster. "My grandfather exhibited a military strictness with his children," Chip Carter's eldest son, James Earl Carter IV, told me. (In the fall of 2012, this grandchild, now a political consultant based in Atlanta, became, as the former President put it, "the most famous Carter," when he passed on to *Mother Jones* the video in which Mitt Romney pronounced 47 percent of voters freeloaders.) Continuing to follow navy protocol, Carter expected his children to keep the peanut fields shipshape. "It was within the capability of even a six-year-old to walk back and forth along the rows and pull up any plants that were not supposed to be there," Carter later wrote about his days as a farming dad, "and just a glance from my pickup truck would reveal any omission in performing their duties."

Carter's exacting standards had roots in his own upbringing. While he idolized his hardworking father, who was not without a playful side, he also feared him. At five, at Earl's insistence, Jimmy would walk five miles to sell bags of boiled peanuts. Whenever his father posed the leading question, "How would you like to pick some cotton today?" he immediately went to work with a smile. "I never even considered disobeying my father," Carter later admitted. Behind these paternal orders was the threat of a whipping with a peach tree switch. While actual physical punishment occurred only a half-dozen times, "these impressive experiences," to use Carter's own words, had a formidable impact.

With his mother, Lillian, working long shifts as a nurse, Jimmy learned to disconnect from his feelings. In his eighth-grade scrapbook, the ambitious adolescent rhapsodized about the benefits of emotional detachment. "A person who wants to build good mental habits," the future President wrote, "should avoid the idle daydream, should give up worry and anger, hatred and envy." Purposeful activity became his all-consuming obsession. As his navy buddy Rod Colegrove put it, "He always wanted to do something constructive."

And like FDR, Carter saw his sons as extensions of himself who could help him achieve his ambitious goals—say, building a booming business or winning a lofty elective office—a sentiment he also expressed through a clumsy use of pronouns. In his quickie autobiography *Why Not the Best?* (1975), Carter used the phrase "When *we* returned home from the Navy," to describe the entire family's move from New York to his native Georgia in 1953 (italics added). Moreover, Carter expected his sons to be as driven to succeed as he was. "Dad sort of believed," Jack remarked in 2003, "that if you were going to do something, you should do it to your absolute best." This intensity was a frequent source of family tension. "And I'm not sure that I ever particularly agreed with that," added Jack. "I felt that you could be much more diffuse in your life."

As a farming dad, Jimmy was only a slightly less extreme version of Earl. "He attempted," wrote a recent biographer, "to mold [his sons] in his and Mr. Earl's image." During the decade of this incarnation, Carter nearly morphed into a full-fledged tiger dad, much like John Adams, another farmer turned President. Like Earl, who rarely offered words of praise, he used more sticks than carrots. If his children failed to keep their rooms spic-and-span or get all As in school, there were consequences. A B would mean a week without TV. "I think I got one C," Jack later recalled. "But that was a horrible thing, and I made As in that course for the rest of the time."

Besides restricting leisure activities, Carter would dish out various other punishments, including extra farm work and spankings with a wooden paddle. When Chip was in eighth grade, he failed a Latin midterm. "Dad became incensed," he told me. To make sure that

Chip passed the course, Carter himself spent a week studying the dead language before beginning daily tutoring sessions. "I got an A in the makeup exam," Chip added proudly. Though Carter enjoyed leisure activities such as fishing with his boys, he could not stop stressing the value of self-improvement. Even vacations were freighted with teachable moments. When the family went to Mexico in the summer of 1965, he insisted that his children order all their meals in Spanish.

While his sons never stopped wanting to please their father, as adolescents, they started to rebel. All three developed a cigarette habit, much to the annoyance of Carter. During the 1976 campaign, Rosalynn admitted that her sons had "experimented" with marijuana. Chip has since acknowledged serious drug problems dating back to college. While living in the White House, Carter's middle son liked to relax by going up to the roof to smoke a joint.

Though Jack was a finalist for a National Merit Scholarship and graduated second in his high school class, he ran into considerable problems in college. Inspired by his father's experience with nuclear-powered submarines, he started out studying physics at Georgia Tech. When he got bad grades because he was spending too much time playing cards, he transferred to Emory, where he also did poorly. He then performed better at Georgia Southwestern before transferring back to Emory. But in the winter of 1968, he wrecked his car—an event he later described as "an excuse" to drop out of college. At his father's insistence, Jack signed up for the navy and went to Vietnam, though he did not do any combat duty. A couple of years later, he was caught smoking marijuana, and in December 1970, he received a general discharge. When later asked about his father's response, Jack issued the following understatement, "Dad was not appreciative, but he was sort of involved in his own things by that time." A month earlier, Carter had been first elected Governor of Georgia.

The farming dad began to fade away during his initial foray into electoral politics—that race for the Georgia State Senate in 1962. As

Carter shifted gears, he continued to rely heavily on his family. As he began campaigning full-time, he promoted his wife from bookkeeper to administrator of the farm and peanut warehouse. And in her spare time, she pumped some flesh. Likewise, his sons emerged as key aides; without the manpower supplied by the Carter boys, his political rise would have been unthinkable. His preoccupations became their preoccupations. "Let's face it, I'm a political animal," the twenty-eight-year-old Chip told a reporter in 1978. "What I breathe and eat and talk is politics." Alluding to the hotly contested 1962 race, which Carter won after a recount, he added, "I've been involved in Dad's campaigns since I was 12 years old and was delivering handbills to shops in south Georgia. I spent three months on the '66 campaign for governor. I'd drive to a town by myself, go out to the fields and talk to farmers. I was 16. We lost that one." Rosalynn has described the 1966 race for the Democratic nomination, in which her still relatively unknown husband fell just twenty thousand votes short of qualifying for the runoff, as "the first family campaign." That summer, all three sons moved to Atlanta and did whatever they could to help. While both Jack and Chip went out on their own, Jeff drove around the state with his mother.

Determined to win the governorship the next time around, Carter took just a month off before beginning anew. "His secret weapon," he later wrote, was "family teamwork." During the last leg on what was essentially a four-year campaign, Chip dropped out of Georgia Southwestern to work full-time on behalf of his father. Then in boarding school in Atlanta, Jeff popped up at the Carter headquarters, which happened to be located in the state capital, at every opportunity.

After Carter's inauguration, his three sons moved into the swanky Governor's Mansion with him. They all went into the new family business—politics—as soon as they could. After graduating from Georgia Tech, Jack worked as a liaison for the Georgia Assembly, where he counted votes on key issues, before going to law school at the University of Georgia. Chip, who lived in a basement room so he could listen to loud music, left Georgia Southwestern a second and final time to work eight hours a day as an unpaid intern in the Governor's office. "My father was always tight with the dollar, and I never got paid for any job I did with him. It's not something he believed in," stated Chip in 2008. Jeff took on a similar gig after finishing high school.

Amy was born in the middle of Carter's second campaign for Governor when he was out almost every evening, and her experience as a child had little in common with that of her elder brothers. She never had to endure any backbreaking farm work. Her father appears to have felt that she may have gotten off a little too easy. "It is almost as though she has four fathers, and we have to stand in line to spoil her," wrote Carter in 1975. Just as Carter would often lean on his sons to be his stand-ins on the campaign trail, so, too, did he ask them to compensate for his being an absentee dad in Amy's early years. While Carter finally had some face time with Amy in the early 1970s—he would read *Henny Penny* to her in the large closet that doubled as her secret retreat, and take her trick-or-treating—their contact was still relatively limited. As Governor, he was already busy laying the foundation for his presidential run, which he announced during his last month in office.

Like LBJ, Carter arranged for a full-time surrogate parent for his daughter. Her nanny was Mary Prince, a young prisoner serving time at the Fulton County Jail, who was assigned to work in the Governor's Mansion in 1971. On January 14, 1975, the day the Carters returned to Plains and Mary to the pen, a disheartened Amy let out a piercing scream. Convinced that Mary had been framed, Carter helped her get released two years later. After he was appointed her parole officer, Carter invited Mary to resume her parenting duties in the White House. Mary and Amy kept each other entertained; they enjoyed doing the robot and the bump—1970s fad dances—in Mary's cozy third-floor bedroom. Like her father, Amy disapproved of smoking and would routinely put out Mary's cigarettes.

As President, Carter saw more of Amy than ever. Besides interacting every night over those policy-heavy conversations at dinner, they also swam and bowled together a few times a week. Bookish and shy like her father, Amy liked to read during White House banquets. Though the press considered her rude, her proud father believed that she was "proceeding with her Carter family habit."

By the time Carter launched his first presidential campaign, his three sons were all married—Jack to Judy Langford, Chip to Caron Griffin, and Jeff to Annette Davis. This private army of six full-time volunteers made all the difference. "Primarily thanks to this all-inclusive family team effort," a still-grateful Carter wrote in 2004, "I became President." Six months into the race, Carter remained a complete unknown. "I was living with Chip in a condemned house in New Hampshire in the spring of 1975," Caron, Chip's first wife, told me. "One day, we passed out a thousand brochures, and only one person had heard of Jimmy. I felt that I was wasting my time working alongside him. We then decided to start doing our own events." Chip estimates that he must have knocked on one-third of all the doors in New Hampshire by the time of his father's victory in the primary the following February. While Amy stayed with Rosalynn's mother back in Plains, Jimmy, his wife, and mother, Lillian, plus the six adult members of the second generation, fanned out all over the country. And this broad reach was instrumental in raising the desperately needed cash. To qualify for federal matching funds under the recently passed Federal Election Campaign Act, the campaign needed to raise at least $5,000 in twenty states in contributions of $250 or less. By the end of that summer, Carter put himself on the map by becoming the fifth Democratic candidate to meet the requirements. Half of the twenty states in which he had raised that minimum amount were in the south—the region to which the industrious Caron was also later assigned.

During Carter's presidency, both Chip and Jeff along with their wives would live in the White House. Chip worked full-time for the Democratic National Committee, while Jeff attended George Washington University. Jack, in contrast, returned to Georgia, where he got his first job as a lawyer. However, with the national press corps covering Amy's every move, many Americans came to believe that she was the President's only child. Chip, who continued to travel around the country raising money in his new post, complained that he was often introduced as "Amy Carter's brother." But all the time away from Washington—often as many as twenty-four days a month—ruined his first marriage. He became unfaithful. "I was a simple guy from Plains and I wasn't used to ladies coming up and saying that they wanted to be with me," Chip confessed to me. "I did not know what I was doing. I was an idiot." Unlike FDR, Carter could listen to his son when he brought up his messy personal life one day in the Oval Office. Eager to fix the problem, the President gave it some thought and eventually sent Chip and Caron off to a marriage counselor in Atlanta. But the therapy did not take, and the couple divorced in 1980.

In contrast to her brothers, Amy never went anywhere near electoral politics. When asked about a possible political future in 1984, she stated, "Never, Daddy. I hate telling people what to do." Even so, father and daughter would continue to bond over hot-button issues. A few years later while she was a Brown University undergraduate, Amy was arrested several times for her political activism. She never doubted her father's support. In April 1987, after being acquitted along with Abbie Hoffman and a dozen other protesters of a disorderly conduct charge for participating in an anti-CIA demonstration in Massachusetts, Amy spoke into a megaphone, urging supporters to attend an upcoming rally at CIA headquarters. "Everyone out there should be at Langley," she stated before adding with a smile, "Tell your parents to come."

———

Jimmy Carter might have remained a preoccupied dad forever had not his eldest son, Jack, confronted him with a thunderbolt a few years into his post-presidency.

One day in the mid-1980s while they were hunting together, a tearful Jack blurted out, "Daddy, I've been wanting to tell you for years. I think the way you treated me as a child almost ruined my life."

"And I, my reaction was anger at this ingrate," Carter later said of this startling moment. "All I did for him, he didn't appreciate. So I went home and told my wife about it, and it took us a long time to realize that we were not good parents."

For a couple of years, father and son refused to see each other, preferring to communicate only through letters, which were often emotionally charged. Rosalynn helped act as an intermediary. While they later reconciled, some tensions remain. "The conflict between Jack and his father remains a sensitive issue," stated Judy Langford, who was married to Jack until 1989 and is still friendly with him, in a recent interview with me.

After much soul-searching, Carter became sympathetic to Jack's concerns, realizing that he had, in fact, internalized the harsh parenting style of his own father, Earl. "When I became a father I emulated my daddy," he reflected in 1996. "I was a naval officer. I gave my three boys orders. If they didn't carry my orders out, they were punished. And it was only later…when my oldest son finally made me realize that I was not a good father." He particularly regretted the severe discipline that he had meted out during his years as a farming dad. Carter, who in 1978 brokered the Camp David Accords and in 2002 won the Nobel Peace Prize for "his decades of untiring effort to find peaceful solutions to international conflicts," was forced to confront that he himself had sometimes strayed from his high ideals in his own home. Chip believes that the further removed Carter was from his navy career, the better his parenting became, noting that Jack probably got punished the most and that Amy was totally exempt from what he calls his "philosophy of spankings." "My father used to tell me, 'I will spank you tomorrow,' and the waiting was always more terrifying than the punishment itself. I guess that's why he did it that way," Chip told me. "But I was probably spanked only about ten times."

As Carter wrestled with his conflicted feelings about how he had unwittingly passed on some of his own childhood pain, this obsessive writer, who has published nearly thirty books since he left the White

House, wrote a poem, "I Wanted to Share My Father's World." Referring to Earl's aloofness, Carter wrote of how he still feels "the need for just a word of praise." No longer blind to how superobedient he had once been, he acknowledged that he "despised the discipline he [Earl] used to shape what I should be."

While Chip flirted with a Congressional run in 1982, Jack has been the only Carter child to seek elective office. In 2006, he ran for a Senate seat from Nevada, but he lost to the Republican incumbent, John Ensign. In 2010, Jason, the elder of Jack's two children from his first marriage to Judy, followed his grandfather to the Georgia State Senate. Four years later, Jason won the Democratic nomination for Governor, but lost in the general election.

Now married to his third wife, Becky Payne, Chip has worked as a consultant on hundreds of campaigns for Democratic candidates. In recent decades, he has spearheaded various humanitarian missions for the Carter Center. For example, in 1997, he helped stave off a civil war in Liberia by monitoring the elections there.

Jeff is still married to Annette, with whom he had three children. A technology wiz, Jeff settled in Georgia where he runs a firm, Computer Mapping Consultants. Amy, who received a master's in art history from Tulane, married James Wentzel in 1996, and they are raising their son, Hugo, in Atlanta. She has illustrated a couple of her father's books, such as his 2001 memoir, *Christmas in Plains*.

After working to repair his relationship with Jack, Carter vowed to be a more nurturing presence in the lives of his large brood. To maintain close connections with his children, grandchildren, and great-grandchildren, for the past two decades, Carter has taken the entire family on a trip every year between Christmas and New Year's. About twenty younger Carters typically accept the annual invitation, so the self-confessed penny-pincher has quipped that he must keep writing his books in order to foot the bill. "I think Dad may still feel a little guilty that he wasn't around much when his own kids were younger and may be trying to compensate," speculated Chip. Destinations have included Belize, Panama, and Tibet. A dab of Carter's military intensity permeates the arrangements. "My grandfather plans the schedule down to the last minute. And he expects everyone to be on time," stated James Earl Carter IV, alluding to Carter's longstanding obsession with punctuality. "On a couple of occasions, some family members almost got left behind."

2

Playful Pals

"My Father Likes Snakes"

I love all these children and have great fun with them, and I am touched
by the way in which they feel that I am their special friend, champion,
and companion.

> President Theodore Roosevelt on his children and
> their Oyster Bay cousins, August 16, 1903

On January 5, 1854, after what he described as "a long and tedious
voyage from San Francisco," thirty-one-year-old Ulysses S. Grant, Captain of the Fourth Infantry Division, reported for duty in his new post
in Humboldt Bay, California. On account of the stormy conditions,
the 250-mile trek on the small sailing vessel, the *John S. McKim*, had
taken two full days. "I can not say much in favor of the place," wrote
the bored and lonely Grant two weeks later to his wife, the former Julia
Dent, who was living at White Haven, her father's farm outside of St.
Louis. Asked to do little but fill out a few forms every now and then,
this West Point graduate of the class of 1843, who had not seen much
of his wife since their marriage six years earlier, whiled away his days
sitting in his room and reading. With the weather too cold for hunting,
his only diversion was an occasional ride on one of the fort's public
horses.

Grant had never found it easy to be away from his family, which
already included three-year-old Fred and one-and-a-half-year-old

Ulysses Jr. After Fred's birth, he had asked for a four-month leave, citing "urgent family reasons." In the summer of 1852, soon after his arrival in California, this Victorian-era soldier lapsed into the patois of twenty-first-century psychology, explaining to Julia, "No person can know the attachment that exists between parent and child until they have been separated for some time. I am almost crazy sometimes to see Fred. I cannot be separated from him and his Ma for a long time." In Humboldt Bay that winter, these feelings of distress were spinning out of control, and the career army officer was starting to snap. "My Dear Wife," Grant wrote on February 2, 1854. "You do not know how forsaken I feel here! The place is good enough but I have interests… which I cannot help thinking about day and night…I feel again as if I [have] been separated from you and Fred long enough and as to Ulys. I have never seen him…How very much I want to see all of you."

Though numerous historians have painted Grant as a heartless "butcher"—given the violent charges that he led as the Commander of the Union Army—he was a devoted father who constantly fantasized about frolicking with his children when he could not do it in the flesh. "I had a long dream about Fred last night," Grant wrote to Julia in early 1853. "I thought I was at home and playing with him. He talked so plain that he astonished me, then too his remarks were so sensible." From Humboldt Bay, Grant kept prodding his wife to fill him in on how Fred and Ulysses Jr. were amusing themselves. "Write me a great deal about our little boys," he insisted on February 6, 1854. "Tell me all their pranks. I suppose Ulys. speaks a great many words distinctly?" In comparison, his military duties seemed completely meaningless. "How very anxious I am to get home once again," he wrote a month later. "Dear little boys what a comfort it would be to see and play with them a few hours every day!" Due to his love for his sons, the American army was about to lose one of its most capable young soldiers.

The legend of Grant the irresponsible alcoholic dates back to his lonely years in the early 1850s, when he often turned to whiskey to mitigate his despair. But he drank not because he was an antisocial misfit, but because he was a sensitive family man who simply could not stand to be without his nearest and dearest. While eyewitness accounts are missing, most Grant biographers assume that by early April 1854, his commanding officer, Robert Buchanan, saw him drunk one pay-day and threatened to court-martial him. Whether prodded by the testy Buchanan or simply overwhelmed by his own anguish, on April 11, 1854, Grant made the fateful decision to resign his commission.

His wife worried about the loss of his military salary, but she was delighted to welcome him back home. "How very happy this reun-ion was! One great boy by his knee," Julia later observed, "one curly-headed, blue-eyed Cupid on his lap, and his happy, proud wife nestled by his side. We cared for no other happiness."

Grant was eager to begin his new life on the one hundred acres of farmland given to him by his father-in-law. "Whoever hears of me in ten years," he informed a friend in 1854, "will hear of a well-to-do old Missouri farmer." But his prophecy did not come close to holding true. Until his return to the armed forces at the beginning of the Civil War, this gentle, five-foot-seven-inch, 135-pound Midwesterner would be an abject failure as a breadwinner. While the macroeconomic collapse behind the Panic of 1857 was partly to blame, Grant never could make ends meet as a gentleman farmer. On December 23, 1857, he was forced to pawn his gold hunting watch for twenty-two dollars. About a year later, shortly after the birth of his fourth child, Jesse—a daugh-ter, Ellen (Nellie), had been born in 1855—Grant sold his house and crops and moved to downtown St. Louis to try his hand at real estate. In the fall of 1859, he suffered another setback when he lost his bid to be appointed a County Engineer in St. Louis, "an office of respect-ability and emolument that would have been very acceptable to me at this time," as he later recalled. Though he was devastated, harmony continued to reign in his family. The evening of his political defeat he sat reading in his drawing room, while, as his wife noted, "our children were happily playing in the garden under a pink cloud of peach and apple blossoms, all unconscious of the anxiety that filled the hearts of their parents."

In May 1860, the family of six relocated to Galena, Illinois, where Grant eked out a modest salary of $60 a month as a clerk at his father's general store. Despite all the hardship and uncertainty, Grant stayed away from liquor. When Eastern salesmen offered to "treat" him to something, he asked for a cigar, not a drink. He also never lost his interest in entertaining his children. He enjoyed reading aloud the novels of Charles Dickens—*Little Dorrit* was a favorite—to the entire family. The cash-strapped father did not hesitate to make his own toys such as paper boats, which his boys would sail in gutters after rainstorms.

In those last couple of years before the war, he and his toddler engaged in a "daily play spell," which the adult Jesse would later describe in his memoir as an "established custom...the one vivid memory of my life in Galena."

"Mister, do you want to fight?" the boy greeted Grant as he hopped up the steps to the family home after spending a day at the store.

"I am a man of peace; but I will not be hectored by a person of your size" was his father's scripted reply. And then the wrestling match began, in which the delighted toddler always came out on top. "In time," Jesse recalled decades later, "the fact that at the end of the bout father always fell upon a bed or the sofa and stretched contentedly there—led me to suspect that he was not doing his best, but it detracted nothing from my enjoyment nor weakened my firm conviction that, with the possible exception of myself, father was the best battler in the world."

Grant's four-year stint in the Union Army did not interrupt his playtime with his children. Far from it. As his staff officer, Horace Porter, observed, Grant's four children, aged from three to eleven at the start of the Civil War, "often romped with him and he joined in their frolics as if they were all playmates together. The younger ones would hang about his neck while he was writing, make a terrible mess of his papers, and turn everything in his tent into a toy."

Ulysses S. Grant related to his children more as a pal than a papa. In their presence, his inner boy came out. And play was the primary means by which he connected with them. But no President exemplifies the playful pal better than Theodore Roosevelt, the father of six children under eighteen during his first year in office. As many contemporaries observed, his wife, Edith Carow, had to manage a household of seven children: Alice, the daughter of TR's first wife (also named Alice, she died soon after giving birth to the couple's only child), her own five, and her husband. In fact, "mother" was the term that TR frequently used to refer to his second wife. And TR often acted as if he were one of Edith's younger children. As Cecil Spring Rice, the veteran British diplomat and the best man at TR's second wedding, put it, "You must always remember that the president is about six." TR eagerly taught his four sons how to shoot, box, swim, row, sail, and ride, and he viewed them as his buddies rather than his boys. On the occasion of the tenth birthday of Ted Jr., Roosevelt presented his firstborn son with a rifle. When the stunned lad asked if it was real, TR shot a bullet into the ceiling, noting, "You mustn't tell mother."

In contrast to both Grant and TR, who also showed their fun-loving side outside the family, Woodrow Wilson came across in public as dour. But in the company of his three daughters, he could often be found singing, dancing, and cracking jokes. At the family dinner table, this playful professor, who was an actor manqué, tended to provide the entertainment.

Other Presidents who fit this description include James Buchanan, Chester Arthur, and George W. Bush. Buchanan, who served from 1857 to 1861, remains our only bachelor President. In 1841, Buchanan, then a Pennsylvania Senator, became the guardian of the two orphaned daughters of his late sister, Jane Lane—the fifteen-year-old Mary and the eleven-year-old Harriet. Harriet lived for a few years at his home in Lancaster before joining her elder sister in a boarding school in

Virginia. Buchanan became particularly close to Harriet, whom he proudly referred to as "his adopted little daughter." Harriet called him Uncle James, or "Nunc." Playful banter cemented their strong bond. The rambunctious and vivacious Harriet, who would grow up to be a talented musician and dancer, would delight Buchanan with her impersonations of leading politicians. In 1854, a year after Buchanan was appointed as Minister to the Court of St. James's, he summoned Harriet to join him in England, where she dazzled the royal family. Noticing that Buchanan and Harriet, who served as his First Lady, had little in common with their predecessors, the melancholy Pierces, one contemporary observer noted at the dawn of his presidency, "Again all is joy and gladness in the Executive Mansion."

While Chester Arthur, who inherited the presidency upon Garfield's death in September 1881, insisted that his children address him as "sir," he had a playful nature. As a young lawyer and Republican operative, he liked to stay up until the wee hours of the morning drinking and smoking cigars with his political cronies. As President, he once climbed in through the window to return to the Executive Mansion after a night on the town. But Arthur also enjoyed taking his family on fancy vacations where he could share his love of sailing and horses. A five-week jaunt to Rhode Island in 1873 cost $600 (then nearly twice the annual salary of the average worker). Fearing that he might lose another child to an early death—his first child, William, had died at two—he indulged both of his surviving children, Chester Jr. ("Alan") and Ellen.

Much to Arthur's disappointment, his son emulated him. Alan was not averse to starting Executive Mansion champagne parties for his Princeton classmates at three in the morning. Dropping out of Columbia Law School, Alan settled into the life of a polo-playing playboy. In 1900, he married an heiress, Myra Townsend, with whom he had a child. The marriage was not happy, and he eventually deserted her. In 1934, the sixty-nine-year-old Alan Arthur married a woman nearly thirty years his junior. He died of a heart attack three years later. Not much is known about the former President's daughter, whom the intensely private Arthur shielded from the press during his time in the limelight. Ellen Arthur married the New York lawyer Charles Pinkerton and died childless at forty-three.

Like Chester Arthur, the jocular George W. Bush had a penchant for drinking with his buddies until he abruptly gave up alcohol the day after his fortieth birthday. Bush's clownish side also frequently came out in his relationships with his twin girls, Jenna and Barbara, who both introduced the sitting President at the 2004 Republican Convention. A Yale graduate like her father, grandfather, and great-grandfather, Barbara mentioned that one of the key things she learned growing up was "the importance of a good sense of humor." Jenna, who had just received her bachelor's degree from the University of Texas, joked that she and her sister kept trying to tell him that "when we are young and irresponsible, well, we are young and irresponsible"—an indirect allusion to the fact that they both had been arrested early in his presidency for underage drinking. Barbara liked to invite her Yale friends down to the White House for Halloween parties. "It was all these gay people tromping around in ridiculous costumes and he loved it," reported a family friend. Since finishing college, both Bush daughters have turned more serious. Barbara is the cofounder and CEO of Global Health Corps, a nonprofit that provides fellowships to young professionals dedicated to fighting for health equity all over the world. In the last year of Bush's presidency, Jenna, who now works as a correspondent for NBC News, married the businessman Henry Hager. The couple has two daughters, Margaret and Poppy, who was named after her great-grandfather, the forty-first President.

Due to their generous and fun-loving nature, playful pals tend to develop affectionate bonds with their children. But this type of parent is typically permissive and unable to set appropriate limits. Alan Arthur became addicted to being spoiled by his father. In 1878, when the elder Arthur lost his cushy job as Collector of the Port of New York, a cousin wrote the fourteen-year-old Alan, "It will now be time for you to reduce your expenses. No more wasting large sums of money on the foaming soda water. And you had better prepare to pawn some of your cravats." But Alan would never mend his high-spending ways. Playful pals also rarely get around to providing much guidance to their children, who often grow up feeling as if they can do whatever they want without considering the consequences. Like Alan Arthur, Grant's two younger sons, Ulysses Jr. (also known as "Buck") and Jesse, as well as TR's son Kermit, would remain irresponsible well into adulthood and never find a meaningful purpose for their lives.

In recent decades, researchers have begun studying the long-term impact of playful fathers on their children. In contrast to mothers, fathers tend to challenge children—particularly their sons—more in play by testing them and teasing them. Not only do the youngsters often prefer this type of play, but it appears to carry a host of benefits. According to a growing body of empirical studies, fathers like Grant or TR, who engage in rough-and-tumble play with their toddlers, may well boost both their intellectual development and language ability. The developmental psychologist Daniel Packet of the University of Montreal, who argues that the "need to be stimulated, pushed and encouraged is as great as [the] need for stability and security," is also convinced that playful fathers can help children adapt to various new situations in the world outside the home—such as school. But positive outcomes are far from guaranteed, as these father-child interactions are just one of many environmental and genetic factors that shape the growth and development of any individual.

───────────

Even the fog of war could not stop Grant from obsessing about how to keep his children entertained. On June 17, 1861, two days after his appointment as the commander of the Illinois Seventh District Regiment, he informed his wife that he "would like to bring Fred [11] and Buck [9] down...with me to spend a month of their vacation if you will let them." Buck had a sensitive disposition and was not interested in being near the front—a decision that Grant respected. But Fred was "perfectly jubilant" to ride beside him, as Grant noted soon after his eldest son's arrival. "The Soldiers and officers call him Colonel," added the proud father, "and he seems to be quite a favorite." In mid-July, Grant sent Fred home when his unit entered enemy territory. "He did not want to go at all," he reported to Julia, "and I felt loathe to send him but...I thought you would be alarmed if he was with me." On the day his firstborn left him, Grant developed a splitting headache, which incapacitated him for a few days. In September 1861, not long after he was promoted to Brigadier General, Grant wrote his wife that he wanted to "take Fred back with me for the balance of the campaign. Won't you let him come?...I will take good care of him." Julia soon relented. As Grant's volunteer aide-de-camp, Fred would live and eat in his father's tent for most of the war. On many a night, father and son would sleep side by side.

In March 1864, Grant shared with his eldest son one of the high-lights of his life. On the eighth, accompanied by the thirteen-year-old Fred, he arrived in Washington where President Abraham Lincoln was to appoint him Lieutenant General—an honor that no other Ameri-can soldier, except for George Washington, had ever received. At the Willard Hotel, he signed the register, "U.S. Grant and son, Galena, Illinois." A stunned desk clerk, who had not recognized the man in the travel-stained uniform, immediately switched their lodgings from a dusty attic room to a sumptuous guest suite. That evening, after putting Fred to bed, Grant met Lincoln for the first time at the Presi-dent's weekly reception. The following day, with Fred at his side, Grant attended a ceremony at the Executive Mansion where he accepted his commission and delivered a short speech. Most Grant biographers agree that his decision to enter Washington with his son rather than with his wife helped to elicit the enthusiastic reception by Lincoln and his cabinet. "The solider who had made his way to the captaincy of the republic," noted William McFeely in his Pulitzer Prize–winning life of Grant, "was coming simply—a father with his eldest boy—to its capital to claim his rank and responsibilities."

Grant repeatedly made special arrangements so that his two youngest children could also visit him during the war. In May 1863, as his troops were fighting the Confederate Army outside of Vicksburg, he managed to procure "the smallest horse I ever saw," so that both eight-year-old Nellie and five-year-old Jesse would be able to take turns riding alongside the troops during an upcoming family visit. As he proudly explained to Julia, "the little Rebel," as the black Shetland pony was named, was "so small that Fred can ride him with one foot dragging on the ground. You must not neglect bringing a little saddle for both Jess and Miss [Nellie], and a small bridle." For Jesse, who accompanied Grant on inspections of Vicksburg, his father's myriad preparations during those "wonderful days" gave him the thrill of a lifetime. As Grant's youngest son later recalled, "The soldiers made me very welcome, carving all sorts of toys and regaling me with molasses candy made over the camp fires." Jesse also loved the pony, which became his steady companion for nearly two decades. For this General, fatherhood provided a helpful tonic, which he freely prescribed to army colleagues. "I believe Ruf," he wrote to the forty-something Maj. Rufus Ingalls in early 1864, "you are still leading a bachelor's life? Don't you regret it? Now I have four children, three boys and one girl, in whose society I feel more enjoyment than I possibly can with any other company. They are a responsibility giving much more pleasure than anxiety. It may not be too late for you yet."

No matter how much strain this Civil War commander was under, he was nearly always gentle and even-tempered in the presence of his family. The exceptions were few and far between. Shortly after the victory at Vicksburg, five-year-old Jesse was seated at a table with some older children during a dinner in Columbia, Kentucky. Missing the attention of his father and his military staff, Jesse rebelled by wearing his hat. When Grant asked him to take it off, Jesse promptly threw the hat on the floor. An exasperated Grant gave Jesse a single spank—the only one the boy ever received—before conceding, "Never mind, son. It was really a mistake for the Governor of Kentucky to expect a man of your size to dine with children."

Grant had a hard time saying no to his children. His permissiveness constituted both a continuation of and a reaction against the parenting that he had received back in Georgetown, Ohio. Grant noted in his memoir that "there never was any scolding or punishing by my parents." While his parents were never mean to either Grant or his five younger siblings, they rarely expressed tender feelings. Grant's father, Jesse, who ran a tannery, could also be judgmental; not understanding the despondent Captain's decision to leave the army in 1854, Jesse went directly to Secretary of War Jefferson Davis to try to get his son reinstated—a ploy that did not work. Grant's mother, Hannah, was distant; as a boy, he never saw her cry, and when he was President, she never visited him in the White House. For his own children, Grant sought to be the parent he never had—the one who gave endless affection. However, in his eagerness not to repeat his past, Grant went too far in the other direction. He refused to lay down any laws at all.

Despite her protestations to the contrary, Julia Grant was just as uncomfortable wielding parental authority as her husband. The couple, who enjoyed one of the more storybook-like marriages in presidential history, shared several core character traits. Though more high-strung than Grant, Julia was also loving and generous. With the children, this southern aristocrat also preached discipline, but was not much of an enforcer. When six-year-old Jesse refused to go to school, Grant gave Julia the following advice from Union headquarters: "I think you will have to show him you are *boss*"—an injunction she had a hard time following.

A year into his presidency, Grant decided to escort fifteen-year-old Nellie from Washington to Farmington, Connecticut, to begin her first year at Miss Porter's Academy, fearing that if his wife did the deed, she would only "cry and bring her back." But he also proved powerless in the face of the teenager's unwillingness to give the exclusive prep school a try. A few days after arriving, Nellie telegraphed Grant, "I shall die if I stay here," and he immediately asked his friend Marshall Jewell, a former Connecticut Governor, to fetch her. Sarah Porter, the school's headmistress, was shocked that none of the adults in Nellie's orbit seemed to set any limits, observing, "It is a pity—[Nellie] is a nice child—but no child could be unhurt by such attentions as she receives...I was somewhat disgusted by Governor Jewell's subserviency." A year later, when thirteen-year-old Jesse wanted to withdraw from Cheltenham Academy, a prep school located near Philadelphia, Grant capitulated before his wife. When Jesse first complained, Julia tried to be firm, responding, "When you have been there longer, you will like it better." But Jesse then pleaded with his father, who immediately sent back a telegram, "We want you, too. Come home at once."

During Grant's first term, Nellie and Jesse lived at home, where both were educated by private tutors. In contrast, his two elder children were rarely in Washington—Fred was at West Point, and Buck attended Phillips Exeter Academy before moving on to Harvard. But neither of his younger children would do all that much studying. Jesse, who saw the Executive Mansion as his personal playground, put much more energy into carrying out his duties as president of the secret boys' club that he cofounded on Christmas Day, 1871, in a tool house—originally given to him by his father as a playroom. Dubbed the K. F. R. Society—the meaning of its initials was also top secret—it was the model upon which Quentin Roosevelt built his "White House Gang" a generation later. In contrast to TR, Grant was not an ex officio member of his son's playgroup. But he did prove supportive; Grant placed ads for Jesse's club in his administration's eight-page literary journal. And though this playful President, unlike TR, did not regularly romp around with his son in the afternoon, he did occasionally take a turn at bat in the baseball games organized by local boys, which took place behind the Executive Mansion. As carefree as her younger brother, the teenage Nellie emerged as a regular on the Washington party circuit, often staying out all night.

Though most political reporters praised Grant for the happy domesticity that reigned in his home, some would rebuke him for failing to rein in his children. "On the whole," wrote Mary Clemmer Ames, one of the first women to establish a foothold in the Washington press corps, "it is a sad sight to see a President's daughter, an only daughter, at an age when any thoughtful mother would shield her from the allurements of pleasure, and shut her away in safety to study and grow to harmonious and beautiful womanhood, suddenly launched into the wild tide of frivolous pleasure."

As President, Grant would also be incapable of disciplining his aides. Ultimately, his tendency to be too trusting would have tragic consequences for his political career. Time and time again, he turned out to be exceedingly loyal to longtime associates, even if they proved ineffective or dishonest. During his second term, his administration was plagued by a series of scandals, such as the Whiskey Ring, in which federal agents conspired to siphon off tax revenues. Though Grant was not personally involved in the bribes, he went out of his way to protect Orville Babcock, his long-serving chief of staff, who everyone, Grant included, knew was guilty. To the surprise of many contemporaries, Grant actually gave false testimony in a deposition to the U.S. Supreme Court to prevent Babcock from going to prison.

The retired President would also be duped by the flamboyant Ferdinand Ward, who, along with his son Ulysses Jr., co-owned the brokerage firm Grant and Ward. In 1884, Grant went bankrupt when Ward absconded with his life savings. As one Wall Street insider then noted, the ex-President seemed to "be a perfect child in financial matters." Worried that his wife and children might end up destitute, a terminally ill Grant began racing against the clock to finish his memoir. "Then I," wrote his former military advisor, Adam Badeau, who helped Grant on this landmark in presidential autobiography, "and I believe even they [his family]—finally discovered how dear they were to him—he revived to struggle on their account...He lived for them and died for them." Completed just before his death in the summer of 1885,

The Personal Memoirs of Ulysses S. Grant netted his family royalties of about $500,000. While his adult children were spared from financial hardship, they would often flounder.

———————

By the time of Grant's death, his beloved Nellie was miserable, as her marriage would prove disastrous. But during his administration, she had captured the heart of the nation and her future appeared to be full of promise.

> *O youth and health! O sweet Missouri rose!*
>   *O bonny bride!*
> *Yield thy red cheeks, thy lips, to-day,*
> *Unto a Nation's loving kiss.*

So addressed Walt Whitman the eighteen-year-old Nellie in his poem "A Kiss to the Bride," which ran in the *New York Daily Graphic* on May 21, 1874. At eleven o'clock that morning, she married Englishman Algernon Sartoris in a lavish East Room ceremony, which has often been described as the premier social event of nineteenth-century Washington. It would not be topped until Alice Roosevelt's wedding thirty-two years later, at which a widowed Nellie would make an appearance. To meet the insatiable public curiosity, that same New York tabloid also published the following day an unprecedented eighteen-page supplement covering all aspects of the extravaganza.

Though the groom came from a prominent family—his mother was the renowned opera singer Adelaide Kemble—the doting dad opposed the union because Sartoris would be whisking off his only daughter from her native land. "I yielded consent," Grant said at the time, "but with a wounded heart." Even so, he pulled out all the stops, buying Nellie a $2,000 wedding dress trimmed with Mechlin lace. During the ceremony, Grant tried to hide his tears by looking down at the floor. Afterward, Grant locked himself in Nellie's bedroom and bawled his eyes out.

As it turned out, the President's fears were well grounded. As the novelist Henry James, who visited Nellie at her new home in Cadogan, England, on several occasions, later put it, Sartoris was a "drunken idiot of a husband." A womanizer, the minor English aristocrat often abandoned Nellie and their three surviving children—the firstborn, a son, died in infancy—by taking long trips to other countries. In 1883, the New York Times humiliated the Grants by reporting that Sartoris, then spending the summer on a farm in Green Bay, was having weekly assignations in Milwaukee with an English widow named Mrs. H. B. Bush. A decade later, while traveling in Italy, Sartoris died of pneumonia at the age of forty-one. The following year, the thirty-eight-year-old Nellie and the children returned to America, moving into her mother's mansion at 2111 Massachusetts Avenue in the nation's capital. In 1912, Grant's daughter got remarried to Franklin Hatch Jones, a Chicago lawyer, but she suffered a stroke just three months later. Fully paralyzed for the last seven years of her life, she died in 1922.

Fred Grant, who served as the best man at Nellie's wedding, tied the knot himself five months later in Chicago. Since his graduation from West Point in 1871, the press had linked him with numerous society women from all over the world. According to one report that circulated during Grant's first term, Queen Victoria had cooked up a scheme to have Fred marry her youngest daughter, Beatrice, so that she could then appoint him Viceroy of Canada, and thus achieve her goal of harmonizing "the feelings of the three countries of America, Canada, and Great Britain...as closely as their interests." Fred settled on Ida Marie Honore, the daughter of an Illinois real estate mogul, whom Grant described as "quite as charming for her manners, amiability, good sense and education as she is for her beauty." Of the four Grant children, only Fred would find happiness in marriage.

Though Fred would be promoted to Major General in 1906 and

become the second most powerful man in the American military, his career did not start well. He nearly flunked out of West Point, which he needed five years to finish. He graduated thirty-seventh out of forty-one in his class and ranked last in discipline. What saved Fred was that the main part of his final examination required him to analyze the Battle of Vicksburg. Having witnessed all the action firsthand with his father, Fred provided a brilliant critique of the Confederate strategy, explaining just what the Rebels might have done to avoid the crushing defeat.

After graduation, Fred toured Europe as Gen. William Sherman's aide-de-camp. A decade later, President Benjamin Harrison appointed him Ambassador to Austria. In the 1890s, Fred served as a Commissioner of the New York City Police Department under Superintendent Theodore Roosevelt before returning to the military, fighting in Puerto Rico during the Spanish American War and then in the Philippines. Upon his death in 1912, the son of "the Union Army's most famous soldier," who still commanded the Eastern Division of the Army on Governor's Island, was given "one of the most impressive funeral ceremonies" in New York history, as the New York Times reported. Numerous luminaries attended, including President Taft, and a crowd of ten thousand viewed the body as it was loaded onto the ferry, which was headed to West Point, where he was buried. Fred's favorite saying was "My father's character is my religion," and he was the child who came closest to living up to Grant's example.

In contrast, Fred's two younger brothers, Ulysses Jr. and Jesse, would remain directionless and would die in relative obscurity. After finishing Columbia Law School in 1876, Buck briefly worked as his father's private secretary in the Executive Mansion. He then turned to finance. Settling in Manhattan, he began romancing a series of heiresses from all over the country. One was Jennie Flood, whose father, James, was a successful investor in northern California. Realizing that the former President's son had considerable social prestige but little money, the elder Flood cut Buck a deal. He promised to provide stock tips for six months so that his future son-in-law could raise sufficient funds to join the Flood family. But after reaping $200,000, Buck broke off the engagement and turned his attention elsewhere. "He started back for Frisco but tarried in Chicago to attend club dinners and meet young ladies," as the *Cincinnati Star* reported. In 1880, Buck married Fannie Chafee, the lone daughter of Jerome Chafee, a former Senator from Colorado who was a wealthy mining executive. "[Buck] has some business dash, but is too confiding like his father," observed the *San Francisco Evening Bulletin* in its wedding announcement. These words would prove prophetic time and time again.

Four years into his marriage, Buck lost hundreds of thousands of dollars when his partner, Ferdinand Ward, ran Grant and Ward into the ground. Afterward, he relocated to California, where he continued his checkered career as an investor and a real estate developer, armed with the million dollars that he had inherited from his father-in-law. In 1899, Buck made an aborted attempt to run for the U.S. Senate; even though he was accused of bribing state legislators—the party officials who, until the passage of the Seventeenth Amendment in 1913, were responsible for selecting the nominees—he just missed making it onto the Republican ticket. In 1910, a year after the death of his wife, with whom he had fathered five children, Buck opened San Diego's elegant U. S. Grant Hotel—"the only dividend paying 'memorial' ever erected by a President's son," as one biographer has put it.

Three years later, Buck married America Will, a widow twenty-five years his junior. Only his youngest son, Ulysses IV, then a student at Harvard, attended the wedding. Unlike his ever-loyal father, Buck punished his four other children by disowning them (though in time, he would reconcile with them all). On their honeymoon, the couple went to Australia, the first stop on a world tour that would last for a year and a half. While Buck did keep his promise to bequeath his wife America two-thirds of his assets, his entire estate amounted to $3,000 when he died in 1929.

Jesse's life ran on parallel tracks. Grant's youngest son never finished any university degree program that he started and took little interest in work or any other gainful activity. In 1907, when the forty-nine-year-old retiree, who was living off the inheritance from his mother's estate, made the surprising announcement that he was running for President—his attempt to wrest the Democratic nomination from William Jennings Bryan would go nowhere—he proudly told the New York Times, "I'm a splendid loafer and with a good cigar I can stare at the wall contentedly for hours." As a Cornell undergraduate, Jesse studied engineering, but he left after his junior year to accompany Grant on the world tour, which followed on the heels of his presidency. In the fall of 1878, Jesse returned to New York, where he put in just a year at Columbia Law School.

In 1880, like his brothers, he married rich; his bride, Elizabeth Chapman, was the daughter of a California real estate tycoon. Often described as a wanderer, Jesse rarely spent any time with her or their two children. In the 1890s, he made many trips to Mexico, where he helped establish Tijuana as a profitable gambling resort town. In 1913, even though Jesse had not been living with his family for four years, he stunned his wife by suing for divorce in Nevada, alleging abandonment. An incredulous judge dismissed his suit and required him to pay all court costs, noting, "I shall never rule, where a family lives in a home and the husband goes to a hotel, the family remaining, the wife deserted the husband." His wife then countersued, claiming that Jesse was no longer supporting her. She said that he was "not engaging in business, but solely pursuing his own pleasure" such as going tarpon fishing in Florida and chasing other women. "I am no more to you than the other women you have thrown over," she wrote to him at the time.

In 1918, a week after finally getting his divorce, Jesse married a wealthy widow, Lillian Burns Wilkins, twenty years his junior. After his second wife died in 1924, Jesse romanced his housekeeper, to whom he left his Los Altos house upon his death in 1934. To help make ends meet, in 1925, Jesse published a sentimental memoir, In the Days of My Father, General Grant, which described the former President as a "quiet, soft-spoken, loving man." However, as Jesse himself knew all too well, the two men had little in common. "The only talent I do inherit from my father," he once quipped, "is my absolute lack of the power of oratory."

At a quarter to seven in the morning, President Theodore Roosevelt and his wife, Edith, were awakened by several knocks on their bedroom door. It was Christmas Day, so the source of the hammering was no mystery. Though the First Family contained only "one or two believers in Santa Claus," as the *New York Times* had recently reported, all six presidential children—Alice, 18, Ted Jr., 15, Kermit, 13, Ethel, 11, Archie, 8, and Quentin, 5—were eager to open their presents. Alice, who had refused to attend boarding school—preferring to educate herself by reading her way through her father's massive library—was already a regular on the Washington party circuit. Ted and Kermit were back from Groton for the holiday. Ethel was enrolled at the capital's Cathedral School, where she lived during the week. Archie was attending a public school, Force Elementary on Massachusetts Avenue, which Quentin was to start the following fall.

The year was 1902, and TR had been living in the White House— the name he himself had recently given to the residence formerly known as the Executive Mansion—for a little over fifteen months. Just forty-two when he replaced the assassinated William McKinley, TR remains the youngest man ever to lead the nation. And no President, before or since, has been surrounded by such a vibrant brood, who injected so much energy and fun into his daily life. During meetings with Congressmen, TR was thrilled to watch from the corner of his eye as Archie and Quentin built mountains in the sandbox just outside his office, calling this play area "a heavenly place for . . . little boys." His two youngest children also explored every nook and cranny of the White House, including the spaces above the ceilings; both also enjoyed bicycling and roller-skating on its wood floors. As Ike Hoover, a White House usher for over four decades, put it in his memoir, "The house became one general playground for [the children]." And rather than trying to curb the games and mischief, TR provided encouragement. In fact, he was a co-conspirator who often could not resist joining in.

After slipping on his robe that Christmas morning, TR shut the window and rekindled the fire. To prepare for the visitors, he placed the six stockings, which had been hanging over the fireplace, on his bed.

After entering the bedroom with his siblings, eight-year-old Archie surprised his father by escorting the entire family into a big closet where, with the help of a carpenter, he had rigged up a small tree with lights. That year, due to environmental concerns, the President had not ordered a White House tree, and his second youngest son felt that this key ingredient to holiday festivities was missing. (The following year, TR would again fail to act, and Archie would put a tree in the sewing room.)

Under his makeshift tree, Archie had placed a present for each member of the family, including Jack the terrier, Tom Quartz the kitten, and Algonquin the pony, whom, as Roosevelt later wrote, "Archie would no more think of neglecting than I would neglect his brothers and sisters."

The children then jumped onto their parents' bed and opened their stockings. This type of family gathering was far from rare. Decades later, the White House staff was still telling stories about how "there was never a morning in the year that the whole five did not go and pile in to the bed with President and Mrs. Roosevelt," according to Ella Riley, Coolidge's housekeeper.

After breakfast, the Roosevelts all headed into the library for another round of gift giving. While TR's eldest child, Alice, received diamond earrings, his youngest, Quentin, got an electric train. All six were delighted, even the rebellious Alice, who rarely got up before noon. As Alice conceded in her diary that night, she enjoyed "great amusement...for the benefit of the family."

TR sought to re-create for his children the delightful Christmases of his own boyhood held in his family's Manhattan town house. The President worshipped his late father, Theodore Roosevelt Sr., who had lavished kindness on him, his brother, Elliott, and his sisters, Anna and Corinne. Sensitive to the plight of the underprivileged, this successful businessman and philanthropist had helped found the Children's Aid Society, the Manhattan-based nonprofit dedicated to improving the lot of abandoned children, which is still going strong. Theodore Sr., TR wrote in his autobiography, was "the best man I ever knew." TR's father was a nurturing parent who had helped him cope with his asthma. In contrast, his mother, Martha ("Mittie") Bulloch, was an eccentric southern belle in the Scarlett O'Hara mold. In fact, Margaret Mitchell, who wrote a feature article on the magnificent wedding of TR's parents at the Bulloch family's Georgia estate for the *Atlanta Journal* in 1923, apparently based the heroine of *Gone with the Wind* on TR's remote and unpredictable mother.

TR always remembered fondly those Christmas mornings choreographed by his father, noting to his sister Corinne in 1903, "I wonder whether there ever can come in life a thrill of greater exaltation and rapture than that which comes to one between the ages of say six and fourteen, when the library door is thrown open and you walk in to see all the gifts, like a materialized fairy land, arrayed on your special table?" For TR's children, "it was," as one biographer has noted, "in a manner of speaking, Christmas every day."

Play was as essential to the President as to his offspring. That Christmas, between lunch and dinner, Roosevelt squeezed in several hours of single stick—a form of fencing—with two friends from his Rough Rider days, Gen. Leonard Wood and Robert Ferguson, whom he dubbed his "playmates." Even though he sustained a few serious injuries that afternoon, including a wounded eye and a swollen wrist, the President did not consider suspending the daily matches. Roosevelt would often invite these adult friends to join the pillow fights that he staged with his children in the White House.

TR designed his eighty-acre estate in Oyster Bay, which contained lush fields and gardens, a turtle pond and tennis courts, to serve as a giant playpen for the family. "It is avowedly the ambition of the President," one guest wrote, "to make Sagamore Hill ever remain in the eyes of his children the one spot on earth which is different from every other." As Ted Jr. noted in his fond 1929 memoir, *All in the Family*, during summer vacations on Long Island, TR would carve out plenty of time to frolic with his children. He would typically start the day with a game of bear before breakfast and end it by recounting vivid ghost stories; in between, he would squeeze in lots of "tickle" and "grabbie," as well as rowing and shooting.

As Roosevelt often said, he was prouder to be a father of six than the head of a nation of eighty million. The man who turned the presidency into his personal "bully pulpit" was, as one recent commentator has put it, a "bully [enthusiastic] father." Upon his reelection in 1904, Roosevelt wrote to his second son, Kermit, that "it was a great comfort to feel, all during the last days when affairs looked doubtful, that no matter how things came out the really important thing was the lovely life I have with mother and with you children, and that compared to this home life everything else was of very small importance from the standpoint of happiness." As TR saw it, the two jobs were closely entwined. He believed that the nation's progress depended on a solid family unit. As he wrote in the foreword to his autobiography, Americans "need to develop all the virtues that have the state for their sphere of action; but...back of them [must] lie the strong and tender virtues of a family life based on the love of the one man for the one woman and on their joyous and fearless acceptance of their common obligation to the children that are theirs." For TR, where there were children, there was always hope, and he opposed families with just one child, arguing that it was the duty of every American couple to have two or more. Once, when he got a bit carried away, TR intimated that "race suicide" would occur if the average family had fewer than four children.

This President defined himself not by his political achievements but by his record as a father. And he considered his children's concerns as important as the nation's business. Like President Obama, who has described his regularly scheduled 6:30 dinners with his daughters as "a prize," President Roosevelt relished his frequent meals with his children, including the daily 8:15 breakfast (attended by the family's kangaroo rat, which Kermit invariably plopped on the dining room table). "At the table the children were always allowed to monopolize the conversation, never mind who or how important the guests were," reported Coolidge's housekeeper decades later.

Late in life, TR culled through his correspondence in order to edit a volume entitled *Theodore Roosevelt's Letters to His Children*. "I would rather," Roosevelt told Joseph Bishop, the journalist who worked as his coeditor, "have this book published than anything that has ever been written about me." Released just after his death, this international bestseller contained dozens of letters written between 1899 and 1911, including several that featured his own line drawings. As these missives document, TR related to his children as equals, no matter what their age. He knew how to adjust his own observations to their particular level of cognitive and emotional development. In a letter from June 1904, when Archie was nine, TR used the salutation "Blessed Archiekins," and both described and drew a picture of an owl that was sent to him at the White House, which he had deposited at the National Zoo. Three years later, in a missive that began with "Dear Archie," TR vividly recounted his excursion on a Mississippi steamboat, adding that the preteen was likely to enjoy his own trip there with "mother" the following year. "Home, wife, children, they are what really count in life," TR wrote to Ted Jr. in the summer of 1911, shortly after his first son's marriage. All his successes, including the presidency, added TR, amount to little "when compared with the joy I have known with your mother and all of you."

The TR who emerges from such tender interactions with his children is the democratic reformer who sought to bring fairness to American society. He vowed not to spoil them and to make sure that they had a normal childhood. "They lead exactly the lives," he wrote to a friend soon after becoming President, "led by any other six children who live in a roomy house with a garden and go to school." Midway through his second term, the New York Times concluded that "the President not only knows how children should be brought up, but...he has put his theories into eminently successful practice." The father who made sure that his youngest child was fed first at the dinner table became the first President to invite a black man—Booker T. Washington—to dine at the White House.

Deviating from the pro-business Republicans such as his predecessor McKinley, Roosevelt argued for a "Square Deal" that stressed the three Cs: conservation, consumer protection, and control of corporations through increased regulation. As President, he repeatedly championed vulnerable segments of the population—from industrial workers to wildlife. He used the same charm that he showered on his children to look out for the nation's interest. To settle the long coal strike of 1902, which threatened to drag on into the winter, TR issued cordial White House invitations to both George F. Baer, President of the Philadelphia and Reading Railroad, and John Mitchell, head of the United Mine Workers. Shortly thereafter, he persuaded both sides to abide by the decision of a fact-finding commission representing various stakeholders, including business, labor, law, and the clergy. For his deft handling of this tense standoff, Roosevelt received kudos from around the world. "In a most quiet and unobtrusive manner," concluded the Times of London, "the President has done a very big and entirely new thing." Both at home and at work, TR preferred to speak softly and carry—rather than use—that big stick to which he often alluded.

TR's fun-loving personality was precisely what bonded him with the electorate and led to his immense popularity; in that 1904 race, he won a stunning 56 percent of the vote—nearly twenty points more than his Democratic challenger, New York Judge Alton B. Parker. To many Americans, he was as cuddly as a teddy bear, the toy that was named after him in 1902 (even though he hated the nickname Teddy). "Everybody is buying a Roosevelt Bear," the *New York Times* reported in 1906. "It has become a fad. Children cry for 'em." The President who could connect with kids ended up giving birth to America's first must-have consumer product for tots.

However, with his children, TR did not always live up to his own lofty ideals. At times, he could be excessively demanding. He insisted that all four boys, but particularly his firstborn, Ted Jr., be warriors. This obsession with manliness and the "strenuous life" dated back to his own early struggles. As a boy, TR had overcome various health ailments, including asthma, by immersing himself in physical activity, just as his father had recommended. "You have the mind, not the body," the elder Roosevelt told the young TR. "You must make your body." But as a father himself, TR often went too far. When Ted Jr. was in grade school, TR asked him to fight a schoolmate who was throwing apples at his sister Ethel, even though the other boy was older and bigger. In the spring of 1898, shortly before TR left his family to fight in Cuba, ten-year-old Ted Jr. began suffering from incapacitating headaches. Fearing that his son was having some "kind of a nervous breakdown," TR sent him to the family doctor, Alexander Lambert, who concluded that TR's high expectations were a big part of the problem. To his credit, TR could honestly examine his own behavior. "Hereafter," he vowed to Lambert, "I shall never press Ted either in body or mind. The fact is that the little fellow, who is particularly dear to me, has bidden fair to be all the things I would like to have been and wasn't, and it has been a great temptation to push him."

But TR would continue to have trouble checking these impulses. According to Edith, their four younger children fared better than Ted primarily because TR had less time on his hands to exert pressure once his political career took off. Egged on by TR, all four sons would later jump at the chance to fight in World War I. But only after TR had witnessed the tragic consequences of his hard-driving ways did he realize that he had once again yielded to temptation.

In the summer of 1905, just seven years after his military triumph at San Juan Hill had first thrust him into the national spotlight, TR was suddenly a peacemaker. The President's pressing concern was to broker a treaty between Russia and Japan, two nations that had been at war for nearly a year and a half. He was also eager to protect America's new territories—Hawaii and the Philippines—from Japanese aggression. On the home front, he needed to mend fences with his rambunctious daughter, Alice. Now twenty-one, she had evolved into the most photographed and talked-about woman in America since her debut in the Blue Room of the White House three years earlier. During his first term, Roosevelt was reported to have told a friend that he could either be President or control Alice, but he could not do both. When later asked if he had actually made this statement, the President responded that if he hadn't, he ought to have. As it turned out, by sending "Princess Alice" on a four-month tour of Asia as his goodwill ambassador, the President managed to achieve both his foreign and domestic goals simultaneously. For his diplomatic efforts, TR would both nab the Nobel Peace Prize in 1906 and cement a powerful bond with the grateful Alice. "The trip to the Far East in 1905," she observed decades later, "was by far the most exciting one I ever made."

TR's relationship with Alice had been strained since her birth. When she was just two days old, he received a double body blow: Her mother, his first wife, also named Alice, died from Bright's disease on one floor of his Manhattan town house while his mother, Martha, just forty-nine, expired from typhoid on another. In his diary on that fateful day, February 14, 1884, he was reduced to placing a big X, under which he wrote, "The light has gone out of my life." Overwhelmed by grief, he sent the infant to live with his sister Anna (Bamie), while he retreated to the Dakota Badlands to bury his emotions in hunting and ranching. Three years later, after he got remarried to his childhood friend, Edith Carow, and settled in Oyster Bay, he took Alice back. But

Alice, who would continue to have frequent visits with her aunt Bamie, would always feel much closer to her than to her stepmother.

Though TR was good-natured, he suffered from a major emotional block, which would dramatically affect Alice. Like many men during the Victorian era, he felt a compelling need to shut out feelings of sadness. He essentially erased his first wife from his memory, refusing to mention her even in his autobiography. As Alice later recalled, "He never ever said her name, or that I even *had* a different mother." If her aunt Bamie had not blurted out the truth, Alice would never have known about the other Alice in TR's past. Summing up her father's inability to acknowledge her identity, Alice noted, "The whole thing was really handled very badly. It was awfully bad psychologically."

By the time the seventeen-year-old Alice moved into the White House with her parents and five half siblings, she was saddled with a host of insecurities. She felt emotionally disconnected from the rest of the family. Though Edith did her best to make up for the loss of her mother, Alice's stepmother was often distant. TR's eldest child developed a lifelong aversion to being touched, suggesting that she had missed out on physical closeness with an attachment figure early in life. Her self-esteem was shot. While an adoring public considered the blue-eyed, golden-haired Alice a great beauty and a fashion icon, she could not understand what all the fuss was about. "Sometimes," she noted decades later, "I look at pictures of myself then, trying to see what they thought was pretty."

As she confided in Edith, she felt as if her father loved her one-eighth as much as his other children. To redress this imbalance and to get her father's attention, Alice "tried to become conspicuous." Much to the delight of the fawning press corps, her behavior became increasingly wild. Alice smoked in public, gambled at the race track, and drove a car at high speeds—all activities few early-twentieth-century society ladies would even contemplate. Her constant companions were her macaw, named Eli Yale, and her snake, Emily Spinach, which she would often whip out of her purse to startle onlookers. Rattling her father was a favorite pastime. When TR demanded that she stop smoking under his roof, she complied by puffing away on top of the White House roof. To protest her father's worship of large families, with the help of three girlfriends, she started the Race Suicide Club to defend Anglo-Saxon women who declined to carry out his directive. Despite many "a serious talk" with her father, Alice continued to do more or less as she pleased.

As opposed to Alice, whom TR called "the liability child," Ethel was "the asset child." Dutiful and obedient, TR's other daughter helped her mother take care of the house and the garden as well as the younger children. A top student, she tutored Archie and Quentin in math and Latin. This anti-Alice, who distinguished herself from her sister by signing off as "your own dauter" in her early letters to her mother, was eager to please both her parents. "Altho she has a tendency to be too nervous and excitable and to do too much," TR wrote in 1906, "she is a very satisfactory child, on the whole." Inspired by the example of both TR and his father, Ethel also taught Sunday school classes to black students at St. Mary's Chapel in Washington. Dubbed "Elephant Johnny" by her father, the stocky and muscular Ethel was a tomboy who would swing from branches and wrestle with her brothers. Ethel was "so strong and rough," Edith noted, "I am almost afraid when she comes near me." An able equestrian who enjoyed long rides with her father, Ethel relished the challenge of controlling her horse, Mollie, when it balked. In describing the 1908 debut of the attractive seventeen-year-old with the silky blond hair at the White House, the *New York Times* highlighted Ethel's modesty, noting that "the contrast between Miss Ethel and [Alice] is most striking—even to the casual observer."

To address Alice's alienation from the rest of the family, TR shifted into an entirely different gear with her. Accepting her for who she was, he stopped trying to change her. And once he realized that her own brand of quirkiness reflected a kindred spirit, he could not help but admire her independence and originality. The President also figured out that this immensely popular daughter could be a tremendous political asset; and that the more that he relied upon her, the more she would feel appreciated. In the spring of 1905, TR arranged for her—along with Secretary of War William Howard Taft—to head a delegation of eighty-three Americans, including thirty-five Congressmen and seven Senators, to Asia. His daughter was delighted, because one of those traveling Congressmen would be Representative Nicholas Longworth of Cincinnati, a thirty-five-year-old bachelor, with whom she had been carrying on an on-again off-again affair for the past year. The stated purpose of the mission was to acquaint the Congressmen with the major stops on the tour—Japan, the Philippines, and China—but TR also asked Taft to conduct top secret diplomatic meetings with high-level Japanese officials.

On June 30, the delegation led by the odd couple of Alice and Taft departed from Washington on two special cars of the Baltimore and Ohio Railroad. Though the Secretary of War was in charge of supervising America's military might, the public regarded Taft merely as Alice's sidekick. As friends of Taft's wife, Helen, then in Europe, would tease, she was "the Mrs. Taft whose husband was traveling with Miss Alice Roosevelt." The trip almost ended a couple of days later—on July 1, TR's Secretary of State, John Hay, suddenly died, and Taft assumed that the President would want him to return to Washington immediately. But in Chicago, the Secretary of War received a wire from the President, informing him that there was no need to change the itinerary.

Arriving in California on July 4, the touring Americans were greeted by five thousand onlookers, the first of many rubbernecking crowds that would come to catch a glimpse of Alice, who was, both at home and abroad, "the party," as one Congressman's wife put it. Excited to be venturing into new terrain—Alice had never been west of the Mississippi—the First Daughter was on her best behavior. In a letter written a few days later aboard the *Manchuria*, which was bound for the Philippines, Alice reassured her father that she had not bothered to visit San Francisco's seedy Chinatown because there was "an opium den" and "a gambling place" on the ship.

Back in Oyster Bay for the summer, TR continued to immerse himself in foreign policy. In the first week of July, he appointed Elihu Root his new Secretary of State. The following week, after intense negotiations with both Russian and Japanese officials, he announced a major diplomatic coup, as the two sides had agreed to sit down in Portsmouth, New Hampshire, to iron out a peace treaty in early August. With this bold stroke, TR had turned America into the premier player on the international stage. For the first time, as the *Boston Globe* proudly reported on July 12, "the world's history... is being made under our hands." Yet despite the complex diplomatic maneuvering that he needed to do that summer—in between preparing for peace talks, which also involved addressing China's concerns about the future of Manchuria, he was consulting with engineers about the construction of the Panama Canal—TR did not sacrifice any playtime with his younger children. On Tuesday afternoon, July 18, he went on his annual camping expedition with his three eldest sons, Ted, Kermit, and Archie, and several of their cousins and friends who appointed him both "chief cook" and "camp director." That night at Lloyd Neck, a five-mile rowboat ride from Sagamore Hill, TR regaled the boys with stories around a campfire.

On July 21, the President fired off one of his charming picture-letters to Alice, who was then closing in on Tokyo, where she was to meet Emperor Meiji a few days later. This high-spirited missive reflected the dramatic new direction that their relationship had taken. At the top of the first page, he wrote, "<u>Not</u> a posterity letter," meaning that she was not to show it to anyone. (Once elected President, TR became acutely aware that his personal letters, including those to his children, would be of interest to future historians.) In lieu of a salutation, TR began with a drawing inside a box, which he described as "a cartouche" (a figure in Egyptian hieroglyphics that contains the characters naming a divine or royal personage). In the center of the box stood the head of a smoking Alice, whom he referred to below as "Her Excellentissima." Continuing to address his daughter in the third person, the President wrote, "She is at present travelling *in partibus* for Her Health. She is remembered at home." The following page contained a few more playful images of Alice, including one of her being whisked around by her chauffeur at forty miles per hour—twenty-five miles over the speed limit—under which he put a caption, "Her chief pastime at home, when not at the races." In a brief news update on the "children"—a category to which Alice no longer belonged—TR briefly wrote about the success of his recent "one-night picnic" where his boys accepted the sandflies "as aids to enjoyment." He concluded by stating that he was pleased to have Root as his Secretary of State, even though "he will not be able really to take hold until the end of September."

From a recalcitrant teenager, Alice had evolved into both a confidante, with whom the President could discuss policy, and a political agent in her own right, capable of flexing her own considerable skills. "Miss Roosevelt," a Japanese reporter noted, "charmed us all…she reminds me of her father and she has the…same way of giving you her undivided attention for the time you are speaking with her." TR's "posterity letter" sent to Tokyo six weeks later, which was typed rather than handwritten and contained no pictures, addressed only politics. "For the last three months," TR acknowledged to Alice on September 2, the day Russia and Japan signed the Portsmouth accord, "the chief business I have had has been the peace business…Now I am overpraised. I am credited with being extremely longheaded, etc.… [but] I would have felt as if I was flinching from a plain duty if I had acted otherwise." Alice, as TR was well aware, had been a big help. Summing up her Asia trip to Kermit a couple of months later, he wrote, "She has behaved mighty well under trying circumstances."

In Asia, the twenty-one-year-old Alice also reconfigured her relationship with another older man, the squat and balding Nicholas Longworth. During the trip, Taft noticed that she and the Congressman were spending lots of time by themselves—except for a few brief separations, which appeared to be caused by lovers' spats—so he asked if they were engaged. Alice responded, "More or less." The engagement was

announced publicly in December, and the White House wedding—
the premier social event of the Roosevelt presidency—took place the
following February. The tenth wedding in the White House since
1812—when Lucy Payne Washington, the sister of Dolly Madison,
married Supreme Court Justice Thomas Todd—is still considered the
grandest in history. Despite all the reports that circulated about Longworth's womanizing and alcoholism, TR, like the rest of the nation,
eagerly embraced this Harvard-educated Republican, who became
Speaker of the House in 1925. (The Longworth House Office Building, completed in 1931, the year of his death, is named after him.)

However, the marriage was not a happy one; both partners strayed.
In 1925, Alice gave birth to a daughter, Paulina, the product of her affair
with Senator William Borah. Paulina married at nineteen, and like her
husband, the artist Alexander Sturm, who drank himself to death at
twenty-eight, could not control her penchant for self-destruction and
died of an overdose of pills in 1957. At the age of seventy-four, Alice
assumed care for her ten-year-old granddaughter, Joanna. Giving back
the love that she had received from TR, Alice delighted in reciting
poetry and riding horses with Joanna. "Mrs L," a friend concluded,
"has been a wonderful father and mother to Joanna: mostly father." A
major player in the capital's social scene until her death at ninety-six,
Alice became known as "Washington's other monument." Known for
her witty one-liners, Alice preached a philosophy similar to her father's.
"The secret of eternal youth," she declared, "is arrested development."

On Thursday, September 26, 1907, nine-year-old Quentin Roosevelt
was back in Washington after spending the summer in Oyster Bay.
On his youngest son's first day home, TR insisted that he skip school
in order "to go about and renew all his friendships." That afternoon,
Quentin roller-skated over to Schmid's animal store, where he obtained
"a large and beautiful and very friendly king snake and two little wee
snakes." With the three creatures draped on his arms, Quentin, still

on his skates, rolled into the office of William Loeb Jr., the President's secretary, asking to show his treasures to his father. "But the Attorney General is with him and they might not want to see the snakes," protested Loeb. "Oh yes, they will," responded Quentin. "My father likes snakes." As soon as the presidential gatekeeper looked the other way, Quentin dashed in to see his father. When Quentin proceeded to deposit the snakes on the President's lap, Attorney General Charles Bonaparte stopped his update on Oklahoman statehood in midsentence. The President smiled, telling his son that he did not think the Attorney General was interested in snakes, but that he should show them to the four Congressmen waiting to see him. Following his son into the next room, TR could not help but laugh. As the President observed, "They at first thought the snakes were wooden ones, but there was some perceptible recoil when they realized that they were alive." Later that afternoon, Quentin again went in to see his father, complaining that something was wrong with the snakes. After quickly pulling one of the small snakes from the mouth of the king snake, TR calmly went back to his paperwork.

Of his six children, TR felt closest to Quentin, who, like Alice, also displayed a fierce independence. In the White House, the President's day began with Quentin's playing a tune on the mechanical piano, to which TR tried to walk in step as he headed to the breakfast table. The precocious Quentin was so much like his father that his sister Ethel felt "as if the two were one." Remarking on the behavior of his youngest son, TR once noted, "There is something very *Theodore* about all this." In contrast to his three brothers, who were all rail thin, Quentin shared his father's muscular physique and was a natural athlete. "He swims like a little duck; rides well; stands quite severe injuries without complaint," TR reported to Kermit in 1906, when the littlest Roosevelt was just eight, "and is really becoming a manly little fellow." Like TR, Quentin also loved to play with words. After disclosing that his favorite nickname for his brother Kermit was "the hermit," Quentin explained, "Of course, he isn't at all; only the name is so app-pree-po."

What TR liked most about his youngest child was his sense of fun. "Quentin is a roly-poly, happy-go-lucky personage," the President wrote in 1907, "the brightest of any of the children but with a strong tendency to pass a very happy life in doing absolutely nothing except swim or loaf about with other little boys." Described by his mother as a "fine little bad boy," Quentin often veered off into mischief. He entertained himself by hurling snowballs at members of the Secret Service and considered the White House elevator his personal toy. Shortly after his fifth birthday, he repeatedly caused the lights to go out during an evening reception by riding it up and down—thereby forcing his father to increase the mansion's supply of electric power. A few years later, when the more easygoing but less academically inclined Archie was lying in bed with diphtheria, Quentin used the elevator to take the family pony, Algonquin, up to his older brother's room for a visit. To his mother, the self-aware Quentin then quipped, "If only I had *Archie's* nature, and *my* head, wouldn't it be great?" In contrast to Archie, whom TR described as "short on pure intellect," Quentin evolved into a stellar student who would read Turgenev and Racine in his spare time.

During TR's presidency, Quentin, accompanied by a few elementary school classmates, would rush back home nearly every afternoon to "engage in escapades which were swept along the wires to national publicity," as one playmate, Earle Looker, later wrote in a memoir. As a miniature version of TR, Q, as he was called, was ideally suited to lead the so-called "White House Gang," which also included Charlie Taft, the preteen son of the Secretary of War, who would take over the reins when his father succeeded TR. Rather than policing the boys, the President joined in. "His active hustling," Looker observed of TR, "his bursts of laughter, made us forget anything else about him, in the fun we were having."

Their favorite haunt was the dusty attic, to which the President would often retreat during his afternoon break. In one game of tag, just as TR was about to catch one of the boys, Looker turned off the lights, causing the President to crash into the wall. "When a block of wood meets a block of wood, there's bound to be a headache. I'm quite all right," an unperturbed TR calmly declared. "But never, never, never again, turn off a light when anybody is near a post."

In January 1908, a few months after starting middle school in Alexandria, Quentin, then the only child still living at home, invited three friends to sleep over at the White House, including Charlie Taft. TR himself watched over the boys, who hardly slept a wink. The play occasionally got rough, and the President had to interfere when Quentin tried to get his guests to ingest sulfureted hydrogen when they were in bed. But rather than feeling annoyed or alarmed, TR was filled with loss. "It made me realize," he wrote to Archie, then in prep school, "how old I had grown and how very busy I had been these last few years, to find that...I was not needed in the play." Like his father, Quentin thoroughly enjoyed everything associated with the presidency. "There is a little hole in my heart," he noted during his father's last year in office, "when I think of leaving the White House." Like his brothers, Quentin would attend Groton and then Harvard, but he dropped out at the end of his sophomore year to serve in the Great War.

In the early morning hours of April 6, 1917, which happened to be Good Friday, Congress voted 373 to 50 to declare war on Germany. Hearing this news that Easter weekend, the retired fifty-eight-year-old hero of the Spanish American War immediately made plans to go from Oyster Bay to Washington. The purpose of the former Rough Rider's hastily arranged trip—he would stay with Alice and her husband at their home on Eighteenth Street—was to ask permission from President Wilson to lead an army division in Europe. The following Tuesday at noon, TR got to make his pitch in person at the White House. When asked afterward about their ostensibly friendly forty-five-minute meeting, President Wilson described Roosevelt to reporters as a "great big boy," adding that "there is a sweetness about him that is very compelling." However, a week later, Wilson's Secretary of War Newton

Baker informed TR that his request was denied for "purely military reasons." Wilson wanted to leave the fighting to the trained professionals, even though, as Baker noted, he could acknowledge the "sentimental value...[of] a representation of the United States in France by a former President." Publicly TR said little, but privately he seethed about the decision by "the malignant coward in the White House." The not easily deterred TR contacted leaders in France and England, but they also turned down his offer of volunteer service.

Frustrated, TR decided to wage this war through his offspring. He pulled every lever he could to place his sons on the battlefield as soon as possible. By the spring of 1917, all of TR's children were married with the exception of Quentin, who was engaged to the Vanderbilt heiress Flora Payne Whitney. And Ethel, whose husband was the Harvard-educated surgeon Richard Derby—later nicknamed "Dusky Dick" by Alice because of his tendency to fall into deep depressions—had actually been the first member of the family to join the war effort. In the fall of 1914, she had accompanied Derby to Paris, where she worked as a nurse at the American Ambulance Hospital.

On May 20, 1917, TR wrote his longtime friend Gen. John J. Pershing about Ted, twenty-nine, and Archie, twenty-three, and the newly appointed commander of the American Expeditionary Force gave them both positions on his staff at the front in Paris. For Kermit, twenty-seven, who had recently returned from Buenos Aires, where he had been working as a banker, TR needed to figure out a different strategy. Unlike his brothers, TR's second son, who had accompanied his father on his post-presidential excursions to Africa and South America, had completed little military training and was not eligible for an American commission. A month later, the former President wrote British Prime Minister Lloyd George about his "exceptionally fit son," and Kermit ended up landing a Second Lieutenant's commission with the British Army in Mesopotamia. Under TR's guidance, Quentin, who at nineteen was a year and a half younger than the youngest men registering for the army that spring, took still another route, signing up for the Flying Corps (the forerunner of the air force). "We boys," Quentin told a friend, "thought it was up to us to practice what Father preached."

In late May 1917, as TR was busy helping all four sons finalize their plans, he wrote to Kermit, with whom he had developed a particularly close bond as a result of their long foreign trips together:

> I am _very_ proud of my sons...I hate to feel that I am out of it, especially because I so strongly believe that—when physical conditions will permit—it's the old, the men whose life is behind them who have drained the cup of joy and sorrow and achievement and failure, who should be in the danger line, for the little sooner or little later matters little to them. But we have to make the best we can of actual conditions and the chief of these...is the presence in the White House of the smooth, cold, treacherous liar and hypocrite who would without a thought ruin this country if his interest lay that way.

Though TR would feel guilty that he no longer faced any of the risks of war himself, he insisted that his sons not shy away from potential danger. Desk jobs would be verboten in the Roosevelt family.

By clinging to a romantic view of war, TR unwittingly placed tremendous stress on his sons. Since military success at San Juan Hill had jump-started his own political career—as soon as he returned from Cuba, he was elected New York's Governor—he equated combat duty with opportunity. "You and your brothers," TR wrote Ted, "are playing your parts in the greatest of the world's great days, and what man of spirit does not envy you?...you have seized the great chance, as was seized by those who fought at Gettysburg, and Waterloo." But such ardent messages, which TR kept firing off from Oyster Bay, both inspired and terrified their recipients; each son began to fear that unless he came home a military hero, his father might consider him a failure. As Ted confided in his superior officer, he was convinced that his father's "dearest wish was that he should lead his battalion in action." In late 1917, after their first exposure to the fighting, both Ted and Archie began teasing Quentin for being "a slacker." In a heartbreaking riposte, the youngest Roosevelt tried to protect himself from such character assassination by writing Archie that it's "no fault of mine that I am not at the front…This having pneumonia rather set me back, but I didn't get it from choice."

Ted and Archie were simply parroting the harsh epithets that they had heard from their father. That spring, TR had accused Archie of being "a slacker" for taking a brief honeymoon after his marriage to Grace Lockwood in Boston. Once the women in the family heard about how TR's paternal prodding had led to such infighting among his sons, they were outraged. Ethel described the baiting of Quentin as "too absurd and too horrid." Edith tried to reassure Quentin by sending him a cable: "AM SHOCKED BY ATTITUDE OF TED AND ARCHIE. IF YOU HAVE ERRED AT ALL IT IS IN TRYING TOO HARD IN GETTING TO THE FRONT."

While TR did worry about his sons' safety, he felt as if the anxiety was "more than offset by pride." Swept up in his own excitement, TR simply could not wait to hear about their war exploits. In February 1918, after learning that Kermit had participated in the Battle of Tikrit, TR wrote to the young man's wife, Belle, "Well, he has been in the game now! I am so pleased; he has the nature which would make it dreadful for him not to have had a hand in the real service." Displaying remarkable courage, the sons would do everything in their power not to disappoint their father. "During the last year," TR wrote to Kermit on July 7, "my chief claim to reputation has been the gallant achievement of you four boys." But though it was true, as TR put it at the end of 1918, that there was not "any family, except the Garibaldis, which comes out of this war with the reputation ours does," the Great War would also exact a huge private toll on TR as well as on all four sons.

Within a few months of Ted's arrival in France, Gen. George Duncan, Pershing's right-hand man who led the First Brigade, was already writing to TR that his eldest son was his "best major." In May 1918, while defending Cantigny from a German onslaught, Ted was gassed; even though he suffered temporary blindness, he laughed off all attempts to remove him from his station. His bravery would earn him a Silver Star and a Purple Heart. That fall, Ted suffered a serious leg injury, but he continued to fight right up until the Armistice. "Your triumph has been great," his father wrote to him on December 3, 1918. "It is simply fine to think of you with your limp commanding your regiment during the last three weeks of the fighting."

The following spring, at a meeting of veterans in Paris, Ted would help found the relief organization now known as the American Legion. But it was in World War II that Ted emerged as a military hero of even greater stature than his father. Whereas the fifty-eight-year-old TR could not get anywhere near the action in World War I, the fifty-seven-year-old Ted managed to become the oldest American and only General to land on Utah Beach with the first wave on D-Day. It took three tries, but the cane-toting Ted, who was slowed down by poor eyesight, a weak heart, and arthritis, did eventually convince the Division Commander that his experience could come in handy. FDR would agree. In awarding Ted a posthumous Congressional Medal of Honor, the President noted that "his valor, courage and presence in the very front of the attack and his complete unconcern at being under heavy fire inspired the troops to the heights of enthusiasm and self-sacrifice." Ted died of exhaustion on July 12, 1944, just as the army was about to name him a Division Commander.

Though Ted excelled as a soldier, his political career stalled. After returning from France, he attempted to follow the path charted by his father—first becoming a New York State Assemblyman and then the Assistant Secretary of the Navy before running for Governor. But in 1924, he was trounced by Democrat Al Smith, who quipped, "The young feller ain't there," an assessment that was widely shared. He never ran for elective office again.

Archie, who served as a captain under Ted in France, also fought valiantly in both world wars. On March 11, 1918, while he was repositioning his men, shrapnel pierced through both his left arm and leg. Continuing to give his men commands after he was struck, Archie received a Croix de Guerre from a French general the next day when he woke up from surgery. Once TR realized that his son was going to survive, he proudly wrote him that most Americans were probably "rather glad that one of _my_ sons had the dangerous honor of being among the first to be wounded in battle."

In September, Archie returned to America, where he was forced to remain for the rest of the war. The aftereffects, both physical and psychological, were deep. Archie walked with a limp and was subject to bouts of trench fever. Saddled with "bad nerves," he showed only a "tepid interest" in his newborn son, Archibald Jr., as TR himself sadly observed. Archie would never develop the same warm bond with his own four children that he had enjoyed with his father.

Yet as a middle-aged man, Archie, just like his father and elder brother, itched to get back into action. In early 1943, the forty-nine-year-old veteran made his pitch to FDR; after the President turned him down, he approached Army Chief of Staff George Marshall, who sent him to New Guinea. While Archie started out as a supply officer, he ended up as a Lieutenant Colonel in the 162nd Infantry Division. Weighed down by a host of medical ailments—including recurrent malarial fever, osteoarthritis, and chronic bronchitis, to name just a few—he was sent back to America a year and a half later. Still eager to fight, Archie asked FDR to reinstate him, but he was forced to retire from the armed services a week before V-J Day. He was the only American to be classified as totally disabled in each world war. Archie earned a Purple Heart and a Silver Star for his heroism; he would repeatedly stand up in a boat in order to draw enemy fire so that he could pinpoint the enemy's position. Reflecting back on World War II in 1966, Archie observed, "[My brother Ted and I] were both too old to be doing the type of work we were doing, and I suppose we were foolish to do it."

In the 1950s, Archie became a successful investment banker dealing in municipal bonds, but he often lapsed into paranoia and despair, which he was prone to drown in Scotch. A rabid McCarthyite—he continued to support the Wisconsin Senator long after he was censured—he became consumed by rooting out "subversives" from every walk of American life. In 1968, Archie published a book containing nothing but quotations from his father that he used to advocate his overt bigotry—"No welfare funds for the lazy, the chiselers, the degenerates and the immoral" and "African savages 50 to 100 thousand years behind whites in development" were typical chapter headings. Embarrassed family members tried to snap up all the copies from bookstores in order to remove them from circulation.

But Archie never lost his sense of boyhood fun. Tweed Roosevelt, the son of Archibald Jr., enjoyed going on hunting trips with his grandfather in the early 1950s. "He could relate well to me when I was a little boy, just as TR had done with him. But when I became an adolescent, he couldn't deal with my desire to be my own man," TR's great-grandson told me. In 1971, Archie was at the wheel when his car crashed, killing his wife, Grace, who was in the passenger seat. He died a depressed recluse in 1979.

Though Kermit was the only son not to be wounded in the Great War, his later life took an even sadder turn than Archie's. After earning the British Military Cross for his bravery against the Turkish forces in Mesopotamia, TR had him transferred to the Seventh Field Artillery Regiment of the First Division in France, where he served until the end of the war. With his "interest in politics nil," as the *New York Times* once noted, Kermit started the Roosevelt Steamship Company in 1920, which he ran for a couple of decades. But his mental health unraveled in the 1930s when he became a heavy drinker and began frequenting prostitutes. In 1936, the bloated father of four started a long-term affair with his German masseuse, Carla Peters, with whom he often disappeared on long cross-country trips.

Described in 1938 by his sympathetic and concerned wife, Belle, as a "very sick man" whose mind and body were in agony, Kermit paradoxically looked to the Second World War for relief from his psychological torment. For this son of TR, in contrast to most middle-aged men, military service was associated less with danger than with regeneration. Kermit served in the British Army in Norway and North Africa for about a year before his alcoholism, combined with several serious physical ailments—including liver disease and malaria—necessitated his discharge. Upon Kermit's return to America, Archie had his elder brother committed to a mental hospital in Hartford. Despite his fragile health, Kermit was insistent on participating in the American war effort. Hearing of his wishes, George Marshall ended up sending him to Alaska, where there was little possibility of combat. But on June 3, 1943, Kermit blew his brains out with his British service revolver. By way of explanation, the Roosevelt scion had sent a telegram to FBI Director J. Edgar Hoover stating that his suicide was "due to despondence resulting from exclusion from combat duties."

Quentin suffered the worst fate of all the sons, as he never even made it back from France. During the spring of 1918, he often felt depressed as he was stuck repeating training exercises in Issoudun, a town in central France 125 miles south of Paris. Due to a lack of combat planes, few of the roughly two thousand American pilots stationed there could get to the front. And with both Archie and Kermit already having received medals, Quentin felt ashamed that he was falling way behind in the race among the brothers for glory. On June 8, Quentin cabled his parents in Oyster Bay, letting them know that he was "moving out at last" and "very glad." In his dangerous line of work— being a chase pilot in a "hot" sector—the average life span was eleven days. Quentin would live a little more than a month, and he would go out in a blaze of glory. His last letter to his father, dated July 11, 1918, began, "I've gotten my first real excitement on the front, for I think I got a Boche [slang term for 'German']. The operations officer is trying for confirmation now." Quentin's hunch was correct. The previous day, after being blown off course eight miles inside of enemy lines, the young Lieutenant had spotted three Pfalz monoplanes and had shot one of them down. But on July 14, an experienced German pilot hit Quentin in the head with two bullets, killing him even before his plane hit the ground in Chamery.

After hearing the news, TR was instantly and dramatically transformed. "The old side of him is gone," observed a family friend, "the old exuberance, the boy in him has died." When asked if he had anything to say to France, TR responded, "I have no message for France; I have already given her the best I had." TR, who now regretted how hard he had pushed his sons, would never be the same. "Since Quentin's death," he declared, "the world seems to have shut down upon me." The man, who had long been known for his emotional control, could be found sobbing, "Poor Quentyquee," as he buried his head in the mane of his son's pony at Sagamore Hill. TR died on January 6, 1919, a few days after learning that the French had given Quentin a posthumous Croix de Guerre.

———————

Early on Saturday morning, June 29, 1912, New Jersey Governor Woodrow Wilson got a call from his agitated campaign manager stationed on the floor of the Democratic Convention in Baltimore. The news was disappointing; the delegates had stayed up all night, and on the tenth ballot, his chief rival and House Speaker, Representative Champ Clark of Missouri, had won 556 votes, compared to his paltry 351. At the time, two-thirds of the 1,088 delegates were needed to secure the presidential nomination, but in every Democratic contest since 1844, the first candidate to reach 50 percent eventually prevailed. Minutes later, Wilson, who was staying in the Governor's summer residence in Sea Girt, New Jersey, sat down to breakfast with his wife, Ellen, and three daughters, Margaret, 25, Jessie, 24, and Eleanor, known as Nell, 22. In contrast to the four Wilson women, who were in tears, the Governor was upbeat. Noticing a catalog advertising coffins in the morning mail, Wilson quipped, "This is certainly prompt service…Will you help me choose a coffin for a dead duck?" Wilson was prepared to release his delegates later that morning. If not for a call a few hours later from his deputy campaign manager, who painted a less grim picture, Wilson's career in national politics might have ended there and then.

That weekend, his wife and children alternated between waiting anxiously for updates next to the temporary phone booth installed underneath the main staircase and battling insomnia in their bedrooms. Jessie began keeping a huge chart on which she dutifully recorded the tallies of all the ballots. In contrast, Wilson himself remained playful and relaxed. On Saturday afternoon, he dashed out to play a round of golf. On Sunday morning, he slept until eleven. Shortly after he got up, he began singing a hymn with his daughters— much to the surprise of the twenty reporters camped out on his lawn. At lunch, the Governor dared not break his own house rule, which prohibited extended discussions about politics during meals. Instead he entertained his family with stories, impersonations, and songs. "It was a little as if we were nervous patients and he the doctor with a beautiful bedside manner," observed Nell years later. Two days later, Wilson won the nomination on the forty-sixth ballot—a development that illustrated Jessie's prescience, as she had created fifty columns on her large sheet of paper. That afternoon, as the press hounded him to insist that his wife and daughters come out to be photographed, the Governor joked, "Gentlemen, my jurisdiction extends all over the state of New Jersey, but when it reaches the front door of the Little White House [the Sea Girt residence], there it stops. You will have to make the appeals yourself."

Though Americans have always thought of Wilson as a dour and distant President, within the confines of his own home, he was warm and accommodating. And like TR, he knew how to have fun. He, too, relished his downtime. A baseball aficionado who had played on his college team as a freshman, he attended four Washington Senators games during his first April in office. As President, he tried to see just about every play that came to Washington, even or especially the latest show at Keith's, the District of Columbia's vaudeville house. If truth be told, the prolific author of history books, who remains the only President with a Ph.D., did not care all that much for serious drama. "He was not interested in anything," Secret Service Agent Edmund Starling, who often accompanied Wilson to the theater, later recalled, "which required the use of his mind. He wanted to laugh at the clowns, admire the pretty legs of the chorus girls...and he loved good dancing." A lively raconteur, the President also liked to mine the jokes he heard for his own comic routines. Until America's entry into the Great War, Wilson rarely worked long days. He, not Eisenhower, set the record for presidential golf outings with one thousand.

But Wilson was not the same species of playful dad as TR, who ran against him in the 1912 election on the Progressive Party ticket. Temperamentally, Wilson had almost nothing in common with TR, his lifelong political enemy. In 1905, after hosting President Roosevelt at the Army-Navy football game, the Princeton University President dismissed his celebrity guest as a "mountebank." In contrast to the gregarious TR, a manly man who enjoyed roughhousing with both his war buddies and his sons, the introspective Wilson connected more easily with members of the opposite sex. As his youngest daughter, Nell, put it, "Father...thought women had 'deeper sensibilities,' 'finer understanding' than most men."

This pattern had roots in Wilson's southern boyhood, where his closest ties were with his mother, the former Janet Woodrow, and two elder sisters. Calling himself a "mamma's boy," Wilson believed that "the love of the best womanhood came to me and entered my heart through those apron-strings." In contrast, Wilson's father, the Presbyterian minister Joseph Ruggles Wilson, the mentor who steered him toward academia, was both domineering and critical. Though Joseph

Wilson had a loving side, Wilson was often on edge around him. In public, President Wilson came across as shy and aloof, but in private, he could be the life of the party. "When one gets access to him," Colonel House, Wilson's foreign policy advisor, noted in his memoir, "there is no more charming man in all the world than Woodrow Wilson."

And nowhere did his playful side come out as much as in his interactions with his daughters. According to his middle child, Jessie, Wilson was "a curious mix of dignity and almost wild gaiety." During his presidency, Wilson and Nell used to play tag with each other and to engage in what southerners of the era called "chicken-fighting." With arms folded, they would repeatedly bump into each other as they marched down the long hallway on the second floor of the White House. Stunned to observe such antics, his brother-in-law Stockton Axson once asked, "What would the great American public think if they could see their 'austere' President now?"

Though the diametric opposite of TR, Wilson enjoyed the company of his children just as much as his nemesis did. Wilson's "family life was singularly happy," noted a colleague from his Princeton days who was a frequent visitor to his capacious home at 72 Library Place, where he resided until becoming the university's president in 1902. Wilson was a hit as the family clown. His facial contortions included blowing out both cheeks until one of the girls would pat them back into shape and pulling out one cheek until it stretched like rubber—a trick which elicited screams of delight. Slapping his hands on knees, Wilson would also metamorphose into a galloping horse. With his wife homeschooling the children, the young professor, who rode home on his bicycle for lunch, ate with the family often. Instead of saying grace after meals, Wilson tended to utter a sing-songy jingle, "Now chickens, run upstairs wash your face and hands brush your teeth and put your bibs away before I count three—or I'll tickle, pinch, and spankdoodle you."

For the girls, "the most important moment of the day" came in the evening after they had finished their homework. That was when Wilson would lock the large rolltop desk in his study that he used to write his influential books, such as his five-volume *History of the American People*. He would then softly jingle his key, signaling that he was ready to come out and play. Afterward, he might lapse into one of his impersonations—say, the staggering drunk, the girls' favorite, or the monocled Englishman. He might even put on a feather boa, or do a turn as a society woman at an afternoon tea. "Come on, Nellie," Wilson was prone to ask his favorite daughter, who also took an interest in drama, "let's run away and go on the stage. We could do a splendid father and daughter act." In the evening, he also had a habit of seizing one of his daughters and beginning to dance, often prompting his wife to question the state of his sanity. "Woodrow, what is the matter with you?" Ellen would exclaim. And the musically inclined Wilson, who often led the trio in song, was no slouch on the dance floor; he could even do the can-can.

While Wilson charmed his girls, he was not as child-centered as the nurturing First Dads such as Truman and Obama covered in Chapter Six. In the dining room, he would rarely steer the conversation around to their daily concerns. He remained first and foremost an entertainer. "We seldom talked at meals, but listened intently," Nell wrote in her memoir, *The Woodrow Wilsons*. "Father had a delightful way of making an engrossing story from the smallest incident that caught his fancy...No one brought troubles or problems of any sort to be discussed at meals." Likewise, Wilson was the chief choreographer in the evening games—and his daughters had to respond to whatever he was in the mood to do. Nevertheless, he was so engaging that they much preferred spending time with him than with playmates their own age.

This playful side of Wilson is not to be confused with the totality of the man. At his core, Wilson was thin-skinned. A perfectionist, he had a tendency toward depression and somatic symptoms, as numerous scholars have argued, including George Washington University professor Jerrold Post, who has authored psychological profiles of world leaders for the CIA. (This body of research is separate from the psychoanalytic hatchet job on Wilson's personality authored by Sigmund

Freud, which was published in 1967 and no longer carries much weight.) Wilson also had a constant need for reassurance. In policy discussions with his staff, the insecure President would often end a thought with a plea for understanding, emitting an interjection such as "Don't you agree?" Whatever the precise extent of Wilson's inner angst, it was not something that typically manifested itself in his relationships with his daughters. Instead the part of Wilson, which repeatedly popped out at home, was thoroughly entrancing.

For the Wilson girls, Mother was associated with discipline and Father with comfort. He was the good cop and Ellen Wilson the bad cop (though she never let her husband in on the details of the infractions and the resulting punishments). As much of an intellectual heavyweight as Woodrow, Ellen was a talented artist and voracious reader, who downed all the major German philosophers, including Kant and Hegel. As a parent, she—and not her husband—fit the bill of the self-absorbed, often downcast scholar. Rattled by a series of family tragedies, she often reminded her husband that he had "married someone who is not gay." A few years before their 1885 wedding, Ellen's mother had died in childbirth, leaving her to be the caretaker of her three younger siblings. Soon thereafter, her father, Samuel Axson, a prominent pastor in Georgia with a history of depression, became violent. Shipped off to the Georgia State Mental Hospital, Axson proceeded to kill himself within a few months. Her brother, Stockton, became an accomplished literature professor who lived on and off with the Wilsons in Princeton, but he suffered periodic nervous breakdowns. In 1905, as her daughters were late adolescents, another brother, Edward, accidentally drowned along with his wife and young child, plunging her into an extended depression. Ellen kept her mind occupied by staying busy—she made all the children's clothes, copy-edited her husband's books, and planned every inch of the garden. "I have never understood how she crowded so many and varied activities into one day," Nell later recalled. And after her brother's death, to keep up her spirits, Ellen immersed herself once again in her painting.

Aware that their mother lacked his playfulness, the girls often turned to their father. In the fall of 1897, seven-year-old Nell came down with a mild case of scarlet fever. Her skin was peeling in minute flakes, and Wilson decided to quarantine his "little chick" in her room out of fear that she might spread the illness to her sisters. (Adults, in contrast, as doctors already knew then, are not susceptible to the infection.) After briefly attending to Nell, Ellen became worn out. Wilson took over and gave Nell a "perfect week." He sang to her, read to her, and played on the floor with her. He also constructed models of his favorite castles and cathedrals out of tiles left over from new Princeton buildings. "We had our meals together," Nell later wrote, "he fed me, petted me, slept in the bed beside me and my bliss was complete. Then...I was well again and had to share him with the others." Despite Ellen's emotional fragility, Wilson loved her deeply, and he was devastated when she died of Bright's disease a year and a half after he became President.

Wilson was as kind to his girls as his mother had been to him. Though Janet Wilson had suffered from a host of psychiatric symptoms, including depression and hypochondria, she passed on to her son a firm belief in his self-worth. "Why my darling, nobody could help loving you, if they were to try," she reassured the adolescent Woodrow when he was nervous about how his fellow high school students would treat him. Like his mother, Wilson was fiercely protective of his children. When the press began prying into their private lives, the newly elected President shot back, insisting that "the ladies of my household are not public characters...are not servants of the government. I deeply resent the treatment they are receiving at the hands of the newspapers...If this continues, I shall deal with you not as President, but man to man." Wilson encouraged his daughters to decide their own futures, such as where or even whether to go to college. He could be picky about the men whom they dated and considered as possible mates, but he kept his objections to himself. "Of course no choice they make will satisfy me. But if they make a distinctly wrong choice," he joked, "I shall never say anything about it. That is one time I shall act a part of the liar to the end." While Wilson has been accused of being an "autocratic" President, he tended to practice the same kind of democracy with the American people as he did with his children. As President, he also attempted to provide guidance, rather than to boss anyone around. His early legislative achievements such as the Federal Reserve Act of 1913 and the Clayton Antitrust Act of 1914 sprang from his belief in a more equitable society. As Wilson saw it, if he articulated his values clearly, he could count on both Congress and the American people to follow his lead.

His daughters, who were establishing their own identities just as he came to Washington, all tended to gravitate toward interests that were connected to some aspect of him. The petite blonde Margaret, who looked just like Wilson, especially when she began wearing glasses, became a professional singer. Jessie, also a blonde and considered the beauty of the family, turned to social work. The dark-haired Nell became obsessed with acting, though she also dabbled in painting—her mother's passion.

His adult daughters, in turn, would influence him. When asked in November 1912, right after her father won the election, how she and her younger sisters felt about giving women the right to vote, Margaret told the *Macon Daily Telegraph*, "We have been too much interested in father, to give that matter any thought yet." In point of fact, his daughters were already committed suffragists who repeatedly challenged their father in the privacy of their own home. In making the case to him, Jessie harped on the injustice that only one-fifth of the family possessed the franchise. Within a couple of years, all three daughters were speaking out publicly. In 1915, Margaret served as hostess for the annual convention of the organization, which eventually became known as the League of Women Voters.

While Wilson was slow to come around, the Nineteenth Amendment did become the law of the land under his watch. In early 1918, he began urging the Democrats in the House to support its passage, citing the "marvelous heroism and splendid loyalty of our women" during the early months of America's involvement in World War I. But his loyalty to the young women in his own family played an equally important role in his evolution. With women in general and his daughters in particular, Wilson could readily engage in give-and-take.

With men, in contrast, this President, who had grown up fearful of his own father, often took a combative stance. In 1922, Wilson abruptly terminated his relationship with Joseph Tumulty, after the aide who had served as his chief of staff for both terms released to the press a statement under his name without his approval. "If Tumulty had been my son and had acted as he did," the retired President told a friend, "I would have done the same thing." But if Tumulty had been a daughter, Wilson would surely have forgiven him. In the most famous example of this pattern, Wilson was unwilling to budge an inch in his negotiations with Henry Cabot Lodge, the influential Republican Senator, over the Treaty of Versailles. This inflexibility led to the nixing of a reasonable compromise by the Senate, which, as most historians agree, was the biggest disaster of his presidency.

Wilson's move to the White House in 1913 coincided with the breakup of his beloved family. The first major separation came just a few months after his inauguration. To avoid the Washington heat, Wilson rented a summer cottage in Cornish, New Hampshire, a resort town populated by numerous artists and writers, including the sculptor Augustus Saint-Gaudens and the poet Percy MacKaye. But after he was forced to call Congress back in session, he insisted that the rest of the family head up to New England without him. In late June, a tearful Wilson wrote Ellen, "The President is a superior kind of slave...I am too lonely. I must think quietly and not with rebellion." Wilson tried to cope by playing golf daily with his aide, Dr. Carl Grayson.

One of the few times that he saw Ellen and his daughters that summer was in a mid-September visit to Cornish to attend *Sanctuary: A Bird Masque*, a play written by MacKaye in which both Margaret and

Nell performed. Worried that her husband might object to his daughters' participation, Ellen had written for his permission; not only did Wilson immediately communicate his approval, he also insisted on seeing their performance. He was not disappointed. "The President," reported the *New York Times*, "was an attentive auditor throughout. He smiled often...[and] expressed himself as much delighted with the piece." Both daughters got good reviews, Margaret for her singing in the prologue and Nell for her starring role as the bird spirit, Ornis. "Miss [Eleanor] Wilson," reported a Boston paper, "threw herself into the spirit of the play with such enthusiasm that it became very evident she had been selected for this trying role because of her ability to play it well quite as much as for her social prominence."

Unbeknownst to her father, Nell carried on the family tradition of wild dancing when, along with a few fellow cast members, she crashed a country dance at the Cornish town hall after the show. Of the locals' response to the surprise guests, who were still wearing their skimpy bird outfits, Nell later wrote, "I have never known whether they thought us a dream, or a visitation from an insane asylum." Nell and her colleagues proceeded to do the fox trot, the tango, the bunny bug, and the "kitchen sink"—a particularly risqué new craze in which the male swung his female partner through his legs. Though some photographers caught the President's daughter in flagrante delicto, Nell managed to persuade them not to print the photos.

On Tuesday, November 25, 1913, the tight-knit Wilson clan was officially rent asunder. At 4:30 that afternoon, Jessie married Francis B. Sayre, a recent Harvard Law School graduate, in front of four hundred guests in the East Room of the White House. "I know; it was a wedding, not a funeral," a sad and pensive Ellen said afterward, "but you must forgive us—this is the first break in the family." After spending their honeymoon in Europe, the couple moved to Massachusetts, where Sayre took up a post at his alma mater, Williams College; for the next few years, he served as an assistant to its president, Harry Garfield, son of another U.S. President. A year later, Jessie gave birth to

Wilson's first grandchild, Francis Sayre Jr., the eleventh and last presidential family member—either child or grandchild—to be born in the White House. Endowed with the intellectual heft of both her parents, Jessie had graduated Phi Beta Kappa from the Women's College of Baltimore (today Goucher College). Inspired by her father's attempt to make Princeton more democratic by abolishing the eating clubs, she resigned from her sorority, Phi Gamma Beta, when it rejected a sister of a charter member for not being "physically charming."

After college, Jessie spent three years toiling at a settlement house for working women in Kensington, Pennsylvania. A fierce advocate for social justice, she managed to help push through some Progressive legislation even before the family got to Pennsylvania Avenue. In February 1913, this eloquent orator gave a speech before the Delaware Legislature, which was instrumental in getting that state to pass a landmark law limiting women to a fifty-five-hour workweek.

After the war, Jessie emerged as a major figure in the Massachusetts Democratic Party. In the fall of 1928, she campaigned actively on behalf of the Democratic standard-bearer, New York Governor Al Smith. That October, she energized a partisan crowd in Boston by describing the philosophy of the Democratic presidential nominee as "Take care of all the people and the rich will somehow manage to save themselves from starvation." Though urged by numerous Massachusetts Democrats to seek a U.S. Senate seat in 1930, the happily married Jessie took herself out of the running in order to care for her family, which by then also included a daughter, Eleanor, and a second son, Woodrow. Jessie died suddenly of gall bladder disease in 1933 at the age of forty-five. Her husband, Francis Sayre Sr., who taught law at Harvard from 1917 until 1933, went on to serve as an Assistant Secretary of State under FDR and as the United States Representative to the United Nations Trusteeship Council under Truman.

Nell, who caught the bouquet at Jessie's wedding, was the next to leave the nest. But first she jilted Ben King, the engineer to whom she had been engaged for two years, replacing him with her father's fifty-year-old Secretary of the Treasury, William McAdoo, who was then busy getting the freshly minted Federal Reserve Bank up and running. "I am so humiliated when I think of my cruelty to Ben, that I can't believe I can keep your respect," she confided to Jessie in March 1914. "Mr. McAdoo…is the only person who can make me happy." Dubbed "Dancing Mac" by the press, the trim and handsome widower could hold his own as Nell's steady partner at the soirees held at the Chevy Chase Golf Club. Less of "a high brow" than her sisters, Nell was "crazy about dancing," as the press reported; eschewing a four-year college, she had attended Saint Mary's, a two-year finishing school in Raleigh, North Carolina. A talented tennis player and golfer, she enjoyed accompanying her father to baseball games. Her wedding took place on May 7, 1914. Due to Ellen Wilson's worsening health, this Blue Room ceremony was relatively modest; only a hundred guests, mostly just the friends and family of the couple, plus assorted administration officials, were invited. Wilson was devastated, as Nell was his "chum," his best pal. "She is simply part of me," he wrote a few days later, "the only delightful part; and I feel the loneliness more than I dare admit even to myself."

Exactly three months later, his wife Ellen died at the age of fifty-four. Though Margaret still officially lived at the White House, his eldest daughter was often in New York taking singing lessons. The loss of his three children, on top of his wife's death, led to a deep depression. "All the elasticity has gone out of me," the President wrote in December 1914. "I read detective stories to forget, as a man would get drunk!" Little did the public know that Wilson stunned his new girlfriend, Edith Galt, by proposing to her in May 1915, just two months after their first meeting; the couple wed six months later. But his daughters readily accepted his second wife. "We can't help loving you, dear Edith," wrote Jessie to her stepmother-to-be in August 1915, "and it isn't only because you have made our darling father so happy, you are so dear and sweet and true that we must love you for yourself."

While remarriage revived Wilson, marriage did not suit Nell. The choice of a much older husband, with whom she sought to re-create her magical connection with her father, did not turn out to be wise. Nell was now a stepmother of McAdoo's six children—two of whom were older than she was. And his younger children could be difficult to manage. McAdoo's third child, his daughter Nona, then in her early twenties, was insanely jealous of the attention that her father paid to Nell. Her irrational outbursts prompted Wilson to hope that someone would marry Nona soon, thus removing her from the family. "That's a hateful remark, I admit," Wilson wrote to his new wife, Edith, "but it must be said that Nona is not an admirable person." Of McAdoo's fourth child, Billy, who evolved into a chronic alcoholic, Nell would note years later, "I fear he is beyond reclaim."

Nell and McAdoo soon had two daughters of their own: Ellen, born in 1915, and Mary, born in 1920. "I seem to have been in a strange daze in 1914 and 1915," Nell later acknowledged. "The war and mother and childbirth and the stress of the McAdoo family all apparently made an automaton of me." Long considered presidential timber, McAdoo led the delegate race after the first ballot in both the 1920 and 1924 Democratic Conventions. In 1920, he never officially threw his hat into the ring, largely because Nell was "thrown into hysterics" by the fear that the stress would incapacitate him just as it had her father, who would never recover from his 1919 stroke. Four years later, McAdoo actively campaigned for the White House. Holding aloft "the torch…carried to such noble heights by Woodrow Wilson," McAdoo still held a slight lead when he released his delegates after the ninety-ninth ballot in the deadlocked Madison Square Garden convention, which eventually nominated John Davis to run against Calvin Coolidge.

After that failed presidential bid, the couple began drifting apart. While their home was in California, McAdoo spent most of his time in Washington pursuing various business interests. "I am in a constant nervous turmoil," Nell wrote in 1928, "and so full of misery and despair that there is no hope of getting myself back into shape again…There is something awfully wrong with me." In 1934, she finally demanded a divorce. Still considered by many "the best dancer in Washington," the youthful, seventy-one-year-old McAdoo, who was elected as a U.S. Senator from California in 1932, married a twenty-six-year-old nurse the following year.

Nell, who continued to struggle with various nervous ailments, turned to writing, publishing a book about her parents' marriage in 1937. In 1946, she was devastated when her elder child, Ellen, a twice-divorced part-time singer, died in a Santa Monica hotel room from an overdose of sleeping pills at the age of thirty-two. That same year, Nell released *Julia and the White House*, a roman à clef for young adults about her own experiences in 1600 Pennsylvania Avenue a generation earlier. In this fictional rewrite of her life, the President's daughter falls in love with a sophisticated older man—Solicitor General George Compton (William McAdoo)—but chooses to remain with her less charming but steadier fiancé, Stephen Brady (Ben King). Ever loyal to her father's vision of international peace, she covered the initial United Nations Conference in San Francisco as a radio journalist. In her last public appearance in the spring of 1959, Nell, who lived until 1967, participated in a "Life with Father" luncheon at Washington's Statler Hotel sponsored by the Women's National Press Club along with eight other presidential offspring, including Alice Roosevelt. When asked about Wilson, Nell stressed his playful nature and his remarkable talents as an entertainer, stating, "He could have been an actor."

Unlike her younger sisters, Margaret would never marry. Though every couple of years, the press would report a new engagement—her husbands-to-be included such prominent men as the Chicago publisher Frank Compton and Wilson's frequent golfing partner, Dr. Carl Grayson—by mid-1914, she was no longer looking for love, telling her sister Jessie, "Music is my husband." Wilson hoped that Margaret might evolve into his "little assistant" who could fill in as First Lady once his wife became ill, but she was not interested. "I guess I am just inadequate to the job of being the oldest daughter of the President," a harried Margaret, who was tired of entertaining White House visitors, wrote to Jessie earlier that year.

Described by the *Atlanta Journal* as "a rather cold intellectual type," the shy Margaret preferred to talk about philosophy rather than to chit-chat about fashion. Chronic interpersonal anxiety had long plagued her. "She has been a nervous child her whole life and is evidently unfitted by temperament to take a full college course," wrote her mother to John Van Meter, the Dean of the Women's College of Baltimore in February 1905, when Margaret was a sophomore. The only education she ever pursued after dropping out of college that spring was private voice lessons. Margaret's love of singing dated back to her Princeton childhood, when she would listen to both her father and to the family's governess, Clara Boehm, who serenaded her with German lieder. In an interview early in Wilson's presidency, she reminded the *New York Times* that her father "has a beautiful tenor. It really is of fine quality except that he has not sung professionally, excepting in a male quartet in college."

Upon her arrival in the White House, she still lacked the courage to appear in public, and her parents were very protective of her. When asked by the head of the National Civic Federation, a prominent business organization, to sing at a banquet about a year into his administration, Margaret turned down the offer, noting that "my father says that the distractions at a banquet are great and inimitable…I have so little experience as a singer I do not dare to trust myself before a large audience." To chase her dream of becoming America's greatest lieder singer, she turned to Ross W. David, a Manhattan-based voice teacher of the world's leading opera stars. With his help and encouragement, she made her professional debut in Syracuse with the Chicago Symphony in May 1915. Buoyed by its success, the lyric soprano embarked on a tour that would last nearly four years. In October 1918, she took her music to France, where she entertained troops for the next nine months. Due to the strain of all those performances, some before crowds of ten thousand or more, she lost her voice, and she would never sing again after her return to the United States. Moreover, the close proximity to the battlefield helped to precipitate a nervous break-down for which her physician recommended an extended stay at the Grove Park Inn in Raleigh, North Carolina.

In the early 1920s, the often flighty Margaret seemed to be a lost soul. One summer afternoon during the last year of her father's presi-dency, she hopped on a bus at Fifth Avenue and Thirty-Fourth Street in Manhattan and handed the conductor, P. G. Lynch, a penny. When reminded that a dime was required to use public transportation, she responded, "I must get off now. That penny is all I have." Lynch, who had no idea that his indigent passenger was a First Daughter, lent her the fare. Margaret proceeded to jot down his name; a few days later, Lynch was startled to get his dime back along with a thank-you note written on White House stationery.

Desperate for money, Margaret, who continued to see doctors for her debilitating anxiety, thought about several options, including pro-moting a prize fight—an idea on which her father put the kibosh, stressing in a telegram that it would bring "deserved disrepute upon our names." As she tried to figure out her next career move, Wilson arranged consultations with several prominent family friends, includ-ing the New York financier Bernard Baruch. She eventually landed a job soliciting new accounts at New York's Blow Advertising Company for a couple of years before turning to selling bonds. Feeling somewhat revived, she also renewed her efforts on behalf of child welfare chari-ties, a cause of long-standing interest. Margaret was at her father's bed-side when his chronically weak heart finally gave way on February 3, 1924. Under his will, she received an annual stipend of $2,500 as long as she remained unmarried.

In the mid-1930s, Margaret immersed herself in Hindu philosophy, particularly the works of Sri Aurobindo, the Cambridge University–educated scholar who had emerged as one of the world's leading practi-tioners of yoga and meditation. By 1938, she considered Sri Aurobindo her master, writing, "It seems as unnecessary now to be assured that I am your disciple as…it would be to be told that I am my father's daughter." In July 1940, she resettled permanently in his ashram at Pondicherry, a French town in South India, where she assumed the name of "Dishta," a Sanskrit word that refers to the presence of the divine in all human beings. Margaret/Dishta died there four years later of uremia.

3

Double-Dealing Dads

"You Know Such Things Happen on Plantations"

My children are my principal treasures.

John Tyler to his daughter Mary, 1831

On Saturday, September 11, 1841, President John Tyler faced a crisis that had never been seen before (and has never been seen again) in the annals of American history. That afternoon, at regular intervals between 12:30 and 5:30, five of his six cabinet members marched into his office in the Executive Mansion to tender their resignations. Only his Secretary of State, the former Massachusetts Senator Daniel Webster, would stand by him.

A year earlier, Tyler had been elected as William Henry Harrison's Vice President—"Tippecanoe and Tyler, too" ran the famous campaign slogan. This Whig ticket would be the most fertile ever, even if we include only the children the public knew about at the time of the election—Harrison's ten and the nine Tyler sired with his first wife, Letitia, who died in 1842. Upon the sixty-eight-year-old Harrison's sudden death in early April, the former Virginia Senator became "His Accidency"—the first Vice President to succeed a President unable to complete his full term.

That summer, Whig legislators, led by the influential Kentucky Senator Henry Clay, began trying to enact key elements of the party's platform. At the top of their agenda was the creation of a national bank.

On July 28, the Senate narrowly approved a banking bill; a week later, the House followed suit by a vote of 131 to 100. In an attempt to guarantee the approval of the President, a former Democrat who had long championed states' rights, Congress added a plank that would allow any state to reject branches of the bank within its borders. With the veto power then a rarely used tool—since the adoption of the Constitution, it had been exercised only twelve times and not once by Tyler's boyhood hero and role model, Thomas Jefferson—passage was widely expected. Even so, Tyler nixed the measure on August 16, frustrating Clay and other sponsors. And after Tyler vetoed a second banking bill on September 9, insisting that he had no choice but to "exercise the negative power entrusted to him by the Constitution...or commit an act of gross moral turpitude," most Whigs could no longer contain their rage. In addition to the walkout by over 80 percent of his cabinet, party members across the country burned the President in effigy. Countless Whig newspaper editors now compared Tyler with Benedict Arnold or Judas Iscariot. Even on his home turf—Charles City County, Virginia—Whigs protested in front of the courthouse, chanting, "Et tu, Brute!"

While the reaction to the second veto was extreme, it could hardly have been a surprise to the President, who knew full well that he was dashing his party's expectations. Expressing the sentiments of the entire cabinet, Secretary of the Treasury Thomas Ewing accused Tyler of betrayal for vetoing "a bill framed and fashioned according to your own suggestion." Ewing was shocked that Tyler had never consulted him before issuing his veto message, emphasizing that "you did not even refer to it in conversation."

Over the years, outside observers have readily understood the pique experienced by Tyler's fellow Whigs. Even scholars sympathetic to Tyler concede that the President was guilty of a serious lapse in judgment. Noting that the President characterized the compromise feature of the first banking bill as "a contemptible subterfuge," an early biographer calls his actions "hasty and not carefully considered." Likewise, another biographer describes his conduct during the controversy that summer as "tricky and deceptive," adding that although the President had often expressed concern about the constitutionality of such federal initiatives, he also had a habit of saying one thing and meaning another. Most historians agree that by being less headstrong and signing either banking bill, Tyler could have both remained true to his ideological position and avoided the debacle that destroyed his presidency.

Two days after the barrage of resignations, seventy Whigs caucused on Capitol Square and denounced the President, insisting that they wanted nothing more to do with him. As Henry Clay put it, Tyler then became "a president without a party." Hardly anyone came to his defense. As the future President Millard Fillmore, then a Whig Congressman from upstate New York, stated on September 23, "I have heard of but two Tyler men in this city [Buffalo]...and both of these are applicants for jobs." The strong-willed Virginian tried to reassert his power by quickly assembling a new cabinet, to whom he demanded absolute obedience to his policies. But he would be severely crippled. The following summer, a House select committee chaired by his northern nemesis, John Quincy Adams, whom the fickle Tyler had supported for President two decades earlier, would consider removing him from office. Though the first impeachment attempt in U.S. history fizzled after several months, with few allies in Congress among either the Whigs or Democrats, the President had little leverage. And his political future was nonexistent. The only party that would nominate Tyler in 1844 was his own, the newly created Democratic-Republican Party, and he ended up dropping out of the race a few months before any votes were cast.

In early October 1841, as he was still recovering from the fallout over the banking bills, the thin, six-foot President with the Roman nose, described by the pioneering nineteenth-century journalist Anne Royall as a "fine-looking man," retreated to his home in Williamsburg for a vacation. Upon his return to Washington, he faced another round of attacks by bitter political foes. In the December 10 issue of the abolitionist newspaper, the *Emancipator and Free American*, editor Joshua Leavitt accused Tyler of betraying members of his own family, reporting that he had fathered numerous slave children, some of whom he had sold. Headlined "Tyler-Ising," Leavitt's article drew on the account of a northern Baptist minister who had visited a Baptist family in Richmond in the mid-1830s. Encountering a white-skinned slave, the minister began asking a series of questions. Much to the cleric's astonishment, the slave reported that he had been born on Governor Tyler's plantation in Williamsburg, adding that "my mother called me John Tyler, because she said Governor Tyler was my father. You know such things happen on plantations." This slave went on to say that Tyler had fathered several other slave children with his mother, whom he had also sold.

Below a transcript of this interview, Leavitt tacked on the story of another alleged slave son named Charles Tyler, who had appeared in Poughkeepsie in the late 1830s before escaping to Canada. According to Leavitt, Charles had served as Tyler's body servant during his tenure as a Senator earlier in the decade. At the time, most Americans, if they heard about these charges at all, considered them fantastical. No other papers picked up the story. And Tyler was able to table the discussion by running a couple of quick rebuttals later that month in the administration's newspaper, the *Madisonian*. "To attempt a refutation of some of the slanderous charges made against President Tyler," its editor, John B. Jones, asserted, "we deem not only useless, but degrading."

But contemporary scholars no longer accept so readily the defenses offered by Tyler's own personal spinmeisters. They have also become increasingly skeptical of the hagiographic view of the tenth President propounded by his early biographers, who had no choice but to rely heavily on a collection of Tyler's papers published by Lyon G. Tyler, a son from the President's second marriage. Though trained as a historian, this longtime President of William and Mary was far from an objective source; until his death in 1935, he continued to describe Lincoln as the "boss slacker" and to insist that southerners "are still political slaves of the North." In stark contrast to his predecessors, Tyler's latest biographer, Ed Crapol, has written that "the claims that John Tyler fathered children by his slaves must be taken seriously and examined thoroughly." In a recent interview with me, Crapol described Tyler as "lusty," and acknowledged that he may well have turned to illicit relationships to satisfy his hyperactive libido.

And these allegations about mulatto children go far beyond just the relatively small number alluded to in Leavitt's article. A handful of late-twentieth-century residents of Charles City County, Virginia—some official white Tyler descendants, others alleged black ones—reported to author Daryl Dance, a professor of English at the University of Richmond, that Tyler often boasted about having fathered a staggering total of fifty-two children with black women over the course of his life. As Doris Christian, a granddaughter of Sylvanius Tyler, a mulatto whose aquiline nose looked similar to Tyler's, stated, "Tyler had fifty-two children. He wrote it down."

Such braggadocio was not uncharacteristic of Tyler, who, in his personal correspondence, repeatedly alluded with pride to his large number of white heirs. For example, when his second wife, Julia, was pregnant with their fifth child—the future historian, Lyon—the ex-President wrote to his elder sister, Martha, "Do you see I am not likely to let the name become extinct." The names of several possible black concubines are known. While no proof in the form of DNA matches yet exists, the considerable amount of circumstantial evidence—including a photo showing the physical similarity between the President and Sylvanius Tyler—strongly suggests that Tyler did father numerous mulatto children, including some whom he sold as slaves. In the antebellum south, sexual encounters with slaves (or free blacks who worked as servants) by the master of the house were not uncommon, and these illicit relationships rarely even caused much friction in marriages. As Mary Chestnut noted in her famous diary written at the dawn of the Civil War, "Every lady tells you who is the father of all the mulatto children in everybody's household, but those in her own she seems to think drop from the clouds, or pretends to think so."

Moreover, during Tyler's lifetime, a handful of allegations involving other types of sexual indiscretions also emerged. In 1845, an administration critic accused the President of staging wild sex parties with his two adult sons, Robert and John Jr., both of whom worked as presidential aides. "Will you deny," Hiram Cumming, a former editor of the *Empire State Democrat*, asked the former President in a massive book entitled *Secret History of the Perfidies, Intrigues, and Corruptions of the Tyler Dynasty*, "that you frequently with them [your two eldest sons] were engaged in bacchanalian reveries in the presidential mansion, which were succeeded by scenes at which the heart recoils, and humanity shudders?" Summing up the matter, Cumming alludes to "blasphemy, debauchery and drunkenness" in the people's house.

While generations of historians have dismissed everything in Cumming's book as malicious gossip, his assertions about the overactive libidos of the Tylers are not far-fetched. After all, in the brief hiatus between the death of his first wife and his marriage to the twenty-four-year-old raven-haired beauty Julia Gardiner in 1844, Tyler was aggressively seeking female companionship. In February 1843, after just a few brief meetings, he stunned the unsuspecting Julia by literally chasing her around the White House in search of a kiss. A few months later, he even made a pass at sixteen-year-old Eliza Fisk Harwood, the ward of his Williamsburg neighbors, Dickie and Mary Galt. As Mary Galt noted in a letter that August, "President Tyler...honored me with a visit, wished E. [Eliza] were only ten years older, she does not admire the President, refused him a kiss, which he thought very strangely of." A disgusted Eliza, as Galt added, also turned down the President's request for a romantic walk by the sea.

Likewise, there is no doubt that John Jr. was a chronic alcoholic who often chased women. By 1840, Tyler's namesake was already living apart from his wife of two years, and the Williamsburg townsfolk often found themselves gossiping about his dalliances and his bar fights, including one that September where he got "his face most dreadfully mangled," as one eyewitness put it. After a dinner with the Tylers on Christmas Eve in 1842, a startled Julia reported to one of her brothers that the still married John Jr. tried to seduce *her*. (Before her marriage, Julia often visited the Presidential Mansion, accompanied by her father, the wealthy Long Islander David Gardiner.) Two years later, the President was forced to fire John Jr. due to his son's outlandish and unpredictable behavior. Of the directionless Tyler scion, Julia would later observe that "The P. [President] says he really believes him part a mad man." Cumming's book does not bear directly on the matter of Tyler's slave children, but it highlights the tenuous nature of long-held assumptions about the private predilections of our tenth President and his second son, John Jr.

While little has been written about Tyler's treachery toward his mulatto children, much ink has been spilled about his treachery toward his country. As the New England historian Henry Wilson, who served as Vice President during Grant's second term, pointed out 140 years ago, Tyler was our "only traitor President." Of the five former Presidents who were alive at the start of the Civil War, he alone joined the enemy. In the fall of 1861, Tyler easily won a seat in the newly established Confederate House of Representatives. He died on January 18, 1862—shortly before the Confederate Congress was to meet for the first time. In an obituary published a few days later, after alluding to his vetoes of the banking bills, the *New York Times* summarized his presidency as follows: "His treachery to all men and parties, his total loss of popularity, and the embarrassment and confusion which he brought upon the country, are matters of history—though they are now all lost sight of in the later and more infamous appellation of traitor."

President Abraham Lincoln refused to acknowledge Tyler's death. A devoted Whig until the party dissolved in the mid-1850s, Lincoln would never forget about Tyler's betrayal of his former colleagues. As the Civil War was ending, President Lincoln still delighted in regaling interlocutors with an anecdote about Tyler, which dated back to the middle of his Accidental Presidency. One day, Tyler's son Robert wanted to order a special train for a presidential excursion. When told by the railroad superintendent, who happened to be a Whig, that his line could not fulfill the order, Robert exclaimed, "What, did you not furnish a special train for the funeral of President Harrison?" To which the superintendent responded matter-of-factly, "Yes, and if you will only bring your father here in *that* shape, you shall have the best train on the road."

Sharing Lincoln's feelings about Tyler, many historians have dismissed our tenth President as a nonentity. "He has been called a mediocre man," wrote a young Theodore Roosevelt in one of his history books published in 1887, "but that is unwarranted flattery. He was a politician of monumental littleness." James Schouler, the author of a highly regarded multivolume history of America that also appeared in the late nineteenth century, labels Tyler a liar, whom "only a casuist in morals" can understand. But this obscure President, remembered today primarily as "the rhyming end of a catchy campaign slogan," as his recent biographer put it, exerted much more influence than is often assumed. On the domestic front, the domineering and self-aggrandizing loner with few political allies could not put his stamp on any legislation. However, he permanently elevated the status of the vice presidency by repeatedly insisting that he was no "Acting President" but the full equal of his nine predecessors.

And in foreign policy, his capacity for double-dealing actually led to a string of achievements that can only be described as impressive. Using a secret slush fund to wage a propaganda war against his political opponents, Tyler managed to negotiate a treaty with Great Britain, which both avoided an impending third war with the mother country and redrew America's northern border. In his final weeks in office, he relied on a parliamentary sleight of hand to bring about the annexation of Texas. Even more significant, Tyler's ideas about American expansionism, which he had first articulated as a young Congressman, formed the template upon which his successor, James Polk, would build. The notion of Manifest Destiny, coined the year he left office, was his stepchild. Tyler also spurred an explosion in America's population, which stood at only seventeen million, including two and a half million slaves, when he took office. "We hold out to the people of other countries an invitation to come and settle among us as members of our rapidly growing family," he declared in his first address before Congress, "and to unite with us in the great task of preserving our institutions and perpetuating our liberties." Responding to Tyler's open invitation, nearly two million immigrants seeking a better life would flock to our shores in the 1840s. But tragically, this compartmentalized man, who refused to free any of his seventy slaves in his will, would never see a contradiction between his determination to promote America as a beacon of liberty and his insistence on preserving the right of some of its residents to buy and sell others, even those whom they had brought into the world.

Tyler's penchant for womanizing is something that he shared with a handful of fellow presidents, including such recent occupants of the Oval Office as John F. Kennedy and Bill Clinton, whose sexual escapades have been all too well documented. Tyler was also a charmer who had a penchant for looking at all human experience through a sexual lens. In his first speech in the House of Representatives, the newly married twenty-six-year-old Virginia Congressman declared, "Popularity, I have always thought, may be compared to a coquette—the more you woo her, the more apt she is to elude your embrace."

Though Tyler meant to stress his lack of interest in appealing to the masses, such explicit sexual language, which was relatively rare in its day, also reveals quite a bit about his own inner world. Thoughts about romantic conquests kept intruding into his consciousness. A man who did not know how to connect, he had an obsessive-compulsive personality, which manifested itself in nearly everything he did. As his second wife observed a couple of years into their marriage, "When he commences business, he does not know when to stop. Today he has bottled and corked fourteen dozen of wine and is wondering now what it is that has made his arms and fingers so to ache." And one of the activities that he could not stop doing was chasing women—even, or especially those he happened to own (his slaves) or happened to work for him (free black servants).

But not every President who pursued numerous extramarital affairs qualifies as a double-dealing dad—defined as one who betrays his children. While Kennedy and Clinton were often duplicitous with their wives, both were caring parents. Tyler belongs to the small subset of promiscuous presidents who have sired illegitimate children they later failed to protect. Other members of this group include Grover Cleveland, whose bachelor fatherhood emerged as the defining issue of the 1884 presidential race, and Warren Harding, whose twenty-four-year-old mistress gave birth to a daughter just as he was launching his run for the presidency. Neither Cleveland nor Harding had much interest in the illegitimate child he had sired. For both men, the youngster was just a blot on his résumé that needed to be covered up, rather than a flesh-and-blood human being who needed to be cared for.

Tyler also alienated the grown children from his first marriage both by marrying a woman five years younger than his eldest daughter, Mary, and leaving all seven out of his will. In most of his personal relationships, Tyler was tempestuous, but with his adored second wife, Julia, he became for the most part "a submissive husband," as he readily acknowledged. A month after their wedding, the smitten President told his bride that the honeymoon was "likely to last forever"—a prediction that held true. He remained deeply in love with Julia, but he was much more solicitous toward her than toward any of the seven children from his second marriage, who for him were more props than people—which provided proof of his exceptional virility. After the birth of their third child, a daughter also named Julia, he wrote to a friend, "You see I have been no idle drone since I parted with politics and the politicians." His youngest, Pearl, was born in 1860 when Tyler was seventy. "The last of the second crop," as President Truman called her, died in 1947. (Truman paid close attention to Pearl's death, "since," as he wrote his wife, Bess, "she's supposed to have been my 92nd cousin once removed and since her pa inherited the Presidency as I did.")

Tyler was not America's first double-dealing dad. As Harvard historian Annette Gordon-Reed has documented in her Pulitzer Prize–winning biography, *The Hemingses of Monticello: An American Family* (2008), Tyler's idol, Thomas Jefferson, fathered six children with his slave Sally Hemings. In 1802, Jefferson's political opponent, the Scottish-born journalist James Callender, first revealed the President's affair with Hemings in the *Richmond Recorder*. But for nearly two centuries, most scholars refused even to look into the matter. The charges, wrote Dumas Malone, author of the definitive six-volume Jefferson biography, "are distinctly out of character, being virtually unthinkable in a man of Jefferson's moral standard and habitual conduct." In 1998, forensic science weighed in, as a DNA test revealed a link between the sixth Hemings child, Eston, and the male Jefferson line. The four Hemings children who reached adulthood worked as their father's slaves during his lifetime, but Jefferson freed them all in his will.

While allegations about illegitimate children are difficult to prove, a scholarly consensus is emerging that Tyler's running mate, William Henry Harrison, also fathered slave children. In his recent biography of Walter White, founder of the NAACP, historian Kenneth Janken, a professor at the University of North Carolina, asserts that White was the great-grandson of the union between Harrison and his slave named Dilsia, with whom he sired six children. According to Janken, in the late 1830s, as he was gearing up to run for President, Harrison decided to dispose of his "bastard slave children." He gave four of them, including a daughter named Marie, to his brother who, in turn, sold them to Joseph Pothyress, an early settler of La Grange, Georgia. At Pothyress's plantation, Dr. Augustus Ware, a surgeon who later became famous for training "the Nancy Harts," as the Confederate Army's only female militia was called, met Marie, with whom he fathered four illegitimate children, including Madeline Harrison, who was Walter White's mother.

In the case of a few other presidents, where there is only limited circumstantial evidence for the existence of love children, contemporary scholars are tentative about saying anything definitive. The descendants of West Ford, a slave owned by George Washington's younger brother, John, have long claimed that he was a product of a 1784 liaison between the future President and a slave named Venus. Acknowledging that "oral history is difficult to interpret," historian Henry Wiencek, author of *An Imperfect God: George Washington, His Slaves, and the Creation of America*, noted that "the possibility still remains that George Washington could have been West Ford's father."

Likewise, longstanding allegations that President Andrew Johnson fathered three slave children have yet to be backed up by much convincing proof. In 1842, when Johnson was a thirty-three-year-old Tennessee state senator, he bought his first slave, a fourteen-year-old girl named Dolly. She would later have three children: Liz, Florence, and William. According to William Johnson, the future President purchased his mother after she made flattering comments about his looks. Having carefully examined the matter, historian David Warren Bowen concluded, "Any relationship of a sexual nature which Johnson may have had with his female slaves is hidden in the fog surrounding that delicate subject. There is simply no conclusive evidence one way or the other. This is particularly regrettable because sex plays such an important part in racist mythology. If Dolly, for example, had been purchased for purposes other than domestic, it might clarify the nature of Johnson's personality." When William Johnson died in 1943, Andrew Johnson's wayward son, Robert, who had committed suicide in 1869, was listed as the father on the death certificate. While this entry could have been correct, it could also have reflected a desire by someone to protect the reputation of the former President.

Though LBJ's promiscuity has not received the same attention as that of the President under whom he served as Vice President for nearly three years, it may well have been even more pronounced. As biographer Robert Dallek has reported, when aides alluded to Kennedy's womanizing, Johnson liked to boast, "Why, I had more women by accident than he had by design." And at least one of these dalliances may have produced a child. In 1948, Johnson started an affair with Madeleine Duncan Brown, then a twenty-three-year-old advertising executive. In a memoir published in 1997, Brown claimed that Johnson fathered her son, Stephen, who was born in 1951 and died of cancer in 1990. According to Brown, she received regular monthly support payments from Johnson until his death in 1973. The Johnson family has long denied Brown's claim of paternity, and Lady Bird Johnson once stated that the affair never even happened. While Madeleine Brown's book may not be entirely truthful, the LBJ she portrays bears a close resemblance to the man as he really was. A few years ago, Marie Fehmer, a loyal aide who worked for Johnson for seven years after finishing college at the University of Texas in 1962, admitted to biographer Randall Woods that in November 1962, the Vice President offered to set her up in an apartment in New York if she would agree to be his lover and to have his child—two propositions she politely declined.

Tyler was also not the only President to betray his first set of children after marrying a younger second wife. In late March 1853—just a few weeks after his presidency ended—Millard Fillmore lost his wife of twenty-seven years, Abigail, with whom he had fathered two children. A year later, after his daughter, Mary, died from cholera at the age of twenty-two, he was comforted by his son, Millard Powers Fillmore, known as Powers. "My good son only, of all my little family remains," the former President wrote his friend, the mental health advocate Dorothea Dix, in September 1854. "I have none other now to sympathize with me in grief or rejoice with me in prosperity." Four years later, over Powers's objection, Fillmore married Caroline McIntosh, a wealthy widow thirteen years his junior. In a prenuptial agreement,

Fillmore, who lived until 1874, promised her rather than his son the bulk of his belongings. When Fillmore's second wife died in 1881, Powers contested her will and sought to regain his father's property, which included wine, silver, and valuable books as well as his personal papers. After winning the suit, Powers would, in turn, ask his executors to destroy his father's letters—a request that was ignored. While it's unclear what motivated Powers to take this action, anger at his father's betrayal is a possible explanation.

President Benjamin Harrison's first wife, Caroline Scott, with whom he had sired two children, died just as his term was ending. Four years later in 1896, Harrison, the sixty-two-year-old grandson of Tyler's running mate, married thirty-seven-year-old Mary Lord Dimmick. Harrison's adult children, Russell and Mary, were both rattled, as Dimmick was his niece by marriage (her mother was the sister of Harrison's late wife). And Harrison's clumsy attempts to smooth over the tension kept backfiring. Shortly before the wedding, which neither Russell nor his sister Mary would attend, Harrison wrote to his son, "It is natural that a man's *former* children should not be pleased . . . with a second marriage" (italics added). Acting like a besotted teenager, Harrison did everything he could to please his young wife. He started going to concerts, declaring, "I am not devoted to music, but Mrs. Harrison is, and I am devoted to her." Harrison eventually fathered a daughter with Dimmick and was still hoping to father a new male heir when he died at the age of sixty-seven. As he noted in the will written shortly before his death, "If a boy shall be born to me, he shall bear my name, and my sword and sash shall be given to him instead of to my son Russell."

Double-dealing dads tend to house two or more contradictory identities within. In Tyler's case, a smooth socialite, an angry rebel, an upstanding family man, and a depressed loner as well as both a prig and a Lothario all somehow managed to coexist with one other. This aristocrat could turn on his southern charm whenever he wanted to. But Tyler also harbored a violent, antisocial side. In 1822, when

Col. John Macon, a witness in a lawsuit that the young attorney was contesting, accused Tyler of not "acting the part of a gentleman," he repeatedly slashed Macon with a riding whip. Tyler later bragged that he had done considerable damage to Macon's face while he himself remained uninjured. Identifying with Robin Hood, Tyler would name his post-presidential plantation Sherwood Forest; there, he would raise his second family with his second wife, Julia.

The deceptive Tyler would routinely demand that his children do as he said—not as he did. This man who often had trouble controlling his own anger counseled his two eldest sons, Robert and John Jr., not to "be too captious or prone to take offense," stressing that "a constant respect for the feelings of others is indispensably necessary for success in life." Tyler also insisted that his daughters from his first marriage hold their temper in check at all times and forgo the waltz, which he considered "rather vulgar." But as President, Tyler would be delighted when composers sold sheet music called "Julia Waltzes," which paid homage to the young and attractive First Lady.

Both Grover Cleveland and Warren Harding had two main identities. As a young man in Buffalo, our twenty-second President was known to his drinking buddies as "Big Steve" (his original first name, which he dropped in late adolescence, had been Stephen). In contrast to "Grover the Good," the duty-bound lawyer and politician, this reckless hedonist enjoyed staying up until the wee hours of the morning, singing lusty drinking songs, chasing women, and getting into bar fights. Likewise, Harding referred to his hypersexual alter ego as "Jerry," and in his correspondence with Carrie Phillips, one of his numerous illicit lovers, he also used this name to designate his penis. "Jerry," Harding wrote in March 1915 to Phillips, "came in while I was pondering your notes in glad reflection...He told me to say that you are the best and darlingest in the world." With Nan Britton, the Ohio woman less than half his age with whom he would father an illegitimate daughter a few years later, he made a slight tweak, calling himself "Jerose."

Tyler's internal divisions dated back to his early childhood. Born in 1790, the first President never to have lived as a British subject was the son of the Revolutionary War hero John Tyler Sr. The elder Tyler roomed at William and Mary with Thomas Jefferson—whose initials, as he liked to point out, were the reverse of his own. An influential state legislator and judge, the father of the future President was elected Governor of Virginia in 1808. The sixth of Judge Tyler's eight children never enjoyed much of a relationship with his mother, who died when he was just seven. Whatever nurturing John Tyler received came from his four elder sisters. As the retired President noted in 1855, when Mary, his last surviving sister, died, "She too who had the charge of my infancy in loco parentis and to whose care and attention I have ever felt myself under the greatest obligations." As a boy, Tyler oscillated between extreme shyness and hyperaggressiveness. His first biographer calls the motherless child "amiable and docile" with a tendency toward "effeminacy." But at the age of ten, he also emerged as the ringleader of a miniature rebellion against a strict Scottish schoolmaster named Mr. McMurdo, whom he and his classmates bound and gagged and left for dead. Temper outbursts would become a fixture of his personality.

This penchant for lawlessness ran in the family. Judge Tyler's first son, Wat Henry Tyler—named after two famous British rebels, Wat Tyler, the leader of a peasant revolt in fourteenth-century England, and Patrick Henry—often mustered even less self-restraint than his politician brother, who was two years his junior. Over the years, these two Tyler boys remained on good terms, and the President entertained Wat at the Executive Mansion on several occasions. Wat Tyler led a conventional life with his first wife, Elizabeth Walker, with whom he fathered six children. After her early death at thirty-two, Tyler's elder brother wed Margaret Govan and became increasingly unpredictable due to his alcoholism. Though this union produced two children and lasted three decades, it was a marriage in name only. As one of Wat

Tyler's former slaves, William N. Taylor, told the Philadelphia-based writer William Still, who conducted thorough interviews with many escaped slaves after the Civil War, "He [Wat] was a doctor, circulated high among southerners, though he never lived agreeably with his wife, would curse her and call her all kinds of names that he should not call a lady."

Not only was Wat Tyler verbally abusive toward his second wife, he was also unfaithful. Judith Ledbetter, a researcher at the Charles City County Center for Local History, told me in a recent interview that Tyler's elder brother "lived apart from his second wife, as he maintained a long-term relationship with a free black woman in New Kent County, which was well known at the time." Calling him a "barbarous man," the former slave Taylor also stated that Wat Tyler had whipped him about a hundred times between the ages of nine and sixteen, adding, "He shot at me once with his double-barreled gun." While there is no evidence that John Tyler ever beat his slaves, he, too, had a reputation for harshness. "Tyler was a very cross man and treated the servants very cruelly," reported one of John Tyler's former slaves to William Still.

Soon after finishing William and Mary at the age of seventeen, the future President, who received his legal training in the Richmond office of former Secretary of State Edmund Randolph, met the black-eyed southern belle Letitia Christian, the daughter of a wealthy landowner. With his "perfectly reserved and modest" fiancée, Tyler was timid and eager to please. More than four years into their courtship, he began a love letter by apologizing for "not entirely obtain[ing] your permission to write to you." Not until year five did he even dare to kiss her hand. While Tyler's first biographer claims that "he seems never to have sown any wild oats" during this extended courtship, such reticence is not likely, given what we know about his various other, less visible selves. In March 1813, two months after his father died, Tyler married Letitia at Cedar Grove, her family's 1,500-acre estate.

From Judge Tyler, Tyler inherited little except thirteen slaves and a small farm, "Mons Sacer," where the couple settled. But when Letitia's parents, Col. Robert Christian and Mary Brown, both died not long after the wedding, he obtained another thirty slaves and about $35,000—enough money to allow him to devote himself to the not-terribly-remunerative career of politics. In 1816, Tyler, who had already served five one-year terms in the Virginia state legislature, was elected to Congress on his first try. Described by one biographer as "a pattern of order, system and neatness, as well as of hospitality, charity, benevolence, and conscientiousness in the discharge of every duty incumbent upon the mistress of a large household," Letitia stayed back in Virginia to manage the farm and raise the children—five of whom were born by 1821. In the spring of that year, figuring that he could make more money if he went back to practicing law, the thirty-year-old Tyler retired from Congress. As he explained to his brother-in-law, Dr. Henry Curtis, "My children will soon be treading on my heels, and it will require no common exertions to enable me to educate them." In that missive, Tyler also noted that his "duty to [his] family" trumped his ambition, which he described as "bounded in a nutshell." But in truth, he would wage an intense internal battle between his political aspirations and his family commitments for the rest of his life.

Tyler would never be free of money troubles. Though he came from a distinguished family, like many Virginia plantation owners in the first half of the nineteenth century—with the notable exception of his father-in-law—Tyler was constantly cash poor. As James Hambleton Christian, one of his slaves, whom he had obtained after the death of Col. Christian, told William Still, "Mr. Tyler was a poor man...I didn't like his marrying into our family, who were considered very far Tyler's superiors." (A light-skinned mulatto, James Christian claimed to be an illegitimate child of Letitia's father.) Northerners also were familiar with the tenuous financial situation of families like Tyler's. This was precisely the reason why the abolitionist editor Joshua Leavitt had little trouble believing the testimony of Tyler's alleged slave son, John Tyler. "From what is known of [Tyler's] pecuniary circumstances," wrote

Leavitt in the 1841 exposé in his paper, "and from the general practice among the slaveholders in lower Virginia, it is altogether probable he has supported the family by selling the increase of his slave stock."

Time and time again, Tyler would sell slaves to plug up his cash-flow deficits. For example, in the fall of 1827, a broke Tyler urgently tried to unload one named Ann Eliza. Having recently returned to Washington as a Virginia Senator, Tyler had many pressing bills. "Do you propose to purchase Ann Eliza or not?" he asked Henry Curtis that September. "If you have concluded not to take her, I should prefer as speedy a sale as can be made." When Curtis declined to buy Ann Eliza, Tyler asked him to bring her to Hubbard's, a public auction house in Richmond, where she was sold. Ann Eliza was not Tyler's daughter, but a favorite house servant; despite this deep tie, Tyler did not hesitate to convert her into cash on the spur of the moment. This was not the first time that Tyler had tried to unload some of his human property onto Curtis. The Tyler papers at the Virginia Historical Society contain a bill of sale, dated January 1, 1816, which documents that Tyler handed off a "mulatto woman named Aggy and her infant child Christiana unto the said Henry Curtis" in exchange for three hundred dollars. While little else is known about either Aggy or Christiana, Tyler, who was then finishing up his last term in the Virginia House of Delegates, may well have been the father of this child. Christiana was also the name of Tyler's youngest sister, whom Curtis had married a few years earlier.

In a recent book based on numerous interviews with contemporary Charles City County residents, the scholar Daryl Dance provides some compelling evidence that Tyler engaged in a string of sexual relationships with black women during his first marriage. One widely suspected concubine is Polly Brown, an unmarried free black woman, who was ten years younger than Tyler and lived nearby. In the 1820s, Polly gave birth to three children—Crawford, Thaddeus, and Joanna. One direct link between Tyler and these children are real estate records showing that in the early 1850s, Tyler sold land next to Sherwood Forest to

Crawford and Thaddeus. Another free black in the Brown line, Martha (Patsy) Brown, born in 1812, worked for Tyler, and her descendants insist that Tyler had two children with her—Sylvanius Tyler Brown and Susan Brown. Likewise, nearly a century ago, Drusilla Dunjee Houston, a prominent early-twentieth-century African-American journalist, reported that Tyler impregnated a Native American slave who worked on his plantation, and that in 1833, the daughter of this union gave birth to her father, John William Dunjee. Tyler may also have been sexually active with black women during his second marriage. According to accounts passed down through the generations in several Charles City County families, Tyler also fathered two of the children born to Sallie Jefferson—Thomas Tyler, born in 1857, and Emma Tyler, born in 1860. "Some of these oral histories—but not necessarily all—must have a basis in fact," Daryl Dance said. "It is very likely that Tyler was a philanderer who had numerous illegitimate children."

However, Harrison Tyler, a son of Lyon Tyler, who was the official family spokesman for many years until developing Alzheimer's disease in 2014, has denied that Tyler fathered any mulatto children. (Lyon Tyler also fathered children with a second wife when he was in his seventies; that's why there is a remarkable age difference of 138 years between the former President and this grandchild.) In an interview two decades ago, using the same argument that Dumas Malone advanced to defend Jefferson, Harrison Tyler said that like other plantation owners of his era, his grandfather adhered to "a strict moral code" against miscegenation. But this Tyler grandson concedes that a member of the family may have been responsible for several mulatto children and has suggested Judge Tyler's tempestuous son Wat Tyler as a probable candidate.

On April 3, 1841, James Lyons, a Richmond lawyer, wrote to Tyler from Washington, "I shall not be surprised to hear by tomorrow that Genl Harrison is no more...It will be particularly unfortunate...thank God that you and not Dick Johnson or any of the other Dicks we might have elected are to take the helm." After his inauguration as Vice President, Tyler had retreated to his home in Williamsburg, and Lyons was eager to let his friend know that he was about to be called to the presidency. Like most Virginians, Lyons could not stand former Vice President Richard M. Johnson, Tyler's immediate predecessor, who had served under President Martin Van Buren. The reason was that the unmarried former Kentucky Senator had lived openly as man and wife with one of his slaves, Julia Chinn, with whom he had fathered two daughters. In the 1836 election, the Democratic presidential candidate, Martin Van Buren, won Virginia's twenty-three electoral votes, but all twenty-three electors refused to vote for his running mate, leaving Johnson one vote shy of a victory. Under the Twelfth Amendment, the race then fell into the hands of the Senate, and Johnson became the first and only Vice President to be elected without receiving a majority of electoral votes. In 1840, due to continued misgivings about Johnson, the Democrats renominated Van Buren but did not endorse any vice presidential candidate. Perhaps what outraged southerners the most about Johnson, as the editor of the *Louisville Journal* suggested, was "the publicity and barefacedness of his conduct, he scorns all secrecy, concealment, disguise." But had Lyons, who upon Tyler's death in 1862 would replace him in the Confederate legislature, known about the secret double life of Johnson's successor, the odds are that he would have been less than thrilled about the upcoming transfer of power.

Lyons's hunch about Harrison's imminent demise was correct, but Tyler was no longer in Williamsburg by the time his missive arrived. At five o'clock on the morning of April 5, the half-asleep Vice President bounded down the stairs from his bedroom to find out who was banging at his front door. The unexpected visitor was Daniel Webster's son, Fletcher, chief clerk of the State Department, who informed him of Harrison's death from pneumonia less than twenty-four hours earlier. Sitting down for a quick breakfast with his family, Tyler made arrangements to travel to Washington with his two eldest sons, Robert and John Jr., and to leave behind his wife, Letitia, who had been partially paralyzed by a stroke. (The delay in bringing her to Washington would lead many journalists to report that month that the new President was a widower.) By four the next morning, the Tylers arrived in the capital. At noon, Tyler took the oath of office, which was administered by a DC Circuit Court judge. Tyler felt that his vice presidential oath would have been sufficient, but he wanted to be sure that no one would doubt his authority.

From the get-go, the headstrong Tyler, who also liked to lord it over his family, took control of the country. When told by Secretary of State Webster at the cabinet meeting that afternoon that Harrison settled policy questions by putting them to a vote, he countered, saying, "I am the President, and I shall be pleased to avail myself of your counsel and advice. But I can never consent to be dictated as to what I shall or shall not do...When you think otherwise, your resignation will be accepted." The Constitution was vague about whether the Vice President inherited the President's office or just his duties, but Tyler would insist on being called the President rather than "the Acting President," as his opponents in Congress such as John Quincy Adams preferred to do. For the rest of his term, Tyler, who, at fifty-one, was the youngest President to date, would refuse to open any mail addressed to the "Vice President" or "Acting President." On April 9, to accentuate his new station, he delivered an inaugural address, in which he promised to turn "to the fathers of the great Republican school for advice and instruction," by which he acknowledged his debt to his Virginian predecessors—Washington, Jefferson, Madison, and Monroe. By what one biographer calls his "master stratagem to win unqualified acceptance as president...from friend and foe alike," Tyler established a template that has guided the eight subsequent Vice Presidents—from Millard Fillmore to Gerald Ford—who have succeeded a President before the expiration of his term. In fact, in 1967, Tyler's view became the law of the land with the passage of the Twenty-Fifth Amendment, which states unequivocally that in the event of the death or resignation of the President, "the Vice President shall become President."

After alienating his fellow Whigs by vetoing the banking bills, Tyler pivoted toward foreign policy—an arena in which he both could flex his power without needing to curry favor with anyone and indulge his penchant for subterfuge to good effect. In the summer of 1842, pushing aside his Secretary of State Daniel Webster, Tyler personally negotiated a treaty with Britain's Foreign Secretary, the first Lord Ashburton, ending a bitter dispute over America's northern boundary, which dated back to the 1780s. For generations, Tyler hagiographers, including his son Lyon, have attributed this towering achievement—the Webster-Ashburton Treaty—to "the President's suavity of manner, conversational ability and familiarity with the amenities employed in diplomacy," as one biographer put it.

But Tyler's charm offensive, of which the moody Webster was incapable, was only the last chapter of the story. As the renowned Harvard historian Frederick Merk reported in his 1971 monograph, *Fruits of Propaganda in the Tyler Administration*, based on the discovery of documents long buried in the National Archives, a year of Tyler's double-dealing also proved critical. In the spring of 1841, Tyler authorized payments from a State Department slush fund to Francis Smith, a veteran Maine journalist, who placed anonymous articles in local newspapers arguing for his plan. Smith's propaganda campaign may well have been unconstitutional, as Tyler had gone around Congress to manipulate domestic public opinion, using federal money that was specifically targeted for the conduct of foreign policy. In early 1846, Congress launched an investigation into these secret payments, which was led by Representative Charles Ingersoll of Pennsylvania, chairman of the House Committee on Foreign Affairs. Though the committee accused the Tyler administration of three counts of official misconduct, it ended up dismissing the charges. The self-righteous Tyler never second-guessed his actions. As he wrote to his son Robert that April, "The late proceedings in Congress relating to the secret service fund need not at all disturb you . . . as to the idea that I had no right to place a fund at the disposal of anybody, it is just absolutely ridiculous." In contrast, Tyler's most recent biographer argues that Congress let him off the hook largely because Ingersoll lacked "curiosity about Tyler's improper use of executive power."

Tyler's most significant foreign policy coup—which, as his proud widow, Julia, later recalled in her memoir, the driven President "consummated" in his last week in office—required even more shiftiness. Ever since Texas had declared its independence from Mexico in 1836, northerners had strongly opposed the annexation of the Lone Star Republic because it would add more slave territory to the nation. After the New Englander Webster resigned as Secretary of State in early 1843, President Tyler made a big push to achieve "the great object of his ambition," as Julia Tyler put it. Once again, he relied heavily on a major propaganda offensive. Tyler tried to frame the issue as a conflict not between abolitionists and slave owners but between America and the still-often-hated mother country, Great Britain. In the summer of 1843, the prominent southern journalist Duff Green, whom Tyler had dispatched to London as his secret executive agent, sent two letters to Tyler and his new Secretary of State, fellow Virginian Abel P. Upshur, which argued that Britain was trying to bribe Texas to abolish slavery. According to Green's dubious thesis, which was supposedly based on authentic information, the Brits were hell-bent on ending slavery everywhere as soon as possible.

Despite this slavery advocate's sloppy intelligence gathering, the Tyler administration's house organ, the *Madisonian*, published editorials promoting Green's view, which Tyler used to open secret negotiations with the foreign minister of Texas. By early 1844, as diplomats were beginning to finalize a treaty, Tyler availed himself of still another disinformation campaign. Eager to convince northern Senators to vote for ratification, the President endorsed the widely circulated pamphlet written by Mississippi Senator Robert J. Walker, which articulated a series of crackpot ideas. Arguing that all blacks—whether free or enslaved—posed a threat to America, Walker insisted that by extending slavery to Texas, America could actually cleanse itself of blacks, who would be inclined to emigrate via the country's newest state. "The outlet for our negro race," maintained the delusional *Letter of Mr. Walker of Mississippi, Relative to the Annexation of Texas*, "through this vast region [Central and South America], can never be opened but by the reannexation of Texas." While most Tyler biographers either ignore Walker's missive or downplay the President's private support of it, the Mississippi Senator was actually leaning on Tyler's own words before Congress two decades earlier. As a young House member, Tyler himself had spoken out on behalf of a similar notion, known as the theory of diffusion, stressing that if America opened up Missouri to slavery, the "peculiar institution" would eventually disappear faster from both the south and the country as a whole. Likewise, as the historian Frederick Merk also discovered a generation ago, in an 1847 letter, the former President praised Walker as a major contributor to the cause of annexation, concluding that his "writings unveiled the true merits of the question."

Insisting that "a love of the Union left the Executive no other alternative than to negotiate the treaty," Tyler submitted it to the Senate for ratification in April 1844. Convinced that such double-talk was just covering up his blatant desire to extend slavery, the Senate voted against annexation by a margin of two to one. Refusing to back down, Tyler then signaled his intention to use any means necessary to gain his objective, declaring, "The great question is not as to the manner in which it shall be done but whether it shall be accomplished or not." The President who had long defined himself as a strict Constitutionalist underwent a sudden ideological conversion and decided to acquire Texas by getting both Houses of Congress to pass a joint resolution. Seeing Tyler's new strategy as an insult both to the Senate and to the Founders, Senator Thomas Hart Benton called it "a base, wicked miserable presidential intrigue." However, the persistent Tyler came out the victor, as in late February 1845, the House passed the Senate's version of the joint resolution.

Many of Tyler's contemporaries regarded the measure as illegal; for example, the venerable Albert Gallatin, the Treasury Secretary under Jefferson, called it an "undisguised usurpation of power." Gallatin considered Tyler a hypocrite, noting that "the provision which requires the consent of two-thirds of the Senate was intended as a guarantee of States' rights." Up until that time, Tyler, along with most fellow southerners, had viewed the willful imposition of federal authority upon states as an evil of nearly unspeakable dimensions. On March 3, two days after signing the joint resolution, Tyler flexed his executive authority one last time by offering Texas immediate annexation, rather than giving incoming President James Polk the option to conduct further negotiations—which is what most Congressmen expected Tyler would do. In an extemporaneous farewell speech in the Blue Room, the President, thinking of his many heirs, sounded a triumphant note. "The acquisition of Texas is a matter of the greatest importance. Our children's children's children will live to realize the vast benefits conferred on our country by the union of Texas with the Republic." Tyler then retreated to Sherwood Forest with his second wife and stayed out of politics altogether—until shortly before the outbreak of the Civil War.

Tyler began wooing Julia Gardiner, then known as the "Belle of Long Island," just five months after the death of his first wife, Letitia. On the evening of February 7, 1843, after a small dinner party, the President teased the twenty-two-year-old Julia in the Red Room, quizzing her about her numerous beaux. "He had quite a flirtation with Julia," reported her sister Margaret, then twenty, "and played several games of *All fours* [a popular card game in the antebellum south] with her." A couple of hours later, once all the other guests had departed, Tyler invited the two Gardiner sisters to relax in front of the fire in his private chambers upstairs. After chatting for a couple of hours, he gave Margaret a good-night kiss. As Margaret recalled, he then began chasing her elder sister around the Executive Mansion. "He was proceeding to treat Julia in the same manner when she snatched away her hand

and flew down the stairs with the President after her around chairs and tables until at last he caught her. It was truly amusing."

Julia's reaction is unknown, but she might well have not been quite as tickled as her sister. Just two weeks later, at a Washington's Birthday Ball at the Presidential Mansion, Tyler moved in on Julia as she was dancing with one of her steady beaux, naval officer Richard Waldron. "I must claim Miss Gardiner's company for a while," the President declared to a dejected Waldron. After dancing with her for just a few minutes, Tyler asked her to marry him. "I had never thought of love," the stunned Julia later wrote, "so I said, 'No, no, no' and shook my head with each word, which flung the tassel of my Greek cap into his face with each word."

Over the next year, Tyler continued to pursue Julia. While she slowly warmed up to him, she was reluctant to get married. But a tragedy on February 25, 1844, suddenly broke down her resistance. That morning, the President, accompanied by a throng of 350 prominent guests, including Senators, diplomats, Cabinet members, and former First Lady Dolley Madison as well as David Gardiner and his two daughters, boarded the new steam frigate, the USS *Princeton*, which featured the world's largest naval gun, "the Peacemaker," for an excursion down the Potomac. Shortly after four that afternoon, as the ship passed Mount Vernon and the champagne flowed, the Captain decided to fire the gun one last time. This time, billows of black smoke shrouded the passengers, including Tyler and Julia, who were celebrating belowdecks. A cannon had exploded, and chunks of red-hot iron were flying around the deck. After the shouting stopped, someone announced that eight people had been killed, including Julia's father and Tyler's Secretary of State, Abel P. Upshur. Picking up Julia, who had fainted, Tyler carried her to a rescue boat. Over the next couple of weeks, Julia was haunted by dreams about her father. By late April, the traumatized daughter finally agreed to set a date for the wedding. "After I lost my father," Julia later wrote, "I felt differently toward the President. He seemed to fill the place and to be more agreeable in every way than any younger man ever was or could be."

This double-dealing dad would also emerge as a surrogate father for his own wife. While Julia was above the age of consent, Tyler's behavior was essentially predatory, as he had seized the opportunity that her temporary helplessness had provided. Thirty years younger than her husband, who was the first sitting President to marry, Julia would never develop her own identity. Her idealization of Tyler would result in a new presidential tradition; at her insistence, "Hail to the Chief" was played every time her husband attended an official event. Like a schoolgirl eager to please her teacher, Julia parroted all her husband's political views, including his avid defense of slavery. Remarkably, just six months after moving to Virginia from Washington, this transplanted Long Islander also could not stop obsessing about the exchange value of the household help. "On returning to Sherwood we found everything pretty much in statu quo," she wrote to one of her brothers in the fall of 1845. "The people had passed about the laziest two months you can well imagine...our absence had been very much taken advantage of. There had been one death on the plantation of a little boy the night before we arrived—who died from the effects of eating <u>dirt</u>. We had heard frequently of his strange taste, and the President before we went away had said all he could to break him of his habit, but to no purpose. It is a loss of several hundred dollars."

The rarely straightforward Tyler hardly told anyone about the wedding; both the press and six of the seven surviving children from his first marriage knew nothing about it until after the fact. On March 24, 1844, in an attempt to put his eldest daughter, Mary, "entirely at ease," he had written that there was "no sufficient foundation" to the rumors that he would marry Julia. And in a missive sent in early June, he added that he had "nothing to write about which would be of any interest to you." Yet on Tuesday, June 25, at 10:30 P.M., Tyler and Julia along with a small wedding party, which included just one of his children—his second son, John Tyler Jr.—slinked into Manhattan unobserved. So determined was Tyler to keep the arrangements secret that he insisted that the proprietor of his hotel, D. D. Howard, lock up his servants for the night lest they divulge a word to anyone. At two o'clock the next afternoon, in front of a dozen guests—the only administration official to witness the nuptials was Postmaster General Charles A. Wickliffe— the Reverend Benjamin Treadwell Onderdonk performed the service at the Church of the Ascension on Fifth Avenue. Once journalists got wind of what had happened, they enjoyed teasing the President, whose official statement explaining his brief trip alluded to his "arduous duties" and need for "repose." "We rather think," opined the *New York Herald* the following day about the only elopement in presidential history, "that the President's 'arduous duties' are only beginning. 'Repose' indeed!" On June 28, Tyler finally wrote Mary to inform her that "what has been talked of for so long a time," was "consummated." But rather than empathizing with her shock, he asked for her approval and encouraged her to "write a suitable letter to Julia...expressive of your pleasure to see her."

Tyler's four daughters were all upset by his sudden remarriage. Mary and Elizabeth slowly began to accept Julia. But Letitia, who was named after his late wife and had served as First Lady until her stepmother replaced her, and Alice, who was still living at home, never did. Devoted only to Julia, Tyler did little to make his children from his first marriage feel cared about. "Whenever Alice has been fractious," Julia reported to her sister Margaret the following year, "her Father has not failed to show severely his displeasure, for he declares I shall find no difficulty in having and doing everything as I wish exactly." His youngest son, Tazwell, fourteen at the time of the wedding, was shipped off to boarding school and, as Julia also informed her sister, "does not interfere with [me] in the least."

Once back in Virginia, Tyler immersed himself in full-time husbandry. Besides superintending his farm, he waited on his new bride hand and foot. As Julia reported to her mother on March 9, 1845, just a few days after the couple had completed the trek from Washington, "The President is puzzling his wits constantly to prevent my feeling lonely and if a long breath happens to escape me, he springs up and says 'What will you have?' and 'What shall I do?'" That year, to please his young wife, who was a superlative dancer, Tyler added a sixty-eight-foot-long ballroom to Sherwood Forest. "The President designed the room himself and he put in a curved ceiling so that the music—the couple liked to dance the Virginia Reel—would sound better," Tyler's grandson Harrison Tyler explained to me when I visited in early 2013.

Romancing Julia became Tyler's constant preoccupation. "The President has just come in," Julia wrote to her mother at the end of 1846—not long after the birth of their first child, David. "He gave me notice of his entrance by suddenly drawing the bow over the strings of a fiddle…He says Time is nothing to him." With his second set of children, rather than being an absentee dad, ensconced in Richmond or Washington in order to attend to politics, Tyler was very much a homebody. But even as his family grew, he continued to reserve almost all his doting for Julia. While he enjoyed taking his sons fishing, he often ignored the new additions, whom he referred to as "Julia's children," as if they were solely members of her family. A decade into the marriage, the first and only former President to become a professional lyricist published the sheet music for his love song to Julia, "I Can Not Live Without Thee." "Thou'rt all the world to me, love," Tyler wrote, "amidst life's troubled sea, love, My heart still turns to thee, love, the star of hope to me." When Tyler turned sixty-five that spring, Julia responded in kind with a poem, which began, "On this natal day, love, I will renew the vow, love, always to keep the lustre on thy brow."

While Tyler would do anything for Julia, he was much less willing to make sacrifices for his children. When Julia suggested that they begin spending the winters at the Villa Margaret, as their summer home in Hampton was called, so that their teenage boys could attend the prestigious Hampton Academy as day students, he immediately vetoed the idea. The "air would be too severe for [my] health," complained Tyler, who insisted that he did not "fancy staying at Sherwood alone."

Though the self-centered Tyler was on the wrong side of history, one cannot help but be moved by the sight of this septuagenarian father as he prepared his family for the horrifying calamity that was to come. In February 1861, Tyler, accompanied by his twelve-year-old daughter Julia, went to Richmond to attend the Secession Convention. The matter at hand was whether Virginia would join the seven other southern states, including his beloved Texas, which had already left the Union. On April 17, the man who never stopped viewing politics through a sexual prism, reported to his wife that "she [his home state] decided on yesterday at three o'clock... to stand before the world clothed in the full vestments of sovereignty" (suggesting that Virginia under the Lincoln administration had resembled a naked woman). Sending "kisses to all," he advised Julia to "live as frugally as possible in the household," adding, "Trying times are before us."

After his death the following January from vascular thrombosis, an aggrieved Julia wrote to her mother that "a truer man, a tenderer husband, a more devoted Father never existed," stressing that "his character was perfect." His wife, as well as the surviving children from each of his marriages, would side with the Confederacy—the middle-aged Robert and John Jr. both served as bureaucrats under President Jefferson Davis, and his two teenage sons from his second marriage, David and John, both fought in the Confederate army. And all these Tylers would also continue to idealize his every thought. As his eldest son, Robert Tyler, noted at the end of the war, "Everything he did or said should be preserved in gold, for a better or purer or a wiser statesman has never lived in these times."

Rebounding quickly from the national tragedy, Robert, who, as a Democratic Party operative, had played a key role in helping James Buchanan win the election of 1856, moved to Alabama, where he became chairman of the state's Democratic Party and the editor of the *Advisor*, Montgomery's main newspaper. In contrast, his younger brother, John Jr., never did overcome his demons. Tyler's fear, which he confided to Robert when his namesake turned forty—"I think his future is a mere blank"—turned out to be well grounded. After the war, an impoverished and lonely John Jr. eked out a living as a clerk in the Treasury Department for a couple of decades before succumbing to paralysis. Like his father, John Jr. also ended up failing to remain true to his party. To keep his string of lowly patronage posts, John Jr. had to support Republican Presidents, even the family's archenemy, the former Union Gen. Ulysses S. Grant, whom he endorsed in the election of 1872. In an editorial entitled "There is a Moral," published upon his death in 1896, the *Omaha Morning Herald* chronicled the precipitous fall of this First Child, who, as the President's private secretary, had once been a mover and shaker in Washington, and concluded: "What a warning to the spirited young men of the United States to shun politics as a pursuit. It were better to be buried alive than to live a life so useless."

———

Was the Democratic nominee vying to become America's second bachelor President actually a responsible father? In the election of 1884, the American voter answered that question in the affirmative, albeit by a narrow margin. And four generations of historians have also been nearly unanimous in their assent. But a close look at all the evidence suggests that Grover Cleveland, who is widely considered a "near-great President," managed to deceive both the public and the academy.

On July 11, 1884, at the Democratic Convention in Chicago, the forty-seven-year-old Cleveland captured the nomination on the second ballot, thereby earning the right to face off against the Republican candidate, former Maine Senator James Blaine, in November. Determined to win back the presidency for the first time since before the Civil War, the Democrats turned to the popular first-term Governor of New York, whose only prior experience in elective office was a brief stint as the Mayor of Buffalo.

Ten days later, Buffalo's *Evening Telegraph* ran an item headlined
A TERRIBLE TALE: A DARK CHAPTER IN A PUBLIC MAN'S HISTORY, alleging that Cleveland—a lifelong bachelor, just like the last Democratic
President, James Buchanan—had fathered an illegitimate son a decade
earlier. According to a "Citizen's Statement" authored by "a leading
minister of the city," which followed a brief editor's note, Cleveland
had a habit of drinking to excess and engaging in "immoralities with
women," and had "seduced...a beautiful, virtuous and intelligent
young lady" named Maria Halpin, the head of the cloak department
at the dry goods store of Flint and Kent. As the minister, later identified as George Ball, who relied on the testimony of several "responsible
and influential citizens" also reported, after Halpin refused to give up
the child, two detectives hired by Cleveland "seized her by force" and
placed her in an insane asylum, where she remained for a few days.
Eventually, Cleveland agreed to pay her $500 in exchange for the boy,
whom he placed in the home of a prominent local family.

"Perhaps personal character," concluded Ball, "originally ought not
to be involved in political discussions, but it would be criminal to allow
the virtuous to vote for so vile a man as this under a false impression
that he is pure and honorable."

Within a week, more than one hundred papers across the country,
mostly those run by Republican partisans, published a version of this
story.

Realizing that his political future was in serious jeopardy, Cleveland
was quick to formulate a response. On July 23, from his Albany office,
the New York Governor fired off a telegram to his lawyer: "Whatever
you do, tell the truth."

Over the next few months, the Governor's campaign would admit
that he had slept with Halpin. But that was not the same thing as telling the unvarnished truth. Cleveland's spinmeisters, who forbade the
candidate to address the matter in his own words, also added several
layers of obfuscation and some outright lies. Their strategy pivoted
around depicting Halpin as both a drunk and a loose woman.

Despite the protestations of a string of hagiographers, Cleveland was certainly not incapable of sliming someone who stood in his way. A decade later, as the journalist Matthew Algeo recently revealed in his engaging book, *The President Is a Sick Man*, Cleveland's team worked closely with the Democratic press to destroy the reputation of the Philadelphia journalist E. J. Edwards, who had exposed the secret operation he underwent for oral cancer in his second term. In a widely circulated interview published in early August 1884, Horatio King, a Cleveland crony whom the Governor had recently appointed to the post of judge advocate of the New York State National Guard, laced into Halpin. King's inflammatory comments originally appeared in the *New York World*, the paper run by Joseph Pulitzer, which was soon to become a synonym for yellow journalism. After admitting that Cleveland had been "sowing his wild oats" at the time of the encounter, King disparaged Halpin as "not a good woman by any means," as she was a "victim of alcoholism" who had been "intimate" with numerous men. According to King, after Cleveland discovered that she had three other lovers, all of whom were married, he decided to assume responsibility for the child. King also asserted that the real father of the child was a close friend of Cleveland's with "an interesting daughter whom he idolized." King was here alluding to Cleveland's former law partner, the late Oscar Folsom, who, as Cleveland himself acknowledged privately, had nothing to do with the child. The candidate was actually upset by this insinuation because he was then courting Folsom's teenage daughter, Frances, who would become his wife two years later.

"Cleveland acted a heroic part," summed up King, "suffering the obloquy [so] that his friends might not bring unpleasantness to their hearthsides."

Remarkably, even though this Cleveland-as-hero narrative was cooked up by his aides to save his presidential campaign, few historians or journalists have ever questioned it. "His friends told the truth," states his authorized biographer in 1923, for whom Halpin remains the woman who shall not be named. In the Pulitzer Prize–winning definitive life published in 1932, Allan Nevins mentions Halpin, but stresses that the affair with her "reveals...a transient weakness on Cleveland's part, but also throws light upon his latent strength." In contrast to King, who portrayed Cleveland as hyperresponsible because he was stepping up to help a child fathered by his law partner, Nevins acknowledges a lapse of some sort. However, he explains away Cleveland's "subsequent indifference to the child"—after the adoptive placement, he would never see the boy again—by alluding to Cleveland's "doubts about his fatherhood." Most contemporary writers continue to recycle one or another of these same myths. In a 2008 op-ed that attempted to provide some historical context on the love child of the onetime presidential hopeful John Edwards, *New York Times* columnist Gail Collins praises the twenty-second President for his honesty, adding that "it probably wasn't Cleveland's child."

Maria Halpin, who was living in New Rochelle, New York, with her uncle when she read the King interview, was disgusted by its contents. To correct the record and to protect her reputation, in late October 1884, she had her attorney release two affidavits, which were reprinted in full in many Republican newspapers. After alluding to "the foul and false statements" by Horatio King, she rebutted the bogus Oscar Folsom innuendo, stating that "there is not and never was a doubt as to the paternity of our child." She also identified the horrifying circumstances of her pregnancy. "While in my rooms," she declared, "he accomplished my ruin by the use of force and violence and without my consent." In her version, Cleveland was not an unmarried gentleman looking for some fun; he was a rapist.

The Democratic newspapers immediately fired back with whatever ammunition they could muster. One line of attack claimed that her own New Rochelle lawyer, Charles Roosevelt, had declared "the alleged scandalous" affidavits to be forgeries, noting that Roosevelt himself would soon sign an affidavit to that effect. No such document was ever produced. (In contrast, the original manuscript pages of Halpin's affidavits have recently been discovered.) On November 2,

just two days before the election, the *New York World*, the same sen-
sationalist paper that ran the King piece, tried another tack, printing
a bogus interview with Halpin. Depicted as a devoted former lover
who supported Cleveland's presidential bid, she is supposed to have
said that she never made any critical statements about Cleveland,
whom she described as "a good, plain, honest-hearted man." Such a
change of heart is highly unlikely, as in an interview with the *Buffalo
Telegraph* that August, Halpin stressed, "Me make a statement exon-
erating Grover Cleveland? Never! I would rather put a bullet through
my heart."

Most Cleveland biographers simply ignore Halpin's affidavits, pre-
tending that they were never published. In *An Honest President* (1996),
H. Paul Jeffers insists that Halpin's whereabouts in 1884 were "untrace-
able," even though numerous newspaper stories that year, such as those
containing her affidavits, describe her as living in New Rochelle, the
city where she would die two decades later. For Jeffers, who dismisses
Halpin as "mentally unbalanced," to arrive at the true story of her pregnancy does not require sifting through a complicated "he-said, she-
said" debate; for him, it's an open-and-shut case involving a paragon
of virtue and a madwoman, which was settled exactly when Cleveland
said it was. "I hope...that the scandal business is about wound up...
I think the matter was handled in the best possible way," declared a
triumphant Cleveland in September 1884. "Matter" and "handled"
are the same words that another double-dealing dad, Warren Harding, would use to talk about his illegitimate child. In the heat of their
respective political battles, both men severed the concept of fatherhood from its relational context.

But Cleveland—or his alter ego, "Big Steve"—might well have suffered from more serious impulse control problems than Halpin. Due
to a penchant for beer and bratwurst, the five-foot-ten Cleveland, who
later admitted that he "had not been a saint" in Buffalo, weighed 250
pounds. On the night in December 1873 that he had sex with Halpin,
Cleveland was no sensation-seeking adolescent, as King suggested, but

an inveterate thirty-six-year-old playboy, who, according to numerous contemporaries besides George Ball, had been frequenting saloons and brothels for decades. As Henry Crabbe, the pastor at Buffalo's United Presbyterian Church, put it in a letter to the *Evening Telegraph* in the fall of 1884, "I am very sorry to say that he is a corrupt, licentious man [who]...is notoriously bad with women...It may be said that these stories are put in circulation for political effect, but it cannot be refuted that they are true." Author Lauren Belcher mined such contemporary accounts in her Buffalo novel *City of Light* (1999), which depicts a lecherous Cleveland. Though "Big Steve" receded as Cleveland aged, he was not entirely dormant during his White House years. During his second term as President, Cleveland cheated on the much younger Frances, with whom he would father five children. As he approached sixty, his sexual yearnings still occasionally trumped other considerations. "I must stop with the assertion," wrote the President to his mistress Kate Nash, a woman about whom little is known, in a Christmas note in 1894, "that I love you dearly and had rather receive the comforts of what you could give rather than any other thing. I am not without hope that I will still see you." More such entreaties followed over the next couple of years and by the middle of 1896, their relationship ended—but only because Kate lost interest. "I do not forget you and never shall," wrote the dejected President in his final billet-doux.

During Cleveland's first campaign in the fall of 1884, Republicans distributed a song, said to be written by composer "H. R. Monroe" (the author's actual name was H. Monroe Rosenfeld) whose chorus began:

Ma! Ma! Where is my Pa?
Up in the White House, darling,
Making the laws, working the cause,
Up in the White House, dear.

After the close contest, which Blaine would not concede until four days after the election, Cleveland supporters came up with a riposte:

Hurrah for Maria
Hurrah for the kid.
We voted for Grover
And we're damn glad we did.

Both Blaine and Cleveland got 48 percent of the popular vote, but Cleveland racked up 219 electoral votes to Blaine's 182. New York State's 36 electoral votes would be decisive, and Cleveland won the Empire State by just 1,000 votes. A key reason why Cleveland prevailed was Blaine's reputation for corruption. Eight years earlier, as he was beginning his career in the Senate, Blaine had accepted a bribe from a railroad company. What was more, as was revealed shortly before the election, Blaine had destroyed letters that implicated him. Noting that Blaine was "delinquent in office, but blameless in private life, while Mr. Cleveland has been a model of official integrity, but culpable in his personal relations," a Cleveland supporter recommended remanding "Mr. Blaine to the private station, which he is admirably fitted to adorn." This argument seemed convincing to many. Even so, the *New York World*'s support, which included that set of sleazy stories about Halpin, was still crucial—a point Cleveland himself acknowledged. Reflecting back on his first presidential run a quarter century later, Cleveland noted, "At any rate, the contest was so close it may be said without reservation that if it had lacked the forceful and potent advocacy of Democratic principles at that time by the *New York World* the result might have been reversed." But in truth, in their efforts to help Democrats like Cleveland, Pulitzer and his crew engaged in lots of unprincipled reporting.

Cleveland's first child, originally named Oscar Folsom Cleveland, grew up in Buffalo, where he was adopted by James E. King, the obstetrician who delivered him, and his wife, Sarah. According to numerous accounts, he died of alcoholism in his late twenties, but this claim has no basis in fact. Renamed James E. King Jr., he finished medical school at what is now SUNY Buffalo in 1896. Following in his stepfather's footsteps, he set up a large medical practice in Buffalo, where he also taught obstetrics and gynecology. Though he was once married for ten years, the intensely private King, who never spoke publicly about the tumultuous first few years of his life or about his famous father, did not leave behind any children of his own.

On June 2, 1886, in a Blue Room ceremony attended by fewer than thirty people, Grover Cleveland became the first—and he remains the only—President to marry in the White House. His wife, Frances Folsom, who had graduated from Wells College the previous spring, was just twenty-one; their twenty-eight-year age gap is the second largest in presidential history, exceeded only by the thirty years separating Tyler from his second wife, Julia. Cleveland had known Frances since her birth; he had bought her first baby carriage. Even his authorized biographer acknowledges that after her father's death, "he had stood almost in *loco parentis*." While he was never her legal guardian, as has often been reported, "Uncle Cleve," as the young Frances referred to him, was both the administrator of her father's estate and an important source of support and guidance. Early in his presidency, most Washington insiders assumed that he would marry another Folsom—Frances's mother, Emma. But the President never had any intention of doing so. "I don't see why the papers," the bachelor with a roving eye told a friend, "keep marrying me to old ladies all the while."

While most late-nineteenth-century Americans looked the other way, today such a presidential union would be bound to elicit considerable discomfort on Main Street in the form of "the yuck factor." After all, by marrying Frances, the President was simultaneously depriving her of a protective father figure—namely, himself. In middle age, most people go through a phase of life—dubbed "generativity" by psychologist Erik Erikson—during which they begin to express love much more readily through nonsexual contacts and to help others make the transition to adulthood. But not Cleveland. Though it's unfair to charge Cleveland with child abuse—his bride, whom he had never officially adopted, was an adult—he had assumed a stepfather-like role in her emotional development. Surprisingly, Cleveland biographers typically transform his questionable behavior into a virtue. For example, Allan Nevins praises the President for "his usual delicacy of feeling" simply because he waited to propose until Frances had finished college.

Cleveland was more of a grandfather than a father to the five children whom he would sire with his young wife—Ruth, Esther, Marion, Richard, and Francis. Sixty-six in 1903, when his last child was born, the cancer survivor battled a slew of health problems during the last decade of his life, including gout, rheumatism, a weak heart, nephritis, and chronic indigestion, which required the use of a stomach pump. He knew full well that he was unlikely to see any of his children reach adulthood. But he felt little guilt, as he was oblivious to their need for a steady, dependable, paternal presence. For Cleveland, who died of heart failure at the age of seventy-one, the very act of fathering constituted a form of neglect. Though he betrayed these children emotionally, he did provide for them financially. Carefully monitoring his investments, he repeatedly expressed an ardent wish to "make everything smug" for his family before his demise.

Unfortunately, money was the only way in which he could express his love, as he lacked an intuitive feel for the inner world of children. He also had no idea how to connect with them. In 1893, when his second child, Esther, was born, he observed that Ruth, who was not yet two, "seems to think the newcomer's advent is a great joke." A decade later, he used similar words to describe his five-year-old son's reaction to the birth of Francis, noting that "Richard was very much tickled as long as he thought it was something in the doll line, and was quite overcome with laughter when he found it was 'a real baby'... He denies with considerable warmth any intention of taking him by the hair and throwing him down." But such thoughts and fantasies appear to reflect Cleveland's own internal musings rather than anyone else's, as he himself had trouble experiencing his children as real; he also was the person addicted to making off-kilter jokes about them. When Francis was just a few days old, he commented to another friend, "In as many languages as are spoken in the wilds of Africa, my youngest son insists that I must promptly convey to you his thanks for the very handsome present you sent to him." For Cleveland, the inarticulate cries of an infant were like some kind of obscure tongue, which he simply could not translate.

Paradoxically, Cleveland's difficulty in forming deep, intimate bonds with others, including his own children, turned out to be a political asset. Freed from feelings of loyalty to his friends and to his party, he could run a much more lean and efficient administration. In contrast to tenderhearted predecessors such as Grant, who got into trouble for appointing incompetent friends, this President repeatedly put principles over people. From the outset of his political career, Cleveland dedicated himself to civil service reform—a passion that emerged as a key element in his campaigns for both Governor and President. In the fall of 1882, the Mayor of Buffalo kicked off his first gubernatorial campaign by vowing to protect New Yorkers from being "defrauded by the displacement of tried and faithful servants…In this way, the interests of the party may be subserved, but the interests of the people are neglected and betrayed." True to his word, during his first legislative session, the Governor worked with the brash young Republican Assemblyman Theodore Roosevelt to enact a comprehensive civil service law. Soon after defeating Blaine, he wrote to reassure the National Civil Service Reform League that "the lessons of the past should be unlearned; and [public] officials…should be taught that efficiency, fitness and devotion to public duty are the conditions of their continuance in public place."

Once he got to Washington, Cleveland stunned both Democratic Party officials and old Buffalo friends by repeatedly insisting on appointing the best man for the job. Like Tyler, this combative President also had no use for party ties. When a prominent Democrat showed up at the Executive Mansion determined to secure a job for a colleague, Cleveland barked, "Well, do you want me to hire another horse thief for you?" He got flak from his former law partner, Wilson Bissel, after he refused to appoint him to the cushy $40,000 post as consul-general in London. But rather than backing down, the President fired back, telling Bissel that "if...I must feel that my friends are calling me selfish and doubting my attachment to them...I shall certainly be very unhappy, but shall nevertheless struggle on...What a nice thing it would be if my close friends could see a compensation in my successful Administration." He set a new standard for presidential conscientiousness by burning the midnight oil to comb through stacks of applications for appointments. He also showed tremendous courage by denying the requests of donors for plum positions. Lauding him for "his freedom from the alliances and obligations to rich men, which have proved the bane of the Republican party," *The Nation* lamented that it was precisely this claim on the public confidence that led to his defeat by Benjamin Harrison in his bid for reelection in 1888.

In the final analysis, the disconnect between the private citizen, who was shallow in his personal relationships, and the public servant, who diligently promoted the national interest, boils down to an intractable case of dual personality. "There were always two Clevelands," concludes Nevins, who despite his attempt to justify all of Cleveland's actions in the Halpin affair, does acknowledge a few of his hero's warts. "To the end of his life, his intimates were struck by the gulf which separated the exuberant, jovial Cleveland of occasional hours of carefree banter, and the stern, unbending Cleveland of work and responsibility, whose life seemed hung round by a pall of duty." As a young man, notes Nevins, Cleveland was often up at 2 A.M. either poring over his law books or carousing in some café while singing his favorite drinking song ("There is a hole in the bottom of the sea"). This was the internal war between "Grover the Good," as his political admirers dubbed him, and "Big Steve."

By and large, the American people got the morally upright "Grover the Good," and the only man to serve two nonconsecutive terms ranks in the top third of most presidential polls. Like Tyler, Cleveland became a fan of the veto, which he repeatedly used to defeat cash grants to voters—such as pensions to specific classes of Civil War veterans. In his first term, Cleveland issued 414 vetoes—more than twice the total exercised by all the previous presidents combined. While Cleveland's second term was marked by a series of disappointments, time and time again, he exerted decisive leadership. When the financial panic of 1893 paralyzed the country, Cleveland immediately called a special session of Congress in order to repeal the Sherman Silver Purchase Act. He was not successful in jump-starting the economy, but he still earned plaudits for his "enlightened conscience and . . . iron firmness," as the *New York Times* put it in an editorial. The following year, Cleveland took a principled stance on tariff legislation. After a few Democratic Senators watered down a comprehensive House bill by putting back protections on products manufactured in their home states, Cleveland tried to fight back against the trusts, which he felt were exerting too much influence. By allowing the bill to pass without his signature, Cleveland managed to get modest rate reductions while still exhorting "the millions of our countrymen who have fought bravely and well for tariff reform . . . to continue the struggle," as he put it in a letter to Congress that summer. When he died in June 1908, his last words to his wife were "I have tried so hard to do right." That sentiment accurately describes what motivated "Grover the Good." But "Big Steve," the alter ego who handled his personal relationships, followed a different script.

———————

In 1917, in the second week of May, as he was mulling over whether to support a bill to send America's young men across the ocean to fight in the Great War, Ohio Senator Warren Harding spotted a letter in his Congressional mailbox.

"I wonder if you will remember me," began Nan Britton, a

twenty-year-old from Marion, Ohio, the quaint Midwestern town where Harding had laid down roots after achieving renown as an editor and a publisher.

Her opening was somewhat disingenuous, as Harding was well acquainted with the entire Britton family. Nan's late father, Samuel, had been a well-respected physician who wrote articles for Harding's newspaper, the *Marion Star*. And after Dr. Britton's death in 1913, Harding had helped her mother land a job as a substitute teacher. The Senator had spoken with the teenage Nan on several occasions. Upon learning during one of her visits to his residence at 380 Mount Vernon Street that Nan had plastered copies of his picture all over her bedroom wall, Harding quipped that he should give her a real picture of himself.

Married to the former Florence Kling for a quarter century, the fifty-one-year-old Senator had been residing in Washington for just two years. As the rising star of the Republican Party, he had nominated William Howard Taft at the 1912 Republican Convention, even though he was then just Ohio's Lieutenant Governor. Harding and his wife had no children of their own, but Florence had had a son, Marshall Eugene DeWolfe, from a previous marriage. Lacking a maternal instinct, his wife passed the boy on to her own parents at the age of four. Harding also experienced some difficulty warming up to Marshall, whom he dismissed as "my good-for-nothing drunken stepson" in 1905—a few years after the young man had dropped out of the University of Michigan. Marshall had recently died from tuberculosis at the age of thirty-four, leaving behind a wife and two children, George Warren and Eugenia. Unlike George Washington, who had helped raise his stepgrandchildren, Harding did not have much to do with his, and they would remain a secret to the national press corps during his presidency. Though Harding often said that he would "rather have kiddies than anything else in the world," like his wife, he never showed much interest in nurturing anyone.

Two years after finishing high school in Marion, the tall, blond Nan was residing in an apartment owned by one of her father's classmates on Manhattan's tony Sutton Place. She was about to graduate from the Ballard Secretarial School located at a nearby YWCA. Having read of "the imperative demand for stenographers and typists throughout the country," she figured Harding might be "in a position to help [her] along this line if there [was] an opening."

Sitting down at his Senate desk, Harding responded right away. "I remember you most agreeably, too," he wrote, adding he expected to be in New York the following week and would be happy to look her up.

They met about ten days later in the lobby of the Manhattan Hotel. After exchanging some reminiscences about Marion on a settee in the lobby, the Senator invited her up to his room.

"We had scarcely closed the door behind us when we shared our first kiss," recalled Britton a decade later in her memoir, *The President's Daughter*.

Published four years after Harding's death, Britton's book chronicles their torrid affair, which produced a child, named Elizabeth Ann Christian, born on October 22, 1919. (Christian was the last name of Harding's private secretary.) As President, Harding did not hesitate to invite his mistress to the White House, where they made love next to the galoshes on the floor of a tiny coat closet near the Oval Office. Though every major commercial house passed on Britton's manuscript, the self-published volume of 439 pages sold one hundred thousand copies. While many readers found her story believable, nearly all cultural arbiters remained skeptical. Except for H. L. Mencken's sympathetic mention in a *Baltimore Sun* piece entitled "Saturnalia," which appeared in July 1927, the mainstream press largely ignored it.

The consensus among both journalists and scholars began to shift in the mid-1960s after a biographer stumbled on a trove of about one hundred love letters that Harding had written to another woman— Carrie Phillips—with whom he had carried on an adulterous liaison from 1905 to 1920. Not long after this discovery, the late *New York Times* reporter R. W. Apple paid a visit to the sixty-seven-year-old

Britton's home in Evanston, Illinois. Though Apple was not granted an interview, he published a sympathetic article about Britton, noting that these "letters tend to give credence to her story of an affair with the President." Sealed for a half century due to a lawsuit filed by Harding's heirs, the letters to Phillips, whose husband had been the owner of Marion's largest dry goods store, were finally released to the public by the Library of Congress in 2014. In adolescent prose that sometimes rambled on for as long as forty pages, Harding wrote frankly of his yearning for the woman he considered the love of his life. "Honestly, I hurt with the insatiate longing," he acknowledged to Phillips on September 15, 1913, "until I feel that there will never be any relief until I take a long, deep, wild draught on your lips and then bury my face on your pillowing breasts. Oh, Carrie! I want the solace you only can give. It is awful to hunger so and be so wholly denied."

As the Great War started, Phillips, who had become a Germanophile after a stay in Berlin in 1911, kept trying to plead the case for her favorite country to the Senator. While Harding listened attentively, unlike Tyler, this double-dealing dad never did side with the enemy. "In spite of your reverence...for Germany (much of which is justified)," he wrote on January 23, 1917, "you are after all an American...there can never be but one answer in the end. 'My country.'" But had the public known that Harding regularly socialized with—much less slept with—this German sympathizer who may well have been a spy for the Central Powers, he never would have had a shot at the presidency.

In the summer of 2015, all doubt about Britton's claim was finally removed when ancestry.com, the genealogical website, performed DNA testing, showing that one of her grandchildren was a second cousin to both a grand-niece and a grand-nephew of Harding. "The technology that we're using is at a level of specificity," Stephen Baloglu, an executive at ancestry.com, told the *New York Times*, "that there's no need to do more DNA testing. This is the definitive answer."

Harding took up with Britton just as his relationship with Phillips was starting to fizzle out. A chief complaint of his longtime mistress was that she could no longer tolerate his flings with countless *other* women. Since late adolescence, this compulsive womanizer, nicknamed the "he-harlot" by his friend, journalist William Allen White, had demonstrated little self-control. As his father had once chided him, "Warren, it's a good thing you weren't born a girl because you'd be in the family way all the time. You can't say *No*." Long after he had sown his wild oats, Harding continued to engage in all kinds of dalliances, including visits to prostitutes and one-night stands with chambermaids and showgirls. As one Senator's wife put it, "He took rash chances with his reputation." In the winter of 1920, as Harding was beginning his presidential run, Phillips offered an ultimatum. If he would not agree to divorce his wife, Phillips threatened to pass on his letters to the press. Giving in to the blackmail, Harding agreed to shell out a lump sum payment of $25,000 plus an additional $5,000 a year.

Britton proved irresistible to this Senator on the rebound, as she had long been infatuated with him. As a high school student, she had proudly broadcast her obsession to her classmates by scribbling "I love Warren Harding" on the blackboard while her teacher was not looking. "She had a case of hero worship, was a little cuckoo for older men," recalled a Marion resident. As soon as Harding sensed the full extent of her ardor, he realized that all he would have to do was to be his usual, accommodating self. Like both Tyler and Cleveland, who would essentially serve as fathers to their own wives, Harding would also emerge as a paternal figure to his much younger lover. "I used to think," noted Britton, "Mr. Harding might have liked to adopt *me*."

Florence Harding may have learned about his affair with Carrie Phillips, who had once been her best friend, as early as 1909. Though initially upset, Harding's wife quickly got over her jealousy by turning to the comfort of homespun nostrums. "Passion is a very transient thing" was one of the many that she jotted down in her calendar book. Harding considered divorce, but he was reluctant to lose his pushy and enterprising wife, whom he nicknamed the Duchess, as she provided invaluable assistance in his various professional endeavors. In her fourteen years as business manager of the *Marion Star*, she turned the paper into a money-making machine. As a Marion neighbor noted, the couple eventually worked out "a perfect understanding," whereby she looked the other way as he carried on with other women and could still continue to watch over his career. Florence never did find out about the relationship with Britton or about his love child. Despite his decades of double-dealing and triple-dipping, Florence could still be easily manipulated by his slick charm. "Had a shampoo yesterday and [put] my hair up again," she wrote to her confidante, the Washington socialite Evalyn McLean, six months before his death. "Mr. Harding says I look twenty years younger. Of course that is not so, but I am glad he thinks so."

Harding's fatherhood can be attributed to the shortsightedness that permeated both his private and public behavior. Lacking guiding principles, this congenial smooth talker tended to think of little but his own momentary desires. Harding was, as historian John Garraty has insisted, "not a bad man, but a weak one." Of the night in January 1919 when his illegitimate daughter was conceived in the Senate office building, Britton observed, "Mr. Harding was more or less careless of consequences, feeling sure he was not now going to become a father." Once he learned of her pregnancy, the emotionally detached Senator immediately waxed practical. "We must go at this thing in a sane way, dearie," he told Britton, "and we must not allow ourselves to be nervous over it." But by the expression on his face, she could tell that he was not fully capable of following his own advice. "It could be handled," he added, attempting to provide reassurance to both his lover and himself.

For this up-and-coming politician with presidential aspirations, despite his frequent protestations to the contrary, fatherhood never would have anything to do with ushering another human being into the world. Instead it was an abstract problem to be solved. Harding proposed "the knife," but Britton balked, saying she could not bring herself "to destroy the precious treasure." Backing down, the eager-to-please Senator then offered generous financial support. Harding gave the pregnant Britton wads of cash at regular intervals, and he set her up in an apartment in Asbury Park, New Jersey. Like his wife, this mistress also lapped up his occasional forays into tenderness. She was moved when he made allusions to a future together by highlighting that Florence, who was five years his senior, might die before him. "I'd take the baby myself and make her a real Harding," he promised the naive youngster.

In late 1919, shortly after the birth of Elizabeth, Britton moved to Chicago, where she placed the baby with a nurse. Six months later, the dark-horse presidential candidate came to town to attend the Republican National Convention. Despite the steep odds against him, the supremely confident Harding was convinced that he would walk away with the nomination, which he won on the tenth ballot. Nearly every day during the proceedings, he managed to sneak in a tryst with Britton, who was staying with her sister and brother-in-law, Elizabeth and Scott Willits. On one occasion, his mistress asked Harding to meet her in the park to see his daughter. He said he was "crazy to do it," but he did not follow through. After his election victory, Harding spoke with Nan's sister, Elizabeth, in Marion and arranged for the Willitses to adopt his daughter. He agreed to fund the child's care, sending the couple $500 a month. During his meeting with Elizabeth Willits, the President-elect could not help revealing that he also found *her* desirable. As Britton reported in her book, he told her sister, "You are looking very stunning, Elizabeth." Like Tyler, this was a man who could not stop sexualizing human connection.

Harding also had trouble separating his paternal affection for his newborn daughter from his longing for the nubile Britton. As he told his mistress, their child must be wonderful "if she's as sweet a baby as her mother's a woman." Unable to stop idealizing her man, Britton never did complain that Harding showed little interest in learning anything about who his daughter really was.

In early January 1923, Britton came to the White House equipped with a new orchid negligee, which she did not get to wear. Worn down by fatigue and high blood pressure, the bloated President, who now weighed 215 pounds, lacked the energy to make love. As they curled up on the couch, she kept asking when Harding would be able to recognize their daughter. He promised little but continued financial support. The man who prided himself on his carefree approach to life was becoming paralyzed by anxiety. "Nan," the President admitted, "our whole matter worries me more than the combined worries of the whole Administration. It is on my mind continually." With the economy beginning a postwar boom, Harding, who had garnered an astounding 60 percent of the popular vote in 1920, was as beloved as ever, but as he also told Britton, he now considered the White House a jail. He spent his days mired in minutiae—doing tasks that could easily have been performed by secretaries. As he confided in his friend, Columbia University President Nicholas Butler, "I am not fit for this office and never should have been here."

This President had no ideas about where he wanted to take the country—much less any sense of how he would go about implementing them. One of the few policy proposals that he floated around was an amendment to the Constitution limiting the President to one six-year term. While he insisted that this measure would enable him to avoid thinking about patronage, he also saw it as his own personal Get Out of Jail Free card. But when his ambitious wife recoiled in horror at this prospect, Harding caved and reluctantly began gearing up for his reelection bid. "My burdens," he told Britton at the end of that January rendezvous, which turned out to be their last, "are more than I can bear." Though Harding was the most powerful man in the world, he was letting others dictate his decisions. Trapped in a life he did not want, he was miserable.

In late June of that year, Britton departed for a tour of France, which included a six-week course in Dijon. Bankrolling the vacation, Harding reassured her, "I wish I might take you, dearie; I wish we might take the trip together." Just as she was sailing across the Atlantic, the President headed west, embarking on what was slated to be a two-month "Voyage of Understanding," which took him to Alaska. On August 2, 1923, as the President was heading back to Washington, he suffered a fatal heart attack in San Francisco. His wife died of kidney failure just a year later. Rushing back from France a couple of weeks after the President's death, Britton was surprised to learn that Harding's will failed to set aside $50,000 for a trust fund for Elizabeth, as he had promised. After the sale of the *Marion Star* in the spring of 1923, Harding possessed assets of $850,000, and he managed to shower each of his four surviving siblings with over $100,000. Two of Harding's sisters were sympathetic to her cause and passed on some support payments. However, his brother George labeled Britton a blackmailer and put an end to the financial assistance—leading her to take pen to paper a few years later.

Even though the former President ended up betraying both her and their daughter, this mistress could find no fault in his behavior. In her memoir, she attributed the death of the man of her dreams to "the burden of fatherhood which he revered but dared not openly confess, combined with the responsibility of the welfare of the United States." In her eighties, Britton, who died in 1991, was still defending Harding, saying, "He never once thought of repudiating his fatherhood." Elizabeth Ann, who married Chicago office worker Henry E. Blaesing in 1938, died in Oregon at eighty-six in 2005, leaving behind three sons.

Harding seduced the entire country with the same charm that he used to captivate Britton. As the *New York Times* noted on the day of his inauguration, the distinguished-looking, silver-haired former Senator, attired in his black overcoat with velvet collar, "looked every inch the President." The veteran newspaperman knew how to talk in sound bites, which could energize his audience. "If I say so myself," he once bragged to a friend, "I do think I turn out a good speech." In his inaugural, he gave voice to a sentiment that, when uttered by another new President exactly four decades later, would inspire an entire generation: "Our most dangerous tendency is to expect too much of government, and at the same time do for it too little." But Harding's mellifluous sentences could also be completely disingenuous, as astute observers picked up right away. Upon reading the speech, the eminent lawyer and Harvard President A. Lawrence Lowell commented, "I can't make out with any precision what his intentions are on any subject; yet I do not believe that that is by any means wholly unintentional on his part. I suspect his ideas are vague."

The new President, who was then paying blackmail to at least two former lovers—without the various cash infusions, Britton, like Phillips, might well have ended his political career—and refused to meet his own daughter, did not shy away from wrapping himself in the banner of domesticity. "We want," he also insisted on that sunny March 4 afternoon, "the cradle of American childhood rocked under conditions so wholesome and so hopeful that no blight may touch it in its development." Harding's frequent mangling of the English language reflected the vast disconnect between his internal experience and his external communications. As many journalists noted, this was a President with a notorious "suffix problem." In Hardingese, *normality* became "normalcy" and *betrothal*, "betrothment"—that this sexually compulsive President stumbled upon the latter concept is not hard to understand. Harding also possessed a penchant for appearing to say something profound while actually saying nothing at all. In his nominating speech for incumbent President William Howard Taft at the 1912 Republican Convention, he had tried to reel Progressives back into the party by stressing that "progression is not proclamation nor palaver. It is not pretense nor play on prejudice. It is not personal pronouns, nor perennial pronouncement. It is not the perturbation of a people passion-wrought, nor a promise proposed." His prose style, noted H. L. Mencken, was "balder and dash." Even though Harding rarely said or did much of substance, during his lifetime, he was widely revered as a heroic leader. In a review of a biography published a year after his death, the *New York Times* alluded to the "stature of his statesmanship," calling Harding "probably our least-hated and best-liked President."

But within a couple of years, countless reports about his duplicitous administration began to spill out, and Harding quickly fell to the bottom of the barrel in the presidential rankings, where he has remained ever since. On January 30, 1925, Charles Forbes, whom Harding had appointed to head the new Veterans' Bureau in August 1921, was found guilty of bribery and conspiracy and sentenced to two years' imprisonment. Harding was not personally responsible for the scandals that happened on his watch, but he could easily have done more to prevent them, or at least to stop them in their tracks. In the case of Forbes, as opposed to his other untrustworthy cronies, the President knew about the graft before he died. However, the emotionally obtuse Harding had been the last person in the administration's inner circle to connect the dots. By early 1923 several staffers, such as White House physicians Charles Sawyer and Joel Boone, had learned that Forbes was collecting kickbacks for both selling off government property at a discount and buying hospital sites at inflated prices. "[Forbes] is and always has been a 'nut' in my estimation," wrote Boone in his diary that January. "Believe his record will reflect adversely on Administration." Forbes's malfeasance did indeed pose a grave threat to the nation, as the Veterans' Bureau with its budget of $500 million—then one-sixth of all federal revenue—constituted the largest federal agency. According to one postmortem analysis, Forbes ended up filching $200 million from the U.S. Treasury. And Harding had long prided himself on the care with which he spent taxpayers' hard-earned dollars. In fact, just before the midterm election of 1922, the President had vetoed a bonus bill for World War I vets, claiming that budget deficits remained the biggest "problem of the world."

In mid-January 1923, Harding's wife, along with both Boone and Sawyer, urged the President to fire Forbes immediately. But Harding dithered because, as Boone noted, he was "loath to believe anything ill." When Attorney General Harry Daugherty tried to fill the President in on all the allegations against Forbes, Harding flew into a rage and refused to speak with his right-hand man for a couple of days.

Finally, Harding came around and apologized to his Attorney General, admitting that the charges against Forbes checked out. "I am heartsick about it," he added. As upset as Harding was—according to one contemporary, the President "never recovered from the shock of Forbes's scoundrelism"—he hardly took any action. In the White House, he put his hands on Forbes's neck and shook him, yelling, "You yellow rat! You double-crossing bastard!" But that was just to blow off steam—to enable him to express his own feelings. Though Harding forced Forbes to resign, he allowed him to do it a few weeks later from Europe, where he was headed on a planned trip.

As with his impending fatherhood, Harding's main concern was the effect of the "matter" on his own career; the consequences for the country never registered. Even Robert K. Murray, author of a sympathetic biography, *The Harding Era* (1969), acknowledges that Harding "did not adopt a wise course…He did not publicly disassociate himself from Forbes or expose his crimes. He did not request immediate Congressional help in a formal investigation or seek court action… Instead…he swept the situation under the rug." The President lost sight of his duty to protect the American people. This carelessness was what Alice Roosevelt Longworth had in mind when she lamented in her 1931 autobiography, "I think everyone must feel that the brevity of his tenure of office was a mercy to him and the country. Harding was not a bad man. He was just a slob."

During Coolidge's second term, other convictions of Harding administration officials followed. In February 1927, Col. Thomas Miller, a former Republican Congressman from Delaware who had served as Alien Property Custodian—the person responsible for handling property acquired during the war—was sentenced to eighteen months in prison for fraud. Indicted along with Miller, Attorney General Daugherty was never found guilty of any crime, but he was widely seen as having been involved in his codefendant's double-dealing. And a few years later, Harding's Secretary of the Interior, Albert Fall, became the first former Cabinet officer to be sent to prison. The key figure in the Teapot Dome scandal, Fall had received kickbacks for leasing federal lands to oil companies at discounted prices.

As with Nixon a half century later, in the wake of the revelations about the spate of scandals, Republican leaders initially dissociated themselves from the former President. In December 1927, the bodies of Harding and his wife were transferred from a temporary resting place in the Marion Cemetery to a newly built marble tomb, which was modeled on the Lincoln Memorial and cost a half million dollars. However, President Coolidge never could find the time for the dedication—a slight that outraged Harding's supporters. Finally, on June 16, 1931, President Hoover tried to rehabilitate Harding by coming to Marion. In his address, delivered before a crowd of twenty thousand, Harding's former Secretary of Commerce, who had accompanied the President on his final trip to Alaska, spoke of his predecessor's "dim realization that he had been betrayed by a few of the men whom he had trusted...It was later proved in the courts of the land that these men had betrayed not only the friendship and trust of their staunch and loyal friend but they had betrayed their country." In contrast to Tyler, Harding was not "a traitor President," but this President, who had betrayed his own child, was all too easily betrayed by others. And the epidemic of double-dealing during his brief stint in the Oval Office would scar America's social fabric for decades.

Franklin Delano Roosevelt with his eldest child, the fourteen-year-old Anna, at a dog show in Washington in May 1920, the year he was nominated for Vice President. Anna enjoyed more time with her pre-polio Pa-pa than her four brothers.

nmy Carter at the Democratic ional Convention in Madison quare Garden in 1976 with his wife, Rosalynn, and mother, Lillian, as well as his daughter, Amy, along with his three sons d their wives. His family's help as critical in propelling him to the presidency.

The former President and his wife along with his four children (from left to right), Amy, Chip, Jack, and Jeff, aboard a cruise during Christmas vacation in 2014.

George H. W. Bush surrounded by his fam[ily] in Kennebunkport, M[aine] on the occasion of Bar[bara] Bush's ninetieth birth[day].

Ulysses Grant, his wife, Julia, and their four children (from left to right), Ulysses Jr. (Buck), Jesse, Ellen (Nellie), and Frederick. In May 1863, the Union General bought "the smallest horse I ever saw," a black Shetland pony, which he named "the little Rebel," so that eight-year-old Nellie and five-year-old Jesse could take turns riding alongside him.

Woodrow Wilson with his first wife, Ellen, and their three daughters (from left to right), Margaret, Eleanor, and Jessie, in Cornish, New Hampshire, where the family often vacationed in the summer.

Not a posterity letter. Sagamore Hill
July 21st, 1905

THE WHITE HOUSE.
WASHINGTON.

The first page of a letter from Theodore Roosevelt to his daughter Alice, written in July 1905 when the President decided to make use of the clever but rebellious child of his first marriage by sending her on a diplomatic mission to Asia.

President Roosevelt with his second wife, Edith, along with their five children in the summer of 1907. Standing behind the president are Kermit (left) and Ted Jr. (right). Seated on his lap is the youngest, Quentin. Holding the dog is Archie. Seated next to Edith is Ethel.

President John Tyler in 1841, the year he became the first Vice President to replace a deceased President. His facial features, particularly his aquiline nose, are similar to those of his alleged black son (below).

Born about 1840, Sylvanius Tyler was, according to his descendants, the son of the union between John Tyler and Patsy Brown, a free black woman who worked at the home of the future President. During the Civil War, Sylvanius tried to help the Union Army, but was arrested and compelled to work as a stable hand for the Confederacy.

Warren Harding's mistress, Nan Britton, with her daughter, Elizabeth Ann. For decades, few Americans believed Britton's claim, made in her 1928 bestseller, *The President's Daughter*, that Harding had fathered an out-of-wedlock child. The tide turned in the mid-1960s when scholars discovered love letters by Harding to another mistress. In 2015, DNA testing proved that Britton was telling the truth.

John Adams in 1797, the year he became President at the age of fifty-one. Adams would age considerably during his four years in office—in part due to the struggles of his children. His youngest son, Charles, died from alcoholism in late 1800. "My children," he wrote his wife, Abigail, in 1798, "give me more pain than all my enemies."

"I am a man of reserved, cold, austere, and forbidding manners," wrote John Quincy Adams in his diary. "My political adversaries say gloomy and unsocial."

The eldest son of John Quincy Adams, George Washington Adams committed suicide in April 1829—a month after his father's term ended.

Jane Pierce with her third child, Benny, who died at eleven in a train crash in January 1853, two months before Franklin Pierce's inauguration. The Pierces had already lost their first two sons, Franklin Jr. and Frank Robert.

Katie McKinley, the first child of William and Ida McKinley, who died in 1875 at the age of three. The couple's other child, Ida, died at six months in 1873. The only surviving picture of either of their children, it hung over the McKinleys' brass bed in the White House.

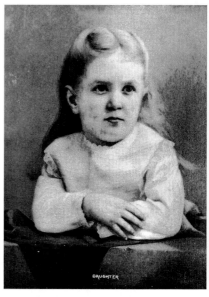

Calvin Coolidge with his wife, Grace, and two sons, Calvin Jr. (left) and John (right) on June 30, 1924. This is the last photo of the whole family. A week later, Calvin Jr. died from a blood wound at the age of sixteen.

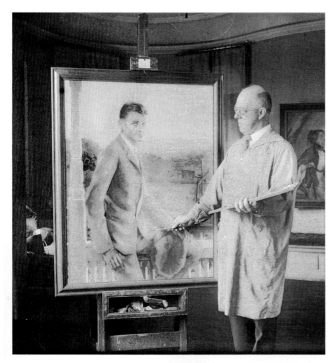

An artist painting a portrait of Calvin Jr. in 1927. In the years following his death, the modest and fun-loving Calvin Jr. was lionized as a national hero.

Rutherford Birchard Hayes with two of his five children who lived to adulthood, Birchard (left) and Rutherford Platt (right) in 1870.

President Harry Truman in 1946 with his wife, Bess, and daughter, Margaret, who considered herself "a total Daddy's girl."

President Obama with his younger daughter, Sasha, on the south lawn of the White House a few days after his forty-ninth birthday.

Tiger Dads

"I Could Feel Nothing but Sorrow and Shame in Your Presence"

You come into life with advantages which will disgrace you if your success is mediocre. And if you do not rise to the head not only of your own profession, but of your country, it will be owing to your own laziness, slovenliness and obstinancy.

John Adams to John Quincy Adams, 1794

At noon on Saturday, August 5, 1809, John Quincy Adams climbed into the hired carriage in front of his house at the corner of Boylston and Nassau Streets in Boston. As the forty-two-year-old statesman, who had recently resigned from the U.S. Senate, noted in his diary, he was embarking on "perhaps the most important of any [enterprise] that I have ever in the course of my life been engaged in." Accompanied by his wife, Louisa Catherine, and his infant son, Charles Francis, President James Madison's new Ambassador to Russia was headed to St. Petersburg.

After crossing the Charles River Bridge, Adams and his family reached Mr. William Gray's wharf in Charlestown, where they boarded the *Horace*. At one o'clock, as both the Boston and Charlestown bells began tolling, the ship commanded by Captain Beckford went out to sea. These three Adamses would not step foot on American soil for another eight years.

The following morning, the temperature remained cool and the southeast wind light, but several passengers, including both Louisa and the baby, got seasick. Not so Adams. "I scarcely perceive," he observed, "that we are at sea." A rarity for an American of his era, he was already a seasoned world traveler who had crossed the Atlantic three times.

On deck, John Quincy Adams thought about his father, the second President, who was living out his retirement in Quincy. In February 1778, when John Adams was himself a forty-two-year-old diplomat, he had taken ten-year-old Johnny, as his firstborn son was then known, to Paris. The elder Adams's mission was to help negotiate America's first set of treaties with France. That midwinter voyage on the *Boston*, John Quincy recalled as the *Horace* lost sight of land, had been fraught with even more danger. A week after leaving Quincy, the *Boston* encountered a hurricane that lasted for three days and nights. To survive this ordeal, John and Johnny Adams spent many hours clasped in each other's arms on the cot that they shared in a lieutenant's cabin belowdecks. Since America was at war in 1778, they also ran the risk of attack. In fact, as they neared the continent, a British cargo ship, the *Martha*, fired several cannonballs toward the *Boston*, a couple of which went whizzing right past their ears. Neither John nor John Quincy Adams could ever bond easily with his fellow man; but in this one instance, they were forced to hold on to one another for dear life.

Like his father, John Quincy Adams would repeatedly put public service over everything else, including his own health and the well-being of his family. In 1778, John Adams sailed to Europe without his wife, Abigail, and Johnny's three siblings—his elder sister, Nabby, 11, and his younger brothers, Charles, 6, and Thomas, 5. Likewise, on his trip to Russia a generation later, John Quincy left behind his two eldest children—George Washington Adams, 8, and John Adams II, 6—with his frail aunt and uncle, Richard and Mary Cranch, in Quincy. In contrast to Abigail Adams—who conceded that her husband had an obligation to "our country... the first and greatest parent [which]...

is to be preferred to parents, wives, children, friends and all things the gods only excepted"—Louisa was "broken-hearted" about John Quincy's decision to separate the family. In her diary, she confided her belief that her husband should have gone on alone. As a mother, her impulse was to "cling to those innocent and helpless creatures whom God himself has given to your charge." She and John Quincy would barely recognize the two boys when they finally joined the rest of the family in Europe in 1815.

The 1778 European sojourn of father and son, which lasted about a year, would launch the careers of two of America's greatest diplomats. While John Adams learned about international affairs from Benjamin Franklin, with whom he shared a house in Passy, Johnny immersed himself in the French language and culture at a nearby boarding school. At the end of 1779, Adams, accompanied by Johnny as well as his second son, Charles, would return to France to assume the position of America's Minister Plenipotentiary. Over the next few years, the elder Adams served as the chief negotiator of the Treaty of Paris, which ended the war with Great Britain. In 1781, he also traveled to Holland, where he secured a valuable loan from Dutch bankers for the fledgling United States. After the revolution, Adams became America's first Ambassador at the Court of St. James's (a post assumed by John Quincy a generation later).

Adams's eldest son ended up spending most of his adolescence in Europe. After studying for a couple of years at the university in Leyden, the precocious fourteen-year-old, whom many Europeans assumed was Adams's younger brother, headed to St. Petersburg, where he served as the secretary to Francis Dana, the U.S. government's representative in Russia. During the Washington administration, John Quincy Adams did stints in the U.S. embassies in both the Netherlands and Prussia. A few years into his second stay in Russia a decade later, President Madison called on this second Adams to end America's second war with Britain—the War of 1812. In Ghent, John Quincy Adams led the

U.S. delegation that settled the various boundary conflicts between the two countries. Perhaps no Secretary of State has ever been more qualified than this scion of John Adams, who formulated the key provisions of the Monroe Doctrine during his distinguished eight-year tenure, which served as his stepping-stone to the presidency.

Though skillful diplomats, America's second and sixth Presidents were both undiplomatic men. Getting along with others was not their strong suit. Feisty and argumentative, both continually preached the wisdom of going it alone. Dubbed by his fellow delegates in Philadelphia as the "atlas of Independence," John Adams emerged as the fiercest advocate for the Declaration on the floor of the Continental Congress. As the physician Elihu Smith observed in 1796, after an extended political discussion with the Vice President, "[Adams] can hardly be called a sociable man." During his presidency, he turned into a party of one, who stressed principle over personal affiliation and ended up abruptly firing two of his five Cabinet officers. The independent-minded John Quincy Adams, who also was limited to a single term in the White House, modeled himself after his father, whom he considered "his oracle." As his younger brother, Thomas, remarked in their childhood, "You seem to differ most always from every one else in company."

But in contrast to his father, this Adams often preferred not to fraternize at all, complaining when he was in Berlin that he was rarely free from "some engagement in company." As a Senator from Federalist Massachusetts, John Quincy Adams tended to side with the opposing party, the Republicans, insisting that "the magistrate is the servant, not...of the people, but of his God." (This credo earned the younger Adams a chapter in Senator John F. Kennedy's Pulitzer Prize–winning collection of essays, *Profiles in Courage*.) At the peace conference in Ghent, the man who acknowledged his "forgetfulness of the courtesies of society" could not even maintain cordial relationships with fellow U.S. delegates such as Henry Clay. Refusing to play party politics,

John Quincy Adams failed to achieve much as President. Adams pere and fils were also two of only four sitting Presidents—the others were Andrew Johnson and Richard Nixon—not to attend the swearing-in of their successors.

The two Adamses ruled over their children in the same way that they governed America. Not all that adept at connecting, they often attempted to control. Though armed with the best of intentions, both John and John Quincy Adams came across as intimidating and unfeeling. These "tiger dads" were obsessed with instilling greatness in their offspring. In the hope of achieving their objectives, they could issue withering criticisms. Rarely was John Adams satisfied with the quality of the young John Quincy's penmanship. "I hope you will take more care to write well. Can't you keep a steadier hand?" demanded the exasperated father in a postscript to a 1780 letter. Upon receiving John Quincy's first missives from St. Petersburg in 1781, John Adams was miffed by the lack of precision. "You have not informed me whether the houses are brick, stone or wood; whether they are seven stories high or only one…You have said nothing about the religion of the country; whether it is Catholic or Protestant."

But by carefully supervising every phase of his eldest son's education—to learn wisdom and virtue, he insisted that the adolescent steep himself in Cicero and Livy—Adams did help him evolve into a brilliant polymath and vibrant writer (whose longhand was very neat). John Quincy Adams would graduate second in his class at Harvard—one spot ahead of his father—and the boy who, at his father's urging, was reading Thucydides in ancient Greek by the age of ten, would eventually master thirteen foreign languages. Unfortunately, with his other children, the strategy seemed to backfire; with Charles and Thomas, John Adams's badgering tended to impede rather than promote success. While his two younger sons, whom he rarely saw until they were adolescents, also graduated from Harvard, both failed miserably as lawyers and became chronic alcoholics. Due to their harrowing struggles for their own sanity, historian Joseph Ellis has described the adult Charles and Thomas as "the kind of human debris subsequently depicted in the plays of Eugene O'Neill."

John Quincy Adams was even more mercurial and exacting than his father. As he once admitted, he was "a man of reserved, cold, austere and forbidding manners." Weighed down by his own insecurities and internal preoccupations, he had difficulty registering the feelings of other adults, much less those of young children. In late August 1809, as the *Horace* made its way across the ocean, his effort to connect with his two boys back in the Bay State took a curious form—a treatise entitled "Letters to My Children." It's hard to imagine that either the eight-year-old George or the six-year-old John could decipher any one of its dense sentences. Beginning with a takedown of Augustus Caesar—who was too much the theatrical performer for his taste—Adams moved on to a discussion of "the obligation of matrimony." In a remarkable under-statement, one biographer describes the epistles as a guide "intended for the father himself perhaps more than for his children." In the five bullet points with which he concluded, Adams alluded to such press-ing concerns for grammar school boys as the need to plan "for an inde-pendent retirement" and to "methodize your studies."

This was not the last time Adams would lecture over the heads of his boys. A couple of years later, he addressed another series of philo-sophical letters to George, which were published a few months after his death in book form as *Letters of John Quincy Adams to His Son, on the Bible and Its Teachings*. These thoughtful missives did merit a close reading by the "young men of America," to whom this 1848 bestseller was dedicated, but not necessarily by the ten-year-old boy to whom they were addressed. (When a brief excerpt was published in newspa-pers during the 1828 presidential campaign, editors were compelled to fib, saying the recipient was a college student.) But Americans perus-ing the volume by this national hero—his post-presidential career as a Congressman who took a strong stand against slavery led to widespread popularity—never learned of this son's name or what had become of him. Tragically, George Washington Adams had committed suicide two decades earlier. George's younger brother, John Adams II, also met an early demise, dying from alcoholism at the age of thirty-one.

Yet John Quincy Adams would also produce one heir who channeled his erudition into an illustrious political career. After arriving in St. Petersburg in October 1809, America's diplomat to Russia began tutoring his youngest son, Charles Francis, several hours a day. To teach the toddler French, he read aloud the fables of La Fontaine from an edition illustrated with woodcuts. Though Charles Francis was gifted, his pedagogue often felt frustrated. "Like my two older boys I find him a child not easy to manage," John Quincy Adams confided in his diary. By the time he started school at the age of six, Charles Francis had also mastered German and Russian. As he withdrew from the daily supervision of his son's studies, John Quincy still made sure that Charles Francis kept an orderly letter book and did not engage in "inordinate" stretches of idleness. In contrast to his older brothers, Charles Francis Adams racked up a series of accomplishments. In 1858, this esteemed editor and historian won a seat in Congress, and three years later, President Lincoln named him Ambassador to Great Britain.

On May 1, 1861, this father of six left for England along with his wife and three youngest children, including the budding journalist, Henry, who would serve as his secretary. As he crossed the Atlantic, Charles Francis Adams, as this son put it decades later in his Pulitzer Prize–winning memoir, *The Education of Henry Adams*, "remembered how John Quincy, in 1809 had sailed for Russia, with himself, a baby of two years old, to cope with Napoleon and Czar Alexander single-handed, almost as much of an adventurer as John Adams [on the little frigate *Boston*] before him. He thought it natural that the government should send him out as an adventurer also, with a twenty-three-year-old son." Remaining in the post held by both his grandfather and father for seven years, Charles Francis Adams would help dissuade Great Britain from forging an alliance with the Confederacy during the Civil War. Yet he served with a certain "uneasiness," as he was eager to be reunited with his six surviving children back in America. The curator of the family's history, who published numerous volumes devoted to his distinguished forebears, Charles Francis Adams was forever haunted by how the "same enemies of separation" conspired to impair the lives of his siblings as well as those of his father, John Quincy Adams.

––––––––––

A few years ago, Yale law professor Amy Chua started a national dialogue about extreme parenting with her bestselling memoir, *The Battle Hymn of the Tiger Mother*, which documents how she raised her two daughters, Sophia and Louisa. Chua chided today's Western parents for not pushing their children hard enough. In contrast, Chinese mothers, she insisted, have long known how to instill success in their offspring. The key is to demand perfection in all endeavors. Chua's house rules included nothing but As; she also expected her daughters to be first in all their classes, except for drama and gym. And backtalk was verboten. "My goal as a parent," Chua often reminded her girls, "is to prepare you for the future—not to make you like me." To ensure compliance with the program, Chua did not hesitate to resort to intimidation; she once called Sophia "garbage" and threatened to burn her stuffed animals.

In a coda to Chua's sometimes tongue-in-cheek manifesto, her elder daughter, Sophia, offered a clever riposte to her mother's offhand remark that her draconian parenting techniques harked back to those of the Founding Fathers, who, so she claimed, possessed "Chinese values." "Mommy, if the Founding Fathers thought that way," responded the youngster, "then it's an American way of thinking."

Authoritarian parenting does have deep roots in America, but its heyday was actually a century before the Founders came on the scene. Chua's assertion that playdates are a waste of time has its analogue in the Puritan idea that most forms of child's play are sinful. Puritan fathers were a lot like Chinese mothers. They, too, worried that "if indolence, selfishness and willfulness were not overcome in childhood, these traits would dominate adulthood," as Steven Mintz noted in his landmark study, *Huck's Raft: A History of American Childhood* (2004). According to Mintz, childhood in America has gone through three phases. During the premodern phase, which lasted until about 1750, patriarchal authority reigned supreme. America's first few generations of fathers considered it their duty to prepare children to enter the working world as early as possible. They were also supposed to choose careers for their sons and spouses for their daughters.

Influenced by the progressive pedagogy of political theorists such as John Locke and Jean-Jacques Rousseau and novelists such as Henry Fielding and Laurence Sterne, Colonists in the second half of the eighteenth century began to develop the modern view, which emphasized love over coercion. Parents were now encouraged to lead by example rather than by rules. The postmodern phase emerged in the 1950s, when mothers gradually started to work outside the home and children started to receive much less adult supervision. Along with these changes came a significant decrease in the acceptability of spanking and other aggressive forms of discipline. By 2000, just twenty-three states allowed corporal punishment in schools, as opposed to all but one sixty years earlier.

Born in 1735, John Adams subscribed to the parenting practices of his Puritan forebears. But while the prickly New Englander expected his own children to heed his every command, this divided man was also well aware that the times were a changin' and that political leaders no longer could expect such blind obedience. "[The people of America]," he reflected in 1818, "thought [England] a kind and tender parent...But when they found her a cruel bedlam, it is no wonder...if their filial affections ceased."

Thomas Jefferson also kept the personal and political in separate compartments. As a father, this diehard revolutionary also placed excessive demands on his two daughters who survived into adulthood— Martha (Patsy) and Mary (Polly). "Nothing is so disgusting to our sex as a want of cleanliness and delicacy in yours," Jefferson reminded the eleven-year-old Martha in 1783, adding that he expected her to dress "in such a stile as that you may be seen by any gentleman without his discovering a pin amiss or any other circumstance of neatness wanting."

Like his father, John Quincy Adams was mired in a Puritan parenting paradigm. But by the early nineteenth century when he was raising his three sons, most fathers relied much more heavily on carrots than on sticks to induce compliance in their children. John Quincy Adams's experience as a father keenly illustrates the perils associated with tiger-dad-dom, which has the potential to either make or break a child. While his actions as a parent cannot be said to have caused the struggles of either George Washington Adams or John Adams II—a genetic susceptibility to depression or alcoholism may also have been at work—his sky-high expectations clearly exacerbated matters. In addition, as John Quincy Adams realized only in retrospect, one factor that put enormous stress on his two elder sons—as well as on his two younger brothers, Charles and Thomas—was that the harsh rebukes were largely unaccompanied by loving affirmations. All four of these Adams boys were forced to endure long separations from their parents, so the constant injunctions to excel, which were issued from afar, no doubt proved particularly unsettling. Fortunately, John Quincy's youngest son, Charles Francis Adams, who benefited from frequent interaction with his father, was careful not to repeat this pattern with his own seven children.

While Puritan parents are no longer to be found, tiger dads have not disappeared. More recent incarnations of these tough taskmasters have tried to apply the lessons learned in their military careers to their offspring. As noted in Chapter One, the former naval officer Jimmy Carter sometimes let his authoritarian streak sneak into his parenting of his three sons. Not surprisingly, Dwight Eisenhower, America's preeminent twentieth-century military commander, had a penchant for issuing orders to his son, John. "I am certain that I was born standing at attention," wrote John in his memoir, *Strictly Personal*, "something like the top sergeant who was not born but issued." John

Eisenhower claims that he felt stuck in that posture until he was about forty. Only when the former President retired to his Pennsylvania farm, and John began helping him write his memoirs, did the son feel that he could really connect with the father. At the same time, John never doubted Ike's love, and he eventually carved out a successful career, in which he both managed to pay tribute to his father and to go his own way. Starting out as a West Point cadet, John served as a staffer in his father's White House before doing a two-year stint as the U.S. Ambassador to Belgium. And over the last forty years of his life, he found his niche as the acclaimed author of a string of bestselling history books, including *The Bitter Woods*, an account of the Battle of the Bulge, and *Yanks: The Epic Story of the American Army in World War I*. "Writing was who he was," his daughter Susan told me, noting proudly that this General's son was finishing up a biography of Stonewall Jackson when he died in 2013 at the age of ninety-one.

———

Looking back over his life at the age of ninety, John Adams observed, "At this time it seems to me to have been wicked to have left such a wife and such a family as I did, but it was done in the service of my country." Clearly, politics did intrude from the moment that Adams became a father. His first child, Abigail (called Nabby), was born on July 14, 1765, at roughly the same time as "the child independence was born," as Adams put it. That was the summer when the Colonists began protesting the Stamp Act. Adams himself marshaled the opposition, publishing an influential critique in the *Boston Gazette* that October just as he was turning thirty. For the first few years of his married life, the requisite appearances in inferior and superior courts all over New England often took the young lawyer away from home. As Adams complained in 1767, "What a desultory life, a rambling roving vagrant, vagabond life, at sessions, then at pleas, now in admiralty, now at superior court." The transition to a full-time political career over the next decade would demand even longer absences from his native Braintree. Immersing himself in the new nation's affairs, he toiled nonstop for about three and a half years at the Continental Congress in Philadelphia where, according to his grandson, Charles Francis Adams, he was "a member of ninety and chairman of twenty-five committees." And then the Atlantic Ocean separated this Odysseus, as Abigail would refer to her husband, from his children during his decade as an Ambassador in Europe.

Upon becoming a revolutionary, Adams would attempt to cope with the guilt for his long separations by considering his new vocation a necessary substitute for flesh-and-blood fathering. "What will come of this labor, time will discover," the exhausted Massachusetts delegate wrote to Abigail from Philadelphia in the spring of 1776. "I am sure the public or posterity ought to get something. I believe my children will think I might as well have thought and labored a little, night and day, for their benefit. But I will not bear the reproaches of my children. I will tell them that I studied and labored to procure a free constitution of government for them to solace themselves under, and if they do not prefer this to ample fortune…they are not my children, and I care not what becomes of them." Though this thin-skinned man was thereby launching a preemptive strike against any future criticism of his career choice by his offspring, he was also articulating his moving vision. As the somewhat less harried diplomat noted without the same animus in 1780, "I must study politics and war so that my sons may have liberty to study mathematics and philosophy." Just as this Founding Father predicted, generations of Americans have benefited precisely because he put the needs of his country over those of his four surviving children—a second daughter, Susanna, born in 1768, lived just a year and a half.

But the call to patriotic duty does not fully explain Adams's emotional unavailability to his kin. As Abigail Adams discovered early in the marriage, her husband was not temperamentally suited to fatherhood. A man who liked his privacy, he could easily feel overwhelmed by the very presence of his "parcel of chattering boys and girls," as he referred to his three sons and the two Abigails, mother and daughter.

Before leaving for Philadelphia to champion America's independence, Adams first fought to achieve independence from his own family. After the birth of Johnny in 1767, he stayed late in Boston almost every day, preferring to chat with friends or colleagues rather than return home to Braintree. By the time the family included Charles and Thomas, Adams established an office in the city where he spent as many as fifteen hours a day. "In the evening," he observed, "I can be alone at my office...I never could in my family." If he had never left New England, Adams might still have preferred delegating nearly all family responsibilities to the capable and resourceful Abigail. For him, the essence of fatherhood was to deliver the proper injunctions. While he never changed his ways, Adams would eventually realize that this definition was too narrow. Decades later, he observed, "Mankind, in general, love their mothers, I believe, rather more tenderly than their fathers, and perhaps have more reason for it." Adams left it up to his wife to figure out how to implement his program, which revolved around instilling a reverence for knowledge, religion, and morality. Abigail often griped about the heavy burden that he placed on her. "The precepts of a mother," she reminded him in May 1776, "would be doubly enforced...with the example of a father alternately before them." But his wife rarely protested for long, as she was forced to concede that Adams was not capable of evolving into a patient, hands-on dad.

A fragmented man with lots of different sides, Adams could wax tender. Writing to Abigail from Philadelphia that same spring, he expressed his longing "to take a walk with you in the garden...I want to take Charles in one hand and Tom in the other, and walk with you, [Nabby] on your right hand and John upon my left, to view the corn fields, the orchards...Alas, poor imagination! how faintly and imperfectly do you supply the want of originality and reality." But such harmony with his children rarely occurred outside the confines of his own fantasy life. In person, he was moody and doled out affection only in brief spurts.

And he had difficulty controlling his emotions. According to most historians, his Federalist Party enemy Alexander Hamilton was not exaggerating all that much when he alluded to Adams's "ungovernable temper" and "gusts of passion" in the pamphlet that he published a few weeks before the 1800 election. "It is a fact," ran the central charge in the widely circulated *Letter from Alexander Hamilton, Concerning the Public Conduct and Character of John Adams, Esq. President of the United States*, "that he is often liable to paroxysms of anger, which deprive him of self command and produce very outrageous behavior to those who approach him." On account of repeated exposure to Adams's wrath, the very thought of displeasing him would make his children squirm. In accordance with the Fifth Commandment, which then held a stranglehold over God-fearing New England, they would forever view blind obedience to their father as a virtue. No matter what this tiger dad said or did, rarely would he face any pushback. But this "filial reverence," which was extreme even by the standards of the day, would exact a toll on all four, and on no one as dramatically as on his firstborn.

If ever there was a dutiful daughter, it was Nabby. As one Adams scholar has put it, "She became a prisoner of the need to please, to obey and to do right." At nine, her father already viewed her as her mother's deputy—as another assistant who could carry out his directives for his sons. "Tell them [your younger brothers] that they must all strive to qualify themselves to be good and useful men," Adams wrote to her from the First Continental Congress, "that they may be blessings to their parents and mankind." Adams rewarded Nabby for passivity, repeatedly praising her "reserve." "[To] be good, and to do good," he stressed, "is all we have to do." While Adams was working day and night in Philadelphia to increase the rights of the Colonists, he tended to oppose expanding his own daughter's intellectual horizons. "By reason of her sex," Adams noted, "[she] requires a different education from [her brothers]." When Nabby, at her mother's direction, began learning Latin grammar from the family tutor, Adams provided little encouragement, noting that this "will do you no hurt, my dear, though you must not tell many people . . . for it is scarcely respectable for young ladies." In the wake of her father's pronouncement, her Latin instruction was soon aborted. To be fair to Adams, his ideas about women's rights were mainstream. In the late eighteenth century, only a select handful of girls such as the daughters of Thomas Jefferson and Aaron Burr would master the classics. With Nabby, as opposed to his sons, Adams did not lay "down any rules for . . . behavior in life," preferring to assign this metatask to Abigail. But he did insist that she, too, learn French and keep a diary in a "handsome hand." Despite her good looks, the blue-eyed, red-haired Nabby grew up to be a painfully shy teenager who lacked even a shred of self-esteem, characterizing herself to John Quincy as "your sister who is so sensible of her own unworthiness." But then something unexpected happened: She fell in love. And though her father was thousands of miles away, his hastily conceived directives would continue to control her daily life.

The suitor was Royall Tyler, a dashing Harvard man with a predilection for ruffled shirts and scarlet cloaks. In the fall of 1782, the twenty-five-year-old lawyer moved to Braintree, where he boarded in the home of Richard and Mary Cranch. That December, as he began courting the seventeen-year-old Nabby, Abigail Adams felt compelled to file a full report with her husband in Paris and to ask for his advice. As she explained, after finishing Harvard, Tyler had frittered away both two years of his life and half of his inheritance. But he had since systematically rededicated himself to his studies and was slowly building a promising practice. "He cannot fail," Abigail concluded, "making a distinguished figure in his profession if he steadily pursues it." The news enraged Adams; everything about Tyler horrified him—and nothing more so than his charm and easy-going manner. "But above all I positively forbid," he fired back, "any connection between my daughter and any youth upon the earth who does not totally eradicate every taste for gaiety and expense." The intensity of Adams's pique had roots in something else besides the facts, and he himself would later acknowledge his own impetuousness. Yet so terrified was Nabby of her father's wrath that she dared not raise any objection. Instead that May, she promised him that she would mend *her* ways:

> I assure you my Dear Sir that I have suffered not a little mortifi-
> cation whenever I reflected that I have requested a favor of you
> that your heart and judgment did not readily assent to grant. 'Twas
> not that your refusal pained me, but the consciousness that there
> was an impropriety in my soliciting whatever you should consider
> incompatible to comply with. It has rendered me so thoroughly
> dissatisfied with my own opinion and judgment that I shall for
> the future take care to avoid the possibility of erring in a similar
> manner.

Despite Nabby's eagerness to please her father, her heart would not budge, and with the support of her mother, she kept seeing her beau. Over the next year, Adams simmered down. The following April, he wrote Tyler that "your connections and education are too respectable for me to entertain any objections to them." But Adams's reversal came too late; by the time Tyler received this missive, the two Abigails were already traveling to Europe to be reunited with him.

During a tearful parting that June, Nabby and Tyler pledged their love to each other in such an open display of affection that it left both her mother and the Cranches feeling rattled. But the romance was doomed. While Nabby wrote to Tyler often from London and Auteuil, where she moved with her parents in the summer of 1784, she received only four letters in return. The following August, an agitated Nabby sent Tyler back his miniature and broke off the engagement. According to Tyler, most of his missives had been lost in transit. Claiming that he was devastated, he soon retreated from Braintree to his mother's home in Jamaica Plain. Embarrassed by the turn of events, the Adamses vowed to speak no more of him—a promise to which the family held true. In fact, when editing his grandparents' correspondence decades later, Charles Francis Adams deleted all references to Tyler.

But Tyler would have the last word, as he would soon immortalize his relationship with Nabby. In early 1787, he dashed off a play, *The Contrast*, which revolves around the doomed courtship by the Anglophile Billy Dimple of the virtuous Maria Van Rough. While this stab at art did not mirror exactly what had just happened, Tyler mined many autobiographical details. Just as Adams and Tyler's late father, a prominent Boston lawyer, were once professional colleagues, so, too, are Dimple's recently deceased father and the elder Van Rough; likewise, while Tyler once squandered half of his inheritance of seventeen thousand dollars, Dimple gambles away some seventeen thousand pounds. The first American comedy to be professionally produced, Tyler's play would be a box-office smash in various cities, including New York, Philadelphia, and Baltimore. This "extraordinary work of genius," as one contemporary commentator put it, turned its author into a celebrity. Central to the plot is the boorishness of Maria's father. Spoofing Adams—who would become America's first Vice President while the play was still being performed—Tyler depicts Van Rough as a money-grubbing control freak who views his daughter as chattel. When she talks of what her heart wants, her calculating father shoots back, "No, no, no! child; it's money makes the mare go; keep your eye on the main chance, Mary!" In the end, Maria Van Rough rejects Dimple in favor of Col. Henry Manly, a Revolutionary War hero modeled on Col. William Stephens Smith, the man Nabby married in London just ten months after she dismissed Tyler. Her jilted suitor would continue to write, publishing a bestselling novel, *The Algerine Captive*, in 1797. Tyler, who settled into a long and happy marriage with the daughter of his Boston landlord, would later achieve success as a lawyer and as the chief justice of the Vermont Supreme Court.

In contrast, William Smith, a graduate of the College of New Jersey (now Princeton University), who hailed from a wealthy New York family, turned out to be the rake that Adams feared Tyler was. An alcoholic who was mentally unstable, he would repeatedly neglect Nabby and their four children over the course of their twenty-seven-year marriage.

General Washington's former aide-de-camp first met Nabby in the
spring of 1785, when he was sent by Congress to serve in the legation to
the Court of Great Britain. Within a few weeks, Ambassador Adams's
thirty-year-old secretary was smitten by his twenty-year-old daughter.
At the time, Nabby was still betrothed to Tyler, so Smith did not press
his case until December, when he returned to London after a four-
month stay in Prussia. Like Tyler, he worked on the shy belle's mother
first, passing on to Abigail a bundle of testimonials from generals in
order to receive permission "to gain the confidence of her daughter
and lay a foundation for a future connection." Both parents immediately approved, with Adams pronouncing Smith a "faithful and agreeable companion" and Abigail describing his character as "fair and
unblemished." Six months later, the couple was married in the Ambassador's residence on Grosvenor Square. A year later, while still in London, Nabby gave birth to a son, William Steuben Smith. At forty-two,
Adams was a grandfather, a role that would suit him much better than
father. Perhaps because this tiger dad would later rue his harshness
with his own children, he would dote on their offspring. Decades later,
Adams would refer to the members of this generation of the family as
"pretty little creatures who, though they disarrange my writing table,
give me much of my enjoyment."

Smith kept his severe character flaws under wraps until the Adamses
all returned to America in 1788. Over the next dozen years, the only
jobs he could land were a couple of federal posts—the U.S. Marshal
for the District of New York and the Surveyor of the Port of New York—
to which he was appointed by his father-in-law during his presidency.
Smith also pursued several get-rich-quick schemes involving speculat-
ing in real estate, all of which went belly-up. He would squander all the
money he borrowed from his new in-laws. Traveling frequently to England and the western United States, Smith also disappeared for long
stretches of time. Isolated with her young children, Nabby was often
miserable and desperate. Yet the girl who never objected to her father's
outbursts evolved into a woman who remained loyal to her abusive

husband. In the mid-1790s, though Smith had not written for nearly two years, Nabby rebuffed her mother's offer to move back home from New York City. Fear of her father continued to paralyze her, as Nabby worried that Adams would be embarrassed if his colleagues noticed that she was living apart from her husband.

She never did learn to say no to Smith. A decade later, when he was incarcerated because of his unpaid debts, she lived with him in a tiny cottage on the prison grounds. Her passivity, however, took its toll. "I only wonder," admitted this stoic woman in a rare moment of candor to her brother John Quincy in 1797, "that I have retained my senses."

During Adams's presidency, Nabby was a source of constant concern. In December 1798, he complained to Abigail that she was likely to "bring down my gray hairs with sorrow to the grave...Unfortunate daughter! Unhappy child!" To protect the President, his wife would often intercept the letters Nabby sent to him from her home in New York. To Smith, toward whom Adams had nothing but contempt, he often let loose. In discussing the possibility of nominating his son-in-law to command a lowly regiment in late 1798, the President decided to be "plain" with him, railing against his "pride and ostentation, which I have seen with inexpressible grief for many years." Warning Smith of a possible rebuff by the Senate, Adams explained that "he whose vanity has been indulged and displayed to the humiliation and mortification of others may depend on meeting their revenge." In this case, Adams's venom was not based on his own dubious assumptions—as in his initial assessment of Tyler—but on years of tangible proof. Nobody liked Smith. As Adams's youngest son, Thomas, put it after a visit the following year, "I never pass a happy hour in Col. Smith's house and never expect to...My dear sister's destiny might have been better."

The lot of the Smith family would scarcely improve, and both husband and wife would meet a tragic end. In the summer of 1813, an emaciated Nabby, ravaged by cancer, made the three-hundred-mile trek from upstate New York to Quincy in order to die "in her father's house." In those final two weeks, in which she was doped up on opium to mitigate the extreme pain, the forty-eight-year-old Nabby may have experienced her most tender moments with Adams. In contrast to her mother, who could not bear to be in the presence of such suffering, he sat calmly by her bedside. Smith, who was then serving an uneventful term in the U.S. Congress, would die destitute some three years later. As the family was horrified to discover, his debts exceeded the staggering sum of $200,000 ($10 million today). An embittered Adams recalled that Smith "undesignedly did more injury to me in my administration than any other man."

If his son-in-law injured Adams the most during his presidency, his middle son, Charles, may have come in a close second. Adams was thinking of both men when he wrote Abigail halfway through his term: "Happy Washington: happy to be childless. My children give me more pain than all my enemies…I have been preserved…I hope for some good, not merely to be punished with the knowledge of the disgrace of my children. My grandchildren I see are to be the poorest objects in the community." Charles, who had married Smith's younger sister, Sally, in 1795, was then a struggling lawyer weighed down by chronic alcoholism.

Born in May 1770—just two months after the Boston Massacre, the event that first put Adams in the spotlight, as he was the lawyer who had defended the accused British soldiers—the handsome Charles possessed attributes rarely found among members of the Adams clan: charm coupled with superior social skills. "Wherever he goes," his father noted shortly before his tenth birthday, "he gets the heart of everybody, especially the ladies." As a boy, Charles received the same directives as his elder siblings, but without as much pressure. From the Continental Congress, Adams, who tended to assume that all his children shared his own pressing anxieties, did not hesitate to ask the six-year-old his thoughts both about the progress of the war and his career goals. "What course of life," the impetuous Adams inquired, "do you intend to steer? Will you be a lawyer, divine, physician or merchant or what?" But he never gave Charles's handwriting the once-over (and, as a result, it did not become ultraneat like his elder brother's).

One reason for the relative restraint is that Adams always placed much higher hopes on "the sublime" John Quincy than on "the beautiful" Charles. Another is that by the time Charles finished Harvard in 1789, Adams hardly knew him, as they had lived under the same roof for a total of just four years.

Adams's second trip to Europe in 1779 had the potential to give father and son a rare opportunity to spend some quality time together. Unfortunately, the experience abroad turned out to be nothing but a series of traumas for Charles. Reluctant to leave home, the nine-year-old was sobbing as he boarded the *Sensible* that November along with John Quincy. Though Charles's tears melted Abigail's heart, she agreed with her husband's plan to take both boys, observing that "they have arrived at an age when a mother's care becomes less necessary and a father's more important." At first, Adams, who shared a tiny cabin with Charles, was able to calm his fears. "Charles," his father reported to Abigail a couple of weeks later, "lies in my bosom at nights."

But Adams himself, like the rest of the passengers, was constantly on edge. This transatlantic crossing, like the one two years earlier, also occurred in the midst of a war; moreover, just a few days out to sea, the ship sprang a leak. After making an emergency landing in northwestern Spain in early December, Adams and his boys traveled the final thousand miles by mule in the dead of winter. Upon arriving in Paris in early February, Adams placed his sons in L'École de Mathématiques, the boarding school in Passy, which John Quincy had previously attended. From then on, Charles's contact with his father was limited to weekends when the Adams trio went sightseeing in Paris. While Charles was a quick learner, the adjustment was much harder for him than for John Quincy, who already spoke French fluently. In his letters home, Adams provided glowing reports, which seem to reveal much more about the father's high expectations than about the son's actual emotional state. "Your delicate Charles," he wrote to Abigail in March, "is as hardy as a flint. He sustains everything better than any of us, even...his brother."

Charles's distress would only intensify once Adams was transferred to Holland that summer. At the Latin School in Amsterdam, where he and John Quincy resumed their education, classes were held in Dutch, a language that neither boy could speak. What was worse, the teachers often relied on thrashings to make their pedagogical points. As soon as Adams discovered what was going on, he fired off an angry letter to the principal and removed both sons, entrusting their instruction to a private tutor instead. The following January, Adams pulled a few strings so that the ten-year-old Charles could matriculate at the University of Leyden along with his elder brother. (Under the rules, the minimum age for attendance was twelve.)

Perhaps because of all the dislocations, by April Charles was felled by a mystery illness, which Adams referred to alternatively as a "fever" and "wound." Just as Charles was recovering, he received another blow when his chief companion, John Quincy, left Holland to begin his diplomatic career in Russia. The dejected eleven-year-old then begged to return to Braintree. Adams consented, explaining to Abigail in July that his sensibility is "too exquisite…for Europe." And the most harrowing part of Charles's European adventure was yet to come. Rather than taking the standard six or seven weeks, his journey home took five months, as he was forced to switch ships in Bilbao, Spain. Little is known about how the youngster fended for himself during this long stopover in a country where he did not speak the language. To his credit, Adams eventually figured out that he had inadvertently over-taxed his son. "I desire I may never have the weakness," he confessed to Abigail in a December letter, in which he alluded to the latest snags delaying Charles's arrival, "to bring a child to Europe. They are infinitely better at home."

Not long after returning to America, Charles was again abandoned, as his mother had to leave for Europe to join her husband. And she was the one person who both could offer sympathetic parental attention and stand between him and his father's hard-charging ways. When Adams recommended placing the preteen at Harvard, she protested.

"You mortify me," she wrote in April 1782, "indeed when you talk of sending Charles to college, who it is not probable will be fit under three or four years." Charles ended up moving to Haverhill along with his brother Thomas to pursue his studies with John Shaw, the husband of Abigail's sister, Elizabeth.

Internalizing the essence of Adams's educational directive, Charles himself was eager to start at Harvard at fifteen—and this feat he accomplished. But in contrast to John Quincy, who was two classes ahead and briefly roomed with him in Hollis Hall, Charles was far from a model student. He drank too much and ran with the fast crowd. From Europe, Adams was unable to keep close tabs on Charles's progress; to his second son, as opposed to his first, this pedagogically obsessed father wrote just an occasional letter and issued only general recommendations such as to "read all the books that are commonly read by the scholars." Fully cognizant of Charles's "sociability," Adams also exhorted him not to "let your companions nor your amusements take up too much of your time." Father and son hardly knew each other when Adams returned to America for good in the spring of 1788. Though Charles kept running afoul of the Harvard administration—in his junior year, he lost his job as a waiter when he refused to testify against fellow students who had smashed windows and chairs in the dining hall—he graduated on schedule the following year. At roughly the same time, his father moved to New York to serve in the administration of the incoming President, George Washington.

Charles's legal career got off to a promising start. Living at the Vice Presidential Mansion at the corner of Varick and Charlton Streets in what is today Greenwich Village, he clerked in the firm run by Alexander Hamilton while he prepared for his examinations. (With formal legal education still in its infancy, college graduates seeking a law license interned with established lawyers.) After Hamilton left private practice to become Secretary of the Treasury, Adams helped Charles land a position with John Lawrence, later a U.S. Senator from New York. Shortly before his 1790 move to Philadelphia along with the rest of the federal government, his difficult-to-please father rendered a surprising verdict to John Quincy: "Charles is uncommonly assiduous in his office and very attentive to his studies."

Charles stayed in New York, where he passed the bar in 1792, the same year he began courting Sally Smith, the younger sister of his brother-in-law, William. Fearing that he lacked the means to support a family, both his father and his mother opposed the union. But Charles was in love, and he could not keep his promise to stop seeing her. In an effort to please both his prospective bride and his parents, he doggedly built up his law practice. By early 1795, Charles had hired two clerks of his own, and Aaron Burr, then a U.S. Senator from New York, was referring to him as "a steady man of business." Though he did not wait to receive his parents' consent before marrying Sally that August, both soon came around. In a visit to New York that December, Adams was delighted to discover that his son's office at 91 Front Street was "large and commodious and well stored with book learning." In a New Year's greeting a few weeks later, Charles's controlling father could find only one thing to quibble about: "I don't approve of your calling her Sally unless to herself... To other people especially in writing, you must call her Mrs. Adams." ("Mrs. Adams" she became in Charles's future correspondence.) And a few weeks before becoming President, Adams wrote his wife, "Charles is doing charmingly. Gets more than he spends without my help."

But sometime over the next year, Charles's life began to disintegrate. What exactly happened is hard to determine, because much of his correspondence has either been lost or destroyed. One cause of his downward spiral was that upon leaving for Europe in 1794, John Quincy had entrusted Charles with his life savings—$4,000—and his younger brother subsequently lost all the money in speculative investments. "I have not enjoyed one moment's comfort for upwards of two years on this account," Charles confided to his mother at the end of 1798, "my sleep has been disturbed and my waking hours embittered." With his once vibrant law practice now foundering, he became nearly destitute. An alcoholic and serial adulterer, he also neglected both his wife and two daughters.

In 1799, Adams encountered Sally and her two children at Nabby's home in Manhattan. After a tearful lament in which Sally filled him in on all the particulars of her husband's behavior, Adams became apoplectic. On October 12, 1799, he wrote to Abigail, "I renounce him…[Charles] is a mere rake, buck, blood and beast." Most biographers assume that Adams was here referring to his disgust with Charles's solicitation of female prostitutes. But it's also possible that he had suddenly learned of his son's penchant for gay sex. (In the late eighteenth century, *beast* carried many of the same connotations as "sodomite," then the operative term for a man who engaged in sex with other men, as *homosexual* had not yet been coined.) To back up this hypothesis, historians point to Charles's close relationship with Baron Friedrich von Steuben, the Continental Army general, whose predilection for gay sex had forced him to flee from his native Germany. Before marrying Sally, Charles had lived in New York with the Baron and his coterie of handsome young male admirers. Charles had repeatedly alluded to his tender feelings for the Baron, noting, for example, in 1794 how his "affection for me calls forth every sentiment of gratitude which can exist in my breast." Whatever the reason for his decision to disown Charles, the stubborn Adams would not budge. He continued to pretend as if Charles no longer existed.

In contrast, Abigail was filled with sadness rather than rage. "When I behold misery and distress," she wrote on October 20, 1799, during her visit to Sally and the two children, "disgrace and poverty, brought upon a family by intemperance, my heart bleeds at every pore." Abigail kept abreast of Charles's worsening condition, and a year later she visited him to say good-bye. "At New York," she wrote to her sister on November 10, 1800, "I found my poor unhappy son, for so I must still call him, laid upon a bed of sickness, destitute of a home. The kindness of a friend afforded him asylum." Saddled with incapacitating depression coupled with cirrhosis of the liver, Charles, who was "at times much deranged," died three weeks later.

Adams learned of this loss on December 3, 1800, just a few weeks before he found out that he had amassed eight fewer electoral votes than both Thomas Jefferson and Aaron Burr, and that his political career was over. The outgoing President immediately tumbled into a deep depression, which would last months. To his youngest child, Thomas, the guilt-ridden father wrote from the Presidential Palace, as the newly built White House was then called, "Oh, that I had died for him [Charles], if that would have relieved him from his faults as well as his disease." Adams rarely spoke of Charles again. Just about the only written remarks the devastated Adams ever made about his intense grief appear in asides in missives to Thomas Jefferson. In March 1801, after thanking the incoming President for forwarding his mail from Washington, he noted that "the papers enclosed...relate wholly to...a son who was once the delight of my eyes...cut off in the flower of his days...by causes which have been...the deepest affliction of my life." Adams would remain tormented by regret over having failed this son. A decade and a half later, in an oblique reference to Charles, Adams lamented to his fellow ex-President that "a man must die before he can learn to bring up his children."

Alcoholism would also destroy Charles's younger brother, Thomas. While most biographers—if they mention him at all—describe Adams's third son as a capable scholar and lawyer who "failed in comparison" to his brother the President, in reality, he too was a constant source of both embarrassment and anxiety to the family.

Born in 1772, the young Thomas Boylston Adams grew up with an even more tenuous connection to his father than Charles. The harried delegate to the Continental Congress often forgot to write to him. "It would have grieved you if you had seen your youngest son," Abigail noted in April 1777, "stand by his mamma and when she delivered out to the others their letters, he inquired for one, but none appearing he stood in silent grief with the tears running down his face." On those few occasions when Adams did think of Tommy while he was in Philadelphia, he could not see him for what he really was—a little boy. "I believe I must make a physician of you," the career-obsessed father wrote to the four-year-old that same year. "It requires the character of rugged and tough, to go through the hardships of riding and walking night and day to visit the sick as well as to take care of an army." In his occasional letters from Europe in the 1780s, Adams would harp on the same theme. "It is generally beneficial," he advised the Harvard freshman in 1787, "to begin early to think of a profession . . . It is never amiss to reflect on the subject." Thomas was essentially a complete stranger until Adams's return to America the following year.

After his graduation in 1790, Thomas briefly lived in New York with his parents before moving with them to Philadelphia. At his father's urging, he studied law. As his mother explained to John Quincy, "I fear it is rather from necessity than inclination and because he finds that his father is fond of having him study it and he does not see any other business." While Thomas passed the bar three years later, his heart was not in defending his indigent clients. In early 1794, as America was briefly considering going to war against England, Thomas acknowledged that he would prefer "the law of arms" to "pursuing my own profession." Later that year, when John Quincy was appointed Minister to Holland and offered Thomas a job as his personal secretary, he jumped at the chance to visit Europe.

In January 1799, Thomas sailed back from Germany on the *Alexander Hamilton*, a schooner named after the Secretary of Treasury turned Major General who was then fighting Adams for the soul of the Federalist Party. The event made the Philadelphia papers because his father still reigned as the most important person in the nation's capital. Before resuming his law practice that summer, the well-connected President's son traveled up and down the country, visiting prominent locals at each stop. On May 24, he talked with George Washington on a variety of subjects for two hours. Impressed by Mount Vernon,

Thomas told him that if the President were to visit, "he would be ashamed of his own place."

But his daily life in Philadelphia turned out to be lonely and frustrating. "Writing all forenoon, destroyed what I had written" ran a typical journal entry. Even with the President's help, Thomas could barely make ends meet. "My ambition does not aspire to anything out of the pale of Bar promotion, but it is by no means an easy task to obtain eminence in this sphere," he confided in a cousin in 1801. "Every opportunity I get, of holding forth at the Bar, invigorates zeal, but I have not yet vanquished the terrors of palpitation incident to inexperienced speakers." With both chronic anxiety and rheumatism weighing him down, he began to turn to alcohol for comfort. At the end of 1803, a dispirited Thomas (who referred to his frequent bouts with melancholia as "the Blue Devils") retreated to his parents' home in Quincy. On May 6, 1805, with the help of his politically prominent father and brother, he was elected as Quincy's representative to the Massachusetts state legislature. With this token achievement in hand, a couple of weeks later, the thirty-three-year-old Thomas finally married his childhood sweetheart, Ann Harrod, and moved with her to Boston. But Thomas was ill-suited to elective office, and in early 1806, he resigned from his new post "owing to some untoward circumstance," as John Quincy put it.

Returning to Quincy, the couple alternated between living at Adams's estate, Peacefield, where Thomas felt like "a pensioner" (which he in effect was, as he depended on his father for financial support), or at the small cottage nearby where Adams had been born. Called "the judge" by the family, Thomas worked part-time as a functionary for an inferior court, which was just about the only steady income he could ever earn on his own. After John Quincy left for Russia, he was paid handsomely to manage the family's investments, a responsibility that he had difficulty carrying out, given his penchant for both binge-drinking and gambling. "There was never any harm in poor Tom," one of John Quincy's grandsons wrote, "except that he would drink.

He nearly drove John Adams and J.Q.A. into insanity with it." John Quincy's wife, Louisa, considered it a "bitter affliction" for the aging patriarch to have to spend his last few years under the same roof as this prodigal son. John Adams himself waxed philosophical. As he told a grandson, the failures of two of his sons were a necessary corrective against too much family pride. "While the world respects us," he remarked stoically, "it at the same [time] pities our misfortune and this pity destroys the envy which would otherwise arise."

Nobody in the family liked Thomas. As the sixteen-year-old Charles Francis Adams described the fifty-two-year-old father of seven in 1824:

> My uncle did not appear until very late at dinner and when he did, in such a humor that he made himself extremely disgusting. He is one of the most unpleasant characters in this world, in his present degradation, being a brute in his manners and a bully in his family. No one addressed a syllable to him and he went off in a rage. The younger part of the family appear considerably affected by it. His wife suffers also.

Thomas's alcoholic binges would cause him to disappear for days at a time, and his terrified children often sought refuge in the home of his brother, John Quincy, in Washington. Late in life, in a drunken rage, Thomas rushed off to Boston, where he rented a chaise that he began driving at breakneck speed. It eventually overturned, leaving him unconscious in the middle of the street. While most bystanders assumed Thomas was dead, some Good Samaritan eventually picked him up and transported him back home.

After his father's death, Thomas's health rapidly declined; he began suffering from severe memory lapses as well as liver disease. He became a pathetic figure—in 1829, one of his daughters could no longer bear to live with him and moved in with John Quincy—and much of the correspondence from his last few years has been destroyed. By 1831, his body twitched every which way, and he was in "an almost constant delirium," as his sister-in-law Louisa put it. Thomas died in 1832 at the age of fifty-nine.

While Charles and Thomas would repeatedly fill Adams with despair, John Quincy would always remain the obedient son, eager to do whatever he could to please his father. After returning from Europe in the fall of 1801, he provided emotional support to the recently retired President. To help his father cope with rejection by the voters, John Quincy supplied him with books and became his muse, inspiring him to write what became his celebrated autobiography. "It is not for the public, but for my children, that I commit these memoirs to writing," noted the elder Adams in October 1802, when he began the book, which was not published in his lifetime. The following year, his eldest son bailed Adams out when he lost his life savings of $13,000 due to the bankruptcy of the London bank of Bird, Savage and Bird. Two decades later, John Quincy gave his father one last gift—when the House of Representatives settled the contested election and elevated him to the highest office in the land. To the eighty-nine-year-old patriarch, the new President-elect wrote, "I can only offer you my congratulations and ask your blessings and prayers." With his own self-esteem tenuous, John Quincy felt as if he were merely the vessel for his father's achievement.

Back in Quincy, the former President was moved to tears at the realization of "his highest wishes," as a friend put it. While Adams shared his joy with numerous family members and friends, he also sounded a cautionary note, telling well-wishers, "No man who ever held the office of President would congratulate a friend on obtaining it."

————————

But John Quincy Adams could never manage to provide the same comfort to his children that he could to his father.

John Quincy had held such high hopes for his first child, a son. By 1801, the former Louisa Catherine Johnson, a British native whom he had married in 1797, had already suffered five miscarriages, so he was greatly relieved by the birth of "the charming and apparently healthy" George Washington Adams in Berlin that April. The name bothered the patriarch, who cursed profusely about it that summer in Quincy; the newly retired Adams did not see the need to commemorate a President who was not a family member. But the boy with the poetic sensibility would become John Adams's favorite grandson, the one who brought the old man "joy and literature." Even after graduating from Harvard in 1821, George would regularly go to Quincy to read to his grandfather. It was George who was seated at Adams's bedside when he died "as calmly as an infant sleeps" at six thirty on the evening of July 4, 1826.

John Quincy Adams spent little time with either George or John, who was born on Independence Day in 1803, during their early years. Like his father, John Quincy was not temperamentally suited to bond with anyone, much less with his two toddlers, whom he found "troublesome." During his Senate term, he arranged for them to stay back in Massachusetts—George with Richard and Mary Cranch, and John with his parents. A disgruntled Louisa complained, but felt she had "no right to refuse what Mr. Adams thought just." John Quincy did also not see either George or John from 1809 until he became Ambassador to the Court of St. James's in 1815. And in his letters, he either lectured—as in those minitreatises on the Bible—or criticized his two eldest boys. Rarely was he satisfied with their handwriting or the speed with which they were learning.

In the spring of 1815, after George and John finally followed John Quincy, Louisa, and Charles to Europe, the Adamses settled on a bucolic estate just outside of London. Over the next two years, this family of five—a daughter, Louisa Catherine, born in Russia in 1811, died at the age of one—enjoyed its happiest times. By day the three boys and their parents would stroll together in the fields, and by night they would study the stars through a telescope. With the "second war of independence" now concluded, John Quincy's diplomatic post turned out to be a sinecure. Lacking many official duties, this erudite poète manqué devoted himself to composing verses, which were, as one biographer has put it, "metrical exercises without warmth or inner feeling"—in other words, just like the man himself.

Though John Quincy's character remained the same, his fathering style seemed to undergo a mild transformation. Realizing that he had failed to "inspire the souls of my three boys with the sublime Platonic ideal of aiming at ideal excellence," the man with the surfeit of leisure time reduced his expectations. He eased up on George, who had been suffering "bilious attacks" in response to the demanding academic program Adams had set up. To prepare George for Harvard, Adams had arranged for tutoring sessions in Latin, Greek, French, and Italian in addition to a full slate of classes at a high-powered local boys' school. Suddenly Adams vowed to let his boys grow up to be just "like other men." "We must be content," John Quincy now asserted, "to take children for children." But this tiger dad's interregnum would not last long.

When Adams returned to Washington in 1817 to become Secretary of State, he was once again separated from his boys, who pursued their education in Massachusetts. While George soon started at Harvard, John and Charles went to Boston Latin High School before crossing the river to attend Harvard themselves. With his new post widely considered a stepping-stone to the presidency—Jefferson, Madison, and Monroe had all made the jump—politics became all-consuming. When John Quincy was not carefully monitoring Spain's attempts to assert itself in the Western Hemisphere—the conduct that led him to pen the Monroe Doctrine—he was busy trying to curry favor with Washington insiders. As Adams was socially maladroit, he relied heavily on the beauty, grace, and charm of his wife, who spent years "Smilin' for the Presidency" and invited as many as a hundred prominent guests to their home every Tuesday evening. Rarely did John Quincy pay much attention to his sons. In the middle of 1818, John Adams, perhaps thinking back on the misfortunes of Charles and Thomas,

wrote to remind his eldest son that "children must not be wholly forgotten in the midst of public duties."

But whenever John Quincy Adams did remember his sons, he
tended to crack the whip. His letters back to New England contained
little but demands and threats. Soon after resettling in Washington,
Adams had second thoughts about lowering his academic standards
and abruptly reversed course. "But this I know," he wrote to John in
November 1817, "the more I indulged you [in England], the more you
encroached upon my indulgence." That fall, George got blasted for
reading the New Testament in Greek. As Adams saw it, since the text
was relatively easy to translate, this decision was a symptom of George's
"propensity to skulk from real study and to idle many hours upon what
was no study at all." John got even more severe tongue-lashings. When
the demanding dad heard about the adolescent's sloppy study habits,
he let it rip: "Are you so much of a baby that you must be taxed to spell
your letters by sugar plums. Or are you such an independent gentleman that you can brook no control and must have everything you ask
for? If so, I desire you not to write for anything to me."

In the fall of 1821, when Adams learned that John ranked forty-fifth
(out of eighty-five) in the junior class at Harvard, he was so horrified
that he denied his son's request to visit the family home in Washington that Christmas. "I could feel nothing but sorrow and shame in
your presence," he insisted. After considerable effort, John rose to sixteenth, but rather than being pleased, Adams made a new demand.
He then announced that he would not attend graduation unless John
made it into the top five. But John never did receive his diploma—at
least not in his lifetime. At the end of his senior year, he was expelled
along with thirty-six other rambunctious classmates for participating in
the campus-wide protest later dubbed the "Great Rebellion" of 1823.
Despite protests from the Secretary of State, Harvard did not back
down—until fifty years later, when the university finally awarded this
scion of the Adams family a belated A.B.

With his first two sons failing to become academic superstars, John Quincy was somewhat more accepting of Charles Francis, who started Harvard two years after John. But even a restrained Adams was not exactly easygoing. As a fourteen-year-old freshman, Charles stood fifty-first (out of fifty-nine) in his class, so he, too, was forced to spend Christmas vacation studying in Cambridge. When Charles announced a few months later that he was thinking of dropping out, John Quincy appeared to be understanding and asked what "alternative course of life" his adolescent son might prefer. But the Secretary of State soon ended these negotiations by threatening eternal damnation. "If I must give up all expectation of success or distinction from you in this life," he requested, "preserve me from the harrowing thought of your perdition in the next." As with his other sons, John Quincy continued to dish out the shame throughout Charles's undergraduate years. In the spring of 1825, noting that his undistinguished academic performance had "destroyed the prospect of his having any part in graduation," President Adams insisted that his son be "as far distant from Cambridge on that day" as possible.

But because of the greater stability in his early life—as a boy, he was rarely separated from either parent—Charles developed much more self-confidence than either George or John. Able to sniff out his father for who he really was, Charles managed to tune him out as needed. In early 1827, after John Quincy upbraided the young lawyer yet again for giving in to "sensual pleasure" by not getting up every morning at five o'clock, Charles wrote in his diary, "I can not but say that his letters are degenerating into sermons and he is as usual missing my character." Unlike his elder brothers, he also was not afraid to talk back. Refusing to alter his schedule, Charles reminded the President of his own tendency to nod off at the dinner table, which he attributed to early risings.

With George, his firstborn, John Quincy, just like his father before him, had initially expected nothing less than the presidency. And this fiercely ambitious tiger dad was not alone in bandying about this notion. Until the mid-nineteenth century, many Americans were still unsure whether Presidents would differ all that much from monarchs, whose male heirs inherited the throne. And of the first five Presidents, John Adams was the only one to have male sons who survived until adulthood. George Washington Adams became aware of his special place in the political firmament as soon as he learned about the former President for whom he was named.

At the age of six, George convinced a playmate on the Boston Common to do him a favor by promising to appoint the boy Secretary of State when he became President. In a brief memoir written in his early twenties, George noted that he "was legally...and absolutely an American citizen"—a necessary qualification for the presidency, according to the Constitution—because the embassy in Prussia where he was born was considered American soil. Intellectually curious, George was the one son who shared his father's literary bent—at Harvard, he won the prestigious Boylston Prize over Ralph Waldo Emerson. However, by late adolescence, his parents already knew that he was not cut out for leadership. Suffering from a nervous disposition—he vomited on the day of his Harvard examinations—he lacked self-esteem; his father's injunctions seemed to haunt him both day and night. The teenager once dumped a girlfriend in the wake of a chilling nightmare; after kissing his beloved, he heard the disapproving John Quincy declare, "Remember, George, who you are and what you are doing." George himself knew that something had gone wrong in his emotional development. "Could my youth have been passed with my parents," he speculated in his memoir, "its present results would probably have been very different." *Eccentric* was the adjective most often used by family members to describe this young man who continually appeared lost in some fantasy world—either that of the novels of Sir Walter Scott or one of his own making.

After Harvard, George worked in Daniel Webster's Boston law office for a few years before setting up his own practice. Still dogged by poetic aspirations, he vowed to devote his mornings to law and his afternoons to literature, but he achieved little at any time of day; to pay his modest expenses, he relied on handouts from his father, who also paid (and criticized) him for managing the family's financial accounts in Quincy.

In the spring of 1826, George was elected to the Massachusetts state legislature; but rather than supporting this fragile son, Adams overwhelmed him with a new set of exacting demands. From Washington, the President tried to control every aspect of George's existence; in a misguided attempt to provide emotional support, Adams sent on list after list, reminding his son which classical authors to read—Plutarch was at the top—and just which Stoic virtues to uphold—prudence, temperance, fortitude, and justice.

That same year, George suffered another disappointment when his engagement to the mercurial Mary Catherine Hellen—"one of the most capricious women ever formed," according to Charles—officially fizzled out. An orphaned niece of his mother, Mary lived with the President and First Lady in Washington, and the couple had been betrothed for three years. The lackadaisical George had miscalculated, assuming that he could keep the flames burning just by dashing off a monthly missive. Even more humiliating was the news that after a brief fling with Charles Francis, Mary had moved on to her housemate, his brother John, whom she was now planning to marry.

George's political career came to an abrupt halt in May 1827 when he lost his bid for reelection to the Massachusetts legislature. The President immediately pounced. "Shall I say," Adams wrote from Washington, "that it [the electoral defeat] gives you time to redeem the arrearages of your promises to me? No—I leave you to say that to yourself." George then retired to his bed, complaining of various physical woes, before tumbling into a deep depression from which he never recovered. By early 1827, he was also carrying on an affair with Eliza Dolph, an Irish chambermaid who was working in the residence of Dr. Thomas Welsh, where he was living. After Eliza had a son that December, George set her up in a rooming house where he continued to visit her. A few months later, he gave up the child for adoption. For George, nothing could have been scarier than the prospect of some extended face time with his often unsympathetic father, to whom he wrote little about his daily struggles.

———————

By the spring of 1829, George could not put off that day of reckoning any longer.

"I wish you to come on immediately upon receiving this letter, to return to us," wrote the sixty-one-year-old former President on Monday, April 20, 1829, to George, then a week past his twenty-eighth birthday. Having left the Executive Mansion a month earlier, John Quincy, who had been trounced by Andrew Jackson in the fall election, was temporarily living at a farm outside of Washington. He was seeking George's help for the move back to Quincy.

But his epistle was also motivated by deep concern. For the past few months, he and his wife, Louisa, had been receiving alarming reports about the health of George from their youngest son, Charles Francis, then twenty-one. While the middle child, John, then twenty-five, also resided in the nation's capital—he had worked in the White House as his father's private secretary—Charles, like George, was beginning his legal career in Boston. From his frequent interactions with George— their Court Street offices were just a few doors apart—Charles knew all too well that his brother was barely getting by. The struggling lawyer who was so deeply in debt that he had trouble paying his rent tended not to come to work until the early afternoon. Sometimes he spent the whole day in his dirty room where, as Charles reported, he "lived like a pig." Charles placed the blame for George's troubles on his "inactivity and indolence, mental and bodily," a view shared by his parents, who figured that they could help George straighten out his life during the trip back home. As Louisa wrote in early April, she and her husband were hoping that George would give up his "expensive and uncomfort-able" residence in Boston and live in Quincy with them.

On the afternoon of Monday, April 27, George announced to Charles that he had just heard from their father and that he intended to start for Washington in a couple of days. "I think this a good plan," wrote Charles in his diary. But Charles remained worried, adding, "He seemed very much disarranged." Their conversation the next day left Charles with the same uneasy feeling. "George . . . [is] quivering," he noted, "under the fear of the merited reproaches which my father can though he will not give them."

On the morning of the twenty-ninth, George took the stage to Providence where he boarded the *Benjamin Franklin,* but he never did make it to Washington. That evening, lost in his own private world of terror, George began hallucinating. He felt as if the ship's engines were speaking to him. "Let it be," he kept hearing them say. "Let it be." He tossed and turned all night. At three in the morning, while the spanking new steamer was whizzing past the Long Island Sound at about sixteen knots an hour, George got out of bed and rushed over to Captain Bunker, asking that he bring the ship ashore. He complained that the other passengers were "laughing at me." Soon after the captain refused his demand, George walked to the upper deck and jumped overboard. His body turned up several weeks later on City Island. George's suicide would devastate his parents. "A more pitiable set I do not think I know," Charles observed that June. And it was only after his death that anyone in the family, including Charles, learned about George's illegitimate daughter.

In the weeks and months that followed, John Quincy repeatedly blamed himself for pushing George "to exertion foreign to his nature." On June 18, 1829, the day he returned to Quincy, Adams made the following prayer to Almighty God, "Grant me health, peace of mind, the will and the power to employ the remaining days which thou hast allotted me on earth to purposes approved by thee and tributary to the well-being of others." Ultimately, this crushing blow would help fuel John Quincy Adams's remarkable political comeback. Just a year and a half later, Adams was elected to a seat in the House of Representatives, where he would serve for nearly two decades. While he accomplished little in his presidency, the principled Congressman racked up a series of legislative victories, including the repeal of the "gag rule," which had prevented House members from discussing the abolition of slavery. Upon his death in 1848, thousands lined the streets to pay tribute as the train bearing his casket made the trek from Washington to Boston. Newspapers throughout the land rhapsodized about this "great man" and his commitment to the national interest, with the *New York Herald* arguing that he "far outstripped" his father in "point of originality and extraordinary talent."

After the death of George, Adams also vowed to be kinder and gentler to his two remaining sons. But for John, this change of heart came too late. In June 1829, Adams gave his second son a loan of $3,000 and installed him as the director of a family-owned mill on Rock Creek in the District of Columbia, as the despairing John wanted nothing more to do with politics. As Charles Francis put it in his diary that summer, "John has decided to desert the state." His final year as his father's secretary had nearly broken him. John's wedding to Mary Hellen on the evening of Monday, February 25, 1828—he remains the first and only presidential son to marry in the White House—was far from a celebratory occasion. Up until the last minute, his disapproving father even failed to acknowledge that it would take place. While the President did appear that evening in the Blue Room, along with some twenty-three guests, neither the spurned George nor Charles could stand to be present. As the conflict-ridden Louisa, who also detested Mary, reported to Charles, "John looks already as if he has all the cares in the world upon his shoulders and my heart tells me there is much to fear."

Two months later, John Adams II faced a major public humiliation. On April 2, 1828, at a soiree in the East Room, the impetuous John referred in a loud voice to journalist Russell Jarvis as "a man, who, if he had any idea of propriety in the conduct of a gentleman, ought not to show his face in this house." This was an election year, and Jarvis, a Jackson partisan, had been sliming the President in recent pieces in the *Daily Telegraph*. John was particularly outraged by the allegation that Adams had pimped the family's nursemaid to Czar Alexander I while serving as the American Ambassador in Russia. Eager to make political hay of the insult, Jarvis rushed up to John, while he was running an errand near the Capitol a couple of weeks later, and pulled his nose. Jarvis was hoping to provoke a duel, but John did not take the bait. At the President's insistence, Congress investigated the journalist's assault on his son by holding hearings, but ultimately failed to issue any reprimand against Jarvis, whose paper repeatedly went after John's manhood, flinging around such disparaging epithets as "the Royal puppy." "The great talk of the day," reported the *Richmond Enquirer* the following month, "still continues to be the distorqueated nose of Prince John." That summer, Charles described John as "looking pale and thin." According to Louisa, this crash course in partisan politics, which also included threats of physical violence, permanently destroyed John's appetite for public service.

At first, the return to private life suited John Adams II well. As his mother informed Charles, he was "steadily industrious and much more cheerful than for years." He and Mary would have two daughters, Mary Louisa and Georgiana Francis—the latter child was named after her father's two brothers (who were also two former beaux of her mother). But the mill business did not turn out to be profitable—John Quincy compared his investment to "gangrene"—and John II was forced to put in long hours. The tentative John also made a series of mistakes, such as selling flour for seventy-five cents a barrel instead of holding out for $2.50 like his competitors.

And having his father breathing down his neck did not help. When John expressed frustration, John Quincy was incapable of providing support. "Your complaints are distressing to me," his father countered, "because they mark an impatience under adversity." By 1832, due to all the stress and to the "dreadfully debilitating climate" at his worksite, John came down with a host of medical ailments, including temporary blindness, fevers, and stiff joints. To make matters worse, John began

drinking heavily. For the next two years, his health steadily deteriorated. By the fall of 1834, though he was only thirty-one, he was terminally ill. On the evening of October 22, John Quincy arrived from
Massachusetts to be by his bedside only to discover that John had lost
consciousness. At four the next morning, as the former President continued to watch for signs of life, John II died. Adams felt an "unutter-
able anguish." "A more honest soul, or more tender heart," he wrote in
his diary, "never breathed on the face of the earth." But as with Nabby,
this dutiful child's unbounded filial affection ended up severely limiting his own personal freedom. Desperate for his father's approval, John
Adams II never became his own man.

Unlike his elder brothers, Charles Francis learned how to cope both
with his overbearing father and with life itself. He took full advantage
of all the privileges that came with being the son of one President and
the grandson of another. After Harvard, he spent two years studying
law with the nation's Chief Executive, which he thoroughly enjoyed.
With his tutor too busy to monitor his reading too closely, Charles
became a regular at Washington parties. He was thrilled to hobnob with
such prominent houseguests as the Revolutionary War hero Marquis
de Lafayette, who stayed in the White House for a few weeks in the
summer of 1825. On February 10, 1827, at a ball given by the French
Ambassador, the nineteen-year-old Charles proposed to the woman of
his dreams, Abigail Brooks, also nineteen, whom he had been eyeing
for about a year. Abby's father was the retired merchant Peter Chardon
Brooks, who happened to be New England's wealthiest man. When
the elder Brooks refused to consent to the union—Charles had yet to
pass the bar—Charles enlisted the help of the President, who wrote a
glowing recommendation, praising his "sedate and considerate character" and "domestic and regular habits." By March, Brooks agreed to a
wedding after Charles turned twenty-one.

Savvy and pragmatic, Charles was careful not to make the same mistakes with his betrothed as his brother George. The following month,
he broke up with his longtime girlfriend, who hailed from a less lofty

social stratum. He also began keeping close tabs on Abigail, writing her at least once a week. After his marriage in 1829, his father-in-law, from whom he would eventually inherit $300,000, began showering him with money. This financial independence would give him the means to curate the family's papers a couple of decades later. And after returning from his diplomatic service in England, Charles would use his wealth to build the nation's first presidential library, the Stone Library in Quincy, which houses his father's fourteen thousand books.

Charles Francis first dipped into politics by serving a few terms in the Massachusetts state legislature in the early 1840s. Soon after his father's death, he jumped onto the national stage. In August 1848, he chaired the first convention of the newly formed Free-Soil Party, which opposed the expansion of slavery into the new western states. The party ended up nominating former President Martin Van Buren for President and Adams himself for Vice President. The ticket earned just 10 percent of the popular vote—and no electoral votes—but this short-lived third party would still exert enormous influence; in 1854, its sizable Congressional delegation was absorbed into the new Republican Party. Though the highest elective office he ever held was Congressman—he served in the House for just two years before becoming the Ambassador to Britain—throughout the 1870s, Charles Francis, who had turned down an offer to become the head of Harvard upon his return to America, was widely considered presidential timber. In the summer of 1872, while serving as President Grant's special envoy to Geneva, where he was skillfully negotiating with the British over Civil War damages, Adams came within forty-nine votes of winning the nomination of the Liberal Republican Party at its Cincinnati convention. Cut from the same cloth as both his father and grandfather, Charles Francis, as the New York Times emphasized in its obituary, possessed a temper that "caused him to couch his opinion in the most offensive terms and to announce it with scornful indifference to the feelings...in others." And just like the second and sixth Presidents, this undiplomatic man who had trouble connecting—in a memoir, Charles Francis Jr., the third of his seven children, lamented that his father was forever an "instructor" rather than a "companion"—managed to carve out an impressive career as both a scholar and a public servant.

On Tuesday, June 6, 1944, John Sheldon Doud Eisenhower, the twenty-one-year-old son of Gen. Dwight David Eisenhower, woke up feeling tired. It was the day of his graduation from West Point, and the only surviving child of the Supreme Allied Commander—an elder brother, Doud Dwight, known as "Icky," had died at three—had hardly slept. Having already returned his mattress, John had spent the night on an iron cot with only blotters as bedding.

As the cadet marched to breakfast, he ran into his battalion commander, who said, "You heard, of course, that the Allies landed in Europe this morning." John was startled. Like most Americans, all he knew was that his father was about to lead a massive Allied invasion of northern France; however, he had no idea exactly when the operation, already referred to as D-Day in the press, would occur. With little time to absorb the news, John continued to prepare for the ceremony in a businesslike manner. In the invocation, the chaplain asked God to bless not only this gathering but also "that other gathering upon the shores of France." The superintendent of the academy, Maj. Gen. Francis Wilby, then read a statement from John's father to the 474 seniors and 8,000 guests, which included his mother, Mamie. "We know," stressed Ike, himself a 1915 graduate, "that in the soldierly qualities of devotion to duty, character and skill you will measure up to the high standards and examples daily being set by your contemporaries from all walks of life, and who are now carrying on the work in which you will soon be engaged." So moved was the audience by the General's inspiring message that when John went to the podium to receive his diploma and the name Eisenhower was uttered, it immediately erupted in a thunderous ovation. Ike's words to the graduates were nearly the same as those he had included in a recent cable addressed to John, which, according to one biographer, "read more like an officer's code of conduct than heartfelt recognition from a father to his son on one of the most important days of his life."

With his sheepskin in hand, 2nd Lt. John Eisenhower was escorted into Major General Wilby's black limousine. He was getting the VIP treatment not because of his academic success—finishing the academy in an accelerated three-year program, he was graduating 138th in his class—but because of orders from the Supreme Allied Commander. As John had learned a couple of weeks earlier, he was to take his leave with his father in Europe. This was top-secret information, which John had kept not only from his classmates but also from his mother, Mamie, who was operating under the assumption that he was to spend his entire four-week vacation with her. A few hours after returning with his mother to her room at the Thayer Hotel, John was picked up by a staff car and taken to the New York Port of Embarkation. There he boarded the HMS *Queen Mary*, which was transporting the U.S. Seventh Armored Division to Scotland.

As he wrote in his 1974 memoir, *Strictly Personal*, John thought that the Army's Chief of Staff, Gen. George C. Marshall, had conceived of the idea of sending him to London, figuring that "during this trying period, it might be beneficial to dad." But Ike had actually been the prime mover. "While it [the visit]," General Eisenhower wrote to Marshall on March 15, "should be a good experience for him as a young officer, my real purpose would be merely an opportunity to become reacquainted with my son. I think I, at times, get a bit homesick." Marshall ended up finalizing all the arrangements, but it was Eisenhower himself who thought through most of the details. Concerned that air travel might prove damaging to his son's health due to a nagging ear infection, he insisted that John go by a fast ship. Eisenhower the dad paralleled Eisenhower the President. As the Princeton political scientist Fred Greenstein has argued in his landmark study, *The Hidden-Hand Presidency: Eisenhower as Leader*, Ike was not the passive bumbler many of his contemporaries assumed him to be. To exert his influence over both the American people and his own son, this demanding perfectionist worked hard behind the scenes.

On Friday, June 9, his first day back in London after returning from Normandy, Ike apologized to his wife for not appearing in person at the graduation. "Due to previous plans it was impossible for me to be with you and John Monday," ran the telegram from the General who, due to the overwhelming stress of the war, often mixed up his days of the week in his correspondence that month. "But I thought of you and hope you and he had a nice time." Later that same Friday, on which a harried Ike also had to address such administrative matters as the appropriate sentence for two GIs convicted of rape, he added in a let-ter, "How I look forward to seeing Johnny. It will be odd to see him as an officer of the Army! I'll burst with pride!" While Ike was full of warm feelings toward his son, he was much more comfortable convey-ing them to Mamie than to John himself.

His son's impending visit was a welcome distraction during this gru-eling week. Ike was forced to remain passive until he could determine how successful the operation would be. According to his chauffeur, Kay Summersby, while waiting for reports from the front, he did little but "smoke and worry."

Not having seen John since he had left Washington in 1942, Ike, who was then stationed at the Supreme Headquarters, Allied Expe-ditionary Force, began counting down the hours and minutes. "John will be in soon—maybe in 1 and ½ hours," he wrote to Mamie, early in the afternoon of D-plus-7 (June 13) from his office at Bushy Park in London. "I'm really as excited as a bride—but luckily I have so much to do I haven't time to get nervous!"

For both father and son, the nearly three weeks that they spent together was a honeymoon of sorts. That first day together, they kept talking "a mile a minute" until one in the morning—the first of many late-night chats. John was thrilled that his father introduced him to the most powerful men in the world, including British Prime Minister

Winston Churchill, whom they visited at Whitehall; Sir Arthur Tedder, Deputy Supreme Commander; Gen. Bernard Law Montgomery, Commander of the Twenty-First Army Group; and Gen. Omar N. Bradley, Commander of the First Army. To John's astonishment, his father now outranked them all—with the exception of Churchill. As Ike confided to his aide, Harry Butcher, he was convinced that his son "would profit greatly if he could...see and sense how the high command is run before...his regular tour of duty on the lower rung of the ladder." And besides the visits to the front, John and his father made the rounds to such sites as Hyde Park and the Tower of London. In northern France, they also took time off to visit Bayeux, the French village where nearly a thousand years earlier, the Norman king, William the Conqueror, had lived. Summing up his visit decades later, John wrote, "London at this time was to me a romantic and heroic place."

John was so excited to be with his adored father that he was one of the few people in London, besides the Supreme Allied Commander himself, who was hardly rattled by the "baby blitz." The day of John's arrival was the same day that the Nazis unleashed their latest weapon, the V-1, which was fired from a pilotless airplane. Over the next eighty days, the Germans would launch some 8,000 "buzz bombs," of which 2,300 would hit London. On Saturday night, June 17, alerts went off repeatedly while the General and John were watching a movie of the D-Day landing at Telegraph Cottage, the small house in the suburb of Kingston where Ike had been living for the past few months. At 1 A.M. on Sunday morning, Harry Butcher was awakened by still another siren and raced into Ike's room. Immersed in a novel—a Western—the General suggested that they all stay in the cottage rather than move to the nearby bomb shelter. But after a couple of additional "pilotless demons came too close for comfort," as Butcher put it, the General and John as well as the entire staff retreated underground. As British antiaircraft fire mounted a response, the fearless Ike could lie down on his cot and begin snoring, but John spent most of the night sitting on a bench. The following day, Ike himself assumed the task of trying to neutralize this new threat, which would continue to pester the Brits until the end of the war.

John also had to cope with the frequent eruptions from Ike himself. While the Supreme Allied Commander had the best of intentions, like both John and John Quincy Adams, he was also "supercritical" of his son, as Summersby later recalled. From Ike's perspective, he needed to be vigilant in order to mold John into a success. But in truth, the high-strung Eisenhower, like most tiger dads, often had difficulty controlling his anger. During the war, one journalist dubbed him "the terrible-tempered Mr. Bang." His short fuse was no secret to his subordinates in the European theater (or to his aides in the White House a decade later). Over the years, perhaps no one would be subjected to more of his legendary rages than John, who would serve on his staff during his second term.

Though Ike did his best to be welcoming during this visit, he slipped on numerous occasions. That first day, after John mentioned that he had hardly slept before his graduation, his father suddenly started glaring at him. When asked to explain this stern reaction by an incredulous Summersby, who reminded her boss that "John was just telling a story," Ike insisted that his son needed to learn to "toughen up." Later that night, in response to John's innocent question about the saluting protocol for officers whose rank was between them, Ike fired back, "John, there isn't an officer in this theater who doesn't rank above you and below me." And whenever John expressed a military opinion, his father would sneer, "Oh, for God's sake."

The criticisms were not limited just to army matters. After the daily bridge games, which were played with a makeshift deck—a joker substituted for the six of clubs—the General analyzed everything his son was doing wrong. His verdict was that John's game needed "sharpening." This browbeating startled everyone at the table, because father and son were on opposing sides—Ike and Summersby teamed up against the young Eisenhower and Butcher—and because this was the only time anyone ever broke the house rule of no postmortems. A decade later, while serving in Washington, John would refuse to play cards with his father. For the ultracompetitive Ike, games were always serious business. In tennis, he would storm off the court after making a poor shot, and Mamie stopped playing with him soon after their wedding in order to preserve the marriage. And as much as he loved golf, Ike exploded with "certain expletives," as John later recalled, whenever his ball ended up in the alfalfa.

This perfectionist often let his frustration spill out onto his son. That June, the General chastised John for allowing his uniform to get dirty during a jeep ride to the front in Normandy. Ike was irate because he considered neatness in dress a sine qua non; the extenuating circumstances for the slipup did not matter. Reflecting on their relationship shortly after his father's death in 1969, John described the incident with his dusty coat as illustrative. "We had," concluded the easygoing and affable John, "a deep mutual affection, but there existed a certain military wall between us." In his later years, John was more direct about this persistent tension. "In intimate relationships, Eisenhower was a very tough character, and he blew up a lot at his son," stated Evan Thomas, who interviewed the octogenarian John for his 2012 Ike biography. While Ike would rarely stay angry for long, the cumulative effect of his outbursts had a significant impact on John—one that the father never fully understood. Fortunately for this presidential scion, as for John Quincy Adams, this constant paternal prodding did not debilitate him so much as spur him on to achievement. "My father did not take granddad's harsh words personally," observed Susan Eisenhower, the second of John's three daughters. "He understood that really powerful people are used to having things made easier for them. He accepted that."

On July 1, 1944, John was "feeling a little choked up" when he said good-bye to his father and headed back to America. His father was sad as well. A week later, Ike wrote to Mamie, "How I miss Johnny. While I was keen to see him, I didn't know how much I appreciated having him by my side until he was gone." Both father and son wished that the visit could have lasted longer, but both believed strongly that duty always came before personal or family concerns. And John was a career officer who needed to attend Infantry Training School at Fort Benning, Georgia, that summer. Upon his return to Europe in February 1945, John, who was eager to fight for his country, was separated from his comrades in the Seventy-First Division and assigned to a noncombat unit, as Generals George Patton and Omar Bradley did not wish to distract Ike by placing his son in harm's way. In April, Ike ordered John to turn up at headquarters so he could have another visit with him. At the end of the war, they toured the death camps together. "These shared wartime experiences bonded father and son," John's youngest daughter, Mary Jean, told me.

In the summer of 1952, John briefly served in an infantry division in Korea while his father ran for President on the Republican ticket. While Ike did not object, he insisted that his son agree to commit suicide if he were captured rather than put the entire country at risk—a condition that John willingly accepted. In 2008, when both the Democratic and Republican vice presidential candidates had an adult son in the military, John argued in an op-ed for the *New York Times*, entitled "Presidential Children Don't Belong in Battle," that his "father was being far too conciliatory in giving me such permission." The country's safety should come first, he insisted. "No matter what the young person's desires or career needs are," wrote John, "they are of little importance compared with ensuring that our leaders are able to stay focused on the important business of the nation—and not worrying about the fate of a child a world away."

————————

When most Americans picture President Eisenhower, they think of a somewhat frail, retired military man, who at his most active played a vigorous round of golf. That's because Ike was sixty-two when he was first elected and suffered both a serious heart attack and a stroke during his eight years in office. But for John Eisenhower, his father conjured up a very different image. "Dad...was," John wrote in his memoir, "a terrifying figure to a boy." In high school in Abilene, Kansas, Ike lived for athletics. He played both center field on the baseball team and defensive back in football. In 1912, a decade before John was born, the "Kansas cyclone," as Eisenhower was dubbed by his teammates, tackled the legendary Jim Thorpe in an Army football game. With his large hands and powerful build, Eisenhower, who was a revered head football coach at both St. Louis College and Camp Meade during the late 1910s and early 1920s, commanded a formidable presence. He was still doing one-handed push-ups well into his forties. Ike never laid a hand on John, who feared that if his father ever had, he would surely have inflicted "serious bodily harm." When the school-age young-ster once irked his father by putting his elbows on the dinner table, Ike escorted the boy to the bathroom, where he put a thumb on the back of his son's neck. "Well," John thought to himself, "your time has come; you're finished." As a child, he was always aware of his father's imposing physical presence. As John admitted to a reporter in the early 1940s, "He had me well frightened from the start...when he told me to do something, I *did it*!"

While Ike "dressed [his son] down smartly on many occasions," he was careful not to repeat the mistakes of his own parents. Described as a "classic German father," Ike's dad, David Eisenhower, who worked as a mechanic at a creamery, was aloof and authoritarian. To keep his children in line—the future President was the third of seven sons—David would whip them in a very businesslike manner. Years later, Eisenhower credited his good-natured mother, Ida, for teaching him to control his temper (a comment that led one presidential aide to quip, "I thought to myself what a poor job she had done"). Despite Ike's lapses, which included his brief outbursts of anger and those all-too-frequent barbs, this dad essentially relied on "gentle persuasion" to keep his son in line.

According to numerous historians, such as Evan Thomas, whose 2012 biography is called *Ike's Bluff: President Eisenhower's Secret Battle to Save the World,* this technique was also precisely what enabled this President to give Americans eight years of peace and prosperity. Though Ike was personally horrified by the use of overwhelming force, he did not mind the fact that leading politicians—both at home and abroad—often feared that he might veer in that direction. After taking office, he refused to consider setting off any atomic bombs in Korea, once telling his advisors, "You boys must be crazy. We can't use those awful things against Asians for the second time in ten years." But he brought that war to a close by using the nuclear option as a deterrent. In both his foreign policy and in his domestic policy with his son, Ike took a hard line, but he was only bluffing.

When John was born on October 3, 1922, both Ike and Mamie were still feeling shattered by the loss of Icky, who had died just twenty-one months earlier. In 1920, right before Christmas, Icky caught scarlet fever from the family maid, and he died about ten days later. Both parents felt personally responsible, and they often quarreled. "John did much to fill the gap that we felt so poignantly and so deeply every day of our lives since the death of our first son," Eisenhower noted. According to John's eldest child—his son, David—Ike, who considered his second child the spitting image of the son he had lost, turned into an overprotective father. In 1944, when John decided to take the plane home from England, Ike consented, but the solicitous dad soon fired off a missive asking about the flight and "whether your ear bothered you any as a result of it." John spent most of his childhood in Washington, DC, but he also lived abroad—in both France and the Philippines—with his peripatetic parents. When John was six, Ike got an assignment to ghostwrite a guide book, *The American Battlefields in France,* and the youngster accompanied his father as he toured all the World War I battle sites. During that 1928 trip to Europe, John "became fascinated with stories of American military valor," and this obsession would consume him for the rest of his life.

The achievement-oriented dad carefully supervised his son's education. While Ike had not been a stellar student at West Point—he ranked sixty-first out of a class of 164—he finished first in his class at Fort Leavenworth's Command and General Staff School. When John started attending the John Quincy Adams elementary school in Washington, Ike reviewed his son's activities with him at the end of every day. In the morning, as they shared the bathroom—sometimes even the bathtub—this military man, like the former President after whom John's school was named, would drill his son "without mercy on the multiplication tables, so that I was always weeks ahead of my class. And no errors were tolerated," recalled John years later. During dinner, his father would also give him pop quizzes about his schoolwork. Due to his father's insistence that he study, as a youngster, John was always second or third in his class of forty.

Though Ike fervently wanted John to go to West Point, he tried his best not to come on too strong. "Through the years," John observed, "he claimed that I was under no obligation whatsoever to attend myself. But...I could detect...his protesting too much." In 1940, as John was finishing up high school in Tacoma, Washington, Ike initiated a frank discussion about his college options, noting the benefits of the more relaxed attitude at other colleges. While John toyed with a couple of other career paths such as journalism and law, he did not deliberate too long. As the seventeen-year-old told his father, "When you talked about the satisfaction you had in an Army career, and the pride you had in being associated with men of character, my mind was made up right then."

When John started West Point, Ike was eager to hear about his every move. "I'm so tied up in him it hurts," he wrote to Mamie in mid-1942. Even in the run-up to D-Day, Ike continued to monitor John's grades closely. In March 1944, when Ike received a report card showing a dip in John's performance in tactics, Ike expressed his hope that it did not "represent a reaction indicated by your bust-up with your girlfriend... because any such reaction should have been reflected more in your English." And while Ike wanted John to follow him into the infantry, he reassured his son in his last semester that "your choice is not only your own but it never occurred to me...to influence you in the slightest degree." In the end, John chose the same branch of service as his father. After the war ended, John taught English at West Point for three years. In the early 1950s, while Ike was President of Columbia, John studied English literature at the university, writing a master's thesis on the character of the soldier in Elizabethan drama.

Once ensconced in 1600 Pennsylvania Avenue, President Eisenhower was as eager to expose his son to the corridors of power as General Eisenhower had been a decade earlier. In 1954, after his brief tour of duty in Korea, John got a "little education" by working in the White House for a month before starting the Army Command School at Fort Leavenworth. Three years later, when Ike's staff secretary, Andrew Goodpaster, went on vacation for three weeks, the President asked John to serve as his replacement. "You're *it* for the time he's gone," stated Ike. The following October, John became Goodpaster's full-time assistant. John has described his two years in the White House as the most stimulating and rewarding period of his life. By then, John, who had married Barbara Thompson in 1947, was the father of four children—David, Anne, Susan, and Mary Jean. During the week, this constant companion to the President lived on the third floor of the White House, and he returned to his family's home in Pennsylvania only on the weekends.

Ike's calendar for those years was dotted with five-minute appointments with John. With John, Ike was particularly gruff. When John entered his office first thing in the morning, his father's standard salutation was "What the hell do you want?" As a junior member of the White House staff, John was often given the unenviable task of delivering bad news, as other aides were reluctant to expose themselves to the President's outbursts. In May 1960, during the embarrassing U-2 affair, which involved the downing of a U.S. spy plane over Soviet airspace, Ike felt guilty for not having fired CIA chief Allen Dulles years earlier. When John once alluded to Dulles's mismanagement, his father exploded. "He was yelling at the top of his voice for me to drop dead,"

John recalled. At the end of his second term, Ike hired John to help him with his memoirs. "He could act a little contemptuously of my opinion at times," noted John. When John suggested criticizing Allen Dulles in the text, Ike again blamed the messenger. "Damn it, John. I'm writing this book." Too intimidated to fight with his father, John responded, "You sure are. Do it your way."

In 1963, John resigned from active duty to become a writer. He was transferred to the Army Reserve, where he was elevated to Brigadier General before retiring in 1975. "Dad had done so well in the military," stated John, "I thought it best to try another profession." As John was carving out his own identity as an author of military histories, he lived next door to his father's farm in Gettysburg. Like John Adams, Ike was less demanding of his grandchildren, but even with them, he lost his grip on his anger every once in a while. In the summer of 1963, Eisenhower's eldest grandchild, David—the future husband of Richard Nixon's daughter Julie, who was then fifteen—worked two days a week at his farm. One afternoon Ike walked into his den and noticed that David, for whom Camp David was named, was taking a long lunch hour—an hour and fifteen minutes—to play cards with a friend. "You are fired," barked Ike. David, who was often lectured by his grandfather about his "deportment," was so scared when he saw Ike open the door that he can no longer recall what else his grandfather said. However, a few hours later, Ike drove by David's house and picked him up for a golf game, during which he got his job back. "I allow all my associates one mistake a year. You have had yours," stated his grandfather.

Ike was more gentle with his three other grandchildren, all of whom were girls. David's youngest sister, Mary Jean, who used to crawl under Ike's White House desk as a toddler, has fond memories of watching TV with her grandfather during the 1960s, when the gentleman farmer's favorite show was *Green Acres*, a sitcom about Manhattanites transplanted to the country. "My father did tell me about Grandad's outbursts, but that was not what I experienced," she told me. "When I informed him that a classmate had just died, his softer side came out.

Moved to tears, the man who never stopped grieving for Icky told me, 'She has not gone away.'"

But Ike would struggle with his temper until his death in 1969. When an interviewer suggested to an octogenarian John that the two sides of his father—the friendly and the cold-blooded—which were instrumental to his success as both a General and a President, were equally balanced, the son offered a correction: "Make that 75 percent cold-blooded."

The Grief-Stricken

"I Always See My Boy Playing Tennis on the Court Out There"

The little boy's brains were dashed out. Gen. Pierce took him up; he did not think the poor little fellow was dead until he took off his cap.

New York Times, January 7, 1853

On November 16, 1852, two weeks after his landslide victory, President-elect Franklin Pierce wrote to the wealthy Boston merchant Amos Lawrence, "Your note of the 11th...manifests a considerate regard for my convenience, which I fully appreciate. It is quite possible that I may desire to avail myself of the kind of accommodation to which you refer." After discussing the matter with his wife, Jane, who was Lawrence's niece, Pierce accepted the generous offer of hospitality. Shortly before Thanksgiving, the former New Hampshire Senator, along with Jane and their eleven-year-old son, Benny, traveled from Concord to Lawrence's Tremont Street mansion, where they stayed for most of the next month. While Lawrence had not voted for Pierce—Massachusetts was one of only four states that had gone to the Whig candidate, Winfield Scott of New Jersey—he was eager to mend fences with the "old-fashioned Democrat," whom he considered "the soul of honor."

In the Bay State capital, Pierce relaxed with his family and began assembling his cabinet. Having won more than half of the popular vote—a feat that would not be achieved by another Democrat until

1932—Pierce sought to unite his party by nominating representatives from all its factions. On Christmas morning, Pierce met with several advisors, including Virginia Senator Robert Hunter and former Massachusetts Congressman Caleb Cushing, who would become his Attorney General, at the Tremont Hotel before dining with the Lawrence family. The following day, Pierce, Jane, and Benny went to nearby Andover in order to ring in the New Year with Jane's sister, Mary, and her husband, John Aiken.

A few days later, the Pierces were shaken by the news that the sixty-six-year-old Amos Lawrence had died of a seizure. On Tuesday, January 4, they traveled from Andover back to Boston to attend both a private funeral at the Lawrence home and a public one at the Brattle Street Church. Reporting on the impressive and solemn services for this beloved philanthropist, the *Boston Transcript* noted, "The death of no man has made a deeper impression on this community than that of Mr. Lawrence."

On Thursday the sixth, the Pierces planned to return home to Concord. But early that afternoon, they were felled by another loss, and this one would forever change their lives as well as the trajectory of American history. At the start of that day, the affable Pierce seemed to be well on his way to charting a path that could mitigate the tensions brewing between western farmers and eastern bankers and between southern slaveholders and northern abolitionists. But by its end, he would be only a shell of his former self. Permanently scarred by a searing trauma, as President, he would lack the wherewithal to do anything to prevent his country from sliding into a vicious civil war.

That morning, the temperature had hovered around zero. At about one o'clock, as the Pierces boarded the Boston and Maine Railroad at the Andover depot, their train was still shrouded in frost. Pierce and Jane found spots on a bench in the fourth row and Benny sat behind them. Five minutes later, all sixty people on board felt a shock as the axle of the front wheel of the passenger car broke off. Within seconds, this car was separated from the baggage car, which was located directly behind the locomotive. After getting turned around, the passenger car rolled over and over before falling twenty feet down an embankment. According to one eyewitness, "The car broke in pieces like a cigar box." Pierce had immediately put his arms around Jane, and both emerged relatively unscathed. But the President-elect had not been able to grab Benny, who tumbled down the aisle. Struck by a fragment of wood— perhaps from a seat—Pierce's son was killed instantly. "The poor boy's head was smashed to jelly," reported the *New York Times*. In addition to Benny, who was the lone fatality, four other passengers were seriously injured. "Gen Pierce," later noted a fellow passenger, a reverend from Manchester, "gave all needful directions about the recovery of his little boy, still entangled in the wreck about him and then afforded all that comfort and sympathy to his partner in sorrow."

Benny's corpse was then taken to the Andover almshouse, where physicians cleaned up his wounds. With the upper portion of his head missing, parts of his brain were exposed. Except for a cut above his right eye, Benny's face was unharmed, though it was bathed in blood. After "the look of life" was restored, his body was carried to the Aiken house where his afflicted parents sat in a stunned silence. Jane could say little but "Why was my boy killed? Oh tell them not to go on railroads!" That weekend, Pierce would come into Jane's room and "throw himself on the bed by her side and mingle his woe with hers," as her cousin, Mary Jane Adams, put it. Numerous relatives and friends flocked to Andover to attend Benny's funeral, which was held on Monday the tenth. At one thirty that afternoon, Pierce accompanied his boy's remains on a special train bound for Concord, where Benny was buried a few hours later in the Old North Church Cemetery. An inconsolable Jane stayed put; she was, as Pierce told a friend, "very feeble and crushed to the earth by the fearful bereavement." She would be unable to think of leaving Andover for weeks. Pierce was not faring all that much better. From their Concord home on the day of the burial, he reported being "overwhelmed with sorrow and a sense of loss which admits of no increase."

Benny's death was beyond devastating to the now childless Pierces, as they had already lost two other sons. Their first child, Franklin Jr., born in February 1836, died after just three days, and Pierce, then a thirty-one-year-old second-term Congressman, never even had a chance to return to New Hampshire to see him. "He who has lived thirty years in this world of ours," wrote Pierce to his sister that month, "seen its vanity, aye its insanity and felt its madness ought not to… weep over the demise of an infant, but alas what has our experience or what has philosophy to do with the feelings of a father." In 1839, two years after Pierce became America's youngest Senator, Jane gave birth to a second son, Frank Robert. Saddled with a stubborn case of depression and various other health woes such as frequent gastro-intestinal distress and respiratory infections, she was eager to have her husband by her side as they started raising children. Less than a year after Benny's birth in April 1841, Jane finally persuaded him to resign from the Senate. Settling into a house on Montgomery Street in Concord, Pierce focused on rebuilding his law practice. Due to his graceful bearing and eloquence, he soon established himself as New Hampshire's "complete master of…twelve men in the jury box," as one contemporary noted.

But then tragedy struck again in 1844 when the four-year-old Frank Robert suddenly died of typhus. In his 1852 campaign biography, Nathaniel Hawthorne, whose friendship with Pierce dated back to their years at Bowdoin College, called Frank's death "the greatest affliction that his father has experienced." Pierce, who described Frank as "the pride and joy of his father's heart—the light and life of our home," felt as if he had been personally responsible. "We should have lived for God," he wrote, "and left the dear ones to the care of Him who is alone Able to take care of them and us…Few have been more entirely absorbed in the whirl of business and cares purely of worldly character than I." To his younger brother Henry, the severely stricken Pierce insisted that "if you ever have a son…you will be able to appreciate the depth of our sorrows, not till then." Frank's death also had a "heavy hold" on Jane, as one family member noted, and she became almost paralyzed by grief. "The dear little one," Jane wrote the following year, "whose social companionship and ever ready affection were my greatest solace—his childish wants and pleasures my care and delight. I hardly know how I go on from day to day without him."

By the mid-1840s, both parents constantly fretted about the health and welfare of Benny, in whom they invested all their hopes for the future. The boy's every cough, cold, or bout of ringworm was a cause for alarm. In the summer of 1846, Pierce turned down the office of Attorney General, telling President Polk, "When I resigned from my seat in the Senate in 1842, I did it with the fixed purpose never again to be voluntarily separated from my family for any considerable length of time except at the call of country at the time of war." The Mexican War qualified as such a special case, and in the spring of 1847, after being commissioned a Brigadier General, Pierce set out for Vera Cruz. His six months of service, from which he emerged a military hero, proved trying for both Jane and Benny. "It is truly such a state of absence and entire separation as almost amounts to widowhood," Jane wrote to her sister a few days after his departure, "and the feeling of dependence on myself alone so different from what I have been accustomed to is excessively painful...I desire to be thankful that Benny has got so well through the measles but at first it tried me a great deal that he should be so sick after his father leaving, and he missed and longed for him so much."

In 1852, the devoted family man was a reluctant presidential candidate. Initially, Pierce viewed the prospect of having the Democrats float his name at the Baltimore convention that spring as "utterly repugnant." On June 5, 1852, he was vacationing with his wife in Boston when the leader of the Massachusetts Democratic Party rode up to his carriage and announced that he had been nominated on the forty-ninth ballot. Pierce was stunned and Jane immediately fainted. Benny was disappointed. "I hope he won't be elected," the youngster wrote to his mother from the home of their Andover relatives, "for I

should not like to live at Washington and I know you would not either."
Benny was right; the shy and sickly Jane, who was consumed by dread
throughout the campaign, prayed for her husband's defeat.

After Benny's death, Jane was never the same. Her hold on reality
became more and more tenuous. She began writing letters to her dead
son, a practice she would continue during her years in the Executive
Mansion. "But you spirit yourself, my dear one," she wrote a couple
of weeks after the accident, "was not your redeeming savior ready to
receive you? Your sweet little brother? Your uncle Lawrence?...But
now I must kneel alone and bear...the burden of your loss which has
brought desolation such as I have never (with all my former griefs)
known." With the pain too much to bear, the devout Calvinist managed to convince her husband that God had taken their son so that he
would no longer be a distraction during his presidency. This interpre-
tation, noted Pierce's first major biographer, "became the fact of the
greatest importance in his life, troubling his conscience, unsettling
him almost completely, and weakening his self-confidence for many
months to come...Much of the difficulty which he experienced in
[his] administration during the next four years may be attributed to
this terrible tragedy and its long-continued after effects."

As news of Benny's death spread, the entire nation shared its
new leader's anguish. "My heart bleeds for you," wrote the historian
George Bancroft to Pierce, "in your sudden and hopeless grief. You
seem...chastened by heaviest afflictions...to find your happiness in
doing high service to your country like the childless Presidents who
have gone before you." (With the exception of Polk, the men in that
category—Washington, Madison, and Jackson—had all been successful two-term Presidents.) Benjamin Brown French, soon to become
Pierce's Commissioner of Public Buildings, spoke for many Americans
when he noted in his diary, "How utterly insignificant to that noble,
warmhearted, affectionate man must at this moment, appear the
Presidency...a mere bauble, ten thousand of which he would give to
restore the breath of life to his dead boy."

Pierce himself acknowledged that he was no longer in the right frame of mind to take on his new job. Returning to the task of putting together his cabinet, he looked "very grave, [with] no smile on his face—but a fixed expression of sorrow and despondency," as one of Jane's cousins put it. On January 12, he confided in his friend Jefferson Davis, the former Mississippi Senator whom he had known since his own days in the Upper Chamber and would soon nominate to be his Secretary of War, "How shall I be able to summon my manhood to gather up my energies for the duties before me, it is hard for me to see. I have no heart to write now." A week later, alone in the home "from which the center of my earthly hopes and the light of my life have departed forever," the President-elect could not stop thinking about Andover and "the dark day that left me childless." To the New York editor George Nicholas Sanders, a Democratic loyalist, he also stressed that he would have to rely on forces outside himself to manage his new responsibilities. "I trust in God...to carry me thro. Recognizing no purposes but those which look to the best and greatest interests of my country I hope that urgent necessity will bring with it adequate strength and wisdom." He now feared for the safety of all the world's children, adding, "When [my private secretary] was describing for me today your four beautiful children, I almost trembled for you."

According to his original plan, Pierce was to take Benny to the Inauguration—with the publicity-shy Jane traveling on her own later—in order that his son "might remember it for future years." But rather than providing a celebratory occasion for father-son bonding, his journey from Concord to Washington, which he undertook in mid-February, resembled a funeral procession. The day before his train arrived in Manhattan, New York's Democratic Party issued the following resolution: "Whereas Gen. Pierce...in consequence of a recent melancholic affliction, has declined a public reception and intimated the desire to avoid on his journey the general demonstrations of popular regard which might otherwise have attended him...we feel bound to defer implicitly to his wishes in this matter, but at the same time we desire to express to him...the profound respect and sympathy we feel for him." As soon as the President and his traveling companions arrived at the Thirty-Second Street depot, they were whisked off in a private coach and taken directly to the luxurious Astor House on Broadway. The fatigued Pierce then immediately informed the hotel's manager, Charles Stetson, that if anyone was permitted to call on him in his private suite, he would take the first train south to Washington. The President-elect did stay a couple of days in Manhattan, but his mood was still dour when he reached the nation's capital at eight thirty on the evening of February 21. There, too, he slinked from the train station into the Willard Hotel, avoiding the mayor and other dignitaries who were eager to greet him. "I did not go to the cars to see him, although I was at the City Hall and could have done so," noted Pierce's friend Benjamin French, "believing he desired to see no one."

————————

Pierce's persistent anguish during his presidency would severely damage his ability to govern. While he previously had exhibited merely a tendency toward indecisiveness, after Benny's death, he was often paralyzed. At the meetings of his diverse cabinet, which included four northerners and three southerners, the man whom Harry Truman later dubbed "our best-looking President" was a moderator rather than a decider. Almost all the leadership skills that he had once possessed were gone.

Pierce was not the only First Dad shattered by the death of a child. On July 7, 1924, just a month after he had earned his party's nomination to run for a full term, Calvin Coolidge's sixteen-year-old son, Calvin Jr., suddenly died. The cause was a blood infection that the adolescent had incurred while playing tennis without socks on the White House court a week earlier. During his last five years in office, Coolidge, like Pierce, was not himself. He, too, was chronically depressed. "That [Calvin Jr.'s] death," noted Robert Gilbert, Northeastern University political scientist, "destroyed his presidency." It is perhaps no coincidence that most historians consider these two grief-stricken dads among our least effective Presidents; in Arthur Schlesinger's 1962 poll of thirty-one Presidents, Coolidge was ranked twenty-seventh and Pierce twenty-eighth. Without these heartbreaking losses, both men might have provided much more determined leadership. If Benny's head had not been split open near Andover, Pierce may well have achieved the modest success of William McKinley, who came in fifteenth in Schlesinger's poll of seventy-five historians and whose reputation has improved since then. In the 1870s, as this former Major in the Union Army was building his law practice, he endured the deaths of two daughters under the age of four. But in contrast to his wife, Ida, who became just as distraught as Jane Pierce, McKinley became energized. Politics became his refuge from despair, and a year after becoming childless, the Ohio native entered politics and was elected to Congress. While many Presidents have endured the deaths of children, in these three cases, the precise manner in which the President processed (or failed to process) his grief had an enormous impact on the nation as a whole.

In the first 125 years of the Republic, the possibility that a child might die an early death was a constant concern for all parents, including the men who would go on to become President. As the Centers for Disease Control and Prevention have reported, as late as 1900 in many cities, three children in ten were still dying by the age of one. John Adams's third child, Susanna, died at thirteen months; his son, John Quincy, also lost a daughter, Louisa Catherine, not long after her first birthday. Four of the six children Thomas Jefferson fathered with his wife, Martha, died before the age of four. Likewise, James Monroe's second child, his only son, known as J.S., never saw his third birthday; and William Henry Harrison's tenth and final child, James, died at about the same age. Both Martin Van Buren and John Tyler lost infants, and both Zachary Taylor and James Garfield lost two children under the age of four. Rutherford B. Hayes also lost three sons who were all just a year old. Unlike Pierce and McKinley, these Presidents all fathered other children who would remain part of their lives, so the impact of these losses was not nearly as profound. In 1863, when Rutherford B. Hayes's fourth child, Joseph, died of dysentery at eighteen months, the Union soldier wrote in his diary, "I have seen so little of him, born since the war that I do not realize the loss." But whenever a firstborn child died early, the distress was invariably intense. Chester Arthur, who was also serving in the Union Army in 1863, was "prostrated with grief" when his two-year-old son, William, the first of his three children, died from convulsions that July.

At the end of his life, the still grief-stricken Pierce would identify strongly with Abraham Lincoln, whose losses eerily paralleled his own. In 1850, Edward, the second son of the thirty-year-old Illinois attorney, fell victim to cancer at the age of three. "We lost our little boy," Lincoln wrote to his stepbrother. "It was not our first, but our second child. We miss him very much." Lincoln's first son, Robert, who later became the President of the Pullman Palace Car Company, would be the only one of his four children to survive into adulthood. Like Benny Pierce, Lincoln's third child, Willie, also died at the age of eleven from typhoid fever in February 1862. Afterward, his wife, Mary, became even more unhinged than Jane Pierce. After witnessing one of her fits, Lincoln pointed to St. Elizabeth's Mental Hospital near the White House and told her, "Try and control your grief, or it will drive you mad, and we may have to send you there." Three weeks after Willie's death, Pierce informed Lincoln that he knew exactly what his successor was going through:

> The impulse to write you, the moment I heard of your great domestic affliction was very strong, but it brought back the crushing sorrow which befell me just before I went to Washington in 1853, with such power that I felt your grief to be too sacred for intrusion...I realize fully how vain it would be, to suggest sources of consolation.
>
> There can be but one refuge in such an hour—but one ready for smitten hearts, which is to trust in him "who doeth all things well," and leave the rest to "Time, comforter and only healer."

In contrast to Pierce, Lincoln did not let his sorrow hijack his presidency. In fact, some historians have suggested that the loss of Lincoln's favorite son marked a turning point in the Civil War, arguing that the numb President suddenly felt less reluctant to step up the use of military force. Mary did end up losing her mind after the sudden death of their fourth son, Tad, at the age of eighteen in 1871. Four years later, her son Robert placed her in an asylum, where she stayed for several months.

In April 1869, as he was heading back to Tennessee after leaving Washington, Lincoln's successor, Andrew Johnson, the father of five, learned that his thirty-five-year-old son, Col. Robert Johnson, had committed suicide. Johnson's fourth child and second son, who had served as his private secretary during his presidency, had been struggling with an addiction to liquor for more than a decade. A year earlier, the frustrated President had sent Robert to St. Elizabeth's Mental Hospital for treatment, even though, as the newspapers reported, "his keepers [had] no expectation of benefitting him." This was the second son whom Johnson had lost to alcoholism. In 1863, Johnson's eldest son, Charles, an assistant surgeon in Tennessee's Tenth Infantry, died in a horseback riding accident, which most historians also consider a suicide. Though Johnson's reactions to those losses were not recorded for posterity, the mental health problems of these two adult sons weighed heavily on him. As he wrote his wife, Eliza, in early 1863, "I feel sometimes like giving all up in despair."

By the time he became President in 1841, William Henry Harrison had lost five adult children, including three in the three years leading up to his election in 1840. The emotional toll might well have impaired the long-term health of Harrison, who died just a month into his presidency. "The most severe affliction I have ever experienced" is how Harrison referred to the death of his thirty-four-year-old eldest son, John Cleves Symmes Harrison, in 1832. Harrison ended up assuming the financial responsibility for the care of John's widow and six children. In June 1840, while Harrison was campaigning for President, his fourth son, Benjamin, a doctor, also died suddenly at the age of thirty-four. "It will be a great shock to the General," reported the *Connecticut Courant*. And it was, as Harrison was forced to suspend his campaign for a month in order to recuperate at his North Bend, Ohio, home with his wife, Anna.

By the end of World War I, improvements in medical science and hygiene sharply reduced child mortality rates, so recent First Dads have not had to deal with quite so many losses. Even so, the early death of a child was not an uncommon experience for twentieth-century presidents. In 1921, Dwight Eisenhower's first child, a son named Doud, known as "Icky," died of scarlet fever at the age of three. "This was the greatest disappointment and disaster of my life," Ike stated. Though both Ike and his wife, Mamie, tried their best to put the pain behind them, it never went away. "For the rest of his life, my grandfather sent my grandmother orchids on Icky's birthday," Susan Eisenhower, a daughter of Ike's second child, John, told me.

George Herbert Walker Bush was also deeply shaken by the death of his second child, Pauline Robinson ("Robin"), who died of leukemia in the fall of 1953 at the age of three. "When I interviewed the President decades later," Dr. Lawrence Altman, who has written thousands of articles on the health of world leaders for the *New York Times*, told me, "he still couldn't talk about it." This death also had a huge impact on another President: Bush's first son, George Walker Bush, who was seven at the time. To help ease the despair of his mother, Barbara, whose hair turned white soon after Robin became ill, George developed his clownish and playful side. He and his mother also formed an intense bond. "Some close to the Bushes do see the death of his sister as a singular event in George W.'s childhood, helping to define him and how he would deal with the world," reported the *Washington Post* in 1999.

On August 9, 1963, John F. Kennedy's second son, Patrick, who was born at thirty-seven weeks, died after just thirty-nine hours from a condition now known as respiratory disease syndrome. Kennedy, who had spent the previous night at Boston Children's Hospital where the infant was being treated in a hyperbaric chamber, was holding Patrick's little fingers when the infant breathed his last breath at 4:19 in the morning. Immediately afterward, JFK slipped into a boiler room, where the often unemotional President exploded in tears for ten minutes. Biographer Thurston Clarke has argued that this tragedy softened Kennedy and brought him much closer to his wife, Jackie. In stark contrast, the death of the day-old Christine Reagan, born four months prematurely in 1947, contributed to the growing tension in the marriage between the future President and his first wife, Jane Wyman, which ended in divorce a year later.

But over the last century and a quarter, a couple of Presidents were comparatively unruffled by the early deaths of children. In January 1904, Grover Cleveland's eldest daughter, known as "Baby Ruth" when she captivated the nation during his second term, suddenly died of diphtheria. Ruth, who was just beginning to outgrow her famous moniker, was only twelve. (In 1921, this First Daughter was back in the news when the Curtiss Company claimed to have renamed one of its candy bars after her; but in reality, the manufacturer was devising an alibi, which it would use to avoid paying the baseball star Babe Ruth any royalties.) Cleveland was not completely unfeeling—he expressed considerable grief in the immediate aftermath—but due to his detached personality style, his distress soon dissipated. "It seems so long since we buried Ruth, and it is only six weeks yesterday," Cleveland confided to a friend in late February 1904. "We are becoming accustomed to her absence. For the rest of it, we have not a shadow of a doubt that all is well with the child."

Likewise, when FDR's second son, Franklin Jr., born in 1909, died of heart failure at just seven months, the young lawyer would not permit himself or anyone else in the family to wallow in feelings of sadness. Just as TR never spoke of his first wife after her untimely death, the hypomanic, chronically upbeat FDR would essentially erase this infant from the family's history, as he gave his fourth son, born in 1914, the same name. Nina Gibson, a daughter of FDR's youngest son, John, has called this inability to mourn the loss of a child "the Roosevelt reaction." As she also told me, when her younger sister, Sally, died in a horseback riding accident in 1960 at the age of thirteen, her father turned mum.

———————

Though Pierce's presidency would turn out to be an unmitigated disaster, it started out on a triumphant note. The inaugural address, which the former trial lawyer delivered without notes in the snow on March 4, 1853, to fifteen thousand people lined up outside the Capitol, was a bravura performance.

Benny's death, to which Pierce alluded several times in his introduction, created an immediate bond between the new President and his fellow Americans. His vulnerability, balanced by his courage and determination, proved to be a winning combination. "My Countrymen," began Pierce, as he removed his overcoat despite the blustery northeasterly wind, "it is a relief to feel that no heart but my own can know the personal regret and bitter sorrow over which I have been borne to a position so suitable for others rather than desirable for myself…You have summoned me in my weakness; you must sustain me by your strength."

Pierce proceeded to set out some broad principles with which he proposed to approach the major issues of the day—slavery, westward expansion, and the wars in Europe. He promised that his overriding concern would be to keep the peace and to foster national unity. Though a New Englander, this small-government Democrat, who considered himself the heir to Andrew Jackson, reaffirmed the need to limit federal authority to the powers specifically prescribed in the Constitution. Invoking the names of Washington and Jefferson, Pierce concluded by taking comfort in the achievements of his predecessors: "I can express no better hope for my country than that the kind Providence which smiled upon our fathers may enable their children to preserve the blessings they have inherited."

Raves came in from every quarter—even before he finished. Several times during his speech, a man standing behind Massachusetts Senator Edward Everett shouted, "By God, he's up to the mark!" Cheers repeatedly interrupted the President. New York's *Weekly Herald* reported that "everyone was delighted" with Pierce's speech except the barnburners (a small faction of New York abolitionists led by former President Martin Van Buren). Given the enthusiastic reception among many Whigs, the paper insisted that the President had "given the coupe de grace" to the opposition party (which would indeed become defunct by 1854). A reader, who identified himself simply as "Ohio," offered this assessment in the *Daily Ohio Statesman*: "Fine as may be the many things Pierce has ever said or done, he has never given to the world anything so perfect as this." The *Baltimore Sun*, which was not affiliated with any party, concluded, "No similar document, that we remember, has met such general favor."

But the loss of Benny also cast an immediate pall over the Executive Mansion, which, with its staterooms draped in black, would become a locus of doom and gloom. Due to his mourning, the President, who would continue to don black gloves for years, canceled the inaugural ball. Jane was still too bereft to even think about politics. On March 2 in Baltimore, she had refused to discuss the upcoming speech with Pierce, prompting her annoyed husband to dash back to Washington right away. Jane did not follow him to the capital until March 22. And she was "brought to Washington more dead than alive," recalled Varina Davis, the wife of Pierce's Secretary of War. As Jessie Benton Frémont, the wife of the influential California politician John Frémont, put it, Jane's "life was over" after Benny's accident. With her sunken, dark eyes and her skin yellowed like ivory, Pierce's wife banished all animation in others. That spring, Henry Watterson, a Washington schoolboy who was about the same age as the recently deceased Benny, was startled when during his first visit to the White House, "a lady in black took me in her arms and convulsively held me there, weeping as if her heart would break." His introduction to Pierce's wife, wrote Watterson years later, was "altogether the saddest episode of [his] childhood."

Jane would not make her first public appearance until the end of the year, when her attire—a black velvet dress worn along with diamonds—elicited pity. For the first two years of her husband's administration, her aunt, Abby Means, would replace her as the nation's hostess. Jane was debilitated both by a deep depression as well as by numerous psychosomatic ailments. "I am troubled with the bilious difficulty a good deal and am not clear headed at all," she wrote in May 1853. "God help my weak soul to bear its sorrow."

The desperately unhappy Jane longed for the comfort of her husband, who was too overworked to pay her much attention. Unable to manage her frustration, she became more and more crotchety. Pierce's college friend Nathaniel Hawthorne was hardly upset that he got few invitations to the White House. "For of all the dismally dull and heavy domestic circles," the novelist observed, "poor Frank's is certainly the most intolerable. It is too bad that the nation should be compelled to see such a death's head in the prominent place among American women." Once when the President was visiting Jefferson and Varina Davis at their country house three miles outside of town, Jane glared when he put his hands in his pockets while talking about his beloved Hawthorne. "No," responded her husband, "I won't take them out of my pockets, Jennie! I am in the country and I like to feel the comfort of it."

Jane's controlling behavior extended to personal humiliation. Eager to make sure her husband refrained from drinking too much—a vice to which he had succumbed during his first incarnation in Washington as a Senator—she resorted to drastic measures. As Ida Russell, a Boston socialite who visited the Executive Mansion, put it, "She makes him sit at table with his glass turned down as a constant advertisement that he has weaknesses that he could not mend & to let the world know that his wife has a hard time taking care of him . . . placing him in a position degrading to his self-respect." No matter how much Jane irritated him, the courteous and eager-to-please Pierce rarely pushed back much.

Facing all this friction and sadness at home, Pierce was much less well equipped to fight his political battles than he might otherwise have been. He was unwilling to ruffle the feathers of any of the seven members of his cabinet. As he once put it, their "daily intercourse" was "happily undisturbed by any element of discord." His cabinet remains the only one in American history that stayed together for four full years. But this dubious achievement, of which he was enormously proud, underlines just how rudderless his presidential leadership was. In January 1854, when Illinois Senator Stephen Douglas proposed a bill that would enable residents of the new Kansas and Nebraska Territories to decide for themselves whether to allow slavery, Pierce quickly gave his assent. The President had promised to protect the Missouri Compromise of 1820, whereby slavery was prohibited in any area north of latitude 36° 30'. He also knew that the legislation would create a firestorm among northerners. Yet it took little pressure to get him to change his mind.

On Sunday, January 22, Jefferson Davis made a quick trip to the family quarters of the Executive Mansion and asked the President to meet right away with Douglas and his Senate colleagues, who were waiting outside. While the increasingly religious Pierce rarely conducted any business on the Sabbath, he graciously gave the visitors two hours of face time. Aided by the President's seal of approval, Congress passed the Kansas-Nebraska Act just four months later. "President Pierce," noted the *New York Times* in an editorial published that May, "professedly wielding his power under a Constitution that guarantees equal rights to all...has been the passive tool of the most-ultra Pro-Slavery fanatics in the union." One such fanatic, the paper noted, was a member of his own cabinet, "one of the most ultra Secessionists in the South," a reference to Jefferson Davis, who, a half-dozen years later, would become President of the Confederacy. As Missouri Senator Thomas Hart Benton later put it, Pierce headed "an Administration in which he was inoperative, and in which nullifiers, disunionists and renegades used his name and his power for their own audacious and criminal purposes."

The Kansas-Nebraska Act dramatically heightened tensions across the country. Those who opposed slavery felt betrayed by the President. For the rest of his time in office, Pierce would be bogged down by a crisis of his own making—"the civil war in Kansas," as newspapers called the series of violent skirmishes that erupted between northern and southern transplants to the new territories. New Hampshirites soon turned against their favorite son.

By 1855, Pierce's home state no longer had a Democratic Governor or any Democratic Congressmen, and the fierce abolitionist John P. Hale held one of its seats in the U.S. Senate. Hale held his Bowdoin College classmate personally responsible for the "murders, arsons...and cruel outrages which have been committed against Kansas." Such animus against Pierce also gripped the entire nation. In the 1854 midterm elections, anxious and disgruntled voters punished the Democrats, who lost nearly half of their 157 seats in the House of Representatives. This sudden reversal paved the way for the birth of the Republican Party, which quickly garnered supporters by promising to contain slavery.

But rather than rallying behind their President, Democrats tended to blame Pierce. As one party operative put it a couple of months before the 1856 Convention, "[Pierce] has no real strength but there is so much weakness in him *personally*, for instance you may hear it often said 'anybody but Pierce.'" In Cincinnati that June, Pierce suffered a humiliating defeat when he became the only elected President to seek his party's nomination and then fail to get the nod. But his heart was no longer tied to politics. As he confessed to Virginia Clay, the wife of Alabama Senator Clement Clay, at the end of his term, "I am so tired of the shackles of Presidential life that I can scarcely endure it! I long for quiet."

As Pierce and his wife prepared to leave Washington, they remained as haunted as ever by Benny's death. The very possibility of the loss of a child continued to trigger the President, who was still obsessed with preventing tragedies such as those that had befallen him. Two months before the end of his term, a blizzard with six-foot snowdrifts would not deter him from paying a visit to an ailing Varina Davis at her F Street home. Though the walk would take an hour each way, the President wanted to be sure to offer support in person, since she had just given birth to her third child, Jefferson Jr. The Pierces felt a special kinship with the Davises, whose first child, Samuel, had died a month before he was to have turned two in June 1854. Pierce and his Secretary of War, whom he called his "strength and solace...[during] four anxious years," were bonded by a common source of anguish. As Varina once put it, "A child's cry in the street well nigh drove [her husband] mad."

When the Pierces traveled to Europe after the inauguration of his successor, James Buchanan, thoughts of Benny still frequently intruded. From Switzerland, in June 1858, Jane, who took along Benny's Bible and locks of hair from all three sons, wrote to her sister, Mary, in Andover, "It is soothing my sister when you speak of my child's picture—does it not seem to say, as he did in my dreams, 'I'm nicely Mother, just as well as I want to be'—precious ones all! God grant that we may meet them in glory, when the ever changing scenes of this life are over—indeed it seems more and more to me like a moving panorama." From Switzerland, Pierce also poured out his heart to his former law partner, Concord's John George, when he heard about the sudden deaths of two of his children. "Great sorrows make another link between us. As you visit the graves...you will meet my thoughts as you pause at the small enclosure, which contains *all* of mine."

A year later, when Pierce was reunited with Hawthorne in Rome, he could not stop thinking about the health of the writer's teenage daughter, Una, then suffering from malaria. He would visit his old friend as often as three times a day to watch over Una, who eventually recovered. "I recollect the first evening that Pierce came to our house," Una's younger brother Julian observed, "listening to the story of Una's illness. 'Poor child! Poor child!' he said occasionally, in a low voice. His sympathy was like something palpable—strong, warm, and comforting. He said very little, but it was impossible not to feel how much he cared."

Upon returning to Concord from Europe, Pierce held to his

longstanding position about a possible Civil War, insisting that north-erners and southerners should figure out a way to compromise in order to avoid slaughtering each other. His primary concern was protecting the members of the next generation. In early 1861, just as Virginia was pondering secession, he sent a telegraph to the state's Governor: "Virginia can yet save her children."

On Wednesday evening, December 20, 1899, in the middle of a meet-ing with his private secretary, George Cortelyou, in the Cabinet Room, President William McKinley suddenly blurted out, "I don't know what in the world to give Mrs. McKinley for Christmas. She has about every-thing she needs." Cortelyou was surprised that the President appeared to be thinking very deeply on the subject. A couple of hours later, right before saying good night to his aide, McKinley again alluded to his domestic anxiety, adding, "I wish someone could tell me what to give Mrs. McKinley."

That month, the President was weighed down by several pressing affairs of state. Though he was proud that he had annexed the Philip-pines at the end of the Spanish American War—a decision that, he insisted, had instantly transformed America into "a world power"—he was worried about the Filipino resistance fighters who had begun to wage a guerrilla war. And a month earlier, he had lost his trusted Vice President, Garret Hobart, to a heart ailment at the age of fifty-five. The worn-out President would soon have to declare whether he wanted to stand for reelection. Unsure if he still felt up to the job, he was waver-ing. "I have had all the honor there is in the place," McKinley admit-ted to his staff that September, "and have had responsibilities enough to kill any man."

Amid these political concerns, McKinley could not stop thinking about the right Christmas gift for his wife, Ida. The President found himself mulling over the possibilities several times a day. What made the selection more difficult than usual was that Ida did not want anything nearly as expensive as the two diamond bracelets he had given her the previous year. But the main reason for the President's obsessive concern about his wife was that her health had deteriorated steadily since June. Troubled by crying spells and memory lapses, she was often ill-tempered. In fact, she was barely able to function at all. Ida hardly ever ventured to come downstairs from her bedroom. McKinley feared that he would soon have to insist that she "retire" from her role as First Lady. The frantic President had recently arranged for a consultation with Dr. Frederick Peterson, a neurologist who had studied with Sigmund Freud in Vienna and now headed the New York State Commission on Lunacy. That December, Peterson came to Washington to study her case. But no interventions seemed to make any difference. As Cortelyou had noted in his diary on the nineteenth, "Mrs. McKinley is not so well. She does not improve at all of late and her friends are beginning to worry about her condition."

Like Jane Pierce, Ida McKinley had been saddled with debilitating illnesses for almost as long as her husband had known her—and hers, too, were exacerbated by the deaths of her offspring. The couple's only two children, Katie and Ida, both died before reaching the age of four. In 1873, two years after their marriage, Ida lost both her mother and her namesake, who lived just four months, within a span of five months. Afterward, she was never the same. Mrs. McKinley became an invalid who was unable to walk more than a few steps at a time. And along with the physical disability, which was probably caused by phlebitis, came epilepsy, which was then little understood. After little Ida's death, she became fiercely protective of her first child, Katie, whom she refused to let out of her sight. "No, I mustn't go out of the yard," the three-year-old told her uncle when he asked her to go on a walk, "or God'll punish mamma some more." The weeping mother would spend hours holding Katie in a darkened room. And when Katie suddenly died in June 1875 from a heart ailment, Ida was inconsolable. Her first reaction was to try to starve herself to death. Depression would hover over her for the rest of her life.

A few days before Christmas, the cautious President passed on the shopping assignment to the White House steward, William Sinclair. At Washington's venerable jewelry store, established by the Galt brothers in 1799, this aide, who doubled as McKinley's body servant, selected a vase and a tiny blue picture frame covered with diamonds. But it was what the President put inside the frame that made all the difference— the family's one surviving picture of Katie. When he gave Ida her present on Saturday evening the twenty-third, she responded with delight. And during the holidays that year, she would begin to experience a small abatement in her nagging feelings of depression and anxiety.

Though Katie and little Ida had been dead nearly a quarter of a century, they were still a constant presence in the psyches of both the President and his wife. As McKinley confided to Cortelyou that winter, he felt especially sad at the end of every year, because his elder daughter "was a Christmas present born on that day. One should feel *holy* at this season that the time should be one of resolution and reflection; the spirit of self-sacrifice should dominate everything." Though the President was connected to his feelings, as a rule, he tended to keep them to himself. Another rare instance when McKinley spoke directly about his grief came a couple of weeks after Christmas, when he learned that the influential New York State Republican politician, Thomas Bradley, had lost an adult son in an accident. As the President noted in his condolence letter, "Only those who have suffered in a similar way can appreciate the keenness of such affliction."

But in contrast to the President, the First Lady could not stop talking about these losses. For Ida, hanging on to the memories of her two children, particularly Katie, was a sine qua non—a crucial weapon in the fight to preserve her sanity. At her insistence, reminders of Katie and little Ida were everywhere in the White House. In the parlor she displayed two rocking chairs—one given to Katie on her first birthday and the other from her own childhood, which was supposed to represent her second child, her namesake. Near the chairs was "a box containing [Katie's] little dresses and shoes and rings," which, as one journalist observed, "partly pain and partly soothe the mother's heart." And it was not as if the First Lady really needed another picture of Katie. She already had several copies of the one she received that Christmas. In their bedroom, a small one stood on a table and an enlarged version, which was hand-tinted to give the child pink cheeks and red lips along with yellow curls, hung on the wall over their brass beds. Katie's blue eyes gazed down on McKinley and his wife every night as they slept.

As was the case with the Pierces, the McKinleys' grief also lent a melancholy tone to the nation's capital. "There was little of real gayety in the White House," recalled Col. William H. Crook, a clerk who worked for every President from Lincoln to Wilson, "during President McKinley's residence… Had he been the father of lusty, growing children, all this might have been altered; but he lived apart from that one element of human life which, more than any other, keeps men and women young, despite advancing years. Furthermore, his wife's ill health was a constant source of anxiety to him, and because of her nervous disorder she was physically unable to endure, much less inspire in others, an atmosphere of singing joyousness."

But Crook's account glosses over the macabre nature of the McKinleys' obsessions. To many a Washington visitor, Ida McKinley offered a peek into the hole of a specially designed artificial Easter egg, through which one could see a diorama showing both her girls playing on the White House lawn. She often pretended as if Katie and little Ida were still alive. As one Senator's wife put it, "She chatted lovingly of what might have been if her own children had lived." McKinley also shared these fantasies about the adult Katie. Once, when a friend spoke of a particular debutante, the President became pensive, explaining to Ida that Katie "would have resembled her."

The First Couple would continue to mourn as if their girls had died only recently. The McKinleys still visited their graves at Canton's West Lawn Cemetery at every available opportunity. On November 6, 1896, three days after the presidential election and the day after all the returns were counted, McKinley stepped out of his carriage to place "tokens in memory of his two daughters, Katie and Ida, who passed away early in life," as the *New York Times* reported. It was as if he was eager to share his victory with his kin. On that day, his wife was too worn out by the rigors of the campaign to accompany him. But they both headed to the cemetery on July 3, 1897—the first time that they appeared in Canton during his presidency. With the press now covering their every move—one reporter identified the precise spot where Mrs. McKinley had "buried hope"—Americans from all over the country got swept up in their grief. Soon tourists from as far away as California would also make pilgrimages to the girls' graves, which were emblazoned on popular postcards. And since the President and First Lady could no longer get there in person as often as they might like, Ida asked her sister, Mary (Pina), who still lived in Canton, to put fresh flowers on the graves every week.

As much as McKinley was forever burdened by his grief, in contrast to Pierce, he was never incapacitated by it. While he, too, was not a visionary leader, his was a successful administration. As the late Stanford University historian Thomas Bailey noted in his book on presidential greatness, "His name is associated with prosperity, sound money, an uninterruptedly victorious war, a triumphant re-election and a substantial closing of the bloody chasm between North and South." McKinley has not always received credit for these achievements because he has been overshadowed by his successor, the hyperactive go-getter Theodore Roosevelt, who, as Assistant Secretary of the Navy in 1898, famously dismissed his boss as having "no more backbone than a chocolate éclair." At the time, the impetuous TR was upset that McKinley was slow to declare war on Spain. Although McKinley used a deliberative approach to establish policy—as well as to select Christmas gifts—unlike Pierce, he had no trouble wielding his executive authority.

In fairness to Pierce, if McKinley had witnessed the violent death of a child just before his inauguration, his capacity for leadership too may well have been compromised. But McKinley was also able to defuse other serious family stressors that threatened to derail his presidency.

His wife was even more helpless and demanding than Jane Pierce. Ida McKinley, as the late Yale University historian John Blum emphasized, "was the most trying First Lady in all American history and surely one of the most trying wives." Weighed down by unremitting anguish about their lost children as well as by numerous psychiatric symptoms, the wheelchair-bound Ida required his constant attention. At dinners in the state dining room, he broke precedent and seated his wife by his side. Her comfort took priority over the pressing affairs of the day. While President McKinley's daughters were long gone, he still had no shortage of fathering responsibilities. "He looked after [his wife]," his aide, Colonel Crook, emphasized, "as if she were a child. When she wanted a pen, or a needle, or a book to read, all she did was to say so, and the President would start at once, hurrying after it as quickly as possible. The devotion to his wife was beautiful; but it was also pathetic when we knew the weight of affairs he was carrying." Ida would not even let the President sleep. During the Spanish American War, McKinley often worked until two in the morning. When he finally came to bed, Ida, who suffered from chronic insomnia, would insist that he sit in an upright position and comfort her with his arm, noting that unless he continued to do so, she could not possibly drop off.

Ever since the mid-1870s, when Ida first made the transition from wife to ward, McKinley had served as her part-time doctor, or "psychiatric nurse," as Margaret Leech, the author of the definitive biography, put it, to manage her epilepsy. She could have a seizure at any moment, and during social gatherings, at the first sign of trouble, McKinley put a napkin over her face so she would not startle anyone. As President, he himself was ordering shipments of several drugs, including sedatives, anticonvulsants, and bromides, from Joseph Bishop, a Manhattan specialist in "nervous diseases and troubles of women." He would administer the cocktail and then file frequent reports with Bishop, who adjusted the various dosages accordingly.

Ida had been relatively stable for the first two years of his administration until she began faltering—the development that necessitated the visit from Dr. Peterson, the neurologist. That December, this outside consultant diagnosed her with "bromism," attributing her constant wooziness to too many bromide pills rather than to any of her underlying health conditions. By early February 1900, after she began relying on other means besides medication to treat her mild seizures—namely, a strict diet combined with regular exercise—her stamina started to come back, and she resumed attending ordinary social functions. But the President was still preoccupied with her ups and downs. In the middle of White House meetings, he would repeatedly ask his staff to give him up-to-the-minute status reports on her health, as she was prone to relapses. On the afternoon of February 24, 1900, for example, Cortelyou passed on the following bulletin: "Mrs. McKinley was very ill this am, having had a bad attack."

———————

For McKinley, as opposed to Pierce, the loss of his children would fuel his political ascension rather than terminate it. To avoid being overwhelmed by sadness, the Canton lawyer threw himself into purposeful activity. A few months after Katie's death, the thirty-two-year-old McKinley jumped at the chance to play a key role in Rutherford Hayes's campaign for a third term as Ohio's Governor. The following year, he won a seat in Congress, where he served for fourteen years. "If a man is to spend his life...in obedience to a sick woman's whims," concluded biographer Margaret Leech, "he must have work to keep him sane. McKinley found his release in his political career. He escaped from his personal tragedy on the floor of the House."

The childless McKinley was a changed man. Suddenly he was all seriousness. He even stopped exercising. To care for Ida, he also had to watch both his words and his every move. After he mentioned that he had come across an attractive woman at President Garfield's funeral, his jealous wife proceeded to have a serious seizure. As President, he even had to check with her before allowing the American opera star Lillian Nordica to sing "Home, Sweet Home" out of fear that an innocuous line like "There is no place like home" might upset her. "Yes, I have learned self-control," he later reflected. "It has been a matter of discipline. Mrs. McKinley has been an invalid for many years. Her life has at times hung by a thread, and her physician believed I could strengthen or weaken that hold on life. I schooled myself, and never went into her presence without a smile on my face."

But as with FDR's polio, her illness ended up teaching him the very skills that he needed to thrive as a politician. McKinley, too, learned how to hide his true feelings—particularly his anxiety and sadness. And his cheerful, unruffled demeanor served him well in Congress, where he became known as the Pacifier because of his ability to smooth over the hurt feelings of fellow House members. "The adroitness gained by constantly tending a nervous, fanciful woman," noted an early twentieth-century biographer, "helped him with irritable opponents." An effective legislator who eventually became Chairman of the powerful House Ways and Means Committee in 1890, McKinley managed to push through the influential tariff bill that bore his name.

McKinley's personal transformation would also enable him to win the adoration of the American people. His identity as the dutiful husband of a helpless wife, with whom he shared an unbreakable bond born out of their mutual grief, became the calling card that propelled him into the presidency. In the weeks preceding the 1896 Republican Convention, which was held in mid-June in St. Louis, McKinley's nomination was a foregone conclusion. As the prominent Washington correspondent George Alfred Townsend put it on June 7, "No other Republican begins to have his gift of love…he is in full rapport with his countrymen's love." Stressing that "the best place to know McKinley well was at home," Townsend made his own visit to Canton to study his family. "For twenty years," he concluded, "McKinley has had a wife bereft of her two children and of her hope of health—a baby on his hands and the exertion of love has steeped him in it: his cross has become his passion." Likewise in an editorial that same week, the *New York Independent* referred to his "beautiful character" and "sweet and spotless life," adding that "his domestic life is a tender romance which touches every true heart."

On June 18, after Ohio Senator Joseph Foraker gave the nominating speech, stressing that "his personality will carry into the presidential lair the aspirations of the voters of America, of the families of America, of the homes of America," delegates responded with a twenty-four-minute ovation. A few hours later, McKinley was selected to head his party's ticket on the first ballot. The second-term Ohio Governor received 661½ votes, crushing the second-place finisher, House Speaker Thomas Reed, who tallied just 84½.

In that fall's election, the fifty-three-year-old McKinley faced off against the thirty-six-year-old William Jennings Bryan, a dynamic orator who had riveted the Democrats at their July convention with his famous "cross of gold" speech. Eager to avoid debating Bryan, McKinley settled on a front-porch campaign. This key strategic decision capitalized on his greatest asset—his exemplary conduct as a head of household. In contrast to Bryan, who would rack up some eighteen thousand miles as he crisscrossed the country giving speeches, McKinley would stay put. Delegations from each state would see him in his element—his home. The gracious McKinleys proved immensely popular with all visitors, particularly with the smallest guests, to whom Ida felt compelled to show her picture of Katie. "And then the children," observed the celebrated novelist Willa Cather—then a twenty-something journalist—"are all very quiet, for they know that that is the picture of Mrs. McKinley's own little girl who died a long time ago." A Canton company began selling a postcard picturing Katie between her parents, as if all three members of the family might soon be moving to Washington. Ida encouraged this misconception by frequently referring to "my husband and little girl," as if her first child were still alive.

But rather than being turned off by the couple's occasional lapses into ghoulishness, most reporters—and voters—were moved by their love for children. As the influential turn-of-the-century Ohio journalist Murat Halstead would later put it, "[The McKinleys]...sought the happiness that their children would have given in closer union and in the enjoyment of the little ones of others...He was like Mrs. McKinley in the respect that little girls could command him for a courtesy and he was always pleased to be in their company...Mr. and Mrs. McKinley were glad to see and gratified to hear the conversation, and notice the smiles and laughter, and the more serious moods of children who happened to be about the age that their children might have been." Right from the start, the twenty-fifth President was widely beloved. "The thing that endeared McKinley to the nation was his slavish protectiveness towards the woman to whom the best had been given—and taken away," as Julia Foraker, the wife of the Ohio Senator, later noted. "The unbroken guard he kept, his patience and gentleness in circumstances of the most trying nature, affected Washington, affected the whole country as nothing coming from the White House ever had." After conducting another front-porch campaign, in which he relied on his new number two—Theodore Roosevelt—to travel around the country in his stead, McKinley won handily the rematch against Bryan in 1900.

Besides reshaping his character, McKinley's losses would also influence one of the most consequential decisions that he made as President. In the middle of 1898, as American diplomats began to negotiate a treaty with their Spanish counterparts in Paris to end the war, McKinley had to stake out a position on the future of the Philippines. Initially, he expressed no desire for "greed of conquest," viewing the annexation of the islands as "criminal aggression." In late July, he informed his cabinet that he "was very conservative in his belief as to the policy of handling the Philippines situation," but wanted "the facts to be carefully considered." However, he soon became wary of the other alternatives, which were to cede the Philippines to Spain or create a self-governing entity under an American protectorate; he then made an about-face that had little to do with any empirical assessment of the conditions on the ground. Publicly, this Methodist President would claim that a religious experience led him to turn America into an imperialist power. As he said in an interview, "I went down on my knees and prayed [to] Almighty God for light and guidance . . . And one night late it came to me . . . that there was nothing left for us to do but to take them all, and to educate the Filipinos and uplift them and civilize and Christianize them."

But members of his administration such as Col. Benjamin Montgomery, the White House telegrapher, would tell a different story. According to these insiders, Ida had been obsessed for years with the possibility that her two girls might have been reincarnated and she nudged the President to take the Philippines in order to reunite the family. "The women and children of the Orient lured McKinley's wife," wrote one biographer. "Out there, perhaps, had there been a paradise of colors and warm flowers, with Katie and baby Ida born again, brown and naked for her kisses, waiting to be brought up as Christian ladies." As Julia Foraker put it, McKinley's daughters were "ghosts in the long-ago moonlight" who were "playing a strangely real part in the national career of the man who became our twenty-fifth President."

In May 1901, while traveling with the President in California, Ida became acutely ill with a blood infection. For about a month, as she was close to death, McKinley was forced to suspend most of his regularly scheduled activities. On June 10, as she finally began to recover, the President, who was now more popular than ever on account of the spate of sympathetic press attention he received that spring, surprised his cabinet by issuing a statement saying that he had no intention of seeking a third term. "My only ambition," he declared, "is to serve through my second term to the acceptance of my countrymen . . . and then, with them, to do my duty in the ranks of private citizenship." These words were perhaps meant more for Ida than for anyone else, as she had been opposed to his reelection bid and was eager to spend more time with him.

Having made this concession, McKinley may well have felt less guilty about turning his attention back to presidential concerns such as the need to set up a civilian government in the Philippines where his appointee, William Howard Taft, would soon become Governor. After all, ever since the deaths of his children, politics had been instrumental in helping him maintain his own psychic equilibrium. And this was the prescription that he recommended to others in similar straits. In late June 1901, Del Hay, the twenty-four-year-old son of Secretary of State John Hay, whom the President had just appointed as Cortelyou's assistant, died from a fall during his Yale College reunion. In response to despairing letters from Hay, in which the Secretary of State mentioned how "every hope of the future was linked with [our boy]," McKinley was sympathetic but practical. Though the President recognized the "sudden and appalling sorrow that has come to your home," he encouraged Hay to get over his "temporary indisposition," noting that a "return to work... will be the best avenue to bring you relief and strength."

By the time McKinley headed to Buffalo that September to attend the Pan-American Exposition, Ida's health "was the best it had been for twenty-seven years," according to her doctor. On September 6, after the President was shot by the anarchist Leon Czolgosz, he stayed in character, saying, "My wife—be careful, Cortelyou, how you tell her— oh, be careful." He died a week later. His grieving widow, who was too shaken to attend his funeral, was reduced to an unremitting state of suicidal depression. "I am more and more lonely and unhappy every day I live," Ida wrote to a friend from Canton in October 1902, "and take no interest in anything... When I go out, I drive to the cemetery in the morning and into the country in the afternoon when the weather permits." Cared for by her younger sister, Pina, she survived for another five years.

"The boys have come home," President Calvin Coolidge wrote from the White House to his father, John Coolidge Sr., on Friday, June 27, 1924, "and I am sure we should think it was very pleasant to have you here on the Fourth of July."

Born on Independence Day in 1872, the thirtieth President was about to turn fifty-two. While Coolidge did not believe in making a fuss about birthdays—he was not planning on having a cake—he was looking forward to spending the day surrounded by his family. His two children, John, 17, and Calvin Jr., 16, had just finished the academic year at Mercersburg Academy, a Pennsylvania prep school. The seventy-seven-year-old John Coolidge Sr. was still living in the family homestead in Plymouth Notch, Vermont. He had not seen his son since the previous August, when in his capacity as a notary public, he had sworn in the President in his living room. Noticing that a new train—the Washingtonian—offered direct service from Vermont, Coolidge was hoping to entice his father to come down for a brief visit. Unfortunately, catching the train in White River Junction required getting up in the middle of the night, and the increasingly frail John Sr. would not feel up to making the trip.

But his father's absence was not the reason Coolidge's first birthday as President turned out to be the most miserable one of his life. On the afternoon of the fourth, instead of leaving with his family for a planned four-day cruise on the *Mayflower*, the presidential yacht, Coolidge began keeping a vigil over an acutely ill son. And Calvin Jr.'s sudden death three days later would be a blow from which Coolidge— both the man and the President—would never recover.

That summer, Coolidge was riding a wave of popularity. During his first eleven months in office, he had shown himself to be an engaged and energetic leader. As with Franklin Pierce, his first major speech to his countrymen—a State of the Union address, given in the House chamber on December 6, 1923—was a smashing success. "The message will increase respect for the President, even among those who do not agree with him," noted the *Baltimore Sun* of the first presidential address to be broadcast on live radio to a national audience. "It invites co-operation with the President and his party by all whose reason is not overmastered by bitter partisanship and fanaticism," raved the *Pittsburgh Gazette*. In the comprehensive seven-thousand-word text, Coolidge set forth thirty policy proposals, several of which he would manage to push through Congress over the next six months. Chief among them was the Mellon Tax Cut, named after Treasury Secretary Andrew Mellon, which reduced the highest income tax rate from 50 percent to 46 percent. "It really was a bold thing for him to appear before the two Houses of Congress to deliver a message," recalled Republican Senator James Watson of Indiana. "He rose to answer the challenge of the hour, and he did so in such outstanding fashion and with such universal acclaim that his future success was assured."

A couple of days after his sparkling radio debut, the President, accompanied by both his boys, attended the winter dinner of Washington's Gridiron Club, where he announced that he would be seeking a full term the following fall. To honor John and Calvin Jr., the first two presidential sons to live in the White House in a decade, the hosts— the capital's newspaper correspondents—also invited all twenty surviving presidential sons, half of whom showed up, including TR's three sons, Theodore Jr., Kermit, and Archibald. Coolidge's speech came after a series of skits that spoofed the upcoming Republican race such as one in which his two likely opponents, Senator Robert LaFollette of Wisconsin and Senator Hiram Johnson of California, appeared in the garb of hostile Indians. With the economy booming and the country at peace, the incumbent, depicted on stage that evening as a well-established Pilgrim by his chief backer, Boston businessman Frank Stearns, would not have much to fear from any challengers. On June 11, 1924, at his party's nominating convention in Cleveland, the Chairman of the Republican National Committee stressed that "the confidence-inspiring character of Coolidge" made him a worthy successor to Lincoln, McKinley, and Roosevelt. The following day, the President was nominated on the first ballot, winning all but 45 of the 1,109 votes cast. LaFollette received 35 and Johnson just 10.

The President's favorite son, the five-foot-ten-inch, 115-pound Calvin Jr., had been feeling fine until Monday, June 30, when he and his elder brother, John, played a few sets of doubles on the White House tennis court. To avoid being late, the youngest member of the family ended up putting his sneakers on directly over his bare feet. During the match, he rubbed a blister on the third toe of his right foot. Though his foot was soon a bit swollen, in typical Coolidge fashion, he did not complain. The following day, Calvin Jr. played some more tennis, but on Wednesday, July 2, he came down with a fever of 102. That afternoon, his mother, Grace, moved a piano into the Lincoln bedroom—where the boys were sleeping on twin beds—so that she could serenade Calvin Jr. while he tried to recuperate. During a thorough physical examination, Joel Boone, a White House doctor, was startled to discover some swollen glands near his groin and red streaks running up and down his leg. Since these symptoms could be a sign of blood poisoning, Boone sent a culture from the boy's toe to a navy lab. Over the next two days, Calvin Jr.'s temperature continued to rise, and Boone called in other doctors for help.

On the night of the third, Coolidge and his wife hardly slept as they made repeated visits to their son's sickbed. Though the President was alarmed, he did not share his anxiety with anyone outside of the White House when he left on the morning of his birthday to give a 10:30 address to the five thousand delegates gathered at the sixty-second annual convention of the National Education Association. As soon as he finished speaking, Coolidge headed back to the White House to check in on Calvin Jr.

After telling his secretary that it was time to notify the press about his son's illness, Coolidge dashed off a missive to his father. "Calvin is very sick," the worried President noted, "so this is not a happy day for me. He blistered his toe and infection got into his blood. The toe looks all right, but the poison spread all over his system. We have five doctors, one from Phila, and 2 nurses. We think his symptoms are a little better now at 1 pm, but he had a bad night. Of course he has all that medical science can give but he may have a long sickness with ulcers, then again he may be better in a few days." Unable to relax, Coolidge paced around the White House grounds. In an attempt to cheer his son up, he caught a small brown rabbit and brought it back to

Calvin Jr., who smiled for a minute before the animal was taken away by an aide.

But the boy would not get any better. The blood tests revealed that his infection was *Staphylococcus aureus* and on Saturday, July 5, he was transferred by ambulance to a room at Walter Reed Hospital. The President and his wife slept across the hall from their son. Both Dr. Boone and the chief White House physician, Dr. James Coupal, also monitored Calvin Jr. around the clock, but his condition continued to deteriorate. On Sunday the sixth, his desperate doctors tried to remove the poison by putting Calvin Jr. under the knife. "Operation on Calvin seems success," Coolidge noted in a Western Union telegram to his father. "He is very low but there is still hope...had bad night." At 8:10 on Monday morning the seventh, Coolidge updated his father: "No real improvement, but symptoms for first time more hopeful. Passed terrible crisis last night. He is struggling hard to get well this morning."

That afternoon, as Coolidge remained at Calvin Jr.'s bedside, the boy began slipping in and out of consciousness. "The President," observed Dr. Boone, "could not believe his son was on the verge of death. He stood there with great dignity, never showing outward emotion, but it was recognized that he was very tense within and stood almost immobile gazing at his son." In the evening, Boone was injured when he was hit in the chest by a piece of metal from an oxygen tank, which had exploded accidentally, and Dr. John Kolmer, a pathologist from Temple University, took over.

At about ten o'clock, Kolmer told the Coolidges that Calvin Jr. was about to die. Suddenly Coolidge lost his characteristic self-control. "The President sprang from his chair," Kolmer later recalled, "and took his dying son in his arms, shouting hysterically into his ears that he would soon join him in the great beyond, and requesting that young Calvin so inform his grandmother (the mother of the President)." In an attempt to calm himself down, Coolidge pulled out a gold locket from his jacket pocket containing a lock of his late mother's hair. As

Coolidge had often remarked, he felt that his son and his mother, who had died four decades earlier, were mirror images of one another, as each had blue eyes, a fair complexion, and sandy-reddish hair. Coolidge put the locket into his son's hand, but the unconscious Calvin Jr. dropped it onto the floor. On the second try, the same thing happened. Finally, the President held his son's hand while the locket was firmly lodged into the boy's palm. With his other hand, Coolidge stroked the boy's forehead. At about 10:20 that evening, Calvin Jr. was no more.

Half an hour later, out of respect for Calvin Jr., the Democrats, who were meeting in Madison Square Garden to nominate an opponent to Coolidge, suspended their quadrennial convention. After Senator Thomas Walsh of Montana, who chaired the proceedings, announced the boy's death on the live radio broadcast, a low moan lasting nearly a minute arose from the delegates on the floor. Suddenly, partisan differences had no meaning. The following morning, on behalf of Chairman Walsh, former Assistant Secretary of the Navy Franklin D. Roosevelt read a resolution that was adopted by unanimous consent. "We bow our heads in sympathy and reverence by the side of our President," said Roosevelt, "as he and his family pass through the valley of the shadow of death." Tens of thousands of calls and telegrams made their way to the White House. The nation grieved as one. As the *New York Times* noted in an editorial, "The President may be sure in his sore affliction of the sincere condolences of all the American people."

In the days and weeks after Calvin Jr.'s death, the usually undemonstrative Coolidge continued to have trouble controlling his grief. On July 8, dressed only in a bathrobe, Coolidge walked into the East Room of the White House, where his son's body lay in state. Peering into Calvin Jr.'s casket, the President could not stop staring at his face and caressing his hair. As aides removed the casket after the White House funeral the following day, the President sobbed uncontrollably, yelling out to his wife, "They're taking our boy away." His remaining son, John, was startled, as he had never seen his father cry before. Later that month, Coolidge's face became flooded with tears during an interview with the journalist John Lambert. "He was not the President of the United States," the shaken Lambert later observed. "He was the father, overcome by grief and by love for his boy."

As time went on, the intensity of his grief did not change all that much, but the way he contained it did. As Senator James Watson recalled after Coolidge's death, "The President was exceedingly devoted to his son, Calvin. The death of that young man made a tremendous impression upon him, and in my judgment it changed the whole course of his conduct from that time on. He never maintained any sadness outwardly, for that would not comport with his Puritanical training. But that he suffered intensely all of the time was quite manifest to those who came into close contact with him." Although the emotional outbursts stopped, Coolidge would still often allude to how devastated he was by the loss. "When I look out the window," the President told many a White House visitor, "I always see my boy playing tennis on the court out there."

Fixating on the gut-wrenching event, Coolidge could never move past it. Instead he became emotionally frozen. According to the grief paradigm laid out by the late psychiatrist Elisabeth Kübler-Ross, those experiencing a loss typically go step-by-step through intense emotional states of denial, anger, and depression before eventually reaching acceptance. In this final phase, the person is still distressed by the loss, but has filed it away as something in the past and is once again fully engaged in the present. Coolidge's denial phase lasted quite a while. For months after the tragedy, he kept saying, "I just can't believe it has happened." And then he became mired in both anger and depression—phases that would evolve into permanent parts of his personality. The post-1924 Coolidge was often both ill-tempered and listless. As one Coolidge biographer noted, "Because of his obsession with his dead son, Calvin Coolidge became a different man and a different President...Instead of being engaged, he became indifferent." For the rest of his life, Coolidge would be saddled with a host of depressive symptoms, including a low energy level, a lack of interest in

daily activities, hypersomnia, digestive problems, and feelings of hope-
lessness and helplessness. Left untreated, his case of major depressive
disorder would turn him into such a shadow of his former self that
upon hearing the news of his death in 1933, the writer Dorothy Parker
was compelled to comment, "How could they tell?"

In contrast, his wife, Grace, though also shaken by their son's death,
had a much easier time achieving closure. The differences between
their reactions are marked. At Calvin Jr.'s burial in Vermont on July 10,
the President was stone-faced, while Grace dabbed her eyes, suggesting that she was more connected to the sadness of the moment. As she
described her emotional state that day to a friend later that summer:

> As we stood beside the grave the sun was shining, throwing long
> slanting shadows and the birds were singing their sleepy songs.
> Truly, it seemed to me God's acre. There was a prayer, a few pas-
> sages of Scripture and two hymns, one the Mercersburg hymn
> which I have seen Calvin sing with the other boys at school and
> I could seem to hear [and] see him then...I came away filled
> with a "peace which passeth understanding," comforted and full
> of courage.

Grace could already imagine a vibrant future without Calvin Jr.—
something that for her husband would never be possible. In May 1928,
when students at Philips Academy in Andover saluted the First Couple
by singing that same Mercersburg hymn, the President stood motion-
less, while his wife joined in. "From the first word to the last," the
Boston Post reported, "she sang it with the boys grouped so simply...
before her—boys of the age of her own Calvin Jr. when he died." Even
as his presidency was coming to an end, Coolidge still could not accept
that time would march on without his son. That same year, after looking out his limousine window and spotting a teenage girl who seemed
to have a mouth like his son's, he immediately asked his wife to find
out more about her.

In the case of the Coolidges, as opposed to the Pierces or the McKinleys, the husband rather than the wife was more debilitated by grief. And in contrast to both Jane Pierce and Ida McKinley, instead of adding to the President's burdens, Grace Coolidge lightened them. As one biographer concluded, she ranks as one of "the most gracious" First Ladies, adding, "The President often showed the world his sorrow. Mrs. Coolidge—never!" Moreover, Coolidge's pain often made him unpleasant to be around. "He never appeared to appreciate any efforts [the employees] put forth to serve him and kept them in a state of constant anxiety," reported Ike Hoover, the White House usher.

A key reason why Coolidge had so much trouble facing the death of Calvin Jr. head-on was that it triggered memories of other excruciating losses. In 1885, when Calvin was just twelve, his mother, Victoria, who had long been slowed by illness—probably consumption—suddenly died on her thirty-ninth birthday. "The greatest grief that can come to a boy came to me," he later wrote. "Life was never to seem the same again." Five years later, his only sister, Abbie, with whom he had been attending the Black River Academy, a Vermont prep school, suddenly died at fifteen. The cause was probably an untreated case of appendicitis. "It is lonesome here without Abbie," the boy wrote that April to his father.

Calvin Jr's death also brought up intense feelings of guilt, which Coolidge was never able to shake off. Sensing the discrepancy between the power of his office and his powerlessness during that excruciating July Fourth weekend, the President experienced a keen sense of failure. "In his suffering," Coolidge later lamented in his autobiography, "he was asking me to make him well. I could not...I do not know why such a price was exacted for occupying the White House."

After his death, the affable and charming Calvin Jr., who embodied the best characteristics of each parent—his mother's engaging manner, and his father's reserve and dry humor—was lionized as a national hero. To feed the public's adulation, newspapers churned out a slew of feature stories about the fun-loving but industrious boy. The oft-repeated anecdotes highlighted his numerous virtues, including his sincerity and modesty. After his father became President in August 1923, Calvin Jr. kept reporting to his forty-cents-an-hour summer job at a tobacco field, as if nothing had happened. When a coworker noted that he would not continue to toil if his father became President, the boy quipped, "If my father was your father, you would." That month, Calvin Jr. also expressed discomfort with his new title. "I think you are mistaken," he wrote in a letter to a young friend that was widely reprinted, "in calling me the first boy of the land since I have done nothing. It is my father who is President. Rather the first boy of the land would be some boy who had distinguished himself through his own actions." In the fall of 1925, the proud but notoriously frugal father paid $350—roughly $5,000 today—for a private printing of a book containing all these newspaper clippings.

The nation's love affair with Calvin Jr. lasted throughout Coolidge's presidency and beyond. In early 1926, the President was asked to intercede in a dispute between neighboring Boy Scout troops from Joliet, Illinois, which both sought to name themselves after his son, a devoted Scout. (Coolidge refused.) That year, a portrait of Calvin Jr. also emerged as the most popular picture at the 121st annual exhibition held by the Pennsylvania Academy of Fine Arts, not because of the artist's abilities, but because of "its human appeal." A few months after the Coolidges left Washington, *Good Housekeeping* printed a poem about Calvin, which Grace had been inspired to write to commemorate the fifth anniversary of his death:

You, my son,
Have shown me God
Your kiss upon my cheek
Has made me feel the gentle touch
Of Him who leads us on.

Her poem, which elicited an enthusiastic response from readers across the nation, was republished many times. The sterling character of the son, who possessed some political skills that the shy and aloof "Silent Cal" could only dream about, would redound to the high esteem in which the country held the father.

———

Until the onset of his debilitating depression at the age of fifty-two, Coolidge had largely been an absentee dad. Before his move to Washington, he boarded at the Adams House Hotel near the State House in Boston, while his boys lived with Grace at the family's home at 21 Massasoit Street in Northampton. He saw them only during weekends and vacations. And as he moved up the political ladder—going from state representative, to state senator, lieutenant governor, and finally, governor—he became more and more preoccupied. In March 1919, two months after Coolidge became Governor, Calvin Jr. wrote of his hope that "mother will let me take violin lessons"—a remark that underlines how uninvolved he was in their daily lives. In that letter, Calvin Jr. enclosed his report card, which he asked his father to sign, adding in a postscript, "Please...send it back right away and try not to lose it."

While Coolidge was stern, he was not unloving—though like most Vermonters of his era, he rarely displayed much affection. As John Coolidge told an interviewer in 1996, "We were expected to behave, of course, and when we didn't, he told us about it." Coolidge never spanked his boys, but he could be quite controlling. He insisted that they wear suspenders rather than belts and told them when to wear their rain gear.

However, in his own aloof way, he did make an effort to connect. As one of Coolidge's college friends, who used to visit the family in Northampton in the 1910s, observed, "Mr. Coolidge is the kind of a father who has the absolute respect of his sons, but he does not easily become their playmate; he occasionally reads to them, takes them on walks, has even gone skating and fishing through the ice with them." On their visits to Boston, Coolidge enjoyed taking Calvin and John to shows at the Colonial Theatre and playing family board games such as Parcheesi and Authors (another popular Parker Brothers creation). When Coolidge became Vice President, he transferred his boys from the Northampton Public School system to Mercersburg Academy, which is located about one hundred miles northwest of the capital. Since he was used to living apart from them, this shift had a much bigger impact on his wife. "The hardest thing for me in going to Washington," Grace later wrote to a friend, "was seeing less of my boys." For both John and Calvin Jr., the bond with Grace was much more critical to their development than the one with their father.

After Calvin Jr. died, Coolidge became a different kind of father to John, who enrolled in his alma mater, Amherst College, in the fall of 1924. Blinded by his despair, the strict but measured disciplinarian morphed into an acerbic nag. In high school, John had performed well academically. Ranking tenth in his high school class, he had been selected to give an honorary address at his Mercersburg graduation—a ceremony attended by his mother but not his father. But partly because of his own distress over his brother's death, John had trouble focusing on his college courses and failed freshman French. As John joked with his college friends, he belonged to the exclusive "Omega Phi Beta Flunk Fraternity" (I made a try, but I flunked).

While Coolidge meant to be helpful, he began unleashing a torrent of harsh recriminations. Disappointed with his son's progress in English—a subject in which he had excelled at Mercersburg—the President let it rip. "It is my recollection," Coolidge wrote John on May 5, 1925, "that you have been taking English practically all your life. I suppose you have learned something out of it, though I cannot see in your writing or your conversation that you are better than I was who have had very little under that name." By early August, the frustrated Coolidge threatened to stop paying for college unless John worked harder. "You had better remember," he stressed on August 10, "that the world is full of people that almost succeed. The trouble is they won't work. Many men are almost President. But only twenty-nine have been chosen. I hope you will not be an 'almost' man." In the summer after his sophomore year, John agreed to take some make-up classes at the University of Vermont. Though the son worked diligently, the father was not easily satisfied. In late July, the President dashed off a missive, insisting that John "get up early in the morning and go to work about 5 o'clock."

During John's junior year, the tension between father and son continued to escalate. That September, Coolidge expressed deep concern about the laziness of John and his entire generation. To find out "what kind of Americans they are," the President ordered his Secret Service agent, Edmund Starling, to go to Amherst to live with his son and shadow him. "John was embarrassed and so was I," Starling later recalled. "He was a thoroughly decent chap...and decided to make the best of it." Returning to Washington with John for Christmas, Starling made a "plea for deliverance," and Coolidge finally relented.

But the President would continue to spy on John by requiring Ira Smith, the White House Chief of Mails, to send him all letters addressed to his son. Sympathizing with John's pique, Smith agreed to make an exception for one correspondent, Florence Trumbull, the daughter of Connecticut's Governor, whom John would marry a few months after his father left the presidency. Coolidge's unreasonableness was clear to everyone but himself. As his backer, Frank Stearns, put it, the President is "very severe on John and bears down on him almost unrelentingly." Likewise, Grace complained to Dr. Boone that her husband "does not understand [John] and makes no attempt to do so...[and] reprimands him almost constantly so that John does not desire to be with his father."

For John, the White House felt like a prison. Coolidge seemed to find fault with just about everything he did. When John asked for money to replace his raggedy tuxedo, his father responded with an emphatic no. Going around the President, John acquired a new tuxedo by trading in his old one. Once he learned what John had done, Coolidge became furious, claiming that the old jacket was good enough for a college boy. And the next night, when John asked to join some young friends for a dinner at the Wardman Park Hotel, a bitter Coolidge struck back, saying, "John, you dine tonight with the President of the United States." Such incidents led the ninety-year-old John to describe his father as "very, very strict." Coolidge also did not attend John's Amherst graduation, claiming that as the sitting President, he would draw too much attention. But throughout John's college years, the President seemed to be incapable of giving John the kind of attention he deserved.

Coolidge's persistent criticism of John for a lack of industriousness may have helped him ward off some of the guilt caused by his own dwindling energy level. After Calvin Jr.'s death, the President's schedule changed drastically. By the second half of 1924, when Coolidge observed that "young men are naturally lazy and require constant prodding to keep them up to a proper standard," he himself was averaging eleven hours of sleep a night, three hours more than in the first year of his presidency. In addition, Coolidge began taking a post-lunch nap, which could last as long as four hours. "He slept more than any other President, whether by day or night," noted *Baltimore Sun* columnist H. L. Mencken, who expressed astonishment at Coolidge's "great gift...for self-induced narcolepsy." The once vibrant President now tended to work just four and a half hours a day. This pattern of behavior constituted a sharp break in his daily routine. In the previous three decades, Coolidge had established a reputation for being a workaholic. As an undergraduate at Amherst, he had put in long hours on his courses, and often remained on campus during vacations to pursue his studies. In Massachusetts, he had been known as a "working Governor if there ever was one." And during his first year in the White House, the diligent President often spent Sundays at his desk.

For Coolidge, as for McKinley, his family's tragedy would also change how he ran for the presidency. In his autobiography, Coolidge claimed that his "participation [in the 1924 campaign] was delayed by the death of my son, Calvin." But the truth of the matter was that he hardly campaigned at all. After returning to Washington from New England, where he and his wife spent the summer of 1924, Coolidge followed the same script as McKinley in the 1900 race. Choosing to remain mostly in Washington, he passed on to his vice presidential candidate, Charles Dawes, the task of traveling around the country. Like McKinley's deputy, Teddy Roosevelt, Dawes would log fifteen thousand miles and give 108 speeches. Explaining the rationale for the strategy in early September to the Washington press corps, William Butler, the Chairman of the Republican National Committee, stated: "There is a tremendous pressure being brought to bear from all parts of the country to have [the President] speak outside, but it is a physical impossibility. I have been amazed by the extraordinary strain the daily work of the White House imposed upon the President." In fact, family matters were draining much more of Coolidge's energy than any affairs of state. But even though the President made only a handful of campaign speeches that fall, he won by a landslide, capturing 54 percent of the popular vote.

To illustrate the extent of Coolidge's depression after Calvin Jr.'s death, consider the President's behavior on March 4, 1925. "It was a most unusual inauguration day, quite different from anything that had gone before," recalled usher Ike Hoover, who had begun working in the White House in 1909. "The occasion had always been looked upon as one for celebration. Certainly there was nothing of the kind this time." Like Jane Pierce and Ida McKinley, a sad Coolidge dampened the mood in his Pennsylvania Avenue residence. Despite the day's "Coolidge weather"—a term then in vogue, which referred to sunny skies—the President showed "no emotion...and was silent, apparently little impressed with the solemnity of the ceremony," according to Secret Service men who accompanied him on his morning walk. At eight, he sat down to breakfast with his family and a few guests. In contrast to the dour President, his father, John Coolidge, and his mother-in-law, Lemira Goodhue, "chatted and seemed to be the only persons...who were fully enjoying the occasion," as one reporter noted. As he was about to get up from the table, Coolidge finally spoke a few words, asking why John was late in arriving from Amherst. At Coolidge's insistence, his son was not allowed to bring a friend, nor was he able to soak in the festivities, as he was told to head back to college early that evening. At noon, Coolidge took the oath of office on the steps of the Capitol and proceeded to give a forty-one-minute speech. As he reviewed the five thousand military men who marched in the parade, the President, reported the New York Times, "was solemn and undemonstrative." As soon as he arrived back at the White House, Coolidge disappeared into his bedroom in order to squeeze in a fifty-minute nap. That evening, he briefly attended a dinner hosted by a special delegation from Massachusetts before going to bed at 9:45. If the President had had his druthers, he would have avoided all social events, concluded Ike Hoover in his assessment of "the inauguration that fell flat." "It was remarked by those who knew," Coolidge's staffer wrote only half-jokingly, "that he would have liked to walk to the Capitol, take the oath of office, and return to the White House for his nap."

During his second term, Coolidge increasingly tailored his job description to match his lethargic mood. While this pro-business Republican had long warned against the perils of excessive government intervention, after his son's death, his position became extreme. "Inactivity is a political philosophy and a party program with Mr. Coolidge," wrote the prominent Washington journalist Walter Lippmann in 1926. Like his shattered and disoriented predecessor, Franklin Pierce, the post-1924 Coolidge rarely asserted himself as a leader, even with his own cabinet. "The way I transact the Cabinet business," he noted in 1927, "is to leave to the head of each Department the conduct of his own business." The President who famously noted that "the business of America is business" also held the view that the business of the federal government was often not his business.

Likewise, Coolidge now believed that the President should strive to be invisible. In the spring of 1925, after Congress went on a long recess, he stated in a press conference, "I would like it if the country could think as little as possible about the Government...so far as I can tell, there won't be any very large governmental matters projected by the Executive." It was as if, noted one biographer, the ship of state had "no functioning captain." According to presidential scholar James David Barber, Coolidge "was a loner who endured in order to serve, while the nation drifted." Fortunately, "Coolidge prosperity" reigned during his years in office, and his do-nothing administration would not do any harm to the vast majority of Americans—at least not in the short run. Alluding to the rising wages and stock prices of the Roaring Twenties, Lippmann concluded that Coolidge's policies suited "the mood and certain of the needs of the country admirably."

Coolidge's relationship with Congress also changed abruptly. Despite the success of his first annual message delivered in the Capitol in December 1923, in subsequent years, the lethargic President insisted that a House clerk read his words to Congress. (This practice became the new normal until President Eisenhower revived the in-person State of the Union address in February 1953.) And instead of trying to influence legislation, Coolidge was now content to be a bystander. "What Congress wants to do for the remainder of the session," the President noted in early 1926, "[is] of course...very largely for them to determine...The Congress ought to be left with a pretty free hand to make its own determination and reach its own decisions." While many Republican Presidents have sought to step out of the way so that "the invisible hand" of the marketplace could work its magic, few have so readily ceded power over the government to Congress. And this minimalist President also was convinced that Congress should not do too much, either. Analyzing the President's message to Congress delivered in December 1926, a *Boston Globe* editorial called Coolidge "a quietist" bent on "counsels of negation." His chief policy recommendation that year was that Congress should "avoid all commitments except of the most pressing nature."

In the last couple of years of his presidency, Coolidge's most decisive actions often involved his persistent refusal to take any action. "In a great day of Yes-men, Calvin Coolidge was a great No-man," quipped one newspaper editor. While a few biographers equate this stance with strength, it often reflected indifference. Take the case of the Great Mississippi Flood—a natural disaster with eerie parallels to 2005's Hurricane Katrina—where his unresponsiveness would have devastating consequences. On April 15, 1927, parts of Mississippi were pelted by up to fifteen inches of rain. Six days later, the levees at Mounds Landing, located twelve miles from Greenville, broke. By the twenty-second, Greenville was flooded by ten feet of water. That morning, Coolidge appointed his Secretary of Commerce, Herbert Hoover, as chairman of a special cabinet committee charged with addressing the flood emergency, which would eventually kill thousands of Americans and uproot nearly a million people from their homes. But after handing off the problem to this capable and industrious technocrat, who spent the next couple of months traveling around the affected states, Coolidge himself did practically nothing. Despite repeated pleas from eight Senators and four Governors of southern states to make a personal visit to help publicize the Red Cross relief campaign, the President refused to leave Washington. That April, he even turned down the request for a telegram from columnist and performer Will Rogers, who had hoped to read a word from the President at his fund-raiser for victims. While Hoover quickly raised some private funds, his credit program could dole out only about $20 per person.

In May, leading Congressmen from both parties urged the President to call a special session to put together a federal aid package. Once again, Coolidge remained unmoved. Though a few newspapers supported the President, most expressed outrage. In a blistering editorial, the *Paducah (KY) News-Democrat* declared: "It's hardly possible that this private credit arrangement will be sufficient to put the refugee population of 700,000 back at work...Either [President Coolidge] has the coldest heart in America or the dullest imagination, and we are about ready to believe he has both." In accounting for Coolidge's insensitivity to the scope of the problem, John Barry, author of *Rising*

Tide, the definitive account of the flood, emphasizes how the President became "more withdrawn [than usual] after his teenaged son died in agony."

Before his son's death, the morally upright and conscientious Coolidge would have been incapable of such a lack of concern for victims of a natural disaster. A month into his presidency, he provided a timely response to the Great Kanto Earthquake, which struck Japan on September 1, 1923, and went on to claim 140,000 lives. In this instance, rather than ignoring pleas for help, Coolidge was an energetic first responder. The next morning, the new President fired off a cable to the Japanese Emperor. "At the moment," Coolidge wrote in his missive of support, which turned out to be the first to arrive from any foreign leader, "when the news of the great disaster which has befallen the people of Japan is being received, I am moved to offer you in my own name and that of the American people the most heartfelt sympathy and to express to your majesty my sincere desire to be of any possible assistance in alleviating the terrible suffering to your people." And the famously budget-conscious Coolidge did not hesitate to put his money where his mouth was. He also ordered Adm. Edwin Anderson, the commander of America's Asiatic squadron, to dispatch several vessels then stationed in China to Yokohama, Japan's second largest city, which had "become a vast plain of fire," as an American visitor observed. American naval ships, which ended up arriving before their Japanese counterparts, were soon providing a wide range of emergency supplies, including gasoline, rice, and canned roast beef. Coolidge also morphed into the fund-raiser in chief. On September 3, he issued a proclamation to the American people, urging them to supplement his federal spending by making generous contributions to the American Red Cross. Buoyed by the President's persistence, this fund-raising drive would quickly result in $12 million of aid.

But after the middle of 1924, Coolidge became disengaged from foreign affairs. When asked for his input on an important national security matter by acting Secretary of State Joseph Grew in 1925, Coolidge stated, "I don't know anything about this. You do…and you're in charge. You settle the problem and I'll back you up." Coolidge no longer was willing to put up much of a fight to achieve his diplomatic goals. In his December 1923 State of the Union address, he had advocated membership in the World Court—a position also included in the platforms of both major parties during the 1924 campaign. Throughout 1925, the President continued to allude to this idea, which was supported by 83 percent of America's newspapers, in major speeches such as his inaugural address.

In January 1926, the Senate decided by a vote of 76 to 17 to join the World Court, subject to five reservations. A key objection was that the United States should have the right to veto advisory opinion, which was held by all the countries belonging to the League of Nations. However, for most of 1926, Coolidge refused to do just about anything but sit back and wait for the forty-eight member nations to agree to all five reservations. He saw the Senate's position as set in stone and instead directed all his pique toward the member nations, whose questions he would not even deign to answer. He also wanted no part of a conference proposed by the League of Nations to discuss the matter. On Armistice Day that year, in an outdoor speech before 175,000 in Kansas City, Coolidge extinguished any lingering hope for U.S. membership by reiterating that he did not "intend to ask the Senate to modify its position." In an editorial a few days later, the *New York Times* saw the President's words as a sign that "he has retreated and…lost heart," arguing that Coolidge "has incontinently abandoned what he was supposed to hold dear." The paper also accused him of passing the buck to "the friends and champions of an International Court of Justice" who would need to pursue their campaign under "a different banner and new leadership." Without Coolidge's support, this opportunity for international cooperation dissolved into irrelevance until it was revived after World War II.

During his second term, the debilitated Coolidge also tended not to think too much about trouble spots in the world such as Mexico and

China. In late 1924, Plutarco Calles took over as President of Mexico, and this populist leader soon began threatening to seize property from U.S. oil companies. By early 1927, the two countries were on the brink of war. For Coolidge, the notion that he should tackle the crisis himself was unthinkable. "I should doubt very much," he said that January, "if it would be at all practicable for the President of the United States to go into conference with the President of Mexico."

To his credit, Coolidge often chose wise advisors, and Dwight Morrow, his Amherst College classmate, whom the President appointed Ambassador to Mexico that fall and to whom he gave a free hand, turned out to be a superlative negotiator. After receiving Coolidge's simple directive on his first day in Mexico City—"Keep us out of war"—Morrow figured out just what to do to protect American interests without antagonizing Mexico's leaders. Coolidge also benefited from the diplomatic skill of his Secretary of State, Frank Kellogg, who managed to defuse tensions with China. In the summer of 1928, Chinese nationalists unified the country and created a new government. As Kellogg began considering the various policy options, he was startled to learn that the President had little interest in talking to him. Coolidge expected his Secretary of State to take charge. "I don't know just what the State Department is planning as to a recognition of the Chinese Nationalist Government," a bewildered President, who had yet to master the central issues, conceded to the press on July 27. "I suppose that making the treaty with a government usually, if not necessarily, constitutes a recognition of that government. It might not, but generally does." Without consulting Coolidge, Kellogg ended up finalizing a new treaty with China, which recognized Chiang Kai-shek's regime and helped bring stability to the region. "If Calvin Coolidge was a lucky man," concluded a sympathetic biographer of his hands-off approach to international affairs, "his luck was best observed in the few foreign crises that confronted his Administration."

But the country suffered serious consequences when he failed to address numerous macroeconomic challenges in his last year in office.

Simply put, his untreated depression may well have helped to cause the Great Depression. In early January 1928, many Wall Street commentators became unnerved when they learned that brokers' loans were approaching $4 billion—about $1 billion more than a year earlier. But rather than expressing concern about a possible economic bubble, Coolidge reassured Wall Street investors, releasing a statement on January 7 that "the increase represents a natural expansion of business in the securities market and…nothing unfavorable." Upon hearing the President's comments, which would end up fueling the speculative boom, an alarmed Secretary of Commerce Herbert Hoover blurted out, "Did that man actually say that?"

The precise reasons for Coolidge's indifference to the emerging economic crisis are not clear. Perhaps he understood the scope of the problem but was unsure what to do about it. According to his Secret Service agent, Edmund Starling, Coolidge saw "economic disaster ahead." Another possibility is that the lackadaisical President simply lacked the energy to familiarize himself with the ABCs of macroeconomics. That April, Coolidge declared, "No information has come to me concerning the increase in rediscount rates, except that which I have seen in the press. That is a matter entirely for the Federal Reserve Board, a matter that I wouldn't happen to know anything about." This stunning acknowledgment later prompted even a couple of his fans—the editors of a volume devoted to his press conferences—to assert the obvious: "The above statement hardly reflects well on his presidential leadership in economic affairs." The Pulitzer Prize–winning journalist William Allen White, author of the first major Coolidge biography, argues that his ignorance of the facts set the worldwide economic collapse in motion, noting that the President was "basically uninformed about either the source or the direction of the great tides that were washing around him."

By early 1928, Coolidge was already a lame duck. Several months earlier, on August 2, 1927, the eve of the fourth anniversary of his first inauguration, he had startled most Americans, including his wife, by announcing that he would not seek a third term. On that drizzly morning, Coolidge, who was vacationing in South Dakota, drove from the game lodge where he stayed for seven weeks that summer to Rapid City High School, the site of his temporary office. At about noon, the laconic President called a press conference in the mathematics classroom where he hand-delivered to reporters folded slips of paper, on which appeared a twelve-word typed statement: "I do not choose to run for President in nineteen twenty-eight." Rather than offering an explanation or answering any questions, Coolidge immediately hopped into his limousine and returned to his residence for lunch and a nap.

In his autobiography, published a year later, he listed several vague reasons such as concern about the "danger of impairment" of his wife's strength before concluding, "My election seemed assured. Nevertheless, I felt it was not best for the country that I should succeed myself." But most administration insiders such as Edmund Starling were convinced that his unresolved grief forced his hand. "The glory of it [the presidency]," wrote his Secret Service agent, "had gone with Calvin's death." In accounting for Coolidge's unexpected withdrawal from a race that he could have easily won, William Allen White also alluded to "the dust and ashes of his fame when he thought of the dead boy and his grave on the Vermont hillside." After the Republican Convention in Kansas City the following summer, the President lost all interest in politics. That fall, the still emotionally numb Coolidge did not do any campaigning for Herbert Hoover. "We who are in a position to observe," reported Coolidge's aide, Ike Hoover, of the mood in the White House in the weeks before the November election, "are convinced that the President would not shed a tear if Mr. Hoover were defeated."

After his retirement, Coolidge moved back to Northampton. Besides his autobiography, he focused on a couple of other writing projects such as a short daily column for the McClure syndicate, for which he was paid handsomely. Keeping a regular but light schedule, he was driven twice a day from his home to his old law office so that he could squeeze in a postlunch nap every afternoon. On the days that he napped until four o'clock, his afternoon shift lasted just fifteen minutes. After finishing Amherst College in the summer of 1928, John took a job as a clerk at the New Haven Railroad that paid just $28 a week. The following fall, he married Florence Trumbull, and the couple settled in a modest apartment on Fountain Street in New Haven. Though Coolidge was still often downcast and lethargic, he became much more sympathetic to his son's concerns. Realizing that the economic collapse was a source of angst to the entire next generation, he tried to offer support and encouragement. "You looked so badly when you were here that I feel worried about you," he wrote to John in April 1932. "If anything is worrying you, you should write me or come to tell me about it. Do not give any thought to your investments. They may come out all right…Get outdoors all you can and walk."

On January 5, 1933, Coolidge died of a heart attack. He was just sixty. About nine months later, John and Florence had their first child, a girl whom they named Cynthia so that her initials would be C.C. like her grandfather's. In 1939, they had another daughter named Lydia. John and Florence remained happily married until her death in 1998; he died two years later at the age of ninety-three. Though John was always bothered by how Coolidge had picked on him during the White House years, as time marched on, he reconnected with warmer feelings toward his father. After his mother's death in 1957, he became increasingly involved in the reconstruction and preservation of the family's homestead in Plymouth Notch, Vermont. Shy and taciturn like his father, John enjoyed telling visitors to the historic site stories about the Coolidges without ever identifying himself.

The Nurturers

"When Is My Daddy Coming?"

You mustn't get agitated when your old dad calls you his baby, because he always will think of you as just that—no matter how old or how big you may get. When you'd cry at night with that awful pain, he'd walk you and wish he could have it for you. When that little pump of yours insisted on going 120 a minute when 70 would have been enough, he got a lot of grey hairs. And now—what a daughter he has! It is worth twice all the trouble and ten times the grey hairs.

Harry Truman to Margaret Truman, 1941

The year was 1878. It was a few days before Easter and a young boy spotted President Rutherford B. Hayes, who had been in office just a year, as he was taking his daily walk near the Executive Mansion.

"Say! Say! Are you going to let us roll eggs in your yard?" the child blurted out.

"I'll have to see about that," the startled President replied.

As Hayes well knew, Easter egg rolls, which were developed by the Scots, who used to roll oatcakes down hills to mark the spring holiday, are an inherently messy affair. After all, the festivities require the smashing and crashing of all the colorful hard-boiled entries.

A relative newcomer to Washington—his only previous stint in the nation's capital had been a single term in Congress a decade earlier—the former three-term Ohio Governor carefully looked into the matter. From his aides, he learned that at the conclusion of the Civil War, Washington,

DC's children began rolling their eggs on the terraces surrounding the Capitol Building every year on the Monday after Easter. As one local paper put it in 1872, "Girls and boys, black and white, big and little, darted in and out of every nook and cranny, romping, with noisy glee, and cracked Easter eggs, and munched their lunches in the Rotunda, littering the floor with debris in utter disregard of the assembled wisdom and majesty in either wing of the building." In the spring of 1876, a few weeks after the egg rollers again trampled on the Capitol's west lawn, Congress pushed back. "That it shall be the duty of the Capitol police," ran the new law signed by President Grant on April 29, 1876, "hereafter to prevent any portion of the Capitol grounds and terraces from being used as play-grounds or otherwise, so far as may be necessary to protect the public property, turf and grass from destruction or injury." The following year, local children were forced to take a hiatus on account of rain. It was now unclear whether Washington's annual event had a home or a future.

After some careful consideration, Hayes "good-humoredly instructed the officer in charge of the grounds to make no objection if the children came on Monday with their eggs," as the New York Evening Post reported. The new President had no qualms about authorizing the use of federal resources to enable the capital's children to frolic worry-free in his backyard. In fact, the nurturing Hayes saw it as his duty to protect their right to celebrate the holiday.

On Monday morning, April 22, 1878, two children walked onto the south lawn of the Executive Mansion. Relieved that the coast was clear, they signaled to a group of boys standing just outside the gates to follow suit. Soon the grounds were covered with throngs of small visitors, who played in the shrubs and rolled their eggs on the terraces behind the people's house.

Each youngster brought between half a dozen to a dozen eggs, most of which were beautifully painted. Some were half pink and half green, with a band of gilt between; others had bright colors only on the ends. The sizes ranged from baby "something" eggs to large goose eggs. And after the rolling of the eggs came "the rolling down hill of *themselves* by the children," as one observer noted. The hills were "alive with heels in the air, and children that were bashful...[found] themselves rolling as freely as the most confident...It was one of the happiest days for children that I ever witnessed, not boisterous in the least, just one constant hum."

The following April, on the Saturday before Easter, another young boy asked the strolling President, "Are you a-going to let us roll eggs in your yard this year?" This time, Hayes immediately reassured his interlocutor that he had no objection. By 1880, the public schools were closed for the occasion and the city's children "seemed to have taken Executive clemency for granted," as the *New York Evening Post* put it, and self-confidently marched through the gates of the Executive Mansion.

Thus began Washington's much ballyhooed Annual Easter Egg Roll, which today is attended by more than thirty thousand visitors. Given the event's immense popularity, ever since 2009 the President has had to restrict admission to those who win tickets through an Internet lottery. As President Barack Obama noted when welcoming the crowd to its 136th incarnation in 2014, "This is the biggest event we have at the White House all year long."

A father of eight children, five of whom lived to maturity, President Hayes bonded easily with youngsters of all ages and stations, whom he "treated as reasonable beings," noted his definitive biographer, "with individual qualities and individual rights, deserving of recognition and respect." By the time of his inauguration, his three eldest sons, Birchard, Webb, and Rutherford, were already adults. But he and his wife, Lucy, were still raising their "second family," which consisted of Fanny, born in 1867, and Scott, born in 1871. (Between his two families came four years of distinguished military service during the Civil War.) Described by his wife as "always calm," the modest and gentle Hayes was a hands-on dad. He did not just preach or moralize, but repeatedly carved out time to both care for and comfort his children—responsibilities that men of his era rarely took on. On July 19, 1875, as he was running for Governor for the third time, he put the welfare of his youngest child, Scott, above everything else. "By reason of my child's sickness with scarlet fever requiring constant attention," he wrote an aide, "I may not be able to get a speech ready so as to send the press advance copies." Ten days later, he resumed his normal campaign activities, reporting, "The boy is still in bed but so improved that I feel it is proper to leave home."

And just a couple of months before welcoming the egg rollers onto his lawn, the President himself had helped chaperone Scott's "noisy, happy, party of thirty young folks" on the occasion of his son's seventh birthday. While Hayes and his three adult visitors—a general, a governor, and a bishop—talked "country and religion," they also "saw the blindman's bluff and other sports in the East Room and halls," as the President recorded in his diary.

Unlike preoccupied First Dads such as FDR and LBJ, who loved the spotlight and could not stop thinking about politics, Hayes was a homebody who enjoyed immersing himself in the daily lives of his children. As Col. William Crook, the Executive Clerk during his administration, put it, "Hayes preferred private to public life."

In May 1873, shortly after returning with his wife to their residence in Fremont at the end of his second term as Governor, the fifty-year-old lawyer wrote to his son Birchard, "We are very glad to get home again after so many years of vagabonding. I have not really felt the fixed home feeling since I went into the army twelve years ago. It was a pleasant life but as people grow older they wish to *settle*." Two years later, when friends and former aides encouraged him to move back to Columbus for a third term, which might propel him to the presidency, he initially balked. "The personal advantages you suggest," he wrote to a prominent Ohio journalist, "tend to repel me. The melancholy thing in our public life is the desire to get higher...But now I can't take the direction, and I will be ever much obliged if you will help me drop out of it as smoothly as possible."

During this two-year retirement from politics, Hayes was delighted to monitor all the micro-milestones in his daughter Fanny's development. He listened carefully to her every syllable. "Little Fanny has a new word, 'exquisite,'" he reported about the five-year-old in the spring of 1873. "Almost all good things are now 'exquisite' and 'exquisitely.' But she doesn't hang on to one word as she used to. She soon drops her favorite and picks up new ones." After hosting her sixth birthday party that September, which featured a hearty meal in the family garden shared with numerous girls her age, he observed with keen interest that his daughter "thinks there is no sense in having only one birthday a year. Two or three a week would be more rational in her view." A couple of months later, he was intrigued by the philosophical turn that her mental meanderings had taken. "Just now she is full of the spirit of inquiry," he wrote to his son Webb, then an undergraduate at Cornell, adding that she was pondering such deep questions as "the paternity of the Saviour, the origin of evil, eternal punishment and the like."

Doting on his only daughter came easily to Hayes. She was named after his beloved elder sister, Fanny, whom he described as "the confidante of all my life, the one I loved best." During his childhood, Hayes had received a double dose of maternal care—as both Fanny and his mother, Sophia, provided steady nurturing. Called a "posthumous boy" by an early biographer, Hayes was born in Delaware, Ohio, on October 4, 1822, a few months after his father died suddenly of a fever at the age of thirty-five. His mother's younger brother, Sardis Birchard, became a surrogate father, but this uncle rarely lived close by. A sickly infant, Rud was not expected to live long. When he was just eight months old, a neighbor told his mother, still overwhelmed by the loss of her husband, "It would be a mercy if the child would die." Though Rud soon recovered, at the age of one, he was still so frail that his uncle Sardis predicted that he would be an invalid for life. His mother, who had baptized the infant as a Presbyterian soon after her own conversion, did not think he would live to see his second birthday. In early 1825, when he was not yet three, his nine-year-old brother, Lorenzo, fell into a frozen millpond while ice-skating and drowned. His mother, again overwhelmed by grief, became overprotective.

Rud was in robust health by the age of five, but his mother refused to send him to public school until he was seven and would not let him play with other boys until he was nine. She also refused to let him do any manual labor, even cut wood for the fire. His confused neighbors considered the sheltered boy who never seemed to do "anything but good" as "timid as a girl." Like the mother of another future President—Ann Dunham, who gave the young Barack Obama English lessons during his early years in Indonesia—Sophia insisted on becoming her son's personal tutor. Using the schoolbooks of his dead brother Lorenzo, she taught him to read, write, and spell. Like Obama, who would also evolve into a nurturing parent, Rud would take his mother's lessons to heart and become an intellectual powerhouse. Coincidentally, Hayes and Obama are the only two Presidents to have graduated from Harvard Law School—the former in 1845, the latter in 1991. These two men with the close ties to their mothers also shared the same cordial temperament, which is averse to personal invective. Like "no-drama Obama," Hayes also managed to avoid emotional outbursts—no matter what the provocation.

For companionship in those early years, Hayes turned primarily to his sister, Fanny, and her female playmates. "Fanny [was]," Hayes later recalled, "my protector and nurse when I was a sickly feeble boy of three or four years old. She would lead me carefully about the garden and barn yard and on short visits to the nearest neighbors. She was loving and kind to me and very generous." According to one biographer, the vivacious Fanny rather than Sophia may even have been "psychologically his true 'mother.'" Brother and sister went to school together and were nearly inseparable until he went off to Kenyon College in 1838. Like his mother, Sophia, Fanny also played pedagogue, teaching him to appreciate both poetry and plays. From the lively and thoughtful Fanny, who had downed all of Shakespeare by the age of twelve, Hayes developed his love of literature. Fanny also encouraged Rud to be ambitious, insisting that he could become "somebody important." When Fanny died in July 1856 at the age of thirty-five, Hayes was deeply shaken. As he confided in a friend later that summer, "It did not seem as if I could bear it." He would continue to mourn her loss for the rest of his life.

Time and time again, Hayes would bestow upon others the same concern and affection that he had received from Sophia and Fanny back in Ohio. The beneficiaries of his nurturing would include not just his own children but the soldiers half his age, whom the forty-something commander led into battle during the Civil War. In May 1861, Hayes, "notwithstanding my unmilitary education and habits," enlisted in the Twenty-Third Ohio Volunteer Infantry Regiment and was appointed a Major. By the time he retired as a Brigadier General in June 1865, he had fought valiantly in some fifty skirmishes. He repeatedly distinguished himself by his calmness under fire. In his first major test at the Battle of South Mountain in 1862, Hayes continued to command his troops after he became faint when a musket ball smashed part of his arm below the elbow. But Hayes did more than just provide inspiring leadership. He also looked to "the comfort, the health, the honor and the morality of his men," observed the esteemed novelist William Dean Howells, "with literally the same studied care, the same enlightened vigilance as a father bestows upon his children." Off the battlefield, he displayed remarkable loyalty and empathy. A frequent visitor to hospitals, he would attend to the wounded, whom he would try to cheer up. For those soldiers who could no longer put pen to paper, he would serve as an amanuensis. To the dying, he promised that he would make sure that their last words reached their wives or mothers. "He shared his blanket," another early biographer wrote, "his last crust, his last penny, with the neediest of his men, and abstained from food when they had none."

As President, the warm Hayes made everyone he came into contact with feel cared about. Longtime presidential staffer Col. William Crook called him "one of the best-natured men who ever lived in the White House." As Crook noted, Hayes treated his clerks and secretaries as his "office family," which "did make one feel like a human being." Hayes was well aware that few politicians were capable of his degree of graciousness. A decade after his retirement, the nineteenth President, who died in 1893, observed that his Republican successor Benjamin

Harrison was "a good man and a good President, but with an unfortunate lack of tact...His coldness and indifference when meeting strangers is sometimes offensive." This nurturing dad was used to deferring to the needs of others. When the First Lady gave in to her penchant for entertaining countless guests from all walks of life, this President did not object. "Father had virtually no privacy," his son Rutherford recalled of Hayes's four years in office. "I have seen him retire to the bathroom, lock the door and prepare some important state papers."

While we may think that nurturing dads are purely a twenty-first-century phenomenon, they have been around for centuries. But it is true that until the last few decades, when women routinely assumed jobs outside the home, their ranks were relatively sparse. In the days when fathers ruled as the undisputed heads of America's households, they were not supposed to be caregivers—an expectation that was captured in our language. After all, the verb *father*, unlike its counterpart *mother*, has traditionally had just one meaning—"to procreate." To this day, *fathering* is rarely used to refer to the act of watching over or providing emotional support to a child. One reason why Rutherford B. Hayes emerged as a paradigm buster was that for him, to parent was to act like a mother. Never having known his own father, he ended up fathering just as he had been mothered—by his coparents, his mother, Sophia, and his elder sister, Fanny.

Barack Obama fits the same mold. He, too, spent little time with his own father, Barack Obama Sr., who abandoned the family soon after the future president's birth. While Harry Truman did grow up with a father—livestock farmer John Truman—the youngster felt more comfortable around his mother, Mary, who shared his interest in the arts and music. Explaining her deep bond with her son, who confided in her about his innermost concerns throughout his adult life, "Momma Truman" said shortly before her death at ninety-four in 1947, "I raised my children right." In both their families and their administrations, these three nurturing dads all sought to lead by being consistent and dependable. Unlike most men, who view morality strictly in terms of abstract principles, Hayes, Truman, and Obama emphasized the importance of "an ethics of care"—to use the term of the feminist psychologist Carol Gilligan. Stressing the interdependence of Americans upon one another, these three presidents advocated policies that addressed the broad social needs of all members of the American family. Inclusiveness reigned in their administrations.

A handful of other Presidents have also provided steady affection to their children, beginning with George Washington. But in contrast to Hayes, Truman, and Obama, the father of our country evolved into an exemplary parent not because of his mother, but in spite of her. Mary Ball Washington was self-absorbed and critical; and as an adolescent Washington, who had lost his father, Augustine, when he was just eleven, vowed to be just the opposite of her. In 1759, when Washington married Martha Dandridge, he became the stepfather to her two surviving children: the four-year-old John (Jacky) Parke Custis and the two-year-old Martha (Patsy) Parke Custis.

The emotionally controlled Washington sometimes came across as stiff and overly formal, but he was kind and generous to both children. One of the ways he connected with them was through music. He encouraged Patsy to study the spinet (a precursor to the harpsichord) and Jacky the violin. When Patsy began suffering from epilepsy—a disease that would kill her at seventeen—a concerned Washington tracked her fits in the margins of his diary. In an attempt to ease her distress, he treated her to extra gifts, including a tortoiseshell comb. Though Jacky showed little interest in his studies, the patient Washington continued to offer love and understanding—even when his nineteen-year-old stepson dropped out of King's College (today Columbia University) to marry the sixteen-year-old Eleanor Calvert in 1774. Jacky, who served as Washington's aide-de-camp during the war for independence, would always have fond feelings for his adoptive father. In June 1776, Jacky wrote to thank him for the "parental care which on all occasions you have shown me...Few have experienced such care and attention from real parents as I have done. He deserves best the name of the father who acts the part of one."

In November 1781, shortly after the British army surrendered at York-town, Jacky died of a fever at the age of twenty-six. His widow, Elea-nor, sent her two youngest children—two-year-old Eleanor Parke Custis and six-month-old George Washington Parke Custis—to Mount Ver-non, where they were raised by George and Martha Washington. While Washington did not officially adopt "Nelly" and "Washy," as he referred to his stepgrandchildren, he certainly doted on them. The vivacious and musically talented Nelly was deeply appreciative of Washington's "grate-ful affection as a parent to myself and family." Despite Washington's gen-tle prodding, Washy, like his father, Jacky, did not apply himself. "From his infancy, I have discovered an almost unconquerable indisposition to indolence," Washington was forced to concede to his stepgrandchild's tutor at Princeton, which the adolescent ended up leaving after just a year. Washington made generous provisions to all four of his stepgrand-children in his will, noting that "it has always been my intention, since my expectation of having issue has ceased, to consider the grandchildren of my wife in the same light as I do my own relations." In 1799, Nelly married Washington's nephew, Lawrence Lewis, with whom she had eight children. She died at her Virginia estate in 1852. George Washing-ton Parke Custis, who dabbled in playwriting, lived the life of a Virginia gentleman until his death in 1857; in 1831, his daughter, Mary, married Robert E. Lee, the future military leader of the Confederacy.

Like Washington, James Madison was also a kind and patient dad to John Payne Todd, the stepson whom he adopted at the age of two in 1794. That was when the forty-three-year-old Congressman mar-ried the boy's mother, the twenty-six-year-old Dolley Payne, who had recently lost both her husband and second child, William, to yellow fever. Whenever John Payne, who would struggle with alcoholism and a gambling addiction for most of his life, racked up huge debts, Mad-ison would simply pay them—no questions asked. In her book, *The*

Founders as Fathers, historian Lorri Glover characterizes Madison as a "supremely reasonable step-father" who provided "ever-steady counsel" to the wayward youth. As President, Madison appointed his stepson to the diplomatic corps, but John Payne continued to carouse and chase women and had to be recalled. A half-dozen years into his retirement, Madison even took out a mortgage on his Montpelier plantation to bail out John Payne, who was then languishing in a debtors' prison in Philadelphia.

Fellow Virginian James Monroe also nurtured his two girls, Eliza and Maria. "Mrs Monroe hath added a daughter to our society, who tho' noisy, contributes greatly to its amusement," wrote the excited young lawyer in announcing Eliza's birth to Thomas Jefferson in 1787. This devoted dad made every effort to avoid separations from his family; when he was elected a U.S. Senator in 1790, both his wife, Elizabeth, and Eliza moved to Philadelphia to be with him. They also accompanied Monroe to Paris four years later when he became Minister to France. A strong advocate of female education, Monroe sent Eliza to the best girls' school in Paris, the one run by Madame Campan, where her classmates included Napoleon's stepdaughter, Hortense de Beauharnais. Decades later, as his presidency was winding down, Monroe visited America's largest female academy in Nashville and made a big pitch for what was still a controversial idea. "The female presents," declared this proud father of two daughters, "capacities for improvement and has equal claims to it, with the other sex."

In 1808, Eliza married George Hay, a prominent Virginia lawyer, who had presented the state's case in the treason trial of Aaron Burr. Monroe would always remain close both to Eliza and to her little sister, Maria, who was born in 1804. During the War of 1812, when Monroe was serving as Secretary of State in Washington, he once rushed back to Eliza's home in Richmond after hearing from her husband that his anxious and depressed daughter was "actually moan[ing] over [his] absence." In 1820, Maria Hester Monroe became the first First Daughter to marry in the White House when she wed her first cousin,

Samuel Gouverneur, who had been serving as the President's private secretary.

Like Hayes and Obama, James Garfield never got to know his father, Abram, who died when he was just eighteen months old. Though his mother, Eliza, was poverty-stricken, she had a buoyant personality and kept Garfield and his two elder siblings entertained in the family's log cabin by singing songs and weaving tales of adventure. Mother and son remained close, and she would later live in the Executive Mansion. While Garfield was not always the best of husbands—during the Civil War, he broke the heart of his wife, Lucretia, by carrying on an affair with a *New York Times* reporter—he was, notes his major biographer, "the most tender and devoted of fathers" to his five children who reached maturity: Harry, James, Mary (Mollie), Irwin, and Abram. Unlike most Congressmen of his era, Garfield chose to take his wife and children with him to Washington, fearing that he would grow apart from them "in experience, culture and knowledge of the world."

Garfield ran the household as if it were a participatory democracy. When eight-year-old Irwin objected to the frustrated Congressman's suggestion that the family's new dog be named "Veto"—in a show of support to President Hayes, who felt compelled to nix key pieces of legislation to keep the Democrats in line—he quickly backed down. "You are quite right," Garfield told his son, "in your view of the way to name the dog. The whole family ought to be heard on the subject. Then we will hold a meeting [in which]...each man, woman and child [will] have a vote."

Gerald Ford also had little contact with his biological father, Leslie King. When he was just a couple of weeks old, his mother, Dorothy, left King, who had beaten her. The future President did, however, have a loving relationship with both his mother and her second husband, Gerald Ford, whom she married when he was two. Ford passed back that affection to his four children—Michael, Jack, Steven, and Susan. Though the Michigan Congressman was constantly on the road, he flew back to the family's Alexandria home every Sunday. In contrast to the preoccupied First Dads, Ford made up for all the long absences by being emotionally present. When his wife, Betty, criticized his daughter, Susan, whose inability to throw a softball precluded her from winning an athletic award given to several other neighborhood girls, this protective dad interjected, "Leave her alone." "From that day forward," Betty Ford later noted, "Susan gave him her unqualified adoration."

Ford urged his children to carve out their own identities. His job as a parent, as he defined it, was to give them "the courage to seek personal challenges and the capacity to make it on their own." Two days after Ford's inauguration, his eldest son, Michael, then a graduate student at the Gordon Conwell Theological Seminary near Boston, told the Associated Press that Richard Nixon should "make a total confession of what was his role in Watergate." When asked to comment, Ford, who would pardon Nixon a month later, responded as a caring dad, not as a politician. "All my children have spoken for themselves since they first learned to speak," the President said, "and not always with my advance approval. I expect that to continue."

———————

In early September 1870, Governor Hayes took a week off to accompany his eldest son, Birchard, to Ithaca, New York. The sixteen-year-old was about to begin his freshman year at Cornell University, then in just its third year of existence. During Hayes's years in Columbus, Birchard and his younger brother, Webb, remained in Fremont to attend high school, where they lived with their great-uncle, Sardis Birchard. But Hayes carefully supervised their education. Six months earlier, when Birchard had expressed an interest in attending Western Reserve College in Hudson (today Cleveland's Case Western Reserve University), Hayes wrote back, "You will have no objection from me if it is finally thought best by you and Uncle to go to that college. But I prefer you would not finally decide about it until I have a talk with you." After consulting with his father, Birchard chose Cornell, even though he lacked sufficient Latin and Greek to enter the classical course. Once in Ithaca, Hayes arranged for his son to substitute German and French for Greek and to make up Latin during the year. But this nurturing dad was not worried just about his son's academic adjustment. He also wanted to make sure that Birchard felt at home in his new surroundings. Writing his uncle Sardis from his son's dormitory on September 13, Hayes reported, "I am glad I came on many accounts...I got this beautifully located room for him...Three windows in front command the finest, noblest view in the region...All Birchie's teachers know him and will give him personal attention...Altogether I leave here feeling very comfortably about Birch."

The Hayes children would also repeatedly look to their father for emotional support rather than to their mother. Dubbed "Lemonade Lucy" by historians due to her advocacy on behalf of the temperance movement, Hayes's wife was not an unfeeling religious zealot, as she has sometimes been portrayed. (And it was actually the President—not the First Lady—who banned alcohol in the Executive Mansion.) But her warmth paled in comparison to her husband's. He was also a much better listener. When Birchard wrote home of "rushes" (fights) between freshmen and sophomores at Cornell, Lucy panicked, but Hayes calmly explained to her that their son was not enlisting in the army, though he added, "It is all right. Life is war." Birchard told his father exactly what he was thinking and feeling, writing early in his freshman year that he had "never studied so hard or laughed so much in [his] life." While Lucy urged Birchard to obey rules—to keep his teeth and nails clean and to blacken his shoes—Hayes did not neglect to emphasize the importance of having fun. At the beginning of his junior year, he encouraged Birchard, who had been obsessed with baseball since high school, to remain on the college's team: "Why can't you play baseball?...You can play if you wish all of your days...You need not borrow trouble as to your future...You are more likely than most men to have agreeable employment after you 'come out,' to use the phrase about young ladies."

Hayes's comforting words were just what Birchard needed. The Cornell of this era was quite competitive; to graduate, students needed to have a minimum grade point average of 3.5 (on a five-point scale). Out of his class of 230 students, the studious Birchard, who had a knack for statistics, was one of only 63 who graduated on time. And after a gap year in Ohio, Hayes's firstborn followed him to Harvard Law School. While Birchard enjoyed visiting his father at the Executive Mansion, he had little interest in politics. "I met none of the big diplomats and their contemporaries," he later recalled. "I did not care for that." In 1886, Birchard married Mary Sherman, with whom he had four children. A prominent tax attorney, he spent most of his life in Toledo, where he died in 1926.

Partly due to Hayes's steady guidance, his second child, Webb, also "overcame the proverbial handicap of being a President's son," as one journalist put it upon his death in 1934, to win distinction as an industrialist, a soldier, and a historian. After receiving Webb's first letter from Cornell, the emotionally attuned father replied, "It was a genuine freshman's letter. A page or two of rushes and the like and a few lines about studies. But that is what I want. Letters that show me just what you are thinking of and what you are enjoying." A few weeks later, Hayes wrote to stress the importance both of giving "solid and honest work to your studies" and of adhering to the virtues of "honesty, truthfulness and sincerity," but then apologized for "a little too much sermon!" During his freshman year, Webb struggled with his courses, particularly German and algebra. He evolved into a prankster, who used to enjoy startling home dwellers in small towns near Ithaca by "horning" at all hours of the night.

At the end of Webb's sophomore year, Hayes was forced to realize that in contrast to Birchard, this scion was not cut out for college. "Webb is not scholarly," he confided to his diary in August 1874. "He will not graduate. A special course is the most he will attempt." But rather than criticizing or browbeating Webb, Hayes continued to offer support and encouragement. "Both boys," he added, "are honest, faithful and affectionate. I am confident both will become respectable and reliable gentlemen." With Hayes's help, Webb switched to an agriculture track during his junior year at Cornell. While Webb then dropped out the following year, he got a chance to apply what he had learned when Hayes asked him to oversee the grove at the family's home in Fremont. During the 1876 Republican Convention in Cincinnati, Webb kept his father abreast of the goings-on with his frequent telegrams from the floor.

When Hayes became President, he hired the twenty-year-old Webb as his confidential secretary. The closely connected father and son worked side by side for the next four years. As opposed to President Eisenhower, who would bark at his son, John, when he served as a White House aide, Hayes was gentle with the young Webb, who also functioned as both a bodyguard—he carried a gun—and special assistant. When the President got flak from southerners for appointing the former abolitionist Frederick Douglass as the United States Marshal of the District of Columbia, he refused to back down. Instead, Hayes asked Webb to act as the official greeter at White House social functions—a duty typically served by the marshal.

After carrying out such delicate responsibilities with considerable aplomb, the self-confident Webb went into business in Ohio. In 1887, he cofounded the National Carbon Company, which later evolved into the multinational behemoth Union Carbide. For decades, Webb served as a company vice president. But it was in the military where Webb would make his biggest mark. The boy, who had been thrilled to spend a few months a year at his father's side during the Civil War would grow up to be the only American officer to do service in Cuba, Puerto Rico, the Philippines, and China. A major at the start of the Spanish American War, Webb fought on San Juan Hill with Theodore Roosevelt, to whom he bore a close physical resemblance. In 1912, the fifty-eight-year-old bachelor, who had been linked with numerous women since his Washington days, married Mary Miller, a Fremont native whom he had known since childhood. The couple had no children. Though he was over sixty when America joined the Allies in World War I, Webb did combat duty in both Southern France and North Africa. To honor his father, Webb erected the Rutherford B. Hayes Presidential Center at the family's former home in Fremont. The first of America's presidential manuscript libraries, it opened in 1916.

With his third son, Rutherford, the youngest member of his "first family," Hayes also adjusted his expectations to the boy's particular strengths and weaknesses. Concerned about Rud's frail health and poor eyesight, Hayes did not want to put too much pressure on him. "He is unfit for hard work or hard study," observed the concerned father of the bright adolescent in his diary. Hayes initially thought Rud should steer clear of "one of the great literary colleges." But while Hayes preferred that he attend the Ohio Agricultural and Mechanical College (today Ohio State University) in nearby Columbus, the sixteen-year-old boy chose the Michigan Agricultural College (today Michigan State University). On the morning of February 22, 1875, Hayes made the daylong trip to Lansing to deposit Rud in his freshman dormitory. Four days later, writing from Detroit where he was stuck in a snowstorm, Hayes sent Rud a $20 bill along with some decorating suggestions. "You should get a substantial carpet (perhaps rag is best), probably a few good new strong chairs...If you get an armchair, get two, so your chum [roommate] can have one. Deal generously with him as you do with yourself." While Hayes was pleased with his son's new living quarters, he did share his discomfort with the "two-in-a-bed-system." To fix the problem, he recommended that Rud purchase two lounge beds. Hayes hoped to visit again in the summer, but on June 3, as the Governor's race was heating up, he was forced to ask Rud to "excuse [his] neglect...This political business smashes my plans for the next four months."

In the fall of 1876, Rutherford transferred to Cornell. Once the youngster got settled, his father offered only one piece of advice. "The golden rule," Hayes wrote on September 27, "is the whole law and the prophet on the subject of intercourse with others." That December, though the Republican presidential nominee was fully immersed in the battle over the disputed election, he still found the time to monitor carefully the developments in Rud's college life. "Write to us often," Hayes wrote on December 3. "Give full particulars of your teachers, friends, studies and amusements." After finishing Cornell, where he wrote a thesis on the history of systematic botany, the intellectually curious Rutherford did graduate work at the Boston Institute of Technology (today MIT). Sharing his father's love of books, he was a founder of the Ohio Library Association as well as a prime mover in the American Library Association. Rutherford eventually settled with his wife, Lucy Platt, and their three children in Asheville, North Carolina, where he became a wealthy real estate developer.

The two children of Hayes's second family, Fanny Rutherford and Scott Russell, spent their formative years in the Executive Mansion. On December 30, 1877, as Hayes celebrated his silver wedding anniversary with Lucy, both the ten-year-old Fanny and the seven-year-old Scott were christened in the Blue Room. A few years after leaving Washington, Fanny headed off to Miss Porter's for high school. Unlike the impulsive Nellie Grant, who left the Connecticut school after a couple of days, Fanny enjoyed her two years in prep school, where her classmates included two other First Daughters, Mollie Garfield and Nellie Arthur. Hayes was limited to lavishing affection on her during her school vacations. When the seventeen-year-old Fanny joined the Methodist Church of Fremont, the former President noted in his diary, "Dear girl! How I love her…she has many of the best traits of my wife and sister. She is a rare sunbeam in the house." After her mother's death in 1889, Fanny was her father's frequent companion. Partially deaf, his daughter vowed not to marry, as she feared passing on her condition to her children. But in 1897, she changed her mind and wedded Ens. Harry Smith, a childhood friend, with whom she would have a son, Dalton. The Spiegel Grove ceremony was attended by President McKinley and his wife, who had become fond of Fanny during her years in Washington. Unfortunately, Smith was not a good match—he had a bad temper—and she divorced him in 1919. Fanny died in 1950 at the age of eighty-two.

Like his elder brother Webb, Scott was not much of a student and left Cornell after just two years. Though Scott was unsure about what he wanted to do, Hayes remained patient and supportive. "Scott is trying his wings," the retired President wrote to a friend in the fall of 1891. "He left the home nest a few weeks ago; has spent time in Columbus, New York, Chicago, and Duluth. He likes Duluth best of all; is there now, and is inclined to settle there. Probably a temporary craze." Hayes was right, as Scott soon moved to Cincinnati, where he took up a position with the Thompson-Houston Electric Company, later General Electric. In an 1896 update on the Hayes family, which it called "still remarkable for the beautiful family life...so noticeable during the life of President and Mrs. Hayes," the *Chicago Record* described Scott as "a practical up-to-date man, with an interest in all the questions of the day." In 1912, he married Maude Anderson and settled in the Hudson River Valley, from where he commuted to his job at an air brake company in Manhattan. A decade later, he died of a brain tumor at the age of fifty-two.

It was the clumsiest handoff in the history of the Republic.

More than three months after the election and just two weeks before inauguration day, President-elect Rutherford Hayes was still not sure when or if he could ever take office. On February 23, 1877, Hayes, who remained in his perch as Governor of Ohio out of fear that critics would charge that he was leading a coup d'etat, wrote President Ulysses Grant from Columbus, "Sinister rumors from Washington leave us in doubt as to the final issue. In case of success," the harried leader added, temporarily forgetting how many days are in February, "I expect to be in Washington next Thurs. the 29th."

On November 7, 1876, the Democratic candidate, Samuel Tilden of New York, won 51 percent of the popular vote, as opposed to just 48 percent for Hayes. But while Tilden led Hayes in the electoral college by 184 to 165, twenty electoral votes in four states—Florida, Louisiana, South Carolina, and Oregon—were still in dispute. Even so, Hayes initially believed that he had lost and that his political career was over. The following day, the relieved father wrote to his son Rutherford at Cornell, "Your mother and I have not been disappointed in the result however much we would prefer it to have been otherwise...We escape a heavy responsibility... great anxiety and care and a world of obliging by the defeat." A month later, though his prospects looked more favorable, the happy family man still had ambivalent feelings about becoming President. "There are many reasons why success may be a calamity to us personally," he wrote to his son Rutherford. "Defeat will be in many ways preferable."

To resolve the impasse, Congress created a fifteen-man Electoral Commission. Upon learning on January 31 that the panel would be composed of eight Republicans and seven Democrats, Hayes wrote in his diary, "In Washington the bets are five to one that the next [President] will be Hayes...If the result is adverse, I shall be cheerful, quiet, and serene. If successful, may God give me grace to be firm and wise and just—clear in the great office—for the true interest of all the people of the United States!"

On February 27, the commission, voting along party lines, completed its work and concluded that all twenty outstanding electoral votes should go to Hayes. However, victory was still not his, because the Senate had yet to confirm the result. Tilden no longer had any hope of becoming President, but Democrats still figured that they could deny the prize to Hayes. The Speaker of the House, Democrat Samuel Randall of Pennsylvania, proposed delaying the count until after March 4, at which time Congress could appoint Secretary of State Hamilton Fish President and call for another election. Embittered supporters of the party, including editors of partisan newspapers, publicly endorsed the idea of assassination. Hayes had reason to fear these threats, as a bullet had recently whisked through a window of his Columbus home, interrupting the family during dinner. As February drew to a close, many Americans were beginning to ponder the unthinkable—an interregnum where chaos would run rampant. Just a decade after the end of the Civil War, the country was in danger of falling apart at the seams once again. It was up to Hayes to steady the ship of state.

Nearly a century and a half after assuming the presidency, Hayes barely registers in our collective memory. The definitive two-volume biography was published in 1914, and only a handful of monographs examining either his life or his career have appeared since then. In his 1935 short story, "The Four Lost Men," the writer Thomas Wolfe lumped our nineteenth President together with three other post-Reconstruction Republican Presidents who also served as Civil War generals, and dismissed them all as nonentities. "Garfield, Arthur, [Benjamin] Harrison, and Hayes," noted this towering figure in early twentieth-century fiction, "time of my father's time, blood of his blood, life of his life…they were the lost Americans: their gravely vacant and bewhiskered faces mixed, melted, swam together in the sea depths of a past intangible, immeasurable, and unknowable as the buried city of Persepolis…Which had the whiskers, which the burnsides: Which was which? Were they not lost?"

In the fall of 2000, when another hotly contested election involving disputed votes in Florida took weeks to resolve itself, Americans reflected back on the resolution of the 1876 race, but not on the man who had won it. Long buried has been how Hayes quietly distinguished himself by meeting head-on an immense challenge. This First Dad, who connected readily with his own children, helped reconnect the American people with one another. The series of sensitive microsteps Hayes took as he assumed power provided the much-needed reassurance that the Constitution could withstand the passions of the moment. However, in his eagerness for peace and reconciliation, Hayes ended up failing to rein in southern Democrats, who were hell-bent on reasserting their control over the recently freed slaves. Unfortunately, this lapse in judgment, which was rooted in his overly sunny view of human nature, would set back race relations for generations.

On February 28, 1877, Hayes announced his resignation as Ohio Governor. At four o'clock that afternoon, he held a reception in the rotunda of the Statehouse in Columbus. The ceremony began when 450 children, who resided at the state's asylum for the deaf and dumb, marched up to shake hands with Hayes and his wife, while 150 young patients from Ohio's asylum for the blind serenaded the crowd with songs. After the blind students received their handshakes, another five thousand children, including two hundred blacks, walked past Hayes, "though the hand-shaking for the most part had to be dispensed with," as the *New York Times* reported. Since his first term as Governor, Hayes had shown a deep commitment to the welfare of all the state's citizens, including the disabled, the orphaned, and the imprisoned. And by the end of his third term, by dint of his frequent visits to Ohio's asylums, he was personally acquainted with many of the blind and deaf students as well as their teachers.

At nine that evening, Hayes addressed the crowd from the stand of the House Speaker. Fully cognizant of his tentative hold on the presidency, the Governor first thanked his supporters and then declared, "As for myself and my family, we go, perhaps to return in a few days to occupy our accustomed place in this community; possibly we go to other scenes and duties not to meet you again."

At about noon on March 1, Hayes, accompanied by Lucy, the twenty-year-old Webb, and his two young children, Fanny and Scott, stepped into an open carriage at the Capitol. As the family traveled the half mile to the Columbus railroad station, they were escorted by a military band and thousands of local citizens. Having refused a palace car offered by a railroad executive, Hayes along with his family and about twenty friends settled into two additional cars set aside for their use on the regular one o'clock Pullman sleeper bound for Washington. When Hayes went to bed that night, he still was not officially the President-elect. But early the following morning, as the train made a brief stop for water in Marysville, Pennsylvania, the telegraph operator received word that at 4:10 A.M., the Senate had declared Hayes the winner. Eager to convey the news, the railroad manager knocked on the door of his stateroom. Once he saw Hayes, he read the telegram; when he did not get a response, he read it again in a louder tone. Holding his own emotions in check, the sensitive family man chose to protect his wife and children rather than celebrate. "I hear you," Hayes responded quietly. "Don't wake everyone in the car. Good night."

On Saturday evening the third, Hayes attended a state dinner hosted

by President Grant. Just before sitting down to eat, Hayes slinked off
into the Red Room to take the oath of office, which was administered
by Chief Justice Morrison Waite. Since the inauguration was not to be
held until Monday the fifth, President Grant wanted to make sure that
his term ended on schedule—at noon on Sunday the fourth. "I did not
altogether approve," wrote Hayes in his diary, "but acquiesced." For the
next half day, for the first and only time in its history, America would
have two co-Presidents.

At noon on the fifth, before an attentive and enthusiastic crowd of
thirty thousand "men, women and children of all ages, colors and conditions of life," as one observer put it, Hayes delivered his inaugural.
Stressing his devotion to national unity, he declared, "He serves his party
best who serves his country best." Half of the speech was devoted to his
plans to address tensions in the south, which were running high because
both South Carolina and Louisiana had two Governors; in the wake of
disputed elections, the Republicans and Democrats in each state had
inaugurated their own candidates. Avoiding any specific proposals, he
sketched some general principles. "Let me reassure my countrymen of
the Southern states," Hayes insisted, "that it is my earnest desire to regard
and promote their truest interests...and to put forward my best efforts in
behalf of a civil policy that will forever wipe out in our political affairs
the color line and the distinction between North and South, to the end
that we may not have a united North or a united South, but a united
country." A century and a quarter later, another nurturing dad would also
move the nation by articulating similar sentiments. In his speech before
the 2004 Democratic National Convention in Boston, which propelled
him into the presidency just four years later, Illinois Senate Candidate
Barack Obama criticized pundits for "slicing and dicing our country into
red states and blue states" before declaring, "We are one people, all of us
pledging allegiance to the stars and stripes, all of us defending the United
States of America." Like Hayes, Obama was also deeply committed to
uniting Americans with one another. But as President, Obama would be
forced to learn the same lesson as Hayes—that though he could often

bring peace and harmony to his family's living room, kumbaya moments rarely happen in the life of a nation.

On Wednesday, March 7, Hayes announced his cabinet selections. In contrast to Obama, Hayes would not borrow Lincoln's "Team of Rivals" approach. He sought to unite not his party, but the nation. Referring to his former rivals, Senator Roscoe Conkling of New York and Senator James Blaine of Maine, Hayes vowed not to "take either of the leading competitors for the presidential nomination." Hayes enraged Republican Party elder statesmen with several of his choices; the most objectionable was Democratic Senator David Key of Tennessee, a former Lieutenant Colonel in the Confederate Army, whom he named Postmaster General.

The following day, Webb Hayes, who was just beginning work as his father's private secretary, wrote in his diary, "The press of the country speak very favorably of the Inaugural and also of the proposed cabinet. The South is particularly pleased. Some southern papers have said 'Actions speak plainer than words' in referring to the Inaugural. The appointment of Senator Key meets this."

Hayes's bold gamble paid off. Letters from across the country began pouring into the offices of his foes in the Senate, urging them to support the President. By Saturday the tenth, all of his nominees were confirmed, either unanimously or with only two dissenting votes. As George William Curtis, the editor of Harper's Weekly, put it that month, "Here was a President who was more of a patriot than a partisan, who regarded public questions with the humane eye of statesmanship, more mindful of the general welfare than of party or personal advantage."

In mid-March, Hayes still needed to address the crisis facing both South Carolina and Louisiana. As he was well aware, unless he was willing to use the army, the Reconstructionist Republican Governors— Daniel Henry Chamberlain of South Carolina and Stephen Packard of Louisiana—would be forced out of office. By March 22, Hayes gave up, concluding that the President was not supposed to impose his will on any state, but instead endorse self-government. On April 3, he ordered the removal of all federal troops from South Carolina; a week later, on the day the army rolled out, the Democrat Wade Hampton took control of the state, where African-Americans comprised nearly 60 percent of the population. "I am pushing my view with practical results," Hayes reported to his son Rutherford that month. "There is some opposition...but I am confident...I can keep calm and serene." In mid-April, a discouraged Governor Packard handed over Louisiana to his Democratic counterpart, Francis Nicholls. On April 22, Hayes noted in his diary, "We have got through with the South Carolina and Louisiana [problems]. At any rate, the troops are ordered away, and I now hope for peace, and what is equally important, security and prosperity for the colored people. The result of my plans is to get from those States by their governors, legislatures, press, and people pledges that the Thirteenth, Fourteenth, and Fifteenth Amendments shall be faithfully observed; that the colored people shall have equal rights to labor, education, and the privileges of citizenship. I am confident this is a good work. Time will tell."

Hayes's confidence was misplaced. Despite their promises, southern states would deny blacks their basic constitutional rights for nearly a century. Former abolitionists such as William Lloyd Garrison were outraged with the President, declaring that he lacked the backbone to fight off "the incorrigible enemies of equal rights and legitimate government." But many northern Republicans felt that he had no choice but to paper over the deep tensions. Surprisingly, among historians, Hayes's biggest cheerleaders have been the archdefenders of the Confederacy. Denigrating as "fanatics" those who applaud "the idea of holding the States of the Lower South in subjection to African majorities," Hamilton J. Eckenrode, the former State historian of Virginia, rhapsodized in his celebratory 1930 Hayes biography that "the South in 1877 once more became definitely Anglo-Saxon is due to Rutherford B. Hayes and to no one else...he was the greatest Southerner of the day, even if he hailed from the north side of the Ohio River." But this eminently reasonable man would never be able to acknowledge the unreasonableness of the Democratic Governors who took over in Louisiana and South Carolina, and their ilk. In 1888, five years before his death, Hayes recorded in his diary a conversation with a friend, a former Civil War General, James McMillan. "The old troubles of 1876–7 in Louisiana were called up. I told him of the good faith of Governor Nicholls...[and] Hampton."

In the summer of 1877, Hayes was once again faced with the decision of whether to send in federal troops to preserve the peace. This conflict pitted neither Democrat against Republican nor white against black but capital against labor. Though the President again chose a moderate course, on this occasion, he did back up his position with a show of military might. On Monday, July 16, 1877, in response to a 10 percent wage cut, striking railroad workers disrupted the service of the Baltimore and Ohio Railroad in both Baltimore and Martinsburg, West Virginia. This standoff, which historians would eventually dub the Great Railroad Strike and which would eventually spread to a total of fourteen states, was under way. Even after one striker was killed in Martinsburg, the West Virginia militia was unable to get the freight trains moving again. On Tuesday the seventeenth, West Virginia Governor Henry Mathews asked the President to send in at least two hundred Marines to maintain "the supremacy of the law." Just as he would later do with that urchin who petitioned for the use of his lawn to roll eggs, Hayes promised the Governor that he would immediately look into the matter. After studying the facts, at 3:50 P.M. on July 18, Hayes ordered 312 men of the Second United States Artillery, who were based in and around Washington, to the scene. While the violence soon ceased in Martinsburg, it began erupting elsewhere. On Friday the twentieth, the Maryland militia killed ten men and boys who were interfering with train traffic near Cumberland. That weekend, terror reigned in Pittsburgh, where a mob caused $5 million in damage to railroad buildings, and twenty protesters as well as two members of the state militia died. Early the following week, Hayes sent troops to several other states, including Pennsylvania, Indiana, and Missouri.

By the end of July, the strike began to peter out. Hayes's firm leadership, which stressed the rule of law, managed to soothe rather than inflame all parties and may well have prevented a revolution. Though this Republican President had received big campaign contributions from the railroads, he was not unsympathetic to the concerns of workers. He wholeheartedly supported the right to strike, but he had no tolerance for agitators, who destroyed property or prevented others from working. In the end, federal troops got both the trains and the entire economy moving again by just showing up; in contrast to the soldiers belonging to the various state militias, they did not kill anyone. His judicious use of presidential authority broke new ground by nudging the federal government away from a laissez-faire policy toward labor disputes. "The strikes have been put down by force," Hayes wrote in his diary of August 5, "but now for the real remedy. Can't something [be] done by education of the strikers, by judicious control of the capitalists, by wise general policy to end or diminish the evil? The railroad strikers, as a rule, are good men, sober, intelligent, and industrious."

Though Hayes—who stepped aside after one term, as he had pledged early in his administration—would be unable to do much to address the evil of inequality, he never stopped thinking about the problem. Several years later, Hayes would tell a friend that he worried about "one tenth [of the population] owning everything." After the passage of the Interstate Commerce Law in 1887, Hayes became an avid proponent of regulation, arguing that "the Government should say to dangerous combinations, 'Thus far and no farther!'" Like TR, this Republican, who easily identified with the concerns of children, would also insist that it was the President's duty to help protect America's little guys from its big guys.

———

As he had emphasized in his inaugural, Hayes would devote his presidency to restoring peace and harmony in a nation still reeling from the aftereffects of a bloody internecine conflict. One of the ways he tried to create a "real union—union of hearts, union of hands," as he put it, was to travel frequently to different parts of the country. Hayes was taking his cue from George Washington, who had also sought to unify America by going on the road. A few months after taking office, President Washington visited all the northern states, which had ratified the Constitution. And in 1791, Washington logged 1,700 miles as he ventured from Philadelphia to all the southern states. Another nurturing First Dad, James Monroe, followed the same script. To celebrate his landslide victory in the election of 1816, in June 1817 the affable Monroe embarked on a fifteen-week tour through New England. In reporting on the warm reception by crowds, the Boston-based *Columbian Centinel* alluded to the dawn of an "era of good feelings"—a phrase later used by historians to capture Monroe's entire presidency. In 1818 Monroe would travel around the Chesapeake Bay, and the following year he would travel all over the south.

On the morning of June 26, 1877, President Hayes, accompanied by his wife, his son Webb, and a handful of aides and cabinet secretaries, arrived in Boston to begin his goodwill tour of New England. That evening, Alexander Rice, the Governor of Massachusetts, hosted a banquet at Hayes's lodgings, the Hotel Brunswick in Copley Square. To honor the President, Boston's éminence grise, the physician Oliver Wendell Holmes Sr., read his commemorative poem, "To R. B. H." In the first few verses, Holmes tried on various monikers for Hayes such as "Great Father," "Your Highness," and "Your Grace" before settling on "Healer of Strife." Comparing the President to "the mother" who knows love "when she clasps her child," Holmes concluded:

Look in our eyes! Your welcome waits you there—
North, South, East, West, from all and everywhere!

The following day, Hayes attended the Harvard commencement where he received an honorary LL.D. on the same day that his son Birchard received his law degree. At a dinner that evening hosted by Harvard President Charles Eliot, Hayes blushed "like a boy" in response to a warm reception. Reluctant to steal the thunder from the next generation, the modest Hayes uttered just a few words to the assembled Harvard graduates. "This is your day. I may not; I ought not to take up any particle of this valuable time…God grant that during the remainder of the term I may be able to do something to deserve…[this hearty greeting]."

That September, Hayes made stops in several towns in his native Ohio before heading to Kentucky, Tennessee, Georgia, and Virginia. In front of a crowd of nearly thirty thousand in Marietta, Ohio, which featured one thousand veterans—including a Mr. Muzzey, who had fought in the War of 1812—Hayes emphasized how in the wake of the Civil War, he saw himself as a re-founding father. "All who are familiar with the history of our country know that a hundred years ago," he insisted, "there was no North, no South. The fathers were one throughout the whole country. Washington and Jefferson were side by side with Franklin and Adams…The whole country belonged to the fathers. It is to that state of harmony, of fraternal friendship, that we desire our country to return." After finishing his remarks, Hayes introduced Postmaster General David Key, the former Tennessee Senator, as "an honest man and a patriotic man." "My friends," Key stated, "the flag I fought for four years has disappeared from the face of the earth…We have but one flag."

Two weeks later, Hayes and his entourage, which again included Key, reached Knoxville. There the President told a cheering crowd, "I want the men of Tennessee to be as much at home on the soil of Vermont as in any State of the South. I want the people of Ohio to feel as much at home in the South as in any State north of the Ohio River… Then shall we be a happier people." This caring First Dad, who had helped his sons settle into their college dormitories, was now eager to ensure that all Americans felt comfortable in every corner of the land.

In September 1880, as his term was winding down, Hayes, along with his wife and his sons Birchard and Rutherford, embarked on a two-month transcontinental journey. Hayes handed off the task of choreographing his excursion to the Pacific to fellow Ohioan William Sherman, then the Commanding General of the Army, who just sixteen years earlier had dealt the south a fatal blow during his triumphant march to the Atlantic. The first sitting President to visit the West Coast, Hayes wanted the residents of the new states such as California and Oregon and of territories such as Utah and Washington to feel more connected to "the people of the older states." Nearly four years after the highly contested election, the nation remained deeply divided. In announcing Hayes's departure from the nation's capital that summer, the *Washington Post*—then a newly minted Democratic party organ—noted that "the fraudulent President...proposes still further to disgrace the office which he stole by making a series of partisan stump speeches [on the Pacific slope]," and warned its readers of the likelihood of "something nauseating" in his "warmed-over political twaddle."

But in fact, Hayes avoided politics—he did not do any campaigning for the Republican presidential nominee, James Garfield—choosing instead to focus on his mission of national unity. He wanted westerners to feel warmly not toward him or his party, but toward the American experiment. "As a mere individual you care nothing for me, and in addressing you, I do it in the sense of representing our nationality and our flag," he told a crowd in Walla Walla, Washington Territory, on October 5. "I trust our meeting will contribute toward the increase of that sentiment of patriotism which makes you free men in the full sense of American citizenship. The better we know each other the more we become attached to each other." Hayes presented himself as the personification of a federal government, which cared about the rights of all its citizens and was, as a result, worth joining. While Hayes "did not have a strong and aggressive character" and "[did not] accomplish great ends," the *New York Times* observed upon his death a dozen years later, "his administration did much to quench the fires of sectional hostility."

One evening in 1927 when the forty-three-year-old Harry Truman was away from home, his wife, Bess, was having trouble getting their three-year-old daughter, Mary Margaret, to go to sleep. "I was giving her the dickens…about her bedtime as usual," Bess wrote to Truman, "and she was sitting down here crying and crying and finally she burst forth with 'When is my daddy coming?'"

Bess had endured two miscarriages before giving birth to Margaret—whom few people ever called by her real first name—and both parents showered lots of attention on their only child. But Margaret would always equate maternal care more with her father than with her mother. While Bess called her Marg with a hard g, Harry opted for the softer-sounding Margie. "I can only say," this First Daughter later recalled, "that Marg still resounds in my ears with orders, impatience, and discipline in it. The other name has none of those things. By five, I was a total Daddy's girl."

Whenever Truman left Independence, Missouri, to go on Army Reserve duty, his young daughter was devastated. Ten days after his departure one summer in the late 1920s, Margaret was playing a family game that involved making up song lyrics. Her contribution: "I saw my Daddy—once he was here." Connecting with Margaret also came more naturally to Harry than to Bess. As a boy, he had felt very close to his own mother, Mary, with whom he enjoyed, as Margaret later put it, "an enormously strong intellectual-emotional bond." Though Harry got along well with his father, John Anderson Truman, a cattle farmer, they were not nearly as close. Like both Hayes and Obama, the youngster was constantly surrounded by women. To correct a rare eye disease, he had to wear thick glasses, so like Hayes, the young Truman also was not able to play sports with the boys in his school. He spent many hours in the kitchen helping Mamma Truman prepare meals for the family of five, which included two younger siblings, Mary Jane and John Vivian. He also pitched in as a surrogate mother by putting his sister to bed and even braiding her hair. As an adult, Truman had few male friends; his closest ties were to the four women in his life—his mother, his wife, his sister, and his daughter.

In contrast, Bess, while she came from a more prosperous Missouri family, had endured a more trying early life. Her adored father, David Wallace, a customs official, waged a lifelong battle with alcoholism. On countless nights, a crew of his Independence chums toted a drunk Wallace back from the local saloon and deposited him on his front porch. On the morning of June 17, 1903, a depressed Wallace blew his brains out with a revolver while the eighteen-year-old Bess was still asleep in her nearby bedroom. In the early twentieth century, a parent's suicide was a great source of shame, and the graphic account of Wallace's death, which was published a few days later in the local paper, mortified the entire family. Bess never fully recovered from this devastating trauma. Margaret would not learn about her grandfather's suicide until she turned twenty—when an aunt told her the truth. In 1944, Truman would be reluctant to become FDR's running mate out of fear that the press would dredge up this family tragedy and push his wife over the edge. To cope with her unresolved grief, Bess, as Margaret noted, exercised "tight control over her emotions." As a mother, Bess would have difficulty relaxing around her daughter. "When it came to worrying," Margaret observed, "Mother was in a class by herself."

After Truman went to Washington in 1935 to take up his seat in the Senate, he saw much less of his daughter. For the next several years, Margaret developed a "split personality," as she later put it. From January through June, "the little Truman girl" resided in an apartment in the nation's capital. The other half of the year, "Mary Margaret" lived at the family home in Independence. The transition was also difficult for her father, because he had always dreaded their separations. In 1925, when he had to abandon his one-year-old daughter to do his annual stint in the Army Reserves, he wrote Bess, "I'm glad that...the baby is all right. I'm so afraid she won't know me when I get home I don't know what to do." When his daughter was back in Independence, Truman wrote her warm letters from his Senate office, where her picture hung under those of his two heroes, George Washington and Robert E. Lee. Like his mother before him, the Senator nurtured his child's mind as well as her heart. And unlike many dads of his era, he did not see her gender as an impediment to achievement. When asked by a reporter if he had any sons, Truman once said, "Yes, my daughter is my son."

The autodidact who had never finished college stressed the importance of academic success. "I just want you," he wrote the fifteen-year-old Margaret in October 1939, "to be properly equipped mentally to hold your own in this great world and maybe some day be the lady senator from Missouri to succeed your pa." He so hated to see her suffer setbacks that he even harbored fantasies about changing the course of world history—just for her. "I am proud of your history test," he wrote the following month, "but I of course wish King Louis had signed that Magna Carta so you could have gotten a hundred. 95 is mighty good, however."

He did not want his daughter to miss out on anything. In the 1930s, when she was limited to an allowance of a dollar a week, he was always slipping her quarters so she could squeeze in another movie. His generosity knew no bounds. After she received her B.A. in history from George Washington University in 1946, the President presented her with a check for $10,000—nearly 15 percent of his presidential salary. While Margaret always felt that she "could twist *him* around her little finger," she rarely took advantage of his good-natured support. Upon receiving the graduation gift, she responded, "Thank you...for the big piece of green lettuce. I'll use it sparingly."

Truman felt genuine concern about the emotional development of all children—not just that of his daughter. In the 1960s, the retired President was giving a speech at a Los Angeles high school, when a student, referring to the Golden State's Governor, Pat Brown, flippantly asked, "What do you think of our local yokel?" Truman's first reaction was to chastise the young man for being disrespectful toward a political leader—an action that elicited applause from the crowd. However, he quickly realized that he had unwittingly humiliated his interlocutor.

After this appearance, he arranged to talk to the student and ask him about his grades. Truman also encouraged the adolescent to write him with updates on his academic progress.

———

"I hope Margie is all right," a nervous Truman wrote to Bess soon after arriving for a week's vacation at the Little White House, a naval base in Key West, on Wednesday, March 12, 1947. "I never wanted anything to be successful in my whole life except her birth." The reason for the President's anxiety? That Sunday, his beloved daughter was to make her debut as a coloratura soprano with the Detroit Symphony Orchestra in a concert, which was to be broadcast live to a national audience on ABC radio. "I'm sure she can do it," he wrote to his wife, who was home in Washington. "If you want me to come home and sit by you I'll do it. But if you think you can stand it without me I'll take some more sun."

That week, Truman reported feeling "worn to a frazzle" by the weight of the world's problems. Less than a half hour before boarding the presidential plane, the *Sacred Cow*, for Florida, he had delivered an impassioned twenty-minute speech in front of a Joint Session of Congress. The subject was the growing threat of Communism. "I believe," Truman declared, "it must be the policy of the United States to support free peoples who are resisting attempted subjugation by armed minorities or by outside pressures." To back up his words, which soon became known as the Truman Doctrine, the President insisted that Congress approve the spending of $400 million to support the hard-pressed Greek and Turkish governments against a possible Communist insurgency. This generous aid package, as most historians now agree, represented the official start of the Cold War. As Truman acknowledged to his daughter the following day, he had agonized over his decision for about six weeks. In the end, he felt he had no choice but to act. "The attempt of Lenin, Trotsky, Stalin, et al., to fool the world... is just like Hitler's and Mussolini's so-called socialist states," he wrote Margaret. "Your pop had to tell the world just that in polite language."

As he tried to relax in Key West, Truman's attention quickly pivoted from Stalin's machinations to Margaret's singing. "I am just as sure as I can be that Sunday night at 8:00 P.M. another great soprano will go on the air," he also told his daughter. "So don't worry about anything… and nothing can stop you—even the handicap of being the Daughter of President Truman!"

Music had long bonded father and daughter. As he told Margaret shortly before becoming President, "sometimes your dad wishes he'd gone on and been a music hall pianist." As an adolescent, he had trekked to Kansas City twice a week to study with a top-notch instructor who introduced him to Ignacy Paderewski when the legendary Polish virtuoso passed through Missouri. Truman learned to play Bach, Beethoven, and Liszt, but he quit at seventeen because he felt he "wasn't good enough." Hoping that Margaret might pick up where he had left off, Truman surprised her one Christmas during the Depression by giving her a baby grand piano. Though Margaret's first reaction was to burst into tears, because she had been dreaming about (and actively lobbying for) an electric train set, she eventually started taking lessons from a talented local amateur—her father. However, she was unwilling to compete with him, and by her late teens, her instrument of choice switched from the keyboard to the voice. After finishing college, Margaret surprised her family by announcing that she wanted to become a professional singer. In contrast to both her mother and maternal grandmother, who considered such a career undignified and tried to nudge her toward marriage, Truman supported her wholeheartedly. As he had informed Mamma Truman the previous fall when Margaret moved to New York to start her singing lessons, "If she wants to be a warbler and has the talent and will to do the hard work necessary to accomplish her purpose, I don't suppose I should kick."

Having received permission from the "boss," as he referred to his wife, Truman stayed put at the Little White House that March. But his daughter's debut continued to leave him feeling rattled. The night before the concert, the normally sound sleeper could not get any rest.

On Sunday, March 16, he emptied his schedule for the entire afternoon, so he could take a long nap after lunch. At ten to eight that evening, Truman retired to the library with several aides to listen to ABC radio's *Sunday Evening Hour* with the Detroit Symphony, led by conductor Karl Krueger. The Key West station, WKWF, was affiliated with the Mutual Broadcasting System, so its owner, John Spottswood, had arranged for the ABC broadcast to be piped into his Key West studio from New York, where it was, in turn, wired to the Little White House. In Detroit, Margaret was still feeling feverish, as she had not quite rid herself of the bronchial pneumonia that had forced her to postpone her appearance for a week. At about 8:25, an announcer began a rambling introduction of who exactly she was, which annoyed many of the fifteen million listeners and none more so than the President. "When that 'bird,'" Truman later wrote, "just kept talking just before she came on, I wanted to shoot him ... but all the gang who were with me at Key West and all the help in the house were seated around listening in at the same time, so I had to sit still and bear it."

At exactly 8:28, Margaret came on the air, singing "Cieleto Lindo," an anonymous Spanish folk song. She then proceeded to launch into an aria from Félicien David's *La Perle du Brésil* before finishing up with "The Last Rose of Summer," a favorite composition of her father's. Truman was beaming throughout her entire performance. To Spottswood, who was pacing up and down the parlor, the proud father asked, "How do you like her?" "I can't stand it," the radio executive responded. "I'm worried something will go wrong." "Just relax," said the President.

Immediately after the broadcast, Truman telephoned his daughter to share his excitement. He "told me that I had performed wonderfully, but of course he's *prejudiced*," Margaret later wrote. Most reviewers concurred with the Commander in Chief. Writing in the *New York Times*, Noel Straus described her phrasing as "careful" and her voice as "sweet and appealing in quality." But the *Boston Globe's* Cyrus Durgin pounced, concluding that "Miss Truman is not yet ready for a serious, professional career," calling the twenty-three-year-old "a young student whose training still has a long way to go." Buoyed by this largely successful debut, which elicited thousands of congratulatory telegrams and letters, Margaret hired a business manager and took to the road. For the next several years—except for a brief hiatus during the fall of 1948 when she campaigned for her father against Republican challenger Thomas Dewey—she crisscrossed the country, singing in many of America's most hallowed concert venues.

In 1956, Margaret married Clifton Daniel, the managing editor of the *New York Times*, with whom she had four boys—Clifton Jr., William, Harrison, and Thomas. That same year, she also released her first book, *Souvenir*, a memoir that traced both her early years in Independence and her life as a First Daughter. Settling in Manhattan, she gave up touring and turned to writing—a career move that might well also have been influenced by her father. A decade earlier, impressed by her letters, he had told her that "you write interestingly and perhaps when...your good voice cracks you can become a good storyteller." Besides an acclaimed biography of each of her parents, she also penned nearly two dozen murder mysteries situated in and around Washington. But Margaret, who died in 2008, never lost her love of music, which she tried to pass on to the next generation. When her eldest child, Clifton Daniel Jr., turned eight—the same age at which she had received her piano from her father—she laid down the law, declaring unequivocally, "You are going to take piano lessons." Though Clifton is now glad that he learned to play, he rebelled as a youngster, just like his mother. "I wouldn't practice all week and never learned to read music," he told me in a recent interview. "To prepare for my lessons, I would ask my mother to play the piece, and I would watch her fingers and copy her."

Margaret's most talked about concert performance took place at Constitution Hall on December 5, 1950. It was the last stop of that year's tour, and her parents attended the event along with British Prime Minister Clement Attlee. The next day at 5 A.M., Truman was stunned to read a scathing review penned by the *Washington Post* music critic, Paul Hume. "Miss Truman," wrote the thirty-four-year-old Hume, who had just started teaching music at Georgetown University, "cannot sing very well... [and] has not improved in the years we have heard her." An enraged Truman immediately fired off a personal letter to Hume, which began as follows:

> I've just read your lousy review of Margaret's concert. I've come to the conclusion that you are an "eight ulcer man on four ulcer pay." It seems to me that you are a frustrated old man who wishes he could have been successful. When you write such poppy-cock as was in the back section of the paper you work for, it shows conclusively that you're off the beam and at least four of your ulcers are at work. Some day I hope to meet you. When that happens you'll need a new nose, a lot of beef steak for black eyes, and perhaps a supporter below!

While the *Post* decided not to run the letter, the *Washington Daily News* printed a slightly edited version. A furor ensued, as many commentators attacked the President for his loss of emotional control. In contrast, the forgiving Hume was not terribly bothered by Truman's temper outburst, which he attributed to a series of recent stressors. On the afternoon of the concert, Truman's press secretary, Charlie Ross, whom he had known since their high school days in Independence, suddenly dropped dead of a heart attack. "This friend of my youth [was] a tower of strength," Truman noted that day in a prepared statement, which he hand-delivered to reporters because he could not bear to read it out loud.

The Commander in Chief had also been blindsided by America's dwindling prospects for victory in the Korean War. In late November, hundreds of thousands of Chinese troops mounted a successful invasion of North Korea. This attack, in turn, led Gen. Douglas MacArthur to criticize Truman publicly for not allowing him to bomb China in retaliation. In addition, several journalists misconstrued the President's comments at a November 30 press conference in which he had alluded to the use of atomic weapons as a last resort and falsely reported that he was strongly considering sending A-bombs to MacArthur. The President was also facing pressure from opponents of the war such as the visiting British Prime Minister Attlee, who was encouraging him to surrender to the Chinese and give up both South Korea and Taiwan.

Given the seriousness of the crisis in Korea, many historians concur with Hume's sympathetic reading of Truman's letter. However, Truman's fiery response was hardly out of character. After all, he was mimicking his own father, John Anderson Truman, who had often directed his pugnacity toward anyone who threatened to push around his three children. As Margaret noted in her biography of the President, "Dad never forgot the warm feeling his father's fights on his behalf aroused in him. I suspect it explains not a little of his own hot temper when he found himself defending his flesh and blood on a more public stage, in later years."

What was more, Truman often expressed violent fantasies toward those who would denigrate Margaret's musical talent. As he wrote his daughter a couple of weeks before her 1947 debut, "Now don't get scared, you can do it! And if anyone says you can't, I'll bust him in the snoot!" That October, after her concert in Pittsburgh, he also vowed to use his fists to protect her, telling her, "I have just been reading the clippings from all the Pittsburgh papers. The write-ups were excellent except for some of the critics. If I ever meet one of them I'll bust him in the nose." Truman was not a violent man, but the southern gentleman in him would simply not allow anyone to attack "his baby." And he was correct in assuming that Margaret would not be embarrassed by his support. When asked for a comment that December during the furor over Hume's review, she told reporters, "I'm glad that chivalry isn't dead."

Truman also had his finger on the pulse of the American people. When aides complained that he had committed a major public relations gaffe, he responded, "Wait til the mail comes in. I'll make you a bet that 80 percent of it is on my side of the argument." A week later, Truman, accompanied by several staff members, headed down to the White House mail room, where clerks had filed the thousands of "Hume letters" in "for" and "against" piles. The final tally revealed that a little over 80 percent supported the President. The vast majority of letters were from mothers who agreed with Truman that fathers needed to be aggressive in standing up for their daughters. "The trouble with you guys is," the President told his aides, "you just don't understand human nature."

Truman never regretted sending the nastygram to Hume. He felt that he had a right to be both the President of the United States and the father of Margaret. "It was Harry S. Truman the human being who wrote that note," he explained. But these two Harry Trumans often thought alike. And his fierce protective streak might well also account for the most momentous decision of his presidency, which he made just a few months after inheriting the office from FDR.

———————

On July 6, 1945, Truman received numerous visitors at the White House, including several Congressmen and the French Ambassador, Henri Bonnet. Two "nice children," as he wrote in his diary, also stopped by to present him with a plaque commemorating the $715 million in war bonds that schoolchildren across the nation had sold. "The nice boy made me a speech," he observed. "At his age, I would surely have passed out if I had had to make a statement similar to his, to the town mayor, let alone to the President of the United States… These modern kids are something to write home about." Over the next month, the youth of America remained foremost on his mind as he became consumed with the desire to end the brutal war with Japan as soon as possible. In the three months since his inauguration, American troops in the Pacific had endured half as many casualties as they had in the three previous years combined. On the night of the sixth, accompanied by about fifty aides, the President secretly boarded a special train for Newport News, Virginia, from where he set sail for Europe the following morning. His destination: the Berlin suburb of Potsdam, where he was to meet ten days later with British Prime Minister Winston Churchill and Soviet Premier Joseph Stalin.

Despite the gravity of his concerns, Truman's mood remained buoyant. A week later, he wrote Margaret, "This has been a great voyage. I
wish you and your mother could have come with me...It seems to take
two warships to get your pa across the pond. The cruiser *Augusta* and
Philadelphia with an admiral in command—he is a rear one. I never
could understand why admirals had to be rear." As he settled into his
temporary quarters in the Cecilienhof, the palace where the last crown
prince of Prussia once resided, Truman still thought that the best way to
achieve his objective would be to induce Stalin to join the war against
Japan. After the first day of the conference, a relieved Truman wrote to
Bess, "I've gotten what I came for—Stalin goes to war August 15 with
no strings on it...I'll say that we'll end the war a year sooner now, and
think of the kids who won't be killed. That is the important thing." He
stressed this same urgency in his first few tête-à-têtes with Churchill,
who was moved when the President alluded to "the terrible responsibilities upon him in regard to unlimited effusion of American blood."

But a week later, when Secretary of War Henry Stimson informed
the President that the atomic bomb stood at his disposal, Truman suddenly changed course. What convinced the President to authorize the
bombing of both Hiroshima and Nagasaki in early August was the
assessment by the Army Chief of Staff, Gen. George Marshall, that
an invasion of Japan was bound to result in the loss of at least hundreds of thousands of American soldiers. "It occurred to me," the President declared later that year, "that a quarter of a million of the flower
of our young manhood were worth a couple of Japanese cities, and I
still think they were and are." Though the atomic blasts ended up killing over a hundred thousand Japanese civilians, Truman had felt duty
bound to protect his American boys.

Truman's eagerness to both care for and protect Americans of all ages
also manifested itself in his signature domestic policy initiative, which
he called the Fair Deal. On January 5, 1949, just two months after his
stunning comeback victory over Dewey, a confident Truman asserted in
his impassioned 3,500-word State of the Union address, "Every segment

of our population and every individual has a right to expect from his government a fair deal." Using language that sounds as if it were plucked from an early-twenty-first-century stump speech, the President wanted to make sure that all Americans benefited from the booming postwar economy, thereby rejecting "the discredited theory that the fortunes of the nation should be in the hands of a privileged few."

Truman urged Congress to pass a host of new bills that would radically alter Social Security, education, civil rights, and medical care. His most ambitious proposal called for a single national health insurance plan, which would cover all Americans. But a conservative coalition, made of Republicans and southern Democrats, opposed most of his ideas. Over the next couple of years, he could claim only a few small achievements, such as the expansion of the Social Security program to include coverage for the totally disabled. In the midterm elections of 1950, Truman suffered a major defeat when the Democrats saw their majority in the Senate shrink from 12 to 2 and their majority in the House go down from 17 to 12. Like the crisis in Korea, this setback also likely served as kindling for Truman's rage attack against Paul Hume the following month. As Korea devolved into a bloody stalemate, which lasted for the rest of his presidency, Truman was forced to abandon his domestic agenda.

But his compassion would still make a mark. In a fitting tribute to Truman, on July 30, 1965, President Johnson traveled to Independence to sign the Medicare bill. Recognizing the eighty-one-year-old Truman's pioneering contribution to health-care reform, LBJ presented Truman and his wife the first two Medicare cards, stating, "The people of the United States love and voted for Harry Truman, not because he gave them hell, but because he gave them hope." As LBJ clearly understood, Truman's legendary anger was always intimately tied to feelings of love.

———

Shortly before the 2004 Illinois Democratic primary for U.S. Senator, which he was to win by a landslide, Illinois state senator Barack Obama was riding high. After about a year of nonstop campaigning, he had raised far more money than any of his rivals, and his path both to the nomination and to the floor of the U.S. Senate seemed assured. But his closest advisors sensed that the forty-two-year-old candidate and father of two—five-year-old Malia and two-year-old Sasha—was feeling a bit down and listless. A concerned Valerie Jarrett suggested that they meet for lunch at Chicago's posh gym, the East Bank Club.

"What's wrong?" Obama asked "the principal," as he referred to his chief aide.

Jarrett replied, "Your heart isn't in it. What's *wrong* with you?"

"I miss my girls," Obama said as tears welled up. "I don't want to be the kind of father I had." But after composing himself, he added, "I'll work it out. I'll be okay."

For Barack Obama, as opposed to George Washington, it was his father rather than his mother who taught him how *not* to parent. In his entire life, the Honolulu native experienced less than two months of face time with his father, Barack Obama Sr., who worked as a government economist in Kenya after completing his education in America. For reasons that remain unclear, in late August 1961, Obama's mother, Ann Dunham, then just eighteen, moved with the nearly one-month-old infant from Hawaii, where she had met Obama Sr. in a college Russian-language class, to Washington State. The marriage would never be repaired, and Ann obtained a divorce in 1964. In 1971, Obama Sr., who had returned to Kenya after receiving his master's degree from Harvard, visited Hawaii in order to spend a month with his ten-year-old namesake, then living with his maternal grandparents. The youngster was fascinated by his exotic African father, but he found the frequent rebukes hard to take. Even though Obama Sr. had no idea what his son's school assignments were, he was convinced that the boy was a slacker. "I tell you, Barry," he barked at his son, "you do not work as hard as you should." Ordering the child into his bedroom, Obama Sr. added, "Go now, before I get angry at you." A couple of weeks into the reunion, the boy had had his fill. "I began to count the days until my father would leave and things would return to normal," Obama noted in his 1995 memoir, *Dreams from My Father*.

Barack Obama Sr. was not just an absentee father. As the future President learned after Obama Sr.'s sudden death at the age of forty-six in 1982, he was also a very troubled man addicted to bullying his nearest and dearest. In fact, if Obama Sr. had spent more time with Barry, he might well have scarred the youngster even more. A woman-izer who was not yet divorced from his first wife when he married Ann Dunham—a fact that he hid from her—Obama Sr. ended up father-ing eight children with four different women. Several of his African children have reported physical abuse. The bitter and quick-tempered Obama Sr. often drowned his anger in large doses of Scotch—a pen-chant that led his fellow Nairobi bar hoppers to nickname him Mr. Double-Double. He was incapable of taking proper care of himself, much less of any of his children, and the car crash in which he lost his life was just the last in a long series of self-destructive acts.

For Obama, one of the most welcome by-products of gaining the highest office in the land at the age of forty-seven was that he could finally differentiate himself from his own father and become the child-centric parent he had always longed to be. As he has often said, the President "lives above the store" and has no commute. No longer would his hectic travel schedule require constant separations from his two girls. Malia was a summer baby—born on the Fourth of July in 1998—and for the first three months of her life, Obama was glad to help his wife, Michelle, by changing diapers and rocking her to sleep. But once fall came, the state senator and part-time law professor had to be away from the family's Chicago home at least half the week. And by early 2007, when he was both a U.S. Senator and a full-time presi-dential candidate, Obama was forced to hand off just about all of the parenting responsibilities to Michelle.

Eager to reconnect with his family, soon after being inaugurated, Obama established what the *New York Times* reporter Jodi Kantor has called "an unusual rule for a president." As he informed all his aides, he vowed to have dinner with his family five nights a week. That left just two nights a week for out-of-town fund-raisers or dinners with fellow politicians. At 6:30, Obama and his wife sat down with the girls for a family dinner—without any outsiders, not even Michelle's mother, Marian Robinson, who typically retreated to her own "home" on the third floor of the White House. The evening meal, observed Obama's former body man, Reggie Love, was treated "like a meeting in the Situation Room. There's a hard stop before that dinner." While aides sometimes call him back to work at 8:30 or 9:00, they rarely dare to go upstairs to bother him during the sacred dinner hour. On most days, Obama also eats breakfast with his daughters. And as part of his commitment to his girls, Obama has been reluctant to visit Camp David, since various school activities typically require the youngsters to be in Washington. Like Hayes, Obama is consumed by family as much as by politics. As early as his first presidential campaign, he joked that the job he would really love is that of ex-President.

Like Teddy Roosevelt, Obama is also extremely proud of his résumé as a parent. He boasts of having read aloud with Malia all seven volumes of the Harry Potter series; in his first fall in office, he also managed to read all of Yann Martel's *Life of Pi* to Sasha. But performing as a head of household did not come easily to him. As this supremely self-confident man, who rarely doubts that he is the smartest person in the room, acknowledged in 2006, "It is in my capacities as a husband and a father that I entertain the most doubt." In sharp contrast to his own neglectful father, this President with the perfect attendance record at his daughters' parent-teacher conferences has emerged as a model father. Out of his own feelings of loss and alienation, which he described in *Dreams from My Father*, has come a road map for both personal and social transformation. "I am a black man who grew up without a father and I know the cost that I paid for that," the President told a panel on Overcoming Poverty at the Catholic-Evangelical Leadership Summit held at Georgetown University in 2015. "And I also know that I have the capacity to break that cycle, and as a consequence,

I think my daughters are better off." As he also noted at that summit, he is eager to tell young blacks whose dads have engaged in reprehensible behavior—for example, by beating their mother and/or refusing to pay child support—how he got over being mad at his own father.

Obama seeks to turn his own story into public policy. The blight that now blankets devastated cities such as Baltimore, he argues, can be addressed if more black men can be inspired to do for their children what their fathers never did for them. This was the impetus behind Obama's decision in September 2014 to set up My Brother's Keeper, a community-based initiative designed to help young men of color reach their full potential. The following May, he announced the formation of My Brother's Keeper Alliance, a nonprofit funded by private corporations devoted to the same mission of providing opportunity to vulnerable inner-city youngsters. "We can remember that these kids are our kids," Obama stated at the launch at Lehman College in the Bronx. "'For these are all our children,' James Baldwin once wrote. 'We will all profit by, or pay for, whatever they become.'" Obama has hinted that he plans to stay involved in this cause long after his presidency is over.

———————

Obama did have a couple of surrogate fathers—namely, his mother's second husband, Lolo Soetoro, with whom he lived for four years in Indonesia, and his maternal grandfather, Stanley Dunham, who helped raise him during his high school years in Hawaii. But these men played a relatively small role in his emotional development. "It was women…who provided the ballast in my life," he wrote in 2006, "my [maternal] grandmother, whose dogged practicality kept the family afloat, and my mother, whose love and clarity of spirit kept my… world centered…From them I would absorb the values that guide me to this day." Like Truman, the adult Obama has always bonded more easily with women than with men. Likewise, as with Truman, his closest ties during his presidency have also been with four females in his family—his wife, Michelle, his two daughters, and his mother-in-law,

Marian Robinson, who moved into the White House right after his first inauguration and has pitched in with the parenting.

It's impossible to understand either Obama the parent—or Obama the President—without taking the full measure of Ann Dunham, whom he has called "the single constant in my life." A voracious reader with a penetrating mind, the precocious Ann possessed a formidable intellect. Having devoured the works of Margaret Mead as a teenager, Obama's mother startled her high school classmates by announcing that she wanted to be an anthropologist. "We had no idea what Ann was talking about," Susan Blake, who attended Mercer Island High School with her, told me. "We had to look up the word in the dictionary." But Ann was also warm and cuddly. Obama's half-sister, Maya Soetoro-Ng, has described Ann as a "softie" who got weepy at the sight of any child being hurt—even on TV or at the movies. According to Maya, her mother would say "I love you" a hundred times a day. While caring for her son meant that Ann took several years to finish her bachelor's degree, she never gave up her dream of pursuing a doctorate in anthropology. Ambitious and demanding, Ann held high expectations both for herself and for everyone in her orbit, especially her two children. When Obama was attending an Indonesian grade school, she taught him English from a correspondence course for three hours five days a week. Classes began at 4 A.M. When her half-asleep son protested, she fired back, "This is no picnic for me, either, buster." Overdrive was the only gear that this determined woman knew. In her early thirties, she left her thirteen-year-old son in Hawaii with her parents while she went back to Indonesia to do the field work for her thesis. "Ann continued to get up at 4 A.M. to write her dissertation, as she had a day job at the time," Bronwen Solyom, an art historian who saw her frequently in Indonesia in the mid-1970s, told me.

Though Obama now realizes that the separations affected him much more than he once thought, he remains deeply appreciative of the solid emotional anchor she provided. As the President told an interviewer in 2010, she gave him "a sense of unconditional love that was big enough that, with all the surface disturbances of our lives, it sustained me, entirely." And when Malia and Sasha came on the scene, he felt an obligation to return the favor. "In my daughters," Obama has written, "I see her [my mother] every day, her joy, her capacity for wonder."

Though she died in 1995 of ovarian cancer at the age of fifty-two, Ann Dunham was the driving force behind the piece of legislation that may well define Obama's domestic legacy—the Affordable Care Act (ACA). As Obama has repeatedly stated, he was heartbroken to watch her fight with her insurance company during the last months of her life. In early 2007, as he was announcing his run for the presidency, Obama had already identified health insurance reform as a pressing issue, which he proposed tackling early in his administration. Harking back to the 1965 Medicare signing ceremony held "in a town called Independence," Obama praised Truman "as the first man who was bold enough to issue the call for universal health care." For Obama, the ACA represented a chance to honor his mother by passing on to future generations some of the nurturing that she had provided for him. When asked what he thought about "Obamacare," the term his political opponents wield to attack his signature legislation, the President calmly answered, "Go ahead, I like that, because I do care. Obama cares."

Inspired by his mother's example, Obama the parent provides unwavering affection to Malia and Sasha, which he combines with frequent prods designed to encourage them to excel. In November 2009, he even went public with one of his elder daughter's slipups, informing the nation about a 73 that she got on a science test. "Malia will tell you" the forty-fourth President admitted to Essence, "that if she comes home with a B, that's not good enough because there's no reason she can't get an A." After finishing the interview, Obama caught himself and apologized to Malia for embarrassing her.

Obama's position on his daughters' grades bears a striking resemblance to that of his Republican predecessor Rutherford B. Hayes. Upon receiving the sixteen-year-old Fanny's high school report card, Hayes conveyed his pride about her top-notch performance in all her academic subjects. However, he was not entirely satisfied. "Deportment 83—," Hayes wrote to her at prep school, "that is fair. But I want to see it go up. Can't you make it one hundred—(100)! Try it."

Like Hayes, this nurturing dad is also not a pushover; he, too, stresses the value of achievement. Used to the ribbing from her father, Malia does not hesitate to egg him on in return. On a family visit to the Lincoln Memorial ten days before his first inauguration, where they read the sixteenth President's prophetic words on the marble walls, Malia told Obama she would not be satisfied with anything less than his best effort in his upcoming speech. "First African-American president," she quipped. "Better be good."

Unlike laissez-faire First Dads such as Grant and FDR, Obama is a strong advocate of household regulations. While Michelle Obama has always had to handle the details, the governing of the girls represents a carefully orchestrated collaborative effort. Since Obama's own childhood was somewhat chaotic, the couple has used Michelle's experience in a loving, two-parent, working-class household as its model. Eager to encourage independence, the Obamas issued both daughters alarm clocks at the age of four. The First Children have long been expected not only to get themselves up and ready for school in the morning, but also to make their own beds every day. (Hospital corners are not necessary; if the girls "just throw the sheet over it," their mother has emphasized, they have done their duty.) And when walking the family's beloved Portuguese water dogs, Bo and Sunny, Malia and Sasha are required to scoop the poop.

To encourage healthy behaviors, the Obamas have not hesitated to set firm limits; desserts are to be consumed only on special occasions such as birthdays, and bedtimes are to be taken seriously. And TV is verboten on school nights. While the Obamas do not approve of spanking, they are not reluctant to enforce discipline. As Obama noted at the beginning of his presidency, Michelle can "holler at them a little bit," and he is "not a softie." To lay down the law, the President tends to give gentle scoldings when they misbehave.

Obama is convinced that all the nation's children could benefit from prolonged exposure to his own parenting paradigm. "In the end," the President said in his first appearance before a joint session of Congress in February 2009, "there is no program or policy that can substitute for a mother or father who will attend those parent-teacher conferences, or help with homework after dinner, or turn off the TV, put away the video games, and read to their child. I speak to you not just as a President, but as a father when I say that responsibility for our children's education must begin at home." Obsessed with the value of his own prescriptions, Obama often brings up the subject of parenting when he meets everyday Americans on his travels. "What time do your kids go to bed?" is a favorite query.

———————

"They should be playing a zone," insisted the President to his wife. "They need to run a play on offense."

It was the middle of Obama's first term, and the First Couple was attending the basketball game of a team composed of Washington, DC, fourth graders, which included their daughter Sasha.

Annoyed by the presidential kibitzing, Michelle Obama proposed some executive action. "Why don't you teach them how to play basketball?"

And thus Barack Obama became the only sitting President ever to double as a part-time basketball coach.

Sasha's team, the Vipers, already had a coach, clinical psychologist Lisa Horowitz, whose day job was conducting research at the National Institutes of Health. But from now on, Horowitz had two new assistants—the President and his longtime body man, Reggie Love, a forward on the 2001 Duke University national championship team, who had accompanied Obama to the gym that day.

Obama became a roundball maniac at ten when he received a basketball as a gift from his father during the one Christmas that they had spent together. "I think there was some cause and effect there," he told

Oprah Winfrey in 2009, "in terms of the degree to which I just ended up taking [up] the sport as a kid who didn't know his dad." A player on his high school team who liked to scrimmage with White House aides, Obama possessed a high basketball IQ. Now it was his chance to connect with the next generation through the game that he loved.

But there was only one problem. The girls were not all that serious about the task at hand. They giggled whenever they accidentally threw the ball out of bounds. In the league face-offs, there are typically five times as many turnovers as baskets, and teams do not always rack up more than ten points in an entire game. "This is not a slumber party," the determined President stated at one of the first practices he ran. "You have to run hard, stand tall, and be strong. You have to listen to your coach."

Obama quickly developed a policy on the three-point shot; no one on the team should even think about attempting one, he insisted, not even in their dreams. Ever the pragmatist, he spent a lot of time helping the girls work on passing and dribbling. "The whole theory was," he noted, "don't practice shots that you are not going to take in a game."

Obama ended up attending all the Vipers games for a couple of seasons. On a few occasions, when the head coach was absent, he took a turn at the helm. "You just want them to win so bad. And when they actually run a play and it works—you're just ecstatic. And a couple of heartbreaking losses and you're feeling terrible. But they're wonderful," the President said.

As Obama geared up for his reelection bid, he began to speak openly about being "an overinvolved sports parent." By early 2012, he was well aware that even his political opponents—no matter how much they disliked his policies—could hardly deny his unqualified success as a father. On those rare occasions when Malia and Sasha appeared in public, they earned raves for both their good manners and their humility. "The value of the family is enormous," Democratic pollster Celinda Lake told the *Washington Post* in February 2012. "The more you know this family and the more you think of Barack Obama in these terms, the harder it is to vilify him." Until then, Obama had alluded to the girls only infrequently—and typically with considerably more aplomb than the preoccupied Jimmy Carter. In May 2010, a few weeks after the BP oil spill in the Gulf of Mexico, the President mentioned a pressing question that Malia had fired at him one morning when he was shaving, "Did you plug the hole yet, Daddy?" Two years later, Obama invoked both daughters when announcing his support of gay marriage. "There have been times where Michelle and I," he told the *Los Angeles Times*, "have been sitting around the dinner table and we're talking about their friends and their parents, and Malia and Sasha, it wouldn't dawn on them that somehow their friends' parents would be treated differently. It doesn't make sense to them and frankly, that's the kind of thing that prompts a change in perspective."

While neither the fourteen-year-old Malia nor the eleven-year-old Sasha did much actual campaigning in 2012, they both popped up regularly in Internet ads such as one released around Father's Day, which featured a montage of their photos over the years. In her voice-over, Michelle Obama alluded to her husband's exemplary attendance record at parent-teacher conferences and at basketball games, adding, "He knows it is important for girls to have the love and support of the most important man in their life, and that's their father."

Americans have fallen hard for numerous other First Children in the past. Noting that Malia and Sasha are the youngest residents of the White House since John and Caroline Kennedy, historian Doris Kearns Goodwin has stated that with young families such as "Theodore Roosevelt's or JFK's, there was a merriment in the White House, a vitality, and the country responded to the presidents even more." But the appeal of the Obama girls has transcended their playfulness and charm. In contrast to those other forty-something Presidents, Obama has also managed to convince the vast majority of Americans that he is raising his children just as they would want to be raised—and his exemplary fathering has emerged as a source of national pride. Obama's "role as father [is]," wrote *New York Times* White House reporter

Jodi Kantor, as the President faced reelection, "one of the most appealing things about him."

By his second term, the integrity of both Malia and Sasha was
unimpeachable. This was a lesson that Elizabeth Lauten, the communications director for Republican Congressman Stephen Fincher
of Tennessee, learned the hard way. In the fall of 2014, after observing
the Obama girls at the 67th annual turkey pardoning, where they both
looked bored during their father's speech, Lauten posted some harsh
words on Facebook: "Dear Sasha and Malia, I get you're both in those
awful teen years, but you're part of the First Family, try showing a little
class. Rise to the occasion. Act like being in the White House matters
to you. Dress like you deserve respect, not a spot at a bar." When the
blogosphere went ballistic, a humiliated Lauten was forced to resign.
Americans were eager to protect not just the teenage Obama girls but
their own hopes and values.

However, the same gentle temperament, which has enabled nurturing dads such as Hayes and Obama to forge strong bonds with their
children, has often led to presidential stumbles. For a President, the
desire to connect deeply with and get along with all constituents can
be a liability rather than an asset. All too ready to trust that locally
elected southern leaders would protect the constitutional rights of
blacks, Hayes ended up removing all federal troops from the south
soon after his 1877 inauguration—a decision that would set back the
cause of civil rights for generations. At times, Obama, too, has been
blinded by the unrealistic hope that gentle persuasion was all that was
needed to achieve his political goals.

Epilogue

Presidential Choices

"I Knew I Had to Share My Daddy"

I had a sense of awe, almost of terror—he was no longer the man with whom we had lived in warm sweet intimacy—he was no longer my father. These people, strangers who had chosen him to be their leader, now claimed him…I had no part in it. I felt deserted and alone.

Eleanor Wilson, recalling her feelings after the election of Woodrow Wilson in 1912

Barack Obama vowed to be an attentive father to his daughters during his presidency—a promise that he has kept. But this course of action, however laudable, may have come at a steep price. That's because in contrast to private citizens, First Dads are fathers not just to their own children, but also to an entire nation. And by attending so conscientiously to the quotidian concerns of Malia and Sasha, so argue critics who hail from both the left and the right, Obama may have neglected his day job. After all, every minute a President spends with his children inevitably takes away from time he could concentrate on the welfare of the countless strangers whose lives depend on his every move. Was Obama perhaps too devoted a parent to be a great President?

After a brief honeymoon period following his first inauguration, in which he signed into law several key pieces of legislation such as the Lilly Ledbetter Fair Pay Act and the $787 billion economic stimulus, this Chief Executive stumbled. With no Republican allies in Congress,

gridlock reigned supreme. Obama's efforts to address such pressing issues as immigration reform and the epidemic of gun violence
went nowhere. Biographer Jonathan Alter attributes these failures of
the forty-fourth President to his lack of a "schmooze gene." According
to this line of reasoning, which has won wide acceptance among the
punditocracy, Obama was uncomfortable building phony relationships
with fellow politicians. Instead he chose to carve out big chunks of
family time with his wife and daughters. Alter describes this penchant
as "a fine quality for an individual, but problematic in a president."
Obama is good at the long game, as evidenced by his ability to promote the long-term health and well-being of his children; however,
Presidents must also be good at the short game—at building temporary coalitions to tackle particular problems. For much of his tenure,
Obama has been attacked for not being another LBJ—a President who
would readily fraternize with Congressional leaders. If only, so goes
the frequent refrain, he had been more obsessed with politics—and
less obsessed with raising his girls—Obama, too, might have been able
to push through landmark legislation such as the Civil Rights Act of
1964.

Can we therefore conclude that preoccupied dads, who dread intimate relationships but often have a knack for developing mutually beneficial superficial connections, make the best Presidents?

The answer would be yes if all the First Dads in this category were
carbon copies of FDR, whose hypomanic temperament was ideally
suited to leading the country, especially in an era of constant crisis.
The American people benefited precisely because FDR was a hands-
off parent who in his first few years in office put all his energy into
persuading Congress to try anything that could possibly jump-start the
economy. That is not to say that all his New Deal programs worked,
but his frenetic activity provided hope. But not every President who
was totally consumed by politics was as good at small talk as FDR.
Like Obama, Jimmy Carter hated it. As his son Chip told me, "During the 1972 campaign, all the major Democratic candidates made a

visit to the Governor's Mansion in Atlanta. A few had five or six drinks. That left a bad impression on my father, who was then a teetotaler. He decided that he would not host any cocktail hours with Congressmen if he became President."

But while LBJ's skill at horse trading enabled him to achieve occasional greatness on the domestic front, in foreign policy he was a disaster. The tragedy of the Vietnam War highlights the potential risks of preoccupied First Dads. Their fierce determination to achieve their goals, no matter what the cost, can easily cause them to go astray. When the military campaign in Southeast Asia faltered, LBJ lacked the reflective capacity to do anything but deepen his commitment to winning the war. In contrast, Presidents with a nurturing parenting style, who eschew impulsive behavior, are a safer bet. These First Dads may not reach stratospheric heights, but they are also less likely to commit grave errors. Like Obama, Hayes and Truman were not among the most effective Presidents, but they provided leadership that was as steady as their paternal affection. Their administrations, which were largely free of corruption, except for the IRS scandals during both the Truman and Obama years, contained few surprises.

Luci Johnson is convinced that her father's driven personality was a good fit for the presidency. "Daddy was the kind of man," she has stated, "who believed it was more important to invite Richard Russell [an influential Senator from Georgia] over for Sunday breakfast than to spend the time alone with his family." In a recent interview with me, LBJ's younger daughter admitted that she used to feel cheated because she saw so little of him as a girl. Luci and Lynda went on only two vacations with their parents—and the one to Disneyland after his heart attack in 1955 lasted just a few days. "As a kid, I wished our family was normal and complained a lot," she said. But Luci also realized that her father was always "living and breathing the next crisis. I knew I had to share my daddy." Today she has no doubt his sacrifices were well worth it. "He was working for the entire country, and he really cared about the causes he was fighting for." To make her case, she mentioned a speech that LBJ gave on the night of December 12, 1972, at a Civil Rights Symposium held at the LBJ Library in Austin. Suffering from severe angina, the former President had been awake all night with Lady Bird. LBJ's doctor could not guarantee that he would walk off the podium alive. "In the middle of his remarks," noted Luci, "he gasped and took a nitroglycerin tablet. When I later asked why he had come, he answered, 'Luci Baines, how could you? If I had died, I would have died for what I had lived for. What more could any man want?'" LBJ would never appear in public again; a little over a month later, he succumbed to a fatal heart attack.

Susan Eisenhower, a granddaughter of the Republican First Dad with whom LBJ had to bargain time and time again during his days as the Senate Majority Leader, shares Luci Johnson's point of view. "I don't think a President should even try to have a normal family life," she told me. "As our public servant, his first obligation is to the people who elected him." Susan Eisenhower, who has run a Washington, DC–based consulting group since 1986, acknowledges that Ike issued some harsh criticisms of her father, John, during his years as a White House aide. But the children of Presidents, especially if they are already adults, she insists, may need to make some sacrifices, too. "My father agreed to serve as my grandfather's sounding board. It was an act of generosity on his part to help Ike, who was alone with lots of pressure and responsibility. The reality is that the presidency is like a combat situation, and family members can provide valuable help with the excessive demands."

When selecting a President, Americans are inclined to want it all— both a caring family man who can exemplify the country's character (and with whom they might enjoy sharing that proverbial beer) and a hard-charging dynamo who can get things done. This longing, which accounts for our enduring love affair with Teddy Roosevelt, probably has something to do with the fact that America has never had a monarchy. Our elected leader does double duty as both a king—a national emblem—and a prime minister—a head of the government.

In contrast, in Europe, where royal families reigned for centuries, voters are much less interested in the family lives of politicians. Americans might do well to give up the fantasy that the President is someone with whom they can ever hope to have a personal relationship. More pragmatic considerations should rule, such as whether a potential candidate has the leadership skills needed to take the country in a particular direction. In appointing someone to head a billion-dollar company, corporate boards do not consider the nature of the executive's family relationships; instead, the focus is exclusively on his or her expected job performance. Like business, politics is also ultimately about producing results rather than about managing people.

But a President's interpersonal style—how he relates to others, particularly his own children—is still far from irrelevant. Playful dads like Ulysses S. Grant may have as much trouble laying down rules for members of their administration as for their own children. And stern fathers, such as the one-term Presidents John Adams and John Quincy Adams, are likely to lack the social skills needed to connect both with fellow politicians and the public at large. Yet these loners may be less reluctant than their better-adjusted counterparts to take unpopular stands; John Adams, for example, deserves credit for his doggedness in keeping the nation out of war with England in the late 1790s. In the final analysis, all character types—even the most unappealing—come with strengths and weaknesses. While compartmentalized men such as Grover Cleveland are often reckless in their personal lives, they can sometimes be conscientious public stewards.

In the decades to come, America will no doubt elect its first First Mom. While women tend to be more nurturing parents than men, those who seek the presidency are also most likely to come from the ranks of the preoccupied. As Hillary Clinton noted a couple of years ago, "Well, you have to be a little crazy to run for President...You have to be totally consumed by [it]...and that's kind of the definition of being a little crazy, I think." But because of the double standard that permeates gender relations in our culture, female politicians may well be judged much more harshly for any parental lapses. When Wendy Davis, a former Democratic state senator from Texas, ran for Governor in 2014, she was vilified for having "abandoned" her two daughters when she moved to Massachusetts to attend Harvard Law School in her late twenties. Men such as John Adams or FDR who spent years away from their children in order to advance their careers have never had to endure such vitriol. And if a female President were to echo Teddy Roosevelt's sentiment—declaring that she was prouder to be the mother of her children than the head of the nation—large numbers of Americans might squirm. Our first First Mom will have to work even harder than her male predecessors to prove that she can hold her own on the chaotic battlefield that is—and has long been—the American presidency.

Acknowledgments

I am grateful to everyone who agreed to be interviewed, but I want to add a special word of thanks to those individuals who not only carved out time to speak to me, but also helped me land other interviews. Their interest in my project proved invaluable. For FDR, this guardian angel was John Boettiger Jr.; for LBJ, it was Tom Johnson; for Jimmy Carter, it was Caron Griffin Morgan; and for Barack Obama, it was Bronwen Solyom. Likewise, while I appreciate the efforts of all the archivists from around the country who helped me locate documents, several deserve a special mention for going above and beyond the call of duty—Heather Cole of Houghton Library, Nan Card of the Rutherford B. Hayes Library, Dave Clark of the Truman Library, Julie Bartlett Nelson of the Forbes Library, Paul Carnahan of the Vermont Historical Society, Robert Clark of the FDR Library, Kendra Hinkle of the Andrew Johnson National Historic Site, Thomas G. Lannon of the New York Public Library, and Elizabeth Shortt of the Woodrow Wilson Presidential Library and Museum.

I am indebted to Robin Lind for arranging my 2013 visit to Sherwood Forest, where I was able to interview John Tyler's grandson Harrison Tyler and his wife, Payne.

Over the past few years, I have been blessed by the fellowship of numerous biographers whom I have met through the Biographers International Organization (BIO), on whose board I proudly serve. Several took time out of their busy schedules to share relevant insights, including Evan Thomas, Irv Gellman, Megan Marshall, Will Swift, and Nigel Hamilton. At BIO's 2014 conference in Boston, I moderated a session on group biography, where I learned a great deal from panelists David Hajdu, Susan Hertog, and Justin Martin. The following June at BIO's meeting at the National Press Club in Washington, I discussed some of the challenges involved in writing this book at a panel on medical diagnosis in biographical subjects, moderated by Robin Rausch, which also featured Dr. Lawrence Altman and Heath Lee.

At Grand Central, I would like to thank Jamie Raab, the president and publisher, for her enthusiastic support. My editor, Mitch Hoffman, provided invaluable counsel, and his assistant, Lindsey Rose, lent a steady hand. Jimmy Franco has also been a devoted publicist. I am also indebted to my agents, Eric Lupfer and Suzanne Gluck of William Morris Endeavor, who both helped give birth to the idea and guide me along the way.

Rachel Youdelman shared insightful comments on an early draft and also helped me track down the photos. I am also grateful to Lauren Smith for help with copyediting.

I would also like to thank the Virginia Center for the Creative Arts for the fellowships that allowed me to do two residencies while I was writing this book.

This is the fourth biography that I have had the pleasure to write from my perch on the fifth floor of the Boston Athenaeum. I appreciate the support of every member of the library's gracious staff, especially Mary Warnement, the William D. Hacker Head of Reader Services.

In February 2015, as I was struggling to meet my deadline, New England was hit by a series of blizzards, which ended up dropping nearly a dozen feet of snow on Boston. When water from ice dams lodged on the roof of my building began leaking into my apartment, several of my Beacon Hill neighbors came to the rescue. I owe a special thanks to Jeff and Jody Black for putting me up in their historic town house, once visited by Teddy Roosevelt, for a couple of weeks.

Unfortunately, as noted in the dedication, my father, George B. Kendall, died while I was working on the book. It is impossible not to think of one's own father when writing (or reading) about America's

First Dads. Of all the First Children, I identified the most with John Eisenhower, whose demanding father also had something to do with his decision to become a writer. I think I have come to know and understand my dad better over the past few years, and I only wish that I could have shared the final product with him.

Sources and Notes

While no previous book focuses exclusively on the fathering experiences of Presidents, several authors have addressed the lives of the First Children. The most thorough studies are *Presidents' Sons: The Prestige of Name in a Democracy* (New York, 1947) by the late Joseph Perling, the longtime publisher of the *Wilmington Record*, and *All the Presidents' Children: Triumph and Tragedy in the Lives of America's First Families* (New York, 2003) by Doug Wead, an ordained Assemblies of God minister who has worked as an advisor to President George Herbert Walker Bush as well as to President George W. Bush. Other overviews include *Our Early Presidents: Their Wives and Children* (Boston, 1890) by Harriet Upton, *Children in the White House* (New York, 1967) by Christine Sadler, *America's First Families* (New York, 2000) by Carl Sferrazza Anthony, and *First Families: The Impact of the White House on Their Lives* (New York, 2005) by Bonnie Angelo. Brief biographies of all the presidential offspring can be found in *America's Royalty: All the Presidents' Children* (Westport, CT, 1995) by Sandra L. Quinn-Musgrove and Sanford Kanter, and *The Complete Book of U.S. Presidents* (Fort Lee, NJ, 2009) by William A. DeGregorio and Sandra Lee Stuart.

To categorize the Presidents, I relied on these books as well as the major biographies. I also consulted memoirs written by various First Dads, First Ladies, and First Children. For the eighteen presidents—three per chapter—whom I covered in depth, I delved into various primary source materials—particularly the published and unpublished presidential papers and family letters—as well as the press coverage. (To track down newspaper articles published before 1922, I used the excellent

online database Archive of Americana, available at most public libraries.)
I also mined the vast secondary literature on their administrations, as I
was interested in drawing connections between how each First Dad led
his family and the nation. In many cases, I also spoke with an influential
biographer or archivist (e.g., James Taylor, an editor of the Adams Papers
at the Massachusetts Historical Society). For the more recent Presidents, I
interviewed family members, family friends, and/or aides. Whenever possible, I also traveled to the President's home and memorial library. The
Library of Congress has microfilmed the collected papers of twenty-three
of the first thirty Presidents, and I was able to view these manuscripts at
Harvard's Lamont Library. I also visited the Library of Congress to look
at the addenda to these collections as well as other relevant manuscripts.

As a Bostonian, I am fortunate to have several outstanding archive
libraries in my backyard such as the Boston Athenaeum, the Massachusetts Historical Society, and Harvard University's Houghton
Library. While the Massachusetts Historical Society is the repository
for the Adams Papers, which includes manuscripts of all the children
of both John Adams and John Quincy Adams, it also contains letters
and diaries of several other early Presidents. Likewise, besides its vast
collection of Theodore Roosevelt papers, Houghton Library also features original letters of dozens of Presidents and countless other manuscripts related to presidential history. At Houghton, I also stumbled
upon various unexpected gems such as a unique annotated edition of
the 1968 Harding biography, *The Shadow of Blooming Grove*, by Francis Russell, a Harvard alumnus. Due to a lawsuit, shortly before publication Russell was forced to remove all the quotations from Harding's
steamy love letters to Carrie Phillips, which he replaced by dashes. In
the edition of the book Russell donated to Houghton, Xeroxed strips
of the original text have been superimposed over the dashes. This was
the only place where researchers could get a peek at those letters until
2014, when the Library of Congress unsealed them all.

Since twenty-two presidential children have attended Harvard—fifteen
more than Yale, the second-most popular academic destination—I also

found it useful to visit the Harvard University Archives, which maintains files of newspaper clippings and other tidbits on distinguished alumni. Among these First Children are the three sons of both John Adams and John Quincy Adams as well as the four sons of Theodore Roosevelt and three of the four sons of Franklin Roosevelt. The penciled annotations of archivists are not without interest. For instance, in the margins of an article about George Washington Adams's death, some university librarian of yesteryear added the word "suicide," in an attempt to clarify a longstanding mystery.

Since the scope of my subject matter is so wide—all forty-four Presidents, who have fathered approximately two hundred children—I have tried to keep the list of references down to a manageable number. I leave out countless books, articles, and manuscript archives that I briefly consulted. For quotations from newspaper and magazine articles, I typically mention the publication and the year in the book. Additionally, for any information easily found on the web such as text from a President's inaugural address, which, for example, is available, at the Avalon Project at the Yale Law School (http://avalon.law.yale .edu/subject_menus/inaug.asp), I do not provide a source.

Throughout the book, archaic spellings have been replaced by their contemporary equivalents.

I mention below the key sources—as well as some explanatory notes and suggestions for further reading—by chapter.

Prologue. *The Sense and Sensibility of James Garfield*

Lucretia Garfield Comer, *Harry Garfield's First Forty Years: Man of Action in a Troubled World* (New York, 1965).

Harry James Brown and Frederick D. Williams, eds., *The Diary of James A. Garfield, Volume IV, 1878–1881* (East Lansing, MI, 1981).

For thoughtful reflections about character and the American presidency, see James David Barber, *The Presidential Character: Predicting Performance in the White House* (Englewood Cliffs, NJ, 1972); Richard Ben Cramer, *What It Takes: The Way to the White House* (New York, 1992); Jerrold M. Post, *The Psychological Assessment of Political Leaders: With Profiles of Saddam Hussein and Bill Clinton* (Ann Arbor, MI, 2003); Matt Bai, *All the Truth Is Out: The Week Politics Went Tabloid* (New York, 2014); Joseph S. Nye Jr., *Presidential Leadership and the Creation of the*

American Era (Princeton, NJ, 2013); and Lorri Glover, *Founders as Fathers: The Private Lives and Politics of the American Revolutionaries* (New Haven, CT, 2014).

Ron Chernow, *Washington: A Life* (New York, 2010).

Dorothy Twohig, ed., *The Papers of George Washington*, Vol. 2 of *Presidential Series* (Charlottesville, VA, 1987).

Richard Nixon, *RN: The Memoirs of Richard Nixon* (New York, 1978).

Paul Raeburn's *Do Fathers Matter? What Science Is Telling Us About the Parent We've Overlooked* (New York, 2014) provides a useful overview of the contemporary literature on fatherhood. For my assessment of Raeburn's book and the new science of fathering, see Joshua Kendall, "'Do Fathers Matter?' Attempts to Redefine 21st Century Fatherhood," *Los Angeles Times*, June 15, 2014.

Michael Beschloss, "The Curse of the Famous Scion," *Newsweek*, August 14, 1995, p. 59.

For a quick discussion of how First Children have often failed to live up to their illustrious fathers, see my op-ed, Joshua Kendall, "Anti-Dynasty Roots Run Deep in USA," *USA Today*, June 18, 2015.

Interviews: Jerrold Post, M.D., and Raymond Levy, Psy.D. (Director of the Fatherhood Project in the Department of Psychiatry at Harvard University's Massachusetts General Hospital).

Chapter 1. *The Preoccupied*

FDR

The FDR Library in Hyde Park contains unpublished letters between FDR and his children as well as files on all the children, which include such intriguing documents as their high school and college transcripts. The Anna Roosevelt Papers feature her diary during the Yalta trip as well as her letters to her husband, John Boettiger Sr.

After FDR's death, his second son, Elliott, emerged as the family's primary historian. In 1946, he published *As He Saw It* (New York), a memoir about his experience as a wartime aide to his father. He then edited a four-volume edition of his father's letters, *FDR: His Personal Letters* (New York, 1947–1950). Two decades later, along with coauthor James Brough, Elliott wrote three family memoirs—*An Untold Story: The Roosevelts of Hyde Park* (New York, 1973), *A Rendezvous with Destiny: The Roosevelts of the White House* (New York, 1975), and *Mother R: Eleanor Roosevelt's Untold Story* (New York, 1977). His elder brother, James Roosevelt, also wrote two memoirs—one with Sidney Shalett, *Affectionately, FDR: A Son's Story of a Lonely Man* (New York, 1959); and one with Bill Libby, *My Parents: A Differing View* (Chicago, 1976). James felt compelled to update his first memoir in order to respond to Elliott's allegation that the polio-stricken FDR had consummated a sexual relationship with his longtime secretary, Missy LeHand.

Two informative books have also been written by FDR grandchildren—John R. Boettiger, *A Love in Shadow: The Story of Anna Roosevelt and John Boettiger* (New York, 1978); and Curtis Roosevelt, *Too Close to the Sun: Growing Up in the Shadow of My Grandparents, Franklin and Eleanor* (New York, 2008).

Geoffrey Ward, *A First-Class Temperament: The Emergence of Franklin Roosevelt* (New York, 1989).

Doris Kearns Goodwin, *No Ordinary Time: Franklin and Eleanor Roosevelt: The Home Front in World War II* (New York, 1994).

Peter Collier and David Horowitz, *The Roosevelts: An American Saga* (New York, 1995).

Conrad Black, *Franklin Delano Roosevelt: Champion of Freedom* (New York, 2003).

Jean Edward Smith, *FDR* (New York, 2008).

John Chamberlain, "FDR's Daughter," *Life*, March 5, 1945, pp. 96–108.

Eleanor Roosevelt, *The Autobiography of Eleanor Roosevelt* (New York, 1961).

Bernard Asbell, ed., *Mother and Daughter: The Letters of Eleanor and Anna Roosevelt* (New York, 1982).

Joseph Persico, *Franklin and Lucy: President Roosevelt, Mrs. Rutherford and the Other Remarkable Women in His Life* (New York, 2008).

Michael Beschloss, *The Conquerors: Roosevelt, Truman and the Destruction of Hitler's Germany, 1941–1945* (New York, 2002).

Interviews: John Boettiger Jr., Irwin Gellman, Nina Roosevelt Gibson, Doris Mack, Eleanor Roosevelt Seagraves, James Roosevelt Jr., and Mary Roosevelt.

LBJ

Robert Caro, *Master of the Senate*, Vol. 3 of *The Years of Lyndon Johnson* (New York, 2002).

Robert Dallek, *Lone Star Rising: Lyndon Johnson and His Times, 1908–1960* (New York, 1991); *Flawed Giant: Lyndon Johnson and His Times, 1961–1973* (New York, 1998).

Randall Woods, *LBJ: Architect of American Ambition* (New York, 2006).

Mark Updegrove, *Indomitable Will: LBJ in the Presidency* (New York, 2012).

Lady Bird Johnson (Claudia Taylor Johnson), *A White House Diary* (New York, 1970).

Michael Gillette, *Lady Bird Johnson: An Oral History* (New York, 2012).

Interviews: Ervin Duggan, Luci Johnson, and Tom Johnson.

Jimmy Carter

Jack Carter's 2003 Oral History (http://www.jimmycarterlibrary.gov/library/oralhistory/clohproject/jackcarter.pdf) and Chip Carter's 2008 Oral History (https://www.youtube.com/watch?v=3dhdwVyaUzA) are available on the web.

Of Jimmy Carter's nearly thirty books, I relied most heavily on *Why Not the Best* (Nashville, 1975), *Keeping Faith: Memoirs of a President* (New York, 1982), *Living Faith* (New York, 1996), *Sharing Good Times* (New York, 2004), and *White House Diary* (New York, 2010).

Dan Ariail and Cheryl Heckler-Feltz, *The Carpenter's Apprentice: The Spiritual Biography of Jimmy Carter* (Grand Rapids, MI, 1996).

Peter Bourne, *Jimmy Carter: A Comprehensive Biography from Plains to Post-Presidency* (New York, 1997).

Frye Gaillard, *Prophet from Plains: Jimmy Carter and His Legacy* (Athens, GA, 2007).

E. Stanly Godbold Jr., *Jimmy and Rosalynn Carter: The Georgia Years, 1924–1974* (New York, 2010).
Elizabeth Drew, *Portrait of an Election: The 1980 Presidential Campaign* (New York, 1981).
Rosalynn Carter, *First Lady from Plains* (Boston, 1984).
Don Richardson, *Conversations with Carter* (Boulder, 1998).
Interviews: Chip Carter, James Earl Carter IV, Kit Dobelle (Chief of Staff to Rosalynn Carter), Muriel Dobbin, Roger Gittines, Judy Langford, and Caron Griffin Morgan.

Other Preoccupied First Dads

Martin Van Buren, *Inquiry into the Origin and Cause of Political Parties in the United States*, edited by Abraham Van Buren and John Van Buren (New York, 1867).
John Niven, *Martin Van Buren: The Romantic Age of American Politics* (New York, 1983).
Wayne Cutler, James L. Rogers II, and Benjamin Severance, eds., *Correspondence of James K. Polk*, Vol. 11, *1846* (Knoxville, TN, 2009).
Charles Sellers, *James Polk: Continentalist, 1843–1846* (Princeton, NJ, 1966).
Silas McKinley, *Old Rough and Ready: The Life and Times of Zachary Taylor* (New York, 1946).
James T. Patterson, *Mr. Republican: A Biography of Robert A. Taft* (Boston, 1972).
Phyllis Robbins, *Robert A. Taft, Boy and Man* (Cambridge, MA, 1953).
Herbert Hoover, *The Memoirs of Herbert Hoover*, Vol. 1, *1874–1920, Years of Adventure* (New York, 1952).
Nancy Beck Young, *Lou Henry Hoover: Activist First Lady* (Lawrence, KS, 2004).
Richard Norton Smith, *An Uncommon Man: The Triumph of Herbert Hoover* (New York, 1984).
Anthony Summers, *The Arrogance of Power: The Secret World of Richard Nixon* (New York, 2000).
Julie Nixon Eisenhower, *Pat Nixon: The Untold Story* (New York, 1986).
Ron Reagan, *My Father at 100* (New York, 2011).
Kiron K. Skinner, Annelise Anderson, and Martin Anderson, eds., *Reagan: A Life in Letters* (New York, 2003).
Kitty Kelley, *The Family: The Real Story of the Bush Dynasty* (New York, 2004).
George W. Bush, *41: A Portrait of My Father* (New York, 2014).
David Maraniss, *First in His Class: A Biography of Bill Clinton* (New York, 1995).

Chapter 2. *Playful Pals*
Ulysses S. Grant

The annotated Library of America volume, *Ulysses S. Grant: Memoirs and Selected Letters*, edited by Mary McFeely (New York, 1990), includes the full text of his two-volume memoir, widely considered one of the best by a former President, as well as several relevant letters. For additional correspondence with or concerning his children, I examined *The Papers of Ulysses S. Grant*, 31 vols., (Carbondale, IL, 1967–2009), which was edited by John Simon.

Jesse Grant, *In the Days of My Father, General Grant* (New York, 1925).

Horace Porter, *Campaigning with Grant* (New York, 1897).

Adam Badeau, *Grant in Peace: From Appomattox to Mount McGregor* (Hartford, CT, 1887).

Brooks Simpson, *Ulysses S. Grant: Triumph Over Adversity, 1822–1865* (New York, 2000).

William McFeely, *Grant: A Biography* (New York, 1981).

Julia Dent Grant, *The Personal Memoirs of Julia Dent Grant* (New York, 1975).

Ishbel Ross, *The General's Wife: The Life of Mrs. Ulysses S. Grant* (New York, 1959).

Mary Clemmer Ames, *Ten Years in Washington: Life and Scenes in the National Capital, as a Woman Sees Them* (Hartford, CT, 1874).

For more on Jesse Grant's tragicomic presidential run, see "Mr. Grant Wouldn't Mind Being President," *New York Times*, May 12, 1907.

Theodore Roosevelt

The Theodore Roosevelt Center (http://www.theodoreroosevelt.org), run by Dickinson State University in North Dakota, has put together a massive digital library containing TR material from a dozen archives, including Houghton Library, which holds the largest collection of TR papers. Houghton contains the papers of all the children, except for those of Theodore Jr., which I combed through at the Library of Congress. Houghton's holdings on Archibald Roosevelt include his 136-page unpublished memoir, written in 1966.

At the Theodore Roosevelt collection in Harvard's Widener Library, I tracked down the newspaper article by the author of *Gone with the Wind*, about the Roosevelt family—Peggy Mitchell, "Bridesmaid of 87 Recalls Mittie Roosevelt's Wedding," *Atlanta Journal Magazine*, June 10, 1923.

The comments about the Roosevelt family by Ella Riley, head of housekeeping at the White House during the last three years of the Coolidge Administration, are drawn from her letters to her mother, Adell, which are held at the Vermont Historical Society in Barre, VT.

Joan Kerr has edited a new edition of *Theodore Roosevelt's Letters to His Children* (New York, 1995), this one titled *A Bully Father*, which includes an introduction by David McCullough. The original edition (New York, 1919), edited by the journalist Joseph Bucklin Bishop, was a bestseller.

Theodore Roosevelt Jr., *All in the Family* (New York, 1929).

Earle Looker, *The White House Gang* (New York, 1929).

Quentin Roosevelt's observation, "My father likes snakes," is drawn from the uncredited article, "Took Three Snakes into White House," *New York Times*, September 27, 1907.

Edmund Morris, *Theodore Rex* (New York, 2001).

Edmund Morris, *Colonel Roosevelt* (New York, 2010).

Edward Wagenknecht, *The Seven Worlds of Theodore Roosevelt* (New York, 1958).

Kathleen Dalton, *Theodore Roosevelt: A Strenuous Life* (New York, 2002).

Stacy Cordery, *Alice: Alice Roosevelt Longworth, from White House Princess to Washington Power Broker* (New York, 2007).

Sylvia Jukes Morris, *Edith Kermit Roosevelt: Portrait of a First Lady* (New York, 1980).
Michael Teague, *Mrs. L: Conversations with Alice Roosevelt Longworth* (New York, 1981).
Robert Walker, *The Namesake: The Biography of Theodore Roosevelt, Jr.* (New York, 2008).
Irwin Hoover, *Forty-Two Years in the White House* (Boston, 1934).
Interview: Tweed Roosevelt.

Woodrow Wilson

The Woodrow Wilson Presidential Library and Museum (http://www.woodrowwilson.org), located at the former President's birthplace in Staunton, VA, maintains an excellent e-library containing copies of the Jessie Wilson Sayre Papers, which are housed at Princeton University, and the Eleanor Wilson McAdoo Papers, which are housed at the University of California at Santa Barbara. I also looked at the unpublished biography of Jessie Wilson by Mary Hoyt, a cousin of Ellen Axson Wilson, which is held in the Presidential Library's own William D. Hoyt Jr. Collection. In the New York Public Library's small collection of Woodrow Wilson documents, I found the letter from Margaret Wilson to the head of the National Civic Federation from which I quote. At the Library of Congress, I viewed letters between Wilson and Edith Bolling Galt, written before their marriage in December 1915, as well as letters between Galt and Wilson's daughters.
At Houghton Library, I looked at the Percy MacKaye Papers.
Wilson's youngest daughter, Eleanor, became the family scribe, writing a memoir about her parents, *The Woodrow Wilsons* (New York, 1937) and editing a collection of their letters, *The Priceless Gift: The Love Letters of Woodrow Wilson and Ellen Axson Wilson* (New York, 1962). Wilson's brother-in-law, the literary scholar Stockton Axson, who lived on and off with Wilson and his children, has also penned a revealing portrait, *"Brother Woodrow": A Memoir of Woodrow Wilson* (Princeton, NJ, 1993).
John Milton Cooper Jr., *Woodrow Wilson: A Biography* (New York, 2009).
A. Scott Berg, *Wilson* (New York, 2013).
Edmund Starling, *Starling of the White House: The Story of the Man Whose Secret Service Detail Guarded Five Presidents from Woodrow Wilson to Franklin D. Roosevelt* (New York, 1946).
Frances Saunders, *Ellen Axson Wilson: First Lady Between Two Worlds* (Chapel Hill, NC, 1985).
For information on the children and stepchildren of Wilson's daughter, Eleanor, I relied on Douglas Craig, *Progressives at War: William G. McAdoo and Newton D. Baker 1863–1941* (Baltimore, 2013).
For an account of the 1959 luncheon at the Women's National Press Club, attended by Eleanor Wilson, see the AP story, "9 Children of Presidents Discuss Dads," *Boston Globe*, May 1, 1959.

Other Playful Pals

George Ticknor Curtis, *Life of James Buchanan: Fifteenth President of the United States*, 2 vols. (New York, 1883).

Thomas Reeves, *Gentleman Boss: The Life of Chester Alan Arthur* (New York, 1975).
Addenda to the Chester Alan Arthur Papers at the Library of Congress.
Carl Swanson, "Barbara Bush's Balancing Act," *Elle.com*, September 24, 2013.

Chapter 3. *Double-Dealing Dads*

John Tyler

I examined Tyler manuscripts at the Virginia Historical Society in Richmond, at William and Mary University's Swem Library, and at Yale University's Sterling Library, which holds the Gardiner Family Papers.

I found the 1841 letter to Tyler from James Lyons, from which I quote, in the Addenda to the Tyler Papers at the Library of Congress.

The letter in which the teenager Eliza Fisk Harwood reports that President Tyler tried to kiss her is contained in the Skinner Papers, which are held in the Southern Historical Collection at the University of North Carolina in Chapel Hill. In 2015, archivist and editor Mary Maillard published Fisk's letters from this period in her life in an Amazon e-book, *The Belles of Williamsburg: The Courtship Correspondence of Eliza Fisk Harwood and Tristrim Lowther Skinner, 1839–1849*.

Lyon Gardiner Tyler, *The Letters and Times of the Tylers*, 3 vols. (Williamsburg, VA, 1896).

Oliver Perry Chitwood, *John Tyler: Champion of the Old South* (New York, 1939).

Edward Crapol, *John Tyler, The Accidental President* (Chapel Hill, NC, 2006).

Robert Seager, *And Tyler Too: A Biography of John and Julia Gardiner Tyler* (New York, 1963).

Daryl Dance, *The Lineage of Abraham: The Biography of a Free Black Family in Charles City, VA* (Richmond, VA, 1998).

Hiram Cumming, *Secret History of the Perfidies, Intrigues, and Corruptions of the Tyler Dynasty, with the Mysteries of Washington City, Connected with That Vile Administration, in a Series of Letters to the ex-Acting President* (Washington, DC, 1845).

Norma Lois Peterson, *The Presidencies of William Henry Harrison and John Tyler* (Lawrence, KS, 1989).

Don Fehrenbacher and Virginia Fehrenbacher, eds., *Recollected Words of Abraham Lincoln* (Stanford, CA, 1996).

Laura Holloway, *The Ladies of the White House, or in the Home of the Presidents, Being a Complete History of the Social and Domestic Lives of the Presidents from Washington to the Present Time* (Philadelphia, PA, 1882).

William Still, *The Underground Railroad* (Salem, NH, 1992).

Frederick Merk with Lois Bannister Merk, *Fruits of Propaganda in the Tyler Administration* (Cambridge, MA, 1971). In an appendix, the Merks include the full text of the "Letter of Mr. Walker of Mississippi, Relative to the Annexation of Texas."

In a manuscript dated January 8, 1938, which is contained in the unpublished book, *Department of Negro History, Heroes of the Negro Race*, journalist Drusilla Dunjee Houston recounts the life of John William Dunjee (sometimes spelled *Dungee* or *Dungy*), asserting that Tyler was his grandfather. This reference was provided to me by Dr. Peggy Brooks-Bertram, who spoke about her research on John Dunjee at a

2005 conference held at the University of Buffalo (http://library.buffalo.edu/exhibits/pdf/foreverfree.pdf).

Interviews: Milton Brown, Peggy Brooks-Bertram, Edward Crapol, Daryl Dance, Judith Ledbetter, Mary Maillard, Randy Ross, Harrison Tyler, and Payne Tyler.

Grover Cleveland

I stumbled upon four love letters of Cleveland to Kate Nash, written between 1892 and 1896, in the Lee Kohns Collection at the New York Public Library.

Robert McNutt McElroy, *Grover Cleveland, the Man and the Statesman: An Authorized Biography*, 2 vols. (New York, 1923).

Allan Nevins, *Grover Cleveland: A Study in Courage* (New York, 1932).

H. Paul Jeffers, *An Honest President: The Life and Presidencies of Grover Cleveland* (New York, 2000).

Matthew Algeo, *The President Is a Sick Man: Wherein the Supposedly Virtuous Grover Cleveland Survives a Secret Surgery at Sea and Vilifies the Courageous Newspaperman Who Dared Expose the Truth* (Chicago, 2011).

Charles Lachman, *A Secret Life: The Lies and Scandals of President Grover Cleveland* (New York, 2011).

Allan Nevins, ed., *Letters of Grover Cleveland, 1850–1908* (Boston, 1933).

Albert Ellery Bergh, ed., *Letters and Addresses of Grover Cleveland* (New York, 1909).

The manuscripts of Halpin's affidavits about the alleged rape by Cleveland were recently rediscovered by biographer Charles Lachman. These affidavits were published in numerous Republican newspapers right before the election of 1884. See, for example, "The Worst of the Cleveland Scandal Has Not Been Told," *Duluth Tribune*, October 31, 1884.

Interview: Charles Lachman.

Warren Harding

In late July 2014, The Library of Congress released the 240 items in the correspondence between Harding and Carrie Phillips, which are now all available online (http://www.loc.gov/collection/warren-harding-carrie-fulton-phillips-correspondence/about-this-collection/). Earlier that month, Jordan Michael Smith published an article, "The Letters That Warren G. Harding's Family Didn't Want You to See," in the *New York Times Magazine*, which described the controversy surrounding their release and included a few excerpts (http://www.nytimes.com/2014/07/13/magazine/letters-warren-g-harding.html). In a front-page story, "Test Results Are In: At Long Last, the Secret About Harding Is Out" in the *New York Times* (August 13, 2015), Peter Baker reported on the recent DNA testing, which, he noted, "has solved one of the enduring mysteries of presidential history."

At the Library of Congress, I looked at the Papers of Warren Harding as well as at the Papers of the Washington socialite Evalyn Walsh McLean, who was a friend and confidante of Florence Harding.

Houghton Library possesses Harding's personal copy—the book is signed by him—of the steamy 1911 novel *The Dangerous Age*, by the Danish writer Karin Michaëlis, suggesting that this sexually promiscuous politician liked to read erotic literature.
At Houghton Library, I also found the observations about Harding of the Harvard President, Abbott Lowell, in a letter to Frederic J. Stimson, his former law partner, which is contained in the Abbott Lowell Papers.
Nan Britton, *The President's Daughter* (New York, 1927).
Francis Russell, *The Shadow of Blooming Grove: Warren G. Harding in His Times* (New York, 1968).
Robert K. Murray, *The Harding Era: Warren G. Harding and His Administration* (Minneapolis, 1969).
Robert H. Ferrell, *The Strange Deaths of President Harding* (Columbia, MO, 1996).
Over the last decade, a new wave of Harding revisionism has emerged. In his brief study, *Warren G. Harding* (New York, 2004), former Nixon aide John Dean, who claims that Britton's "purported confessional" was responsible for "trashing Harding's personal life," defends the twenty-ninth President from the charge that he was an ineffective leader. So, too, does James Robenalt, in *The Harding Affair: Love and Espionage During the Great War* (New York, 2009), where he accuses Harding's critics of suffering from an "obsession" with the former president's sex life. Though Robenalt argues that Phillips may have been a spy, he also denies that the affair with Britton ever took place, insisting that the "close study of the Phillips letters tends to discredit Ms. Britton's story." But six years later, when he was confronted with the new DNA evidence by Peter Baker of the *New York Times*, Robenalt renounced that position.
Francis Russell, "The Shadow of Warren Harding," *Antioch Review* 36 (Winter 1978).
Excerpts from H. L. Mencken's article, "Balder and Dash," originally published in 1921 in the *Baltimore Evening Sun*, are reprinted in *Lapham's Quarterly* 7 (Winter 2014).
Carl Sferrazza Anthony, *Florence Harding: The First Lady, the Jazz Age, and the Death of America's Most Scandalous President* (New York, 1998).
Eugene Trani and David Wilson, *The Presidency of Warren G. Harding* (Lawrence, KS, 1977).
Robert Murray, *The Politics of Normalcy: Governmental Theory and Practice in the Harding-Coolidge Era* (New York, 1973).

Other Double-Dealing Dads

Annette Gordon-Reed, *The Hemingses of Monticello: An American Family* (New York, 2008).
Kenneth Robert Janken, *White: The Biography of Walter White, Mr. NAACP* (New York, 2003).
Henry Wiencek, *An Imperfect God: George Washington, His Slaves, and the Creation of America* (New York, 2003).
David Warren Brown's comments about President Andrew Johnson are included in the chapter "Presidents, Race, and Sex" by Werner Sollors, in *Sally Hemings and*

Thomas Jefferson: History, Memory, and Civic Culture, edited by Jan Ellen Lewis and Peter S. Onuf (Charlottesville, VA, 1999).

Madeleine Duncan Brown, *Texas in the Morning: The Love Story of Madeleine Brown and President Lyndon Baines Johnson* (Baltimore, 1997).

Robert J. Scarry, *Millard Fillmore* (Jefferson, NC, 2000).

Houghton Library contains the extensive correspondence between Fillmore and Dorothea Dix covering the years 1850 to 1869.

Harry Sievers, *Benjamin Harrison, Hoosier President: The White House and After* (Indianapolis, IN, 1968).

Chapter 4. *Tiger Dads*

John Adams

The Massachusetts Historical Society holds the papers of John Adams. Valuable information about his family life can be found in *Diary and Autobiography of John Adams,* 4 vols., edited by L. H. Butterfield, Leonard Faber, and Wendell Garrett (Cambridge, MA, 1961). The *Adams Family Correspondence,* of which twelve volumes, covering 1761 to 1798, have been published to date (Cambridge, MA, 1963–2013) and whose current editors are Sara Martin, James Taylor, Neal Millikan, Amanda Mathews, Hobson Woodward, Sara Sikes, Gregg Lint, and Sara Georgini, includes numerous letters between John Adams and his children.

At the Massachusetts Historical Society, I viewed additional unpublished letters between Charles Adams and his father. Eight letters that Charles sent to John Adams have long been reported as missing. Given the tragic circumstances surrounding Charles's early death, some historians suspect that the family may have destroyed them.

David Musto, "The Youth of John Quincy Adams," *Proceedings of the American Philosophical Society* 113 (August 15, 1969), pp. 269–282.

The family's foremost historian, Charles Francis Adams, completed a biography, which his father, John Quincy Adams, had started, *Life of John Adams,* 2 vols. (Philadelphia, 1871). Charles Francis Adams also edited a twelve-volume edition of his father's massive diary, *Memoirs of John Quincy Adams, Comprising Portions of His Diary from 1795 to 1848* (Philadelphia, PA, 1877).

John Ferling, *John Adams: A Life* (Knoxville, TN, 1992).

Joseph Ellis, *First Family: Abigail and John Adams* (New York, 2010).

Joseph Ellis, *Passionate Sage: The Character and Legacy of John Adams* (New York, 1993).

David McCullough, *John Adams* (New York, 2001).

Page Smith, *John Adams,* 2 vols. (Garden City, NY, 1962).

Peter Shaw, *The Character of John Adams* (Chapel Hill, NC, 1976).

Jack Shepherd, *Adams Chronicles: Four Generations of Greatness* (Boston, 1975).

Paul Nagel, *Descent from Glory: Four Generations of the John Adams Family* (New York, 1983).

Paul Nagel, *The Adams Women: Abigail and Louisa Adams, Their Sisters and Daughters* (New York, 1987).

Caroline DeWindt, the daughter of Abigail (Nabby) Adams, has edited some of her mother's writings, in *Journal and Correspondence of Miss Adams, Daughter of John Adams, Second President of the United States. Written in France and England in 1785*, 2 vols. (New York, 1841–1842).

Victor Hugo Paltsits, ed., *Berlin and the Prussian Court in 1798: Journal of Thomas Boylston Adams* (New York, 1916).

Charles Washburn, ed., "Letters of Thomas Boylston Adams to William Shaw Smith," *Proceedings of the American Antiquarian Society* 27 (1917), pp. 83–176.

Interview: James Taylor.

John Quincy Adams

At the Massachusetts Historical Society, I looked at George Washington Adams's unpublished memoir.

Information on the illegitimate child of George Washington Adams can be found in the pamphlet *Report of a Trial: Miles Farmer, versus Dr. David Humphreys Storer* (Boston, 1831).

Charles Francis Adams's diaries, which run from 1820 to 1880, are also housed at the Massachusetts Historical Society. In 1964, under the editorship of Aida Donald and David Donald, Harvard University Press (Cambridge, MA) began publishing them. So far, eight volumes, which go up to 1840, have appeared.

The papers of Russell Jarvis, which are held at Houghton Library, contain several interesting letters and documents on the violent April 1828 encounter between this Washington journalist and John Adams II.

At Houghton Library, I found a letter from John Quincy to his mother-in-law, Mrs. Joshua Johnson, dated April 18, 1801, in which he alludes to his feelings upon the birth of his first son, George.

John Quincy Adams, *Letters of John Quincy Adams to His Son, On the Bible and Its Teachings* (Auburn, NY, 1848).

Judith Graham, Beth Luey, Margaret Hogan, and C. James Taylor, eds., *Diary and Autobiographical Writings of Louisa Catherine Adams*, 2 vols. (Cambridge, MA, 2013).

Paul Nagel, *John Quincy Adams: A Public Life, A Private Life* (New York, 1997).

Harlow Unger, *John Quincy Adams* (Boston, 2012).

Martin Duberman, *Charles Francis Adams, 1807–1866* (Boston, 1961).

Henry Adams, *The Education of Henry Adams* (New York, 1990).

Jack Shepherd, *Cannibals of the Heart: A Personal Biography of Louisa Catherine and John Quincy Adams* (New York, 1980).

Dwight Eisenhower

John Eisenhower, *Strictly Personal* (Garden City, NY, 1974).

Stephen Ambrose, *Eisenhower*, 2 vols. (New York, 1983–1984).

Michael Korda, *Ike: An American Hero* (New York, 2007).

Joseph Hobbs, ed., *Dear General: Eisenhower's Wartime Letters to Marshall* (Baltimore, 1971).

Dwight D. Eisenhower, *Letters to Mamie*, edited by John S. D. Eisenhower (Garden City, NY, 1978).

Alfred D. Chandler, ed., *The Papers of Dwight David Eisenhower*, vols 1–6 (Baltimore, 1970–1978).

Francis Trevelyan Miller, *Eisenhower: Man and Soldier* (Philadelphia, 1944).

Dwight Eisenhower, *At Ease: Stories I Tell to Friends* (Garden City, NY, 1967).

David Eisenhower, *Going Home to Glory: A Memoir of Life with Dwight D. Eisenhower, 1961–1969* (New York, 2010).

Steve Neal, *The Eisenhowers: Reluctant Dynasty* (Garden City, NY, 1978).

Harry Butcher, *My Three Years with Eisenhower: The Personal Diary of Captain Harry C. Butcher, USNR, Naval Aide to General Eisenhower, 1942 to 1945* (New York, 1946).

Kay Summersby Morgan, *Past Forgetting: My Love Affair with Dwight D. Eisenhower* (New York, 1976).

Carlo D'Este, *Eisenhower: A Soldier's Life* (New York, 2002).

Fred Greenstein, *The Hidden-Hand Presidency: Eisenhower as Leader* (New York, 1982).

Evan Thomas, *Ike's Bluff: Eisenhower's Secret Battle to Save the World* (New York, 2012).

Interviews: Mary Jean Eisenhower, Susan Eisenhower, and Evan Thomas.

Tiger Dads Overview

Amy Chua, *Battle Hymn of the Tiger Mother* (New York, 2011).

Steven Mintz, *Huck's Raft: A History of American Childhood* (Cambridge, MA, 2004).

Chapter 5. *The Grief-Stricken*

Franklin Pierce

The Amos Lawrence Papers at the Massachusetts Historical Society contain the correspondence between this Boston merchant and his niece Jane Pierce and her husband, President Franklin Pierce.

The Frederick Dearborn Papers at Harvard's Houghton Library feature a few Pierce letters, often overlooked by scholars, such as the moving one quoted in the chapter, which the President-elect sent to editor George Nicholas soon after he lost his son in the train accident.

Jane Pierce's heartbreaking missive of January 23, 1853, to her dead son, Benny, is available on the web (http://nhhistory.org/libraryexhibits/manuscriptcollection/mom/5-01janepierce/janepierce3.html).

Norman F. Boas, *The Pierce-Aiken Papers: Letters of Jane M. Pierce, Her Sister Mary M. Aiken, Their Family and President Franklin Pierce, with Biographies of Jane Pierce, Other Members of Her Family, and Genealogical Tables* (Stonington, CT, 1983).

Peter Wallner, *Franklin Pierce*, 2 vols. (Concord, NH, 2004–2007).

Roy Nichols, *Franklin Pierce, Young Hickory of the Granite Hills* (Philadelphia, 1931).

Anne Middleton Means, *Amherst and Our Family Tree* (Boston, 1921).

Lloyd Taylor Jr., "A Wife for Mr. Pierce," *New England Quarterly* 28 (September 1955), pp. 339–348.

Nathaniel Hawthorne, *Life of Franklin Pierce* (Boston, 1852).

Jane Walter Venzke and Craig Paul Venzke, "The President's Wife, Jane Means Appleton Pierce: A Woman of Her Time," *Historical New Hampshire* 59 (2005), pp. 44–63.

Allan Nevins, *Ordeal of the Union: A House Dividing, 1852–1857* (New York, 1947).

Benjamin Brown French, *Witness to the Young Republic: A Yankee's Journal, 1828–1870*, edited by Donald B. Cole and John J. McDonough (Hanover, NH, 1989).

Varina Davis, *Jefferson Davis, Ex-President of the Confederate States of America: A Memoir by His Wife*, 2 vols. (New York, 1890).

Jessie Benton Frémont, *Souvenirs of My Time* (Boston, 1887).

Henry Watterson, *"Marse Henry": An Autobiography*, 2 vols. (New York, 1919).

James Mellow, *Nathaniel Hawthorne in His Times* (Boston, 1980).

Peter Wallner, "Franklin Pierce and Bowdoin College Associates Hawthorne and Hale," *Historical New Hampshire* 59 (2005), pp. 23–43.

Virginia Clay-Copton, *A Belle of the Fifties: Memoirs of Mrs. Clay of Alabama, Covering Social and Political Life in Washington and the South, 1853–66* (New York, 1905).

Interview: Peter Wallner.

William McKinley

McKinley's words expressing his concern about what to buy his wife for Christmas in 1899 come from the George Cortelyou Papers, which are held at the Library of Congress.

Margaret Leech, *In the Days of McKinley* (New York, 1959).

At Houghton Library, I examined Leech's papers, which include copies of McKinley letters in addition to various newspaper clippings and articles that she used to write her Pulitzer Prize–winning biography.

H. Wayne Morgan, *William McKinley and His America* (Syracuse, NY, 1963).

Margarita Spalding Gerry, ed., *Through Five Administrations: Reminiscences of Colonel William H. Crook, Body-guard to President Lincoln* (New York, 1910).

Carl Sferrazza Anthony, *Ida McKinley: The Turn-of-the-Century First Lady Through War, Assassination, and Secret Disability* (Kent, OH, 2013).

Thomas Bailey, *Presidential Greatness: The Image and the Man from George Washington to the Present* (New York, 1968).

Thomas Beer, *Hanna* (New York, 1929).

Murat Halstead, *Illustrious Life of William McKinley, Our Martyred President* (Chicago, 1901).

Murat Halstead, *Life and Distinguished Services of William McKinley, our Martyr President* (Chicago, 1901).

Charles Dawes, *A Journal of the McKinley Years* (Chicago, 1950).

Julia Foraker, *I Would Live It Again* (New York, 1932).

Calvin Coolidge

I looked at Calvin Coolidge manuscripts at the Vermont Historical Society in Barre, VT, the Forbes Library in Northampton, MA, and the Library of Congress.

Calvin Coolidge, *The Autobiography of Calvin Coolidge* (New York, 1929).

Robert E. Gilbert, *The Tormented President: Calvin Coolidge, Death, and Clinical Depression* (Westport, CT, 2003).

Claude Fuess, *Calvin Coolidge: The Man from Vermont* (Boston, 1940).

Donald McCoy, *Calvin Coolidge: The Quiet President* (Lawrence, KS, 1988).

Amity Shlaes, *Coolidge* (New York, 2013).

William Allen White, *A Puritan in Babylon: The Story of Calvin Coolidge* (New York, 1938).

James Watson, *As I Knew Them: Memoirs of James Watson, Former United States Senator from Indiana* (New York, 1936).

The Library of Congress has put the unpublished memoir of Coolidge's doctor, Joel Boone, on the web (http://memory.loc.gov/cgi-bin/ampage?collId=cool&hdl=amrl m:mb01:0001).

Dr. John Kolmer's brief account of the death of Calvin Coolidge Jr., "A President's Grief," was published in *Time*, July 18, 1955.

Elisabeth Kübler-Ross, *On Death and Dying* (New York, 1969).

Edward Lathem, *Meet Calvin Coolidge: The Man Behind the Myth* (Brattleboro, VT, 1960).

Ishbel Ross, *Grace Coolidge and Her Era* (New York, 1962).

Grace Coolidge, *Grace Coolidge: An Autobiography*, edited by Lawrence E. Wikander and Robert H. Ferrell (Worland, WY, 1992).

John Barry, *Rising Tide: The Great Mississippi Flood of 1927 and How It Changed America* (New York, 1997).

Howard Quint and Robert Ferrell, eds., *The Talkative President: The Off-the-Record Press Conferences of Calvin Coolidge* (Amherst, MA, 1964).

Other Grief-Stricken Dads

Elwin Page, "Franklin Pierce and Abraham Lincoln," *Abraham Lincoln Quarterly* 5 (1949), pp. 455–472.

Hans Trefousse, *Andrew Johnson: A Biography* (New York, 1989).

I looked at Robert Johnson's unpublished diaries from 1866 and 1868, which cover his stint as a patient at St. Elizabeth's Hospital and are held at the Andrew Johnson National Historic Site in Greenville, TN.

Freeman Cleaves, *Old Tippecanoe: William Henry Harrison and His Time* (New York, 1939).

Thurston Clarke, *JFK's Last Hundred Days: The Transformation of a Man and the Emergence of A Great President* (New York, 2013).

Interviews: Lawrence Altman, Susan Eisenhower, and Nina Gibson.

Chapter 6. *The Nurturers*

Rutherford B. Hayes

The Rutherford B. Hayes Library possesses files on the five Hayes children who reached maturity, containing both letters and newspaper clippings. Webb Hayes's papers include the diary that he kept during the years that he lived in the White House and served as his father's private secretary. I also drew on the microfilmed edition of the Rutherford B. Hayes Papers as well as on additional Hayes manuscripts at the Library of Congress.

For the history of the Easter Egg Roll, see C. L. Arbelbide, "With Easter Monday You Get Egg Roll at the White House," *Prologue* 32 (Spring 2000).

Charles Richard Williams edited a five-volume set, *The Diary and Letters of Rutherford B. Hayes, Nineteenth President of the United States* (Columbus, OH, 1922), which can be viewed on the web courtesy of the Hayes Library (http://www.rbhayes.org/hayes/diaries/).

Harry Barnard, *Rutherford B. Hayes and His America* (Indianapolis, IN, 1954).

Russell Conwell, *Life and Public Services of Gov. Rutherford B. Hayes* (Boston, 1876).

Hamilton Eckenrode, *Rutherford B. Hayes, Statesman of Reunion* (New York, 1930).

Charles Richard Williams, *The Life of Rutherford Birchard Hayes, Nineteenth President of the United States*, 2 vols. (Boston, 1914).

William Dean Howells, *Sketch of the Life and Character of Rutherford B. Hayes* (New York, 1876).

J. Q. Howard, *The Life, Public Services and Select Speeches of Rutherford B. Hayes* (Cincinnati, OH, 1876).

Emily Apt Geer, *First Lady: The Life of Lucy Webb Hayes* (Kent, OH, 1984).

Ari Hoogenboom, *The Presidency of Rutherford B. Hayes* (Lawrence, KS, 1988).

Kristine Deacon, "On the Road with Rutherford B. Hayes: Oregon's First Presidential Visit, 1880." *Oregon Historical Quarterly* 112:2 (Summer 2011), pp. 170–193.

Interview: Stephen Hayes (a great-great-grandson of the former President).

Harry Truman

At the Truman Presidential Library in Independence, Missouri, I looked at the correspondence between Margaret and her father, which begins in 1925 when she was just a year old.

Margaret Truman has published some of these letters in a book, which she edited, *Letters from Father: The Truman Family's Personal Correspondence* (New York, 1981). She also wrote a memoir (with Margaret Cousins), *Souvenir: Margaret Truman's Own Story* (New York, 1956), as well as biographies of both her father, *Harry S. Truman* (New York, 1973), and her mother, *Bess W. Truman* (New York, 1986).

David McCullough, *Truman* (New York, 1992).

Robert Ferrell, *Harry S. Truman* (Washington, DC, 2003).

Harry Truman, *Memoirs*, 2 vols. (New York, 1956).

Robert Ferrell, ed., *Off the Record: The Private Papers of Harry S. Truman* (New York, 1980).

Truman's Little White House in Key West has some useful resources on its website such as the log for his visit in March 1947 (http://www.trumanlittlewhitehouse.com/logs/log2.pdf).

Interview: Clifton Truman Daniel Jr.

Barack Obama

Barack Obama, *Dreams from My Father: A Story of Race and Inheritance* (New York, 2004).

Barack Obama, *The Audacity of Hope* (New York, 2006).

Jodi Kantor, *The Obamas* (New York, 2012).

Janny Scott, *A Singular Woman: The Untold Story of Barack Obama's Mother* (New York, 2011).

David Remnick, *The Bridge: The Life and Rise of Barack Obama* (New York, 2010).

Sally Jacobs, *The Other Barack: The Bold and Reckless Life of President Obama's Father* (New York, 2011).

Obama's remarks about missing his girls come from Richard Wolffe's interview with Valerie Jarrett, as recounted in his book, *Renegade: The Making of a President* (New York, 2009).

In his memoir, *Power Forward: My Presidential Education* (New York, 2015), Reggie Love discusses Obama's decision to coach Sasha's basketball team.

Dinesh Sharma, *Barack Obama in Hawaii and Indonesia: The Making of a Global President* (Santa Barbara, CA, 2011).

Interviews: Susan Blake, Maxine Box, Dinesh Sharma, and Bronwen Solyom.

Other Nurturing Dads

Harlow Unger, *The Last Founding Father: James Monroe and a Nation's Call to Greatness* (Cambridge, MA, 2009).

Theodore Clarke Smith, ed., *The Life and Letters of James Abram Garfield*, 2 vols. (New Haven, CT, 1925).

Margaret Leech, *The Garfield Orbit* (New York, 1978).

Betty Ford with Chris Chase, *The Times of My Life* (New York, 1978).

Epilogue. *Presidential Choices*

Jonathan Alter, *The Center Holds: Obama and His Enemies* (New York, 2014).

Hillary Clinton, interview with Gwen Ifill, *PBS Newshour*, June 25, 2014.

Interviews: Chip Carter, Susan Eisenhower, and Luci Johnson.

Photo Credits

FDR and Anna
National Photo Company Collection/Library of Congress Prints and Photographs Division [LC-DIG-npcc-01568]

Carter Family, 1976
Warren K. Leffler/Library of Congress Prints and Photographs Division [LC-DIG-ppmsca-09738]

Carter Family, 2014
Courtesy of Chip Carter

Bush Family, 2015
Evan Sisley/Office of George Herbert Walker Bush

Grant Family
General Grant and His Family (1868), Fred B. Schell (design) and Samuel Sartain (engraving). Published by Daughaday & Becker, Philadelphia. Library of Congress Prints and Photographs Division [LC-USZ62-70725]

Wilson Family
Pach Brothers, New York (1912)/Library of Congress Prints and Photographs Division [LC-USZ62-88078]

TR Letter to Alice
Houghton Library, Harvard University [MS Am 1541.9 (69)]

TR Family
Pach Brothers, New York (1907)/Library of Congress Prints and Photographs Division [LC-DIG-ppmsca-35755]

John Tyler
John Tyler (1841), Charles Fenderich. Lithograph, 31.8 x 28.3 cm/Library of Congress Prints and Photographs Division [LC-USZ62-7266]

Sylvanius Tyler Brown
Charles City County Historical Society

Nan Britton and Daughter
Library of Congress Prints and Photographs Division [LC-USZ62-73646]

John Adams
Portrait of John Adams (1797), William Joseph Williams/Adams National Historical Park

John Quincy Adams
John Quincy Adams (1843), Philip Haas (lithograph from daguerreotype). Library of Congress Prints and Photographs Division [LC-DIG-pga-06984]

George Washington Adams
Portrait of George Washington Adams (ca. 1820), Charles Bird King/Adams National Historical Park

Jane Pierce and Benny
Jane Pierce and son Benjamin ("Benny") (ca.1850). Daguerreotype. The Pierce Brigade/The Pierce Manse

Katie McKinley
McKinley Presidential Library and Museum Ramsayer Research Library Permanent Collection

Coolidge Family, June 1924
National Photo Company Collection/Library of Congress Prints and Photographs Division [LC-USZ62-93275]

Calvin Coolidge Jr.
Harris & Ewing Collection/Library of Congress Prints and Photographs Division [LC-DIG-hec-34338]

Hayes and Sons
Brady-Handy Photograph Collection/Library of Congress Prints and Photographs Division [LC-DIG-cwpbh-04816]

Truman Family
Library of Congress Prints and Photographs Division [LC-USZ62-71726]

Obama and Sasha
Official White House Photo by Pete Souza

Index

Gordon-Reed, Annette, 140
Gouverneur, Samuel, 305
Grant, America Will, 87
Grant, Elizabeth Chapman, 88
Grant, Ellen "Nellie," 73, 80, 81–82, 84–85
Grant, Fannie Chafee, 87
Grant, Fred, 71–72, 78–80, 82, 85–86
Grant, Hannah, 81
Grant, Ida Marie Honore, 85–86
Grant, Jesse, 73, 74, 78, 80–81, 82, 86, 87–89
Grant, Jesse, Sr., 81
Grant, Julia Dent, 8, 71, 72, 73, 78, 79, 81
Grant, Lillian Burns Wilkens, 88
Grant, Ulysses S., 71–74, 78–89, 136, 161, 170, 295, 312, 316
  appointed Lt. General, accompanied by son, 79–80
  career problems, 73–74
  character, 73, 80–81, 86, 89
  children in the White House, 82–83
  Civil War, family time and, 74, 78–79, 80
  as devoted father, 72, 78–80
  domestic harmony of, 73–74
  failings of associates and scandals, 83
  grief at daughter's marriage, 85
  happy marriage of, 81
  as permissive parent, 8, 78, 81–82, 342
  as "playful pal" parent, 9, 71–75, 78–89, 351
  presidential autobiography, 83–84
  upbringing of, 81
  White House wedding of daughter, 84–85
Grant, Ulysses S., IV, 87
Grant, Ulysses S., Jr. (Buck), 71–72, 78–79, 82, 83, 86–87
Greenstein, Fred, 228–29
Griffin, Caron, 66, 67
Guiteau, Charles, 3

Hager, Henry, 77
Hale, John P., 257
Halpin, Maria, 162, 163, 164–66, 167, 171
Halsted, James, 43
Hamilton, Alexander, 207, 211
  letter about John Adams, 198
Hamilton, George, 53
Harding, Florence Kling, 173, 178, 179, 180, 182
  husband's affairs and, 176–77

Harding, George, 180
Harding, Warren G., 20, 172–85
  affair with Carrie Phillips, 174, 175–76
  affair with Nan Britton, 173–80
  character of, 177
  as compulsive womanizer, 176, 178, 181
  contradictory identities of, 144
  death of, 180
  illegitimate daughter, 9, 139, 144, 165, 174, 175, 177, 178, 179, 180, 181, 184
  inaugural address, 180–81
  internal-external disconnect of, 181
  marriage to Florence Kling, 173, 176–77
  nominating speech for Taft, 181
  popularity of, 179, 180, 181–82
  presidential performance, 179, 181–84
  scandals in administration of, 182–84
  stepson and stepgrandchildren, ignoring of, 173
  tomb of, 184
  White House trysts, 174, 177, 179
Harding Era, The (Murray), 183
Harriman, Averell, 33, 38
Harriman, Kathleen, 38, 39
Harrison, Anna, 251
Harrison, Benjamin, 19, 86, 171, 300–301, 314
  as "double-dealing dad," 143
Harrison, Caroline Scott, 143
Harrison, John Cleves Symmes, 250
Harrison, Mary (daughter of Benjamin), 143
Harrison, Mary Lord Dimmick (second wife of Benjamin), 143
Harrison, Russell, 143
Harrison, William Henry, 130, 149, 150
  death of adult children, and grief, 250–51
  death of tenth child, 248
  slave children fathered by, 140–41
Hart, Gary, 4, 23
Hawthorne, Julian, 258
Hawthorne, Nathaniel, 243, 255, 258
Hawthorne, Una, 258
Hay, George, 304
Hayes, Birchard, 296, 297, 306–8, 321–23
Hayes, Fanny (daughter), 296, 297–98, 311, 341–42
Hayes, Fanny (sister), 298, 299, 301
Hayes, Lucy, 296, 307, 311
Hayes, Mary Miller, 309

About the Author

Joshua Kendall is the author of *The Man Who Made Lists*, a life of Peter Roget, the inventor of the legendary Thesaurus; *The Forgotten Founding Father*, a biography of Noah Webster; and *America's Obsessives: The Compulsive Energy That Built a Nation*, a group biography of seven American icons, including Thomas Jefferson, Henry Heinz, and Charles Lindbergh. An award-winning freelance journalist, he has written for numerous publications, such as the *Boston Globe, BusinessWeek*, the *Los Angeles Times*, the *New York Times, Psychology Today*, and *Slate*. He is a Board Member of Biographers International Organization. An Associate Fellow of Yale's Trumbull College, he lives in Boston, Massachusetts.